About Island Press

Island Press is the only nonprofit organization in the United States whose principal purpose is the publication of books on environmental issues and natural resource management. We provide solutions-oriented information to professionals, public officials, business and community leaders, and concerned citizens who are shaping responses to environmental problems.

In 2006, Island Press celebrates its twenty-first anniversary as the leading provider of timely and practical books that take a multi-disciplinary approach to critical environmental concerns. Our growing list of titles reflects our commitment to bringing the best of an expanding body of literature to the environmental community throughout North America and the world.

Support for Island Press is provided by the Agua Fund, The Geraldine R. Dodge Foundation, Doris Duke Charitable Foundation, The William and Flora Hewlett Foundation, Kendeda Sustainability Fund of the Tides Foundation, Forrest C. Lattner Foundation, The Henry Luce Foundation, The John D. and Catherine T. MacArthur Foundation, The Marisla Foundation, The Andrew W. Mellon Foundation, Gordon and Betty Moore Foundation, The Curtis and Edith Munson Foundation, Oak Foundation, The Overbrook Foundation, The David and Lucile Packard Foundation, The Winslow Foundation, and other generous donors.

The opinions expressed in this book are those of the author(s) and do not necessarily reflect the views of these foundations.

DESIGNING GREENWAYS

DESIGNING GREENWAYS

SUSTAINABLE LANDSCAPES
FOR NATURE AND PEOPLE

Paul Cawood Hellmund & Daniel Somers Smith

ISLANDPRESS

WASHINGTON • COVELO • LONDON

Library of Congress Cataloging-in-Publication Data

 Designing greenways : sustainable landscapes for nature and people / Paul Cawood Hellmund and Daniel S. Smith, editors.
        p. cm.
  Includes bibliographical references and index.
    ISBN 1-55963-329-8 (cloth : alk. paper) -- ISBN 1-55963-325-5 (pbk. : alk. paper)
  1. Greenways. 2. Landscape ecology. I. Hellmund, Paul Cawood. II. Smith Daniel S. (Daniel Somers)
   HT241.D47 2006
   711'.41--dc22

                                                        2005031595

British Cataloguing-in-Publication data available.

Printed on recycled, acid-free paper ✪

Design by Joan Wolbier

Manufactured in the United States of America
10 9 8 7 6 5 4 3 2 1

For my father,
who reminds
me that conservatives
can also be conservationists.
—DANIEL SOMERS SMITH

For Joan, Andrew, and Noah,
who help me see the world and
mean the world to me.
—PAUL CAWOOD HELLMUND

CONTENTS

⋮ PREFACE

We live in a world of fragmentation. Natural areas are penetrated by development, diminished in size, and split apart. Wildlife cannot move freely across the landscape. Waterways and the vegetation that protects them are bisected and exposed to contaminants moving downslope. People live their lives separated from the natural world, their habitat defined in large measure by automobiles, and the built environment. Neighborhoods are segregated by race and class, even as income gaps continue to grow. Turbulent economies require relocation and migration, displacing people from family, community, and place.

As troubling as they may be, however, these aspects of fragmentation are only one side of the story. We live amidst fragmentation but we also live *by* fragmentation, and it is important to remember that this is neither new nor an accident. Science operates by reducing the world to narrow, manageable questions, while technology proceeds to rearrange those fragmented pieces, hopefully, though not always, to useful ends. Likewise, the capitalist economy that has helped to produce a remarkably high standard of living for a minority of the world's inhabitants relies on the constant dissolution and reconstitution of nature and society into new forms. Economists aptly refer to this as "creative destruction" and it is, for better or worse, the lifeblood of our economy. Thus, even in the midst of disconcerting fragmentation, new connections are formed and new wholes emerge.

Although we are, like many, deeply troubled by both the history and current course of these transformations, that important question is not what this book is about. Our aim here is more immediate and tangible. Regardless of one's opinion of the current state of the modern world, there are problems of fragmentation around which consensus more readily forms. The loss and fragmentation of natural areas proceeds unarguably to the detriment of both wildlife and water resources. People clearly yearn for the serenity, healthfulness, and adventure that come with the direct experience of nature. The increasing separation of people from different social and economic backgrounds weakens civil society and chips away at the social basis of democracy. These are problems that most people would agree deserve public attention. They offer a common ground from which discussion and pragmatic action can proceed.

They are also problems that greenways can help address because of the simple fact of their linearity and their ability to wind through and connect a variety of habitats and communities. Greenways, when designed with care, can tie together and restore a significant measure of ecological function to what would otherwise be isolated natural areas and exposed waterways. They can bring nature and people into closer contact, providing regular opportunities to experience and learn about nature close to home. And they can connect people to one another—both physically, as people use trails for recreation and transportation, and because greenways lend themselves to grassroots involvement and community collaboration. Finally, by providing for nonmotorized transportation, raising environmental awareness, and strengthening civil society and grassroots participation, greenways have the potential to help promote sustainability at both local and global scales. However, none of these *possible* benefits should be taken for granted. In fact, they will sometimes be in conflict, as when local greenway initiatives draw attention and resources away from more pressing problems in other places and at larger scales. But greenway designs that face such tensions head-on and that are informed by an awareness of context, by sound science, and by broad-based public participation have the potential to help restore ecological health and social well-being—or, jointly, what we call *landscape integrity*.

This book explains how greenways function ecologically (including both biophysical "natural" function and social-ecological function), illustrates how they can help solve problems of natural and social fragmentation, and provides a practical guide for how planners, designers, and conservationists can implement those solutions in real world contexts. Toward those ends, we emphasize two principles.

First, greenway design (and the design of landscapes more generally) should be holistic, integrative, and contextual to achieve long-term results in a world with finite resources. Although the idea that "everything is connected to everything else" is the cardinal rule of ecology, this maxim is too often lost in the push to develop specific expertise regarding particular, isolated problems. Although expertise is crucial, increasing the health and integrity of landscapes requires simultaneous consideration of multiple biophysical and social issues, as well as multiple scales, from local to regional to global. Sometimes those issues and scales will be mutually reinforcing; other times they will require hard compromises. They should always be taken into consideration. In this sense, practitioners such as landscape architects, planners, and conservationists, whose work is fundamentally integrative and interdisciplinary, have a special role to play.

Second, there is a need to bridge the gap between science (both natural and social science) and practice. Anyone involved in conservation these days knows that there is an extraordinary wealth of talent and energy being devoted to both the science and practice of conservation, but the two realms often do not communicate adequately. Although specialization on both ends of the science-practice continuum is good and necessary, there is a great need for scientists to ask practical questions and make sure that their results are "translated" and made available for nonspecialists, and a concomitant need for practitioners to become scientifically literate and go the extra mile in understanding complex, technical information. This book aims to help establish closer collaboration by presenting thorough scientific information in a way that is accessible to nonspecialists and by integrating scientific principles into a comprehensive design method. Ideally, information should also flow in the other direction; we hope that scientists will benefit from this book by gaining insight into the sorts of questions that are most relevant to practitioners.

The arts and humanities also play an important role. Scientific understanding and sophisticated techniques are useful only when they are guided by serious regard for the values, ethics, and matters of the heart. Although somewhat less of a focus than science in this volume, the arts and humanities, by helping us to understand and reflect on these questions of meaning and value, deserve the attention of scientists and practitioners alike.

Designing Greenways owes a great deal to our previous collaborative volume, *Ecology of Greenways*, which emphasized a triad of largely biophysical themes: wildlife, water resources, and the ecological impacts of recreation. That work originated with our simultaneous experience with, on the one hand, the emerging science of landscape ecology and its theoretical insights into corridor function, and on the other hand, proliferating efforts in the late 1980s and early 1990s to protect, restore, and promote greenways as a new form of public greenspace. At the time, it was clear that these two realms of science and practice would benefit from cross-pollination. *Ecology of Greenways* was the result, aimed at filling an empty niche on ecological design in the literature of its day.

The current volume takes a similar approach but incorporates important changes in our understanding of landscapes—especially their social components—that have occurred in the past dozen years. Chapter 1 sets the stage for the book by outlining greenway functions, their role in holistic, ecological landscape planning, and the integrative approach used throughout this volume. The chapter also introduces several important case studies. Chapter 2 provides a more detailed theoretical foundation based on the discipline of landscape ecology—the conceptual glue that gives unity to the book's technical chapters.

Chapters 3 through 5 focus on more specific aspects of greenway function and design. Chapters 3 and 4 provide clear and robust summaries of the scientific basis for corridor design related to wildlife and water resources, respectively, and explain how practitioners can best make use of basic principles and technical information. Chapter 5 introduces a social-ecological perspective on greenways and landscapes. In this chapter, and throughout the volume, we stress the importance of viewing human society and social groups not simply as *causes* of environmental change but as complex systems that are of vital concern in their own right. Drawing on advances in fields such as ecosystem management, ecological economics, and environmental justice, this approach draws attention to a host of new and important questions for greenway designers related to ideas and education; institutions, participation, and democracy; communities and social interaction; and economics and environmental justice.

Chapter 6 draws together the conceptual and technical threads from preceding chapters and integrates them into a flexible method that can be used to guide a wide range of greenway projects. The method is based on a series of questions that brings important issues to the attention of the greenway designer. It can be used from start to finish, adopted in part, or reviewed as a general guide.

This book would never have happened without the inspiration and assistance of many people. We are especially grateful for the constructive criticism we received on draft chapters. Reviewers included Kevin Crooks, Colorado State University, Craig Johnson, Utah State University, David Theobald, Colorado State University, and Susan van den Heever, Colorado State University. Several anonymous reviewers also made important contributions.

Others have supported this effort in diverse and meaningful ways. We have benefited tremendously from the writings of and conversations with Richard T. T. Forman, Larry Harris, Bill Burch, and Jusuck Koh. We have been encouraged by discussions with colleagues and students at Colorado State and Wageningen universities, as well as the Yale School of Forestry and Environmental Studies, Ramapo College, the Conway School of Landscape Design, and the Graduate School of Design at Harvard University. Support and inspiration for the early stages of our work came from the National Park Service River and Trail Conservation Assistance Program, especially the staff of the Northeast Regional office. Insights and feedback on specific topics were provided by George Wallace, John Armstrong, Jack Ahern, Rob Jongman, Enrique Peñalosa, Liana Geidezis, Bill Wenk, and many others.

We thank landscape architects Joe McGrane and Jane Shoplick for their drawings, which add an important dimension to the book. Stephen Wallner and his colleagues at Colorado State gave important support to the project, without which this book might not have been completed.

The members of Colorado's Chatfield Basin Conservation Network, especially founders Ray Sperger and Brooke Fox, provided important feedback on the practicality of many of the components of the design approach and inspiration through their dedicated examples.

At Island Press, our former editor, Heather Boyer, was quick to see the potential of our project, and her successor, M. Jeff Hardwick, was a staunch and good-humored supporter. Shannon O'Neill helped keep us on track and organized and remained patient even when we were late. We thank Joy Drohan for her thoughtful editing of the text, Joan Wolbier for book design, and Cecilia Gonzalez and Jessica Heise for shepherding the book through design and production.

Island Press also provided generous financial support that allowed us to substantially improve the book's quality. The trustees of the Conway School of Landscape Design provided generous support for this project. The L'Aiglon Foundation provided funds for additional illustrations.

Joan Cawood Hellmund helped edit countless drafts and helped in many other ways.

CHAPTER 1

INTRODUCTION: GREENWAY FUNCTIONS, DESIGN, AND HISTORY

Greenways and Landscape Integrity: An Overview

Greenways are being designated in cities and countrysides throughout North America and elsewhere. Sometimes these conservation areas are a response to environmental problems, such as flooding or degrading water quality. Other times their creation is an act of pure vision—people imagining a better community—one where people and natural processes coexist more closely. Often, despite this recent popularity, people fail to recognize the full range of contributions greenways can make to society and the environment. It is as if open spaces, especially in metropolitan areas, have been thought of as just so much generic greenery, mere backdrops for people's activities.[1]

In this chapter we suggest why greenways are deserving of their newfound popularity and how their functions can be enhanced, but also consider their limitations. We discuss how the *greenway* concept came to be, how it has been defined, and how its spatial form and content have varied. We also highlight the significant social and ecological functions of greenways, in advance of a fuller discussion of greenway ecology and design in subsequent chapters.

Greenways Vary Widely in Type and Name

Greenways are bands on the landscape, designated for their natural or recreational resources or other special qualities. Greenways—known by a variety of monikers (table 1.1)—straddle waterways, traverse ridgelines, and sometimes cut across the landscape independent of topographic features. They range from narrow urban trail corridors to winding river floodplains to very wide, wildernesslike landscape linkages. Although they exist in varied landscapes, from cities to farmland to commercial forests, historically they have most frequently been created in suburban areas. All greenways have in common their linearity and official designation, or at least popular identification, as distinct areas of the landscape with recognized qualities.

TABLE 1.1. Greenway and greenwaylike designations.
Greenways vary widely in function, situation, and name. What they all have in common is that they are primarily linear or networks of linear lands designated or recognized for their special qualities.

TERM	OBJECTIVE OR CONDITION	EXAMPLES
Biological corridor (biocorridor)	Protect wildlife movement and accomplish other aspects of nature conservation.	Mesoamerican Biological Corridor through Central America; Chichinautzin Biological Corridor, State of Morelos, Mexico
Bioswale	Filter pollutants from storm runoff (usually at the scale of a site).	Numerous examples in various localities. See, for instance, the bioswales that are part of the City of Seattle Public Utilities' Street Edge Alternative (SEA) project in northwest Seattle.
Conservation corridor	Conserve biological resources, protect water quality, and/or mitigate the impacts of flooding.	Southeast Wisconsin environmental corridors
Desokota	Blend rural and urban areas in a dense web of transactions, tying large urban cores to their surrounding regions in the same landscape. (From the Indonesian words "desa," for village, and "kota," for town. Also known as the McGee–Ginsburg model.[1])	Indonesia and China
Dispersal corridor	Facilitate migration and other movement of wildlife. Can also be a road corridor that unintentionally facilitates movement of weeds.	Owl dispersal corridor in the Juncrook area of the Mt. Hood National Forest in Oregon; Marine dispersal corridors for blue crab in the Chesapeake Bay
Ecological corridors (eco-corridors)	Facilitate movement of animals, plants, or other ecological processes.	North Andean Patagonian Regional Eco-Corridor Project
Ecological networks	Facilitate movement or other ecological processes.	Pan-European Ecological Network for Central and Eastern Europe
Environmental corridor	Conserve environmental quality.	Southeastern Wisconsin environmental corridors
Greenbelts	Protect natural or agricultural lands to restrict or direct metropolitan growth.	City of Boulder, Colorado, greenbelt; London, England, greenbelt
Green extensions	Put residents in contact with nature in their day-to-day lives through a system of residential public greenspace, shaded sidewalks, and riparian strips.	Nanjing, China[2]
Green frame	Provide a network of greenspace for a metropolis or larger area.	San Mateo County, California, Shared Vision 2010 for the county's future development green frame; Addis Ababa, Ethiopia, green frame
Green heart	Protect a large area of greenspace that is surrounded by development. Originally referred to a specific area in the Netherlands, but now more widely used.	The agricultural open space surrounded by the Randstad, Holland's urban ring, consisting of the cities of Amsterdam, The Hague, Rotterdam, and Utrecht
Green infrastructure	Protect greenspace for multiple objectives on equal grounds with gray infrastructure (i.e., roads, utility lines, etc.).	Maryland Greenprint Program; Chatfield Basin Conservation Network—Denver, Colorado, metropolitan area
Green fingers	Purify stormwater through bioswales.	Buffalo Bayou and Beyond for the 21st Century Plan, Houston, Texas, area
Green links	Connect separated greenspace.	Green Links initiative to connect isolated patches of habitat throughout the lower mainland of British Columbia
Greenspace or green space	Protect lands from development.	Countless systems (usually called "open space") across North America
Green structure or greenstructure	Connect separated areas of greenspace and provide a structure around which development may occur. Term is commonly used in Europe.	Greater Copenhagen Green Structure Plan

Green veins	Help protect biodiversity in agricultural landscapes through networks of small, mostly linear landscape elements.	Term has been used by scientists in the Netherlands, France, and other European countries
Green wedges	Keep developed areas apart while bringing greenspace closer to the heart of a settlement. Almost the reverse of the greenbelt concept. [3]	Melbourne, Australia; 1971 General plan for Moscow, Russia
Landscape linkages	Connect large ecosystems across broad linear bands, including undisturbed rivers.	Pima County, Arizona, Critical Landscape Linkages
Natural backbone	Facilitate ecological processes.	Central and Eastern Europe
Nature frames	Provide recreation, protect water quality, serve urban design, and mitigate for environmental impacts.	Lithuanian's Nature Frame
Open space	Protect lands from development.	Countless systems in cities and counties across North America
Recreational corridors	Provide recreation.	Hillsborough County, Florida, Greenway System; Alberta Recreational Corridors
River or other linear parks	Protect or at least follow river or other corridors, sometimes with scenic drives and trails.	Rock Creek Park, Washington, D.C.
Scenic corridors	Protect scenery.	Scottsdale, Arizona, Scenic Corridors; Clayoquot Sound, British Columbia, Scenic Corridors
Trail corridors	Provide recreation.	Applachian Trail, eastern United States
Utilitarian corridors	Serve utilitarian functions, such as routes for canals or power lines, but also may protect nature and provide recreation.	Metro Phoenix, Arizona, Grand Canal
Vegetative or riparian buffers	Buffer a stream or body of water and protect water quality by planting or maintaining a riparian strip.	Numerous examples in various localities, especially in agricultural landscapes in the midwestern United States and Canada
Wildlife corridors	Protect wildlife movement between areas of habitat.	Yellowstone to Yukon Conservation Initiative (Canada and U.S.); Mountains to Mangroves South East Queensland Wildlife Corridor (Brisbane, Queensland, Australia)

[1] Sui, D. Z., and H. Zeng. (2000). "Modeling the dynamics of landscape structure in Asia's emerging desokota regions: A case study in Shenzhen." *Landscape and Urban Planning* 758: 1-16.

[2] Shuang, C., and C. Y. Jim. (2003). *Green space planning strategies compatible with high-density development in the urban area.* Internet Conference on Ecocity Development, http://www.ias.unu.edu/proceedings/icibs/ecocity03/papers.html.

[3] Lynch, K. (1981). *A Theory of Good City Form.* Cambridge, MA, MIT Press. p. 441.

People have been setting aside greenways of various sorts for more than one hundred years. In North America in the late 19th and early 20th centuries, parkways—early prototypes for greenways—were created to connect urban parks. During the same period, broad greenbelts were designed to encircle some cities and limit urban sprawl. In the 1960s, citizens, ecological planners, and landscape architects recognized the need to protect waterways and other corridors that included a high concentration of important natural features. More recently, natural scientists and conservationists have considered the significance of corridors for wildlife management and biodiversity protection. Social scientists have explored how greenways affect things such as economics, community and civic life, and social interaction among diverse users. At the same time, citizens, alarmed by the rapid loss of open space to development, have expressed strong desires for opportunities for outdoor recreation near where they live.

Ideally, greenways are corridors of land and water (and networks of such corridors) designed and managed for multiple purposes, such as nature conservation, recreation, stormwater management, community enhancement, social equity, and scenery protection, with an overall aim of sustaining the integrity of the landscape, including both its natural (biophysical) and social components.[2] The term *greenway* has gained wide acceptance among landscape architects, greenspace planners, conservationists, and citizen groups.[3] But the terms used to identify greenways and other greenspaces are used imprecisely. This confusion is apparent in the range of terms shown in table 1.1.

Networks of greenways are sometimes known as *green infrastructure*—"interconnected networks of green space that conserve natural ecosystem values and functions and provide associated benefits to human populations."[4] In Europe greenway networks, along with the nature reserves they connect, are likely to be known as ecological networks, even if their purpose is more than just nature conservation.[5] In this book we primarily use the terms *greenway*, the more encompassing *greenspace* (rather than the vague *open space*[6]), *green infrastructure*, and *ecological networks*.

Greenways Help Retain or Re-Create Important Landscape Functions

A greenway exists within a landscape. Many landscapes today, especially those on the urbanizing metropolitan fringe, are being transformed dramatically. With these transformations there is a great opportunity to intervene to sustain more of a landscape's unique qualities or integrity—its cultural and natural richness—by designating greenways.

What is vital to sustaining landscape integrity is not just the overall quantity of land area lost or conserved. The pattern or configuration—and especially the connectedness—of what remains is extremely important. This is where greenways can play a role. If implemented carefully, greenways can help conserve some landscape connections and functioning.

When people designate a greenway they nominate it for special status in the landscape. They are saying that they value this special corridor because it plays, or, with restoration, could play important roles in the community. With the designation, they commit to managing that greenway for its overall health or integrity. They recognize that the greenway is not something distinct from the landscape; it is integral to the landscape. With this perspective they easily see that a greenway never provides just one function, such as recreation along a bike path, but it always, even if unintentionally, does many things at the same time, such as nature conservation, floodwater management, and water quality protection. A greenway is most effectively designed and managed, then, when all of these dimensions are recognized and coordinated.

When a landscape is largely free of development, the mosaic of patches and corridors and their surrounding matrix are naturally filled with connections and interactions. Water ebbs and flows. Wildlife moves to fulfill a range of needs. But as people build communities and supporting infrastructure, they tend to disrupt and restrict these flows, sometimes intentionally. They may attempt to dampen disturbances, such as wildfires and floods, to reduce impacts to human lives and development. But often, alterations to the landscape are so gradual and incremental that their cumulative effects go unnoticed, in a "tyranny of small changes."[7]

If we assume that development is, to some extent, inevitable in many metropolitan areas, greenways do more than stem the tide of loss of natural features. They also help to create new,

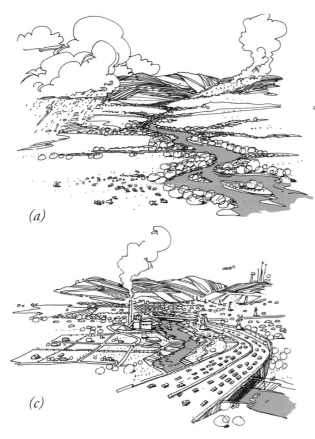

(a)

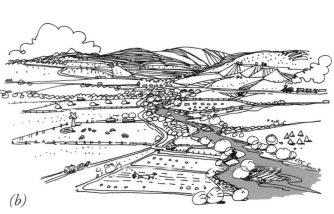

(b)

(c)

FIGURE 1.1

The evolution of a developing landscape in western North America: the "tyranny of small changes." As people increasingly dominate landscapes, natural flows and disturbance patterns may be intentionally and unintentionally interrupted, as new social connections are created. (a) Hypothetical western landscape before settlement, (b) with early settlement patterns, and (c) contemporary scene with human patterns overwhelming natural processes. (Drawing by Joe McGrane, courtesy of Colorado Department of Transportation.)

positive social functions in the midst of what might otherwise be haphazard development patterns (figure 1.1). Just as water and wildlife move and flow in the landscape, there are myriad social connections in the landscape that increase with greater human presence. Greenways create opportunities to steer these new connections in socially positive ways. In addition to their obvious recreational uses, properly designed and managed greenways can tie diverse neighborhoods together in ways that increase civic interaction and expand and deepen people's sense of community. The linearity of greenways allows them to wind through a variety of neighborhoods, making them more accessible than nonlinear greenspace and contributing to goals of social equity. Especially where communities take responsibility for design and management, greenways can help strengthen the capacity for collaboration and overall democratic process. As with greenways' biophysical functions, however, these benefits are not a given but require thoughtful investigation and planning.

Although greenways share certain general characteristics, the diversity of greenway types and forms, combined with geographic differences, means that different greenways may function very differently ecologically and socially. Ecologically, greenways can protect natural areas and diminish the isolating, disruptive effects of habitat fragmentation on wildlife and water resources. Their effectiveness on both of these counts, however, will vary according to factors such as their width, shape, location, and context. From a social and community perspective, greenways can provide important places for recreation, help maintain the scenic quality of landscapes, or serve as regional separators between towns and cities.

Consider Landscape Integrity

Although there is widespread concern today about environmental degradation, there is considerable difference of opinion as to how to gauge that degradation or even measure the quality or health of landscapes in general. Biological diversity (or biodiversity) and ecological integrity, health, fit, and sustainability are several of the concepts offered as possible landscape metrics or goals. Each term addresses various aspects of goodness or quality of the environment, and how changes made by humans affect that quality. With many of these terms, such as biodiversity, the focus is, and the primary goals relate to, nature and natural processes. Sustainability, by definition a broader concept, deals with both socioeconomic and natural features. Sustainability is sometimes described as looking at the "triple bottom line" of economic, environmental, and social conditions of systems. English landscape architect Ian Thompson conceived of sustainable design as incorporating "ecology, community, and delight,"[8] with the last of the three terms referring to the beauty of the landscape and the prospect of creating art with the environment. Sustainability and sustainable development have been adopted as goals by a number of conservation organizations and projects, drawing suspicion from some biologists, who are concerned about introducing economic advancement into an evaluation of conservation activities.[9]

In considering which concept to suggest here for greenway designers, we felt that each of the earlier mentioned approaches has merit, but none was as comprehensive and as practical as needed for real-world, multiobjective greenway projects. Therefore, we propose a broader concept we believe holds promise as a goal appropriate for greenway creation and management, a concept we call *landscape integrity*. Although this term has sometimes been used with a meaning more focused on natural systems, the pairing of these two words suits the broader goal of ecological and social quality for greenways.

To evaluate landscape integrity is to consider the overall quality or health of the landscape, including ecological and social functions. It includes the health of plants and animals, and other qualities embodied in the term *ecological integrity*, as well as social functions related to economic, recreational, and aesthetic resources, improving the quality of social and civic interaction, and ensuring equitable access to public spaces and the benefits, both economic and intangible, they offer. A place with strong landscape integrity has a good representation of ecological and cultural resources and a strong sense of place. There is a good fit between people and place and opportunities for both to flourish. Natural processes are sustained, while humans have access to jobs, housing, and services. There is environmental justice, civic interaction, and opportunities for people to participate in decisions that affect the landscape.

As a start, Richard Forman's suggested measures of ecological integrity can appropriately be thought of as part of landscape integrity. He recommends[10] pursuing near-natural conditions of:

- plant productivity;
- biodiversity;
- soil/soil erosion; and
- water quality and quantity.

With the broader concept of landscape integrity, Forman's above-listed natural conditions can be complemented with social issues that contribute to a sense of place, such as historical, cultural, and recreational resources. It is also crucial to examine the socioeconomic impacts of greenway conservation, such as influences on communities, civic interaction, and environmental justice.

Landscape integrity, as we propose it, is not a checklist of easily quantifiable factors, but instead, a broad set of essential items—focused reminders of the significant values that are behind a greenway project and the landscape to which it is integral. Conservationist Aldo Leopold advised readers of his 1933 book on wildlife management that the techniques given in the book "represent examples of how to think, observe, deduce, and experiment, rather than specifications of what to do."[11] Similarly, we suggest that greenway designers use this working concept of landscape integrity as a guide to thinking, observing, deducing, and experimenting with greenway design and management.

By their very nature, landscapes are dynamic, and a landscape with integrity has room to accommodate—and even requires—changes for its health. For example, if channelization shunts floodwaters downstream, eliminating historic flooding of adjacent areas, then some trees or other organisms dependent on flooding may not be able to regenerate. Flooding, drought, and other disturbances may affect or even eliminate resources being conserved by a park or greenway. At times conservationists have taken a more static view of conservation, setting aside reserves with the assumption that resources would be accommodated within that area. Yet aspects of landscape integrity, including the resources that were the initial impetus for conservation, can be lost when landscape dynamics are compromised.

Landscape integrity cannot be effectively evaluated without examining an area of interest in its broader spatial and temporal contexts. This is because some ecological patterns are not obvious if they are considered within too narrow a time or space perspective. A broader perspective may reveal, for instance, that a greenway design may simply be shifting a problem, such as flooding, to a downstream location. Similarly, if greenways only exist in affluent neighborhoods, benefits for the larger goal of landscape intergrity may be compromised. Or, greenway managers may have future problems if fire, flooding, drought, or other regularly occurring natural disturbances are not anticipated in the design.

Greenways offer a strategic approach to conserving and enhancing landscape integrity by focusing on some of a landscape's most important connections and dynamics related to such objectives as wildlife conservation, stormwater management, water quality protection, recreation, and urban design. Because typically there is a coincidence of resources found along riparian corridors,[12] conserving a skeleton of open lands along riparian and other corridors can be an effective way of conserving a disproportionately large amount of a landscape's important features. Not to be forgotten in conserving greenways, however, is that although they may be linear in nature, they must have adequate width if they are to sustain many resources.

Greenways Can Help Conserve Landscape Integrity

Although there is no simple, single recipe for designing a greenway, there are many useful principles and systematic steps that can contribute to successful greenway design and landscape integrity. Some general principles are presented in this chapter with more detailed guidelines interspersed throughout subsequent chapters. Because they highlight background issues and concerns, these guidelines should prove useful to greenway designers, although they will still need to ground the guidelines in local conditions and objectives.

Some of the most important, overarching principles for greenway design are:

- Greenway designers should strive to conserve and enhance the connectivity of natural features of the landscape and thereby contribute to landscape integrity, including connectivity of many sorts.
- Greenway plans should keep nature near where people live, no matter how urban the area. People, especially children, benefit from having access to nature nearby, even if that nature is not pristine.
- Greenways should be distributed as equally as possible, with special emphasis on low-income areas, so that their benefits are available for all.
- Most landscapes have both natural and cultural resources, and greenways should be designed and managed with these multiple objectives in mind.
- Greenways and systems of green infrastructure are as deserving of careful planning and management as are utility corridors, roads, and other forms of gray infrastructure.
- Unlike gray infrastructure, green infrastructure must be designed and managed with its ecological dynamics in mind. This may mean, for example, that greenway widths must be determined not only on what is within a greenway, but also what is adjacent to it.
- Greenways should reclaim degraded areas to accommodate natural processes and serve people's needs.
- Planners should design gray and green infrastructure at the same time so they do not degrade each other.
- Community gardens, farms, and forests should be included where possible within or adjacent to greenways.
- It may be more important to provide short connector trails than long-distance ones.
- Existing landscape lines such as canals or abandoned railroad corridors created for one purpose can have greenway potential today.
- A carefully planned greenway project with a broadly inclusive process could be an important vehicle for overcoming social conflict or aspects of environmental inequity.

Applying these and other greenway design principles can help designers implement a greenway that contributes to the integrity of landscapes, and more broadly, landscape sustainability. Some of these principles are illustrated in the prototypical landscape illustrated in figure 1.2.

Greenways Are Not a Conservation Panacea

A number of greenway observers from very different perspectives voice the same sentiment: greenways should not be considered a conservation panacea.[13] They warn against a common human tendency to take an attractive concept to extremes, ending up with solutions that may be simplistic or even harmful. Greenways alone are no cure-all for nature conservation because they are just one form of conservation, better planned in concert with other elements in conservation networks.

Developing a balanced view of greenways also requires acknowledging some of their potential

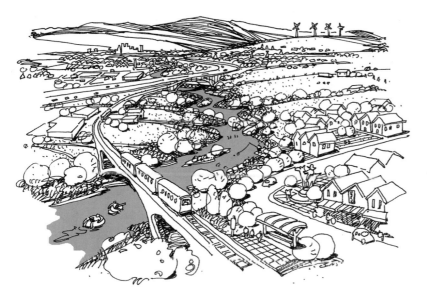

FIGURE 1.2

With networks of greenways and an aggregation of land uses, it may be possible to guide a landscape toward greater sustainability than typically results without planning. With a broad protected band along the river in this western U.S. city, there is room for many of the river's dynamic processes, as well as recreation. Development is clumped in contiguous areas and relates to transportation corridors without sprawl.

(Drawing by Joe McGrane, courtesy of Colorado Department of Transportation.)

negative characteristics for wildlife (chapter 3). Foremost among these is the preponderance of edge conditions found in human-dominated landscapes. Greenways, especially when very narrow, are greatly exposed to influences from outside their borders. Assessing these intrusions, whether they are human activity, predation by pets, or disruption of native communities by invasive species, is of prime importance. Greenways may also be ineffective as wildlife movement corridors if they are severed by roads. Because of these potential shortcomings, some have suggested that wildlife corridors should be thought of only as last resorts or even "bandages for a wounded natural landscape."[14]

As with wildlife conservation, people sometimes overestimate the potential of greenways in urban design and especially their ability to resolve social problems. Although greenways can be important elements in urban settings, contributing to a sense of place and providing access to nearby nature for urban dwellers, they may add to some urban problems or shift problems from one population to another. (This is discussed in more detail later in this chapter and in chapter 5.) "We need to understand urban ecosystems far beyond the point of believing that making them 'greener' will be enough," comments one urban observer as he describes the grim irony of urban youth conservation workers successfully restoring wildlife habitat within a city, only to have some of their fellows lose their lives to violence in their own neighborhoods.[15]

Other important social impacts can be economic. For instance, although greenways have been documented as increasing values[16] of properties adjacent to them, much less frequently discussed is the impact of such increased values on those financially less well off, who may be displaced or excluded by increased property values. Similarly, there needs to be more frank discussion of how greenways are used by the homeless, rather than assuming that use by the homeless and successful greenway management are always incompatible.[17]

Beyond these tangible impacts, it is important to view the benefits offered by greenways in their larger social context. Because of their benefits, great popular appeal, and relative ease of implementation, greenways tend to attract attention and foster a sense of optimism and empowerment. This is good as far as it goes, but these positives can have a downside if they overshadow and draw attention away from other pressing concerns that are less popular and more intractable. There is reason to be concerned that greenways, along with other popular and relatively easy solutions (recycling, hybrid cars, donations to one's favorite environmental group) may unintentionally generate a false sense of security and commitment. In a world where fundamental trends, such as energy use, resource consumption, and population, all point in troubling directions, we should not let local conservation, as important as it is, obscure the need for deeper changes in behavior, politics, and economics.

Such concerns become even more pressing when we consider ecological sustainability and social justice beyond the local and regional scales at which greenway planning typically occurs. This is especially true in places such as North America and Europe. Here both the history of colonialism and current levels of wealth and consumption made possible by exploitation of labor and natural resources around the globe make clear that our society's negative impacts extend far beyond the local environment. From this standpoint, it is vital to compare the relative priority of local improvements to environment or quality of life with those that might be accomplished with the same resources in other places where needs may be far greater. We are not suggesting that resources can easily be shifted away from local concerns or that improving people's lives at home may not have far-reaching benefits. But in a world where needs are great and resources finite, priorities should always be critically examined beyond the scales at which we are accustomed to thinking.

These are heavy issues not often considered in conservation planning, and introducing them here may discourage some greenway proponents. It is our belief, however, that embracing rather than avoiding these issues, combined with a flexible and adaptive orientation, will lead to greater commitment and confidence in our greenway efforts, not less. If there is concern that greenways may unintentionally create complacency about more difficult issues, this concern can be incorporated into educational displays and programs or environmental art. Paying attention to such issues allows us to learn about them and adjust course. Likewise, in areas that are wealthy or already well endowed with greenspace, perhaps some or all of the excitement about a new greenway project can be channeled into supporting similar efforts in a sister city where needs are far greater. Perhaps a greenway conceived by a small group of enthusiasts simply isn't needed, and careful analysis can point them toward other, more worthy goals. If a project is still compelling once potential downsides and other priorities have been considered, then greenway enthusiasts can proceed with confidence and conviction that their goals are well founded and important.

Landscape Problems and Greenway Opportunities

Greenway projects tend to be initiated because people perceive a problem in the landscape, such as flooding or a decline in greenspace. But greenway projects also get started because someone has a vision of what things could be like in the future, that it would be great, say, to have an interconnected system of greenspace that precedes additional development and gives form to it, while allowing for wildlife movement and trails.

Landscape Problems: Ecology and Society

Landscapes everywhere are experiencing a loss of habitat and the attendant problems of habitat fragmentation and isolation. Individually and collectively, these problems can lead to loss of species, degraded water quality, and increased flooding, among other things. On the human side of the equation, landscapes can become fragmented in ways that make them fail to provide direct access for residents, fail to provide people with a coherent visual framework that reinforces the local identity of that place (i.e., sense of place), and fail to allow people to see and experience natural processes directly. Furthermore, these landscape shortcomings may affect people differently based on their situation, ethnicity, and other factors that call into question environmental justice.

Development Fragments Greenspace

In many parts of North America, an unprecedented amount of open lands is being developed. In the five-year period between 1992 and 1997, the rate of development in the United States (2.2 million acres [890,308 ha] per year) was more than one and one-half times that of the previous ten-year period, 1982–1992 (1.4 million acres [566,560 ha] per year).

Over the fifteen-year period 1982–1997, the total amount of developed land in the United States increased by more than 25 million acres (10,117,141 ha), or one-third (34 percent).[18] That is nearly the total area of the Commonwealth of Virginia or almost twelve times the size of Yellowstone National Park. Certainly, this trend has been underway since the first Europeans settled on American shores and began importing a new and exotic way of life and use of the land. Only recently, however, has it been widely recognized that the proliferation of intensive human activities and the loss of natural areas are leading to serious decline of ecosystems and ecological processes and an alienation of people from nature.

With fewer acres of undeveloped land there is less habitat and less diversity of habitat for wildlife of all sorts, including birds, mammals, reptiles, fish, and plants. This problem is especially serious for those native species that are poorly adapted to human-dominated landscapes and most grave for rare and endangered species that cannot adjust. Habitat loss clearly contributes to the fact that, as of 2004, 1,265 species of animals and plants in the United States were listed as threatened or endangered by the U.S. Fish and Wildlife Service.

Development Pollutes and Disrupts the Water Cycle

Development generates contaminants such as eroded soil, excess nutrients, and toxic chemicals, which reduce water quality in wetlands, streams, and aquifers. Buildings, roads, and other impermeable surfaces redirect the drainage of water that would otherwise soak into the soil. They increase the amount of surface drainage conveyed directly to waterways and can thus radically alter the hydrology of streams and rivers. Stripped of their natural vegetation, waterways are susceptible to contamination from an array of materials moving downslope, including sediment, excess nutrients, and other pollutants.[19] Aquatic habitats and their biota become degraded by these contaminants and also suffer from decreased inputs of organic debris (see chapter 4).

FIGURE 1.3

Loss and fragmentation of forested areas in Cadiz Township, Green County, Wisconsin, between 1831 and 1950. The township is six square miles. Shaded areas represent remaining forest cover and, in some areas, land reverting to forest from presettlement grassland. As forests are cleared and patches created, straight edges replace curved ones and patches become smaller and more isolated. (After Curtis, J. T. [1956]. "The modification of mid-latitude grasslands and forests by man," p. 721–736, in *Man's Role in Changing the Face of the Earth.* W. L. Thomas, ed. Chicago, University of Chicago Press.)

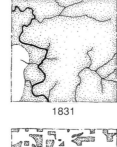
1831

1882

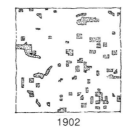
1902

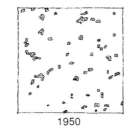
1950

Isolated Fragments Can Become Islands in a Development "Sea"

Human activity is not only reducing the size and number of remaining natural areas fragments, but also isolating those areas from each other. Taken together these problems result in configurations of these remnants that may be poorly suited to maintaining ecological function because areas are too small to be viable for some wildlife or too remote for recolonization. Remaining wildlife habitats have become isolated from one another, sometimes by inhospitable land uses such as agriculture, roads, suburbs, and cities (figures 1.3 and 1.4). As will be explained in subsequent chapters, this phenomenon of habitat fragmentation can be just as serious a problem for native wildlife as overall loss of habitat acreage.

Small and isolated habitat areas tend to support fewer native species as well as smaller (and therefore less secure) populations of those species that do persist. Developed areas that isolate habitat fragments tend to discourage dispersal of individuals among populations, thus making them more vulnerable to genetic inbreeding and localized extinctions. Fragmentation encourages the spread of invasive plants and animals that often displace or prey upon native species.[20] This last point is discussed in more detail in chapters 3 and 4.

The spatial configuration of natural areas also has far-reaching effects on water resources. If arranged haphazardly within a watershed, areas of natural vegetation may not fulfill the protective functions performed by continuous riparian forests.

Virtual Communities Fragment Habitat

In our postmodern world, at least some people have the option of piecing together their own virtual communities in ways that were not possible in times past. This can lead to habitat fragmentation. Digital communications have made it possible to work from home and only occasionally or almost never visit a traditional office. The network infrastructure that has made such communications possible consists of servers (as nodes), routers and switches, and personal computers, cell phones, and other user devices. These are linked by various wired and wireless connections.[21] This new infrastructure is transforming urban land-use patterns, loosening spatial and temporal linkages among urban activities. You don't have to be in the same place at the same time to work with someone else. Over time, some have suggested, new social linkages and recombinations will develop, resulting in new land-use patterns.[22] But, will these new patterns based on new technologies necessarily favor interconnected natural areas and other open space systems?

Massachusetts Institute of Technology architect William Mitchell warns of *exurbia*, or "unmanaged, scattered development enabled by widely available telecommunications, distributed small-scale electric power generation, and micro-water treatment technologies."[23] This side of the telecommunications revolution is having and will continue to have significant impacts on natural

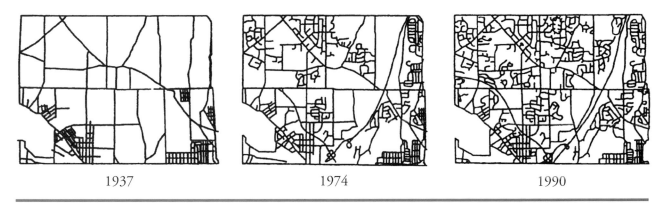

1937   1974   1990

FIGURE 1.4

This landscape time series demonstrates the patterns by which development (roads are shown here) fragments the landscape for a smaller area than the previous example. With a greenway plan in place in advance of at least some of the development, this area would have been much different today. (Courtesy of Natural Lands Trust.)

and social systems. But Mitchell sees a significant transition underway in the contemporary landscape, in which land uses are realigning in response to these new telecommunications possibilities. This suggests that it will take conscious choice and design for metropolitan landscapes to support nature conservation and other greenway functions. It isn't likely we can trust that smatterings of leftover nature will have the integrity we may desire in the landscape.

Greenways Support Diverse Landscape Functions

Greenways can help meet various challenges facing the integrity of landscapes because they can help to preserve connectivity for a wide variety of reasons and also function in other important ways.

Recreational greenways are easily the best known among greenway types. They include trails for walking or bicycling and sometimes areas for organized sports and other group activities (figure 1.5). Linear urban parks, often located along rivers, usually have a strong recreational focus, as do converted human-made corridors such as canal towpaths or railroad rights-of-way ("rail-trails"), which often make effective routes for bicycle commuters in suburbs and cities.

At the other end of the spectrum, conservation biologists and landscape ecologists typically describe and study, and conservationists seek to protect, wildlife corridors and streamside buffers from the standpoint of understanding, enhancing, or protecting ecological integrity.

FIGURE 1.5

A recreational greenway along the Ottawa River in Ottawa, Canada, provides opportunities for walking, jogging, and commuting in a scenic urban setting. (Photo by P. Hellmund.)

For example, ecologist Larry Harris defined a "faunal dispersal corridor" as "a naturally existing or restored native linear landscape feature that connects two or more larger tracts of habitat and functions as a dispersal route for native fauna and flora and for the occurrence of natural ecological processes such as fire."[24] Although human beings are technically part of the native fauna of North America, typically this approach does not consider human needs, instead viewing humans as a major source of problems.

Although the functions of some existing greenways are largely limited to either recreation or nature conservation, most support some combination of the two, as well as other important functions. Greenways devoted mostly to conservation are likely be established in more rural areas (although such areas may undergo development in the future). Recreational greenways tend to be in or connect metropolitan areas, especially suburbs.

It is important to recognize that greenways of all sorts, in all kinds of locales, have both natural and cultural aspects (figure 1.6). For example, greenways that incorporate rail-trails or other human-engineered corridors can be enhanced with native vegetation, and remnant natural corridors, such as riparian greenways, that have been isolated by human actions exist within human-modified landscapes. (Even the mere act of designating a greenway, no matter how undisturbed its ecosystems may be, in some ways makes it a cultural system by putting human boundaries around it.)

We often differentiate greenways according to the natural features they include. Ridgeline and riparian greenways trace natural but different physiographic corridors. Upland greenways may follow neither ridges nor waterways, instead being defined by human needs. Connectors can tie together other, longer greenways to provide multiple linkages and network connectivity ("green infrastructure"). These greenways provide useful descriptive terms that relate less to characteristics that may change over time or along a greenway's length, like recreation intensity or the type of adjacent land use, and more to primary physical and biological characteristics.

For instance, the city of Boulder, Colorado, has designed multipurpose greenways that include walking trails, paved bike paths, and habitat for urban wildlife, while Boulder County has designated corridors in rural areas primarily to protect elk migration routes. In a five-county area of southeastern Wisconsin, a network of "environmental corridors," mostly along waterways, has been protected in both rural and urban areas, with many of the most significant ecological corridors occurring outside of cities. Perhaps because the greenway concept has been so closely associated with recreation, conservation-oriented corridors are often given other designations, such as wildlife corridor. Nonetheless, as linear greenspace, conservation corridors fit the greenway definition.

Philadelphia's Fairmount Park includes a broad greenway along Wissahickon Creek, which is both an urban natural area and a popular recreation corridor (Figure 1.7). The Appalachian Trail takes hikers on a 2,100-mile (3,379-km) journey through a nearly continuous corridor of protected land, ranging from less than 1,000 feet (305 m) to several miles wide. The Bay Circuit Trail, encircling the Boston metropolitan area, is billed as a recreation way for public use. It runs through a series of natural areas, and by making those areas available to the public serves as a catalyst for continued land protection along its length. Even converted rail lines, which are apt to be quite narrow, can be valuable havens for some animal and plant species if native vegetation is maintained or restored.

FIGURE 1.6

In short proximity, the opposite banks of the St. Charles River in Quebec illustrate very different ecological conditions. In the 1960s (a) flood control walls were built with an adjacent recreational path. (Photo by P. Hellmund.) *Since 1996 a less structural approach has been the norm (b), with the installation of plants that benefit wildlife and provide enjoyment to people.* (Photo by Hannah Whipple.)

FIGURE 1.7

Wissahickon Creek in Philadelphia's Fairmount Park is a major urban natural area that contains both trails and developed recreational areas. (Photo by D. Smith.)

Greenway Functions: Ecology

Like other types of conserved lands, greenways support many ecological functions simply because they keep areas clear of most development, providing habitat for plants and animals. Riparian corridors are especially important in this regard because they can include a diversity of habitats—aquatic, riparian, and upland—within a relatively small area.[25] Greenways and other natural areas can supply clean water to aquifers, wetlands, and waterways. If they occupy enough area, they can help to counteract excessive heat buildup in cities by shading adjacent areas and also through evapotranspiration within the corridor, both of which cool the air.[26] Greenway vegetation can contribute to urban air quality by filtering out particulate matter, especially pollutants emanating from adjacent roadways.[27]

If properly designed, streamside greenways and those linked to other natural areas can also perform many functions that traditional preserves cannot. As ecologists Richard Forman and Michel Godron stressed in developing a conceptual framework for landscape ecology, corridors are not only structurally prominent in most landscapes but also strongly influence the flow of organisms, materials, and energy.[28] Because greenways have the high ratio of edge to interior that characterizes corridors, they are very much exposed to surrounding elements. They thus interact with adjacent lands—sometimes for the better, sometimes for worse—to a much greater degree than nonlinear conservation areas, which have less edge for each unit of interior. These interactions between greenways and their surroundings can involve the movement of animals, plants, and inert materials, such as dust. Conservation biologists and landscape ecologists have suggested that naturally vegetated corridors can play a key role in allowing wildlife to move between habitat areas that would otherwise be isolated from one another.[29] In recent years, this suggestion has been supported by empirical studies of animal movement, including small and large mammals in North America,[30] small mammals in Australia,[31] and numerous birds in North America and Europe.[32]

FIGURE 1.8

Upland greenways
can be used to connect habitat patches that would otherwise be
isolated, thus allowing animals to avoid inhospitable areas and move in
relative safety from one patch to another. (Drawing by Jane Shoplick.)

Greenways for Plants and Animals

Greenways can benefit wildlife in many ways (see chapter 3). Enhancing connectivity between habitat areas can increase the area available to wide-ranging species and can allow individuals to travel between different habitat types to meet daily or seasonal needs (figure 1.8). Enhanced connectivity may also increase the long-term health of populations by increasing genetic exchange and by maintaining natural demographic processes, such as recolonization following local extinctions. Greenways can serve as movement corridors for plant species as well, allowing for recolonization of disturbed areas or for long-term genetic exchange. Finally, broad (both wide and long) corridors may help entire biotic communities adapt to long-term climate change by allowing plants and animals to migrate along latitudinal or elevational gradients. Without sufficient regional connections between habitat areas, both fauna and flora may become locked into locations whose suitability for their survival may gradually decrease.

Services from Stream Corridors

Not only do stream corridor greenways often support significant vegetation and associated wildlife, they also provide many other important services. Greenways can help reduce damage from flooding by soaking up and storing excess water. They also maintain the quality of water resources in important ways. Naturally vegetated riparian corridors, located between waterways and adjacent lands with intensive human use, filter excess nutrients in groundwater through vegetative uptake before they reach streams and rivers. In a similar fashion, microtopography, vegetation, and natural ground coverings such as leaves, logs, and other debris form a physical screen for materials moving downslope. Eroded sediments and associated pollutants emanating from agricultural fields, roads, construction areas, or other disturbances are thus filtered out of surface water before they have a chance to cover streambeds or fill in reservoirs. Streamside greenways, especially those containing wetlands, help maintain natural stream levels and rates of flow. By providing areas for water storage, wetlands can significantly reduce the magnitude and thus the damage of floods.

Protection of water quality is not only important for people but crucial to the existence of healthy aquatic organisms and communities. Riparian vegetation helps to sustain these communities by providing shade that lowers water temperatures, by producing organic matter that feeds aquatic animals, and by helping to create diverse and dynamic stream structures such as pools, riffles, and waterfalls that aerate the water and provide shelter for organisms (see chapter 4).

Likewise, healthy streams and aquatic communities are important to many land animals as a source of both food and water. Land and water are thus intimately connected. Ecologist Larry Harris wrote that "animals such as raccoons, weasels, mink and otter forage from the aquatic food chain, but spend most of their time in terrestrial habitats. Like fish, they do work by moving energy and matter up the gradient, against the gravitational field; they link the aquatic system to the adjacent upland."[33]

A river presently known for few of these qualities is the Los Angeles River. Featured in popular films such as *Terminator 2*, *Repo Man*, and *Grease*,[34] it is probably one of the best known urban river corridors in North America, but more often thought of as a ditch than a river (figure 1.9). Its current state is the result of a thirty-year channelization program by the U.S. Army Corps of Engineers, who have overseen the transformation of the once-lush linear desert oasis into a concrete channel. Los Angeles County has developed a greenway vision for the river's future.

A river transformation is already underway in San Jose, California.[35] The greenway known as the Guadalupe River Park is currently being developed along the banks of the river in the heart of downtown San Jose (figure 1.10). It combines goals of flood protection, habitat enhancement and restoration, and recreation in an urban area.

FIGURE 1.9

Heavily channelized portions of the Los Angeles River lack most characteristics of healthy riparian corridors and are designed for flood control.
(A composite made from photographs from the U.S. National Park Service's Historic American Engineering Record, Cal, 019-Losan, 83j-6.)

FIGURE 1.10

A greenway known as the Guadalupe River Park is currently being developed along the banks of the San Jose Guadalupe River, through downtown San Jose. (Drawing by Joe McGrane.)

Greenway Functions: Social

Mainstream environmentalism has had a long focus on distant nature, on wild and scenic places that provide an exotic escape for city dwellers and tourists of all sorts. Although these places and experiences are important, for many years insufficient emphasis was given to nature close to home, to places where people could have regular outdoor experiences, learn about natural history and the environment related to their homes and daily lives, and simply relax and enjoy. Although greenways are obviously not the only sort of nearby nature, they can play a special role because they tend to incorporate diverse environments of particular value in the landscape and because their linearity makes them more accessible than other sorts of greenspace. Greenways have come to play an important role in reconnecting people to nature in their daily lives, providing places for recreation and leisure and shifting ideas about nature away from an infatuation with the distant and wild and toward engaging with the places where most people live.

Much like with wildlife, the movement of people across the landscape is complex and variable. Social connectivity and interaction can be affected by the existence, configuration, and design of greenways. On a physical level, greenways offer the possibility of connecting diverse neighborhoods and, if well designed and managed, of fostering positive social interaction. In a more strictly social sense, because greenways tend to reflect grassroots activism and community involvement, they also have great potential to bring people together and build community through planning and management activities. The result can be more effective and responsive management, stronger social ties and collaboration, and the cultivation of civic interaction and democratic participation.

Greenways have the potential to promote social justice and equality. Because of their linearity, greenways increase accessibility in an absolute sense (i.e., for a given area of greenspace). For the same reason, they also tend to run through diverse neighborhoods, further increasing public access. At the same time, in the context of adjacent private lands and a market economy, there is potential for greenways to contribute to neighborhood gentrification, rising land prices, and, in the long term, increased spatial segregation of higher and lower income groups. Similarly, to the extent that greenways may increase certain types of business activity there is the potential for public investments to distribute benefits disproportionately to certain economic interests. Although the linearity of greenways offers important benefits, all else being equal, fostering social justice requires thinking through how greenways are likely to function in specific social and economic context and working cooperatively with agencies and organizations that operate at that broader scale.

Greenways play a wide range of roles, some active and some passive—in the life of a community and its residents. It is not surprising that many corridors attractive as greenways have cultural, historical, or other community significance, in addition to natural resource qualities. They may be a source for drinking and irrigation water, power generation, building materials, shade, hunting, and other resources.

Recreation

Of all the uses greenways have been put to, recreation is the best known. A growing urban population with significant amounts of leisure time, combined with an overall surge in health consciousness, has led to increasing demand for outdoor pursuits such as jogging, walking, biking, and cross-country skiing.

It is no coincidence that increased demand for outdoor recreation has occurred simultaneously with the growing popularity of greenways, because many greenways are well suited to active travel-oriented sports. Greenways lead somewhere and can connect with other greenways that go to still more places, which is exactly what bikers, in-line skaters, runners, and walkers want to do. Greenways' frequent location along streams and rivers further enhances their aesthetic and recreational appeal. Also, greenways are often designed for recreation because it is the most immediate and tangible benefit for the public and thus can yield a strong and vocal recreation constituency.

Some forms of recreation, like those that use trails or rivers, are especially compatible with greenways because they take advantage of their linear form. Others, like bird watching, may not require linear greenspace, but may be more readily accessible to more people in such a space. Offering nature close at hand seems especially important for children.[36]

Beauty

Greenways have other social benefits that are less tangible than recreation, but equally important. Like other types of parks and natural areas, they add to the aesthetic appeal of landscapes. Greenways often follow natural physiographic corridors, such as streams, rivers, and ridges that have historical and cultural significance. This significance adds to the sense of history and culture that is so important to people's experience of a landscape and their overall sense of place. Greenways can also tie communities together by linking features such as parks, historic sites, residential areas, and shopping districts and by allowing people to travel from place to place without the noise and rush of automobiles.

When designed to encircle cities and towns, greenways can function as greenbelts and help maintain the distinct character of both urban and rural areas. They may, however, have negative impacts on such things as housing affordability, especially if not carefully coordinated with other policy decisions. In Boulder, Colorado, for example, housing prices rose dramatically in the 1990s when the effects of a strict urban containment system (i.e., the greenbelt) collided with residents' unwillingness to accommodate increased densities.[37] Greenbelts in such situations can spawn a demand for exurban housing, which can increase the average commute time[38] and spawn transportation or other problems.

Economic Development and Increased Property Value

Greenways and other linear conservation areas can "create jobs, enhance property values, expand local businesses, attract new or relocating businesses, increase local tax revenues, decrease local government expenditures, and promote a local community," suggest their promoters.[39] Sometimes, however, greenways can create situations in which social justice is called into question if the greenway benefits one group of people but becomes an economic barrier to others who can't afford to live nearby because of increased property values.

People enjoy seeing open, undeveloped lands within a metropolitan context, even if they don't enter such places. Even more basic is what economists call existence value: people may value knowing that there are places set aside, in this case as greenways, even if they never see or visit them.

Historic Preservation

People create roads, railroads, trails, canals, and other lines and corridors in the landscape that over time may take on historical significance. Designation as a greenway may be an appropriate way of preserving aspects of these linear, historical resources. Also, the manner in which the corridor has been used, or not used, over its history may endow it with significant natural resources or other important qualities. Rail corridors through prairie landscapes, for example, sometimes host native plants that once were common to the broader area but have been displaced by development (figure 1.11). Occasional fires sparked by passing trains may have replicated the burning necessary for these plants to sustain themselves.

Sometimes the greatest significance of these corridors is simply that they have been preserved in the face of development as unbroken or largely unbroken lines in the landscape, not necessarily because of the qualities within their bounds. When such a corridor becomes available for a trail or is managed for wildlife this can be unexpected gift to the community. In such cases these greenways are much greater than the sum of their parts. For example, when the abandoned right-of-way of a railroad is divided up and returned to adjacent landowners, there are small gains for many people. When the corridor stays intact, however, something unique has been preserved for the community as a whole. In the last thirty-five years, the Rails-to-Trails Conservancy estimates that 12,650 miles (20,358 km) of abandoned railroad tracks have been converted to rail-trail greenways in the United States, serving approximately 100 million users per year.[40]

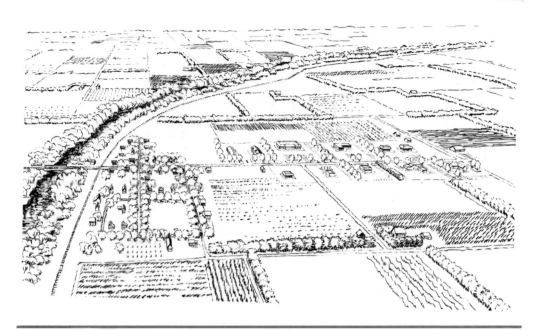

FIGURE 1.11

Fields of corn and soybeans now grow in what was once a native grassland landscape in the American Midwest. The abandoned railroad corridor along the river serves as a refuge for the original prairie species. Trees are now common only along the river and where planted as windbreaks. (Drawing by Jane Shoplick.)

BOX 1.1

Sometimes significant natural resources have been preserved because they were corridors where people were excluded, such as protected national boundaries. The Korean Demilitarized Zone, the last remaining Cold War–style frontier in the world, is the largest contiguous, intact ecosystem left on the Korean peninsula and is home to rare and endangered species, including leopards and possibly tigers as well as endangered migratory birds, such as the white-naped and red-crowned cranes and the black-faced spoonbill. For similar reasons, Europe's Iron Curtain corridor (below) represents one of the greatest opportunities for a greenway anywhere in the world, with its unique combination of natural, historic, and recreational potential. For 40 years this 4,000-plus-mile corridor was strictly off limits to people and, as a result, wildlife abounded. For one hundred years the United States protected the forests of the Panama Canal area because they provided watershed functions important to the functioning of the canal. Now under Panamanian jurisdictions, many of these forests, including some that were parts of U.S. military bases, have become national parks and part of the Mesoamerican Biological Corridor.

Iron Curtain corridor at Salzwedel, Germany.

A Strategic Greenway Design Approach

Some of the most significant ecological and social functions of greenways have been outlined in this chapter. The chapters that follow will examine these functions in greater detail and will consider how they relate to the practical task of designing greenways. A broad aim of this book is to illuminate the intersections of science and design and to find ways of effectively communicating scientific information to greenway designers and greenway objectives to scientists. Chapter 6 presents a strategic greenway design approach that embodies concepts presented earlier.

Greenway design, like any manipulation of natural/cultural systems, can be a highly complex endeavor. Each project involves unique local conditions and presents different problems to be solved.

From a broader perspective, because greenways interact with surrounding lands, it is crucial to consider a greenway's context within the landscape. Understanding context may mean deciphering the ways in which animals use neighboring unprotected lands in addition to a greenway itself. Or it may mean determining the type and magnitude of contaminants flowing toward a greenway from adjacent areas. Contextual design also requires understanding the social and economic impacts of a greenway on nearby human communities.

Greenways function in multiple dimensions whether or not they are designed and managed for multiple objectives. Along with these multiple objectives come multiple stakeholders, representing disparate interests. With the active participation of stakeholders, greenway designers are more likely to obtain better information and an understanding of varied values and perspectives and to make better decisions. Without the participation of these stakeholders it will be very difficult to get the cooperation that is necessary to implement and manage the greenway.

To complicate greenway design, the professionals in North America who deal with most greenway issues aren't necessarily accustomed to collaboration. At times there is a kind of intellectual fragmentation among a project team, with biologists focused on biological issues, stormwater engineers focused on drainage management issues, and watershed scientists focused on water quality. Greenspace and recreation are the concerns of greenspace planners. Social concerns are often reduced to consideration of recreation, aesthetics, and historic preservation, with issues such as environmental justice and social interaction left out of greenway planning entirely.

Certainly there are many crossdisciplinary efforts underway, but the compartmentalized nature of most government agencies and other sources of information can make it challenging to obtain a broader perspective. Although collaboration is useful and important, also needed are broad integrators who see connections and relationships and who can envision futures that combine the best aspects of a range of issues. Because greenways combine social and natural objectives and because they frequently sit within highly disturbed settings, visions for their future need to be integrative and creative. Sometimes this kind of vision may start with a single person, but such a vision risks being too personal to be broadly supported or relevant. Sometimes it may actually be easier for nonspecialist, nonprofessionals to see the possibilities for integration than it is for people who may be thought of as leaders.

A part of the metropolis that may be overlooked in selecting corridors for greenways is degraded lands. Formerly degraded areas (e.g., restored brownfields) may serve as important links or nodes in a greenway network. Artist Timothy Collins, who has worked with the Nine Mile Run Greenway Project in Pittsburgh, Pennsylvania, suggested that "the enormous potential for significant changes in thinking about urban development, public space, ecology and sustainability make brownfield properties ideal subjects for democratic discourse."[41]

Of particular significance to the design approach presented in this book is sensitivity to scale and asking the right questions at the right point in the process. This is important because different phenomena are relevant or observable at different scales and the responses to them are best accomplished at an appropriate scale. For example, some landscape patterns, such as connectedness, may not be readily apparent at the wrong scale, or scientists may not realize that a wildlife species is rare if the geographic perspective is too narrowly focused.

Fundamental to this design approach is an understanding that a greenway is an element of urban design that must be considered within a design context and as a design element. Thus designers will consider how a greenway responds to topography, helps fit the city to its landscapes, helps cultivate a sense of community, helps frame views of other areas of nature as well as of developed parts of the metropolis, provides an edge or boundary to parts of the metropolis, engenders a sense of place, provides opportunities for regeneration and sustainability, and highlights change and continuity over time, among other design objectives.[42] Thus, in cultural aspects greenway design goes beyond just including cultural elements, such as historic sites, in a corridor to considering the greenway as a whole as an element of urban and community design.

Landscape architect Jack Ahern noted that greenways are a strategic planning approach. The greenway approach "substitutes the difficulty/futility of planning the entire landscape, with a strategic effort to build a linear network as a kind of sustainable framework,"[43] he wrote. The challenge then in making sustainable greenways and greenway networks is understanding the landscape well enough to identify its strategic elements.

The design approach described in chapter 6 is strategic. It uses rules of thumb or master principles[44] and is adaptive, so decisions can be made with the information at hand.

Greenways and Sustainable Design: The Significance of Scale and Equity

Greenways are sometimes presented as a component of sustainable landscapes and communities, something good for the environment. Sustainability, however, as discussed earlier, is a rather vague term. It tends to mean what people want it to mean, which can be quite variable. This may account for its popularity and wide acceptance, which can have both positive and negative aspects. On one hand, it gets people interested in the concept, at least at some level. On the other hand, it opens the door for anyone to put a "good" label on things that may be relatively short-sighted or provincial, or even disingenuous and self-serving, as with corporate greenwashing. (This may involve presenting a business practice as environmentally friendly when it may not actually be.) Although landscape sustainability may not exist in an absolute sense, as a process of learning and moving toward landscape integrity, it has considerable value. Working toward sustainability is a valid and vital goal.

Although sorting out all the issues related to sustainability and greenways is clearly beyond the scope of this book, it may be helpful here to consider two critical issues related to sustainable design of greenways and landscape design in general: scale and social inequality/injustice.

A Greenway's Larger Context Influences Sustainability

People tend to look at projects at one or sometimes two spatial scales. The first is the local scale—the bounds of the project itself—and a second scale may be global. For the latter, there is a general desire to make the planet sustainable and to manage resources and pollutants and population in aggregate, at the global scale. This is useful to some extent, but all too easily leads to a tendency of global environmental managers telling the real people in specific places what they can or should do based on what is happening globally. The challenge with this approach is remembering to pay attention to how things will play out at the local level and encouraging bottom-up solutions as much as possible.

From the local perspective, we focus on and seek sustainability in places to which we feel attached. We often feel that if we can just get the greenway right ecologically and socially here in our own community, that we must be making a contribution to global sustainability. It is true that local initiatives can make a significant contribution to both local quality of life and to global sustainability. For instance, a greenway may maintain biodiversity and productive ecosystems, reduce energy used for transportation, and provide beauty and recreation. But true sustainability is more complicated than that. If we focus on the range of ecological connections, we see that even the most well meaning local actions can have at least some negative effects at broader scales. If a greenway is used for tourism, for example, it encourages more travel and pollution. It may also take resources that might do much more for overall sustainability if used elsewhere. Thus there may be cases where we should question spending $50,000 or more per acre on conservation in a metropolitan area, when such a sum could achieve far more in other parts of the world, where needs may be far greater.

The problem is not that we don't think about sustainability at multiple scales, but that we sometimes don't connect the scales. When focusing on local opportunities, we sometimes fail to look at the larger picture. So, for instance, we assume that land conservation is always in support of sustainability without asking questions such as: How much did that land cost, and how great were the needs and benefits, especially in comparison with needs and benefits elsewhere or for other purposes? What else could have been done with the money? Where is the land and how will people get to it? What are the implications of the land's location for development (local scale), transportation (regional scale), energy consumption, and pollution (regional and global)?

The Variable Impacts of Greenway Projects across Society

Unlike the problem in considering scale, which is typically a failure to link the local to the global, the problem with social inequality is almost the opposite. Often there is a failure to disaggregate "we" into distinct nationalities, races, classes, or other groups and thereby understand differences in needs and impacts.

Community is, by definition, both inclusive and exclusive. Some people are in a community, others are out. You can't have community without excluding and discriminating. Ideally what we should seek is the common ties of community combined with tolerance and concern beyond the bounds of the community. But community does tend to mean some negative things for those who are outside it. To the extent that we associate sustainability with community, it opens the door to improving local quality of life while ignoring other people and places that in reality lie within the sphere of our material connections and impacts. Community can be defined as that sphere of impacts, or better, of interconnections. But we don't typically use that definition because many of those connections are out of sight, out of mind, and sometimes those connections are troublesome, difficult, and unpleasant. So often we restrict our view of community to those who are near us physically and socially, excluding people who are either physically or socially distant.

The tendency is often to look at a greenway situation in the aggregate and say that "we all" need to use resources more efficiently and that the greenway will help. This makes it easy to overlook the fact that some of us have an enormously unfair share of the world's resources. So to the extent that a focus on sustainability ignores questions of distribution of resources it helps to reinforce the status quo.

The key here is not that justice automatically leads to or is required for sustainability, as is sometimes suggested, but that, from an ethical perspective, the two run parallel. They both relate to our impacts on things that are distant from us—in time or in space or in terms of social groups. When we have an impact on things, we have a responsibility to them. Just as we are increasingly recognizing that we have an ethical responsibility to consider the effects of our actions over time (e.g., leaving sufficient resources for our children, which is one definition of sustainability), there is an ethical imperative to consider the effects of our actions across space as they affect people in different groups, different places, and different parts of the world.

We need to be aware that, if we really look at all the connections a greenway may make, both natural and social, what often pass for win-win solutions aren't always that. What may appear at first look to be just great for everyone may have a lot more complexity, contention, and conflict as we look deeper. This is not a reason to abandon the idea of harmonizing interests so that everyone wins, and we should still aim for that. The point is that achieving justice and moving toward true sustainability for a greenway—on both ecological and social grounds—is much more of a challenge than we frequently are led to believe. However challenging, it is very useful to identify and resolve conflicts rather than avoid them to gain the appearance of harmony.

Hard-Headed Analysis Is Needed to Keep Greenway Enthusiasm from Mere Boosterism

It is easy to get excited about a greenway project and all it might accomplish. Boosterism, however, can have negative aspects. We should not let our aspirations and hopes drive our understanding and analysis. Sure, it would be great if the things we get excited about could save the world, but that doesn't mean they will. Maybe they will, maybe not. Maybe they will make a small contribution overall, and maybe they will just make a particular place better. Whatever the case, it is important to be analytically hard-headed, looking beyond mere local benefits, while still retaining big-hearted aspirations.

Evolution of Greenways from Linear Conservation and Transportation Corridors

Greenways have an interesting history in North America. Although the term *greenway* is relatively new, having emerged only in the late 1950s, the design of linear greenspace in North America predates the name by nearly a century.

Parkways: The First Greenways

As early as the 1860s, the eminent American landscape architect Frederick Law Olmsted recognized the great potential of linear greenspace for providing access to city parks and extending the benefits of parks into nearby neighborhoods. By designing tree-lined carriageways—which he called parkways—that linked parks to each other and to surrounding neighborhoods, Olmsted enhanced the recreational and aesthetic experience of park visitors and city dwellers in general.

In 1866 and 1867, Olmsted and his partner, Calvert Vaux, designed Brooklyn's Prospect Park. As part of that design they proposed two connecting parkways, one leading south to Coney Island, the other linking Prospect Park with Central Park in Manhattan, which had also been designed by Olmsted and Vaux. Although the linkage to Central Park was never implemented, the parkway to Coney Island and another leading northeast to Queens, called Ocean Parkway and Eastern Parkway respectively, were later constructed.[45] These parkways included broad, six-lane carriage roads and walking paths and were flanked on each side by thirty-two-foot–wide (10 m) wooded strips.[46]

Olmsted and Vaux continued to include linear connections in many of their later projects, including parkways and open-space systems in Buffalo and Chicago. They emphasized social and aesthetic issues in most of these projects because these were seen as some of the most pressing needs of their day.

Basis of Some Early Greenways in Ecology

Olmsted's design for Boston's Emerald Necklace, which he developed in stages between 1878 and 1890, addressed concerns about drainage and water quality. Encircling the city with a ring of green that included the Back Bay Fens and the Muddy River, as well as other parks and parkway segments, the Emerald Necklace, as it has come to be known, is one of Olmsted's most famous designs (figure 1.12). Here, he expanded upon his earlier aesthetic emphasis by modifying the river to better drain surrounding neighborhoods and by reshaping the fens to provide increased flood storage[47] (figure 1.13). These actions were combined with the construction of sewers for human waste, which had previously flowed directly into the river, and flood gates to regulate periodic flooding tides. The project enhanced flood storage, improved waste disposal, and linked the area to the rest of the Emerald Necklace for recreation and transportation. Although these modifications were more akin to modern engineering solutions than to an ecological approach, Olmsted nonetheless established an early and strong precedent for the idea of using greenways to accommodate multiple uses.

Landscape architect and Olmsted protégé Charles Eliot proposed the Metropolitan Boston Park System in the 1890s, which included a regional greenspace system of ocean fronts, river estuaries, harbor islands, large forests, and small urban squares. This system was a more extensive, regional version of the closer-in Emerald Necklace.

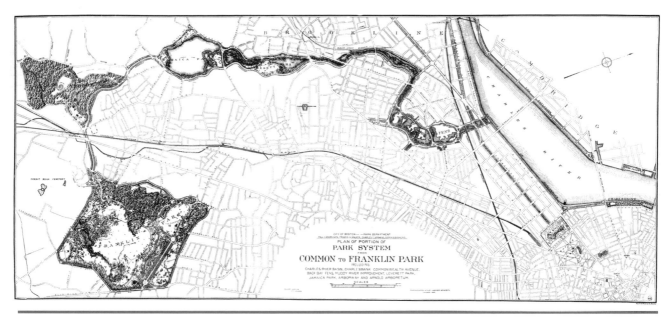

FIGURE 1.12

Plan view of Frederick Law Olmsted's design for Boston's Emerald Necklace. Designed in stages between 1878 and 1890, the Emerald Necklace includes a series of urban parks linked together with parkways. (Courtesy of U. S. National Park Service, Frederick Law Olmsted National Historic Site.)

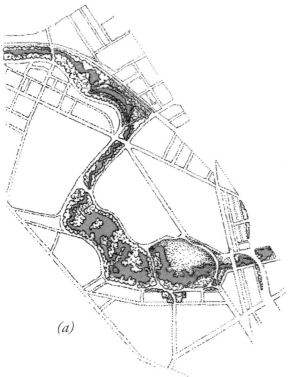

(a)

(b)

FIGURE 1.13

Olmsted's design for the Muddy River and the Back Bay Fens, both part of the Emerald Necklace, involved modifications that increased the flood storage capacity of the fens and helped treat raw sewage flowing into the river.
(a) Plan view. (b) Historic photograph of construction along the Muddy River.
(Photo courtesy of Public Library of Brookline, Massachusetts.)

Parkways Become More Common

Around the turn of the century, parkways and other greenspace connectors became more common in American cities as others followed Olmsted's lead. Between 1890 and the 1920s, similar linkages were designed by H. W. S. Cleveland for Minneapolis and St. Paul, Charles Eliot for the greater Boston area, and by Jens Jensen for South Chicago.[48]

These early greenspace corridors, even when fairly narrow, could usually accommodate carriage roads and walking paths while maintaining a pleasing, naturalistic setting.[49] This situation changed as the automobile became a common means of transportation in the early decades of the 20th century. With the addition of automobiles, many parkways designed after about 1920 took on a very different character, first as paved roads for pleasure driving and later as high-speed commuter routes.[50]

Some of these later parkways were designed with wide buffers of natural land, especially those built in the 1920s and 1930s, such as the Bronx River Parkway in New York and Virginia's Skyline Drive, flanked by Shenandoah National Park. Later, as cars sped up, traffic became heavier, and people traveled greater distances, these winding, leisurely roads gave way to straighter parkways designed for faster, safer travel and eventually were rendered largely obsolete by today's utilitarian highways and freeways.[51]

Greenbelts as Part of British and North American New Towns

An independent but somewhat related concept was developed in England at about the same time. In 1898, Ebenezer Howard proposed the design of a model "Garden City." In this idealized scheme, the inner residential part of the city would be encircled with a "Grand Avenue." The avenue was to be "420 feet [128 m] wide, and, forming a belt of green upwards of three miles [4.8 km] long."[52] Farther out, beyond commercial and industrial areas, Garden City was to be surrounded by extensive farms and forests.[53] Howard meant to insulate cities with belts of rural land to limit urban sprawl and to tie city and country together, thus offering the benefits of both to society. Howard's concept, including the use of greenbelts, as they came to be called, was later adapted with various degrees of success in numerous town-planning efforts in England and elsewhere (figure 1.14).[54] After World War II, a greenbelt was implemented around London, mostly by means of land-use controls.[55]

Greenbelts were later used in the United States in the design of several planned communities. A key figure in the United States was Rexford Guy Tugwell, who proposed and headed the Resettlement Association within the U.S. Department of Agriculture (USDA) during the New Deal. To provide low-income housing during the Depression, from 1935 to 1937 Tugwell oversaw the design and implementation of three new towns surrounded by greenbelts: Greenhills, Ohio; Greendale, Wisconsin; and Greenbelt, Maryland.[56] Garden City concepts embodied a blending of city and nature and included greenbelts as a specific linear conservation zone—a proto-greenway.

Benton MacKaye Proposes "Open Ways"

The greenbelt concept was further developed by the American regional planner Benton MacKaye. MacKaye proposed systems of wooded greenspace that "would form a linear area, or belt around and through the locality."[57] His intent was more than just to surround cities with greenspace as a means

FIGURE 1.14

Even though development has leapfrogged portions of the Ottawa greenbelt, the greenbelt still makes significant contributions to the livability of the city. Shown here are hiking opportunities in the 9,140-acre (3,700-hectare) Mer Bleue Conservation Area, an internationally significant peat bog. (Photo by P. Hellmund.)

of blocking urban sprawl. He also suggested bisecting settled areas with spokes of green and including recreation as a primary use of these "open ways," as he called them. MacKaye thus combined, in effect, the greenbelt concept with elements of the early parkways and urban open-space networks.

MacKaye also proposed the Appalachian Trail in 1921, which he saw not just as a hiking trail, but as a broad-scale version of his regional greenspace, containing the spread of development from the eastern seaboard and providing a primeval pathway for the adventurous hiker. Today, the 2,100-mile (3,379-km) Appalachian National Scenic Trail is protected with a nearly continuous corridor of land that averages about 1,000 feet (305 m) wide. The trail connects many larger federal and state land holdings.

Ecology Becomes Prominent in Planning and Design

In the 1960s, the ideas of Olmsted, Howard, and MacKaye were followed by the emergence of a new emphasis on ecology in planning and design, which has had a major impact on the development of greenways. Early in the decade, Phillip Lewis, Jr., a professor of landscape architecture at the University of Wisconsin at Madison, stressed the importance of ecological features in guiding land conservation. By overlaying and analyzing natural resource maps on transparencies, Lewis found that the bulk of important resources were typically located along waterways and in areas of pronounced topography; he referred to these alignments as "environmental corridors."[58]

Using this technique, Lewis systematically identified corridors in statewide studies of Wisconsin and Illinois. In Wisconsin, these corridors (figure 1.15) formed the basis for a statewide trails plan that subsequently became a focus of state land acquisitions.[59] Lewis's work also paved the way for successful efforts to preserve an extensive regional network of corridors in southeastern Wisconsin.

FIGURE 1.15

Map of Wisconsin showing the pattern of environmental corridors identified by Phillip Lewis, Jr., including waterways, wetlands, and, especially in the southwestern portion of the state, areas of pronounced topography. (From Wisconsin Department of Resource Development. [1962]. *Recreation in Wisconsin.* Madison, WI.)

Ian McHarg Proposes "Design with Nature"

In 1969, Ian McHarg, of the University of Pennsylvania, published his influential book *Design with Nature*, in which he outlined a theoretical and technical basis for ecologically based planning and design. McHarg stressed the importance of systematic land-use planning according to the relative ecological value and sensitivity of each part of the landscape: "The distribution of open space must respond to natural process. . . . The problem lies not in absolute area but in distribution. We seek a concept that can provide an interfusion of open space and population."[60] The idea was not so much to exclude development as to distribute it in such a way as to minimize disruption of ecological processes.

McHarg's method, like that of Lewis, was based on a system of transparent map overlays. Each overlay represented a different category of natural feature, such as hydrology, geology, and plant communities. For each type of feature, the more sensitive an area was to development impacts, the darker shading it received. (Sensitivity was determined previously through ecological inventory and analysis.) The overlays were then placed atop one another to form a composite that revealed the combined shading, and thus sensitivity, of all locations (figure 1.16). In this way, the relative suitability of different areas for development of various kinds and intensities, or for conservation, was determined. Because stream and river corridors nearly always have important combinations of natural features—as Lewis had earlier demonstrated—this method provided an important objective rationale for corridor protection.

Although similar systems of overlays had been used since at least as early as 1912,[61] McHarg's development and application of the technique, together with his articulation of a comprehensive approach to ecological planning and design, marked a major step in the development of the field.[62] Importantly, this method addressed much more than the delineation of corridors and has been used to develop spatial frameworks for both development and conservation across large areas. Variations of the method have been adapted to computerized geographic information systems (see chapter 6 for further discussion).[63]

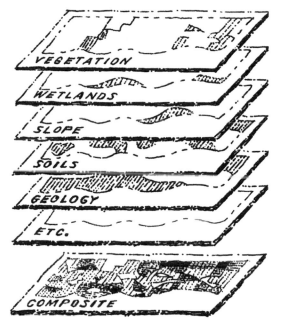

FIGURE 1.16

The map overlay process combines maps of various environmental features to create a composite map. As promoted by Ian McHarg, such overlay systems have been widely used to determine appropriate locations for different kinds of land use, including conservation. This process has been greatly facilitated by geographic information systems.

Island Biogeography Helps Launch Spatial Conservation Thinking

Two years before McHarg published his influential *Design with Nature*, two scientists, Robert MacArthur and Edward Wilson, articulated a theory of species equilibrium and islands that has had a profound influence on terrestrial nature conservation, including wildlife corridor planning.[64] Significantly, their theory of island biogeography (see chapter 2) got ecologists and conservationists thinking spatially about the patterns of elements in the landscape. The work of MacArthur and Wilson, seen today as groundbreaking, set the stage for other ways of understanding the spatial dimensions of landscapes. It still informs the language, if not the practice, of conservation.

A Sudden Interest in Wildlife Corridors

Growing out of island biogeography was a considerable interest in and application of the conservation of wildlife corridors. Such corridors seemed to make intuitive sense. If the landscape was being increasingly fragmented, then saving or reinstating connections for wildlife made sense. There was vigorous debate about the potential problems of pursuing corridor strategies, problems such as the potential spread of disease or predators, but still there was a push for corridors, which continues today. Although vestiges of the debate survive, more frequently the warning today is to view corridors as one of a number of conservation strategies, not a panacea. Rather than focus on physical connections through the landscape—such as corridors you might draw on a map—there is more discussion about facilitating movement across a range of landscape elements, in a process called functional connectivity.

Nature Is in Cities Too

After generations of viewing nature as something safely distant from the city, more often people today are aware that natural processes are better planned for, accommodated, and even celebrated than fought or ignored. Instead of channelizing or burying streams, for example, today there are greater attempts to keep some natural characteristics of urban streams, as well as daylighting buried ones. With this realization has come a greater appreciation of the environmental services greenways can provide.

Conservation Meets Recreation

In the 1980s, increased interest in open-space conservation converged with the growing popularity of outdoor recreation, resulting in many new greenway projects, along with vigorous support across the country.[65] As the loss of greenspace became increasingly apparent on the national level and particularly striking in many urban areas, interest in all types of land conservation rose to an unprecedented level. At the same time, the cost of land continued to rise, especially in metropolitan areas, while federal funding for land conservation plummeted. Land protection thus became difficult in many parts of the country.

Meanwhile, the increased demand for outdoor recreation in recent years has spurred on greenway initiatives. The linearity of greenways makes them well suited for trails, while their common location along water encourages boating and fishing and helps retain beautiful scenery. Recreationists, therefore, have a strong affinity for greenways and often have become their greatest supporters among the general public, playing a significant role in greenway advocacy.

Further evidence for support of greenspace protection in the United States came on election day in 2003, when voters approved 64 ballot measures in 16 states to set aside approximately $1.2 billion in public money to protect land for parks and other greenspace.[66]

Proposal for a National System of Greenways: The Launch of a Movement

The trends toward greenspace conservation and outdoor recreation were recognized by the President's Commission on Americans Outdoors, appointed in 1985 to study the state of greenspace and outdoor recreation in the United States.[67] The commission found strong support across the country for increasing land conservation and recreation facilities and proposed a national system of greenways as a means of achieving both ends: "We have a vision for allowing every American easy access to the natural world: Greenways. Greenways are fingers of green that reach out from and around and through communities all across America, created by local action. They will connect parks and forests and scenic countrysides, public and private, in recreation corridors for hiking, jogging, wildlife movement, horse and bicycle riding."[68]

Estimates put the number of greenways in the United States in 1989 at more than 250[69] and today more than 3,000.[70] The actual number of greenways may be higher because many protected linear greenspaces that lack organized management, administration, or publicity often go unrecognized. Also the term *greenway* can appropriately be applied to many linear greenspaces not necessarily so named.

Thousands of greenway projects are now underway across the country in urban, suburban, and rural settings. Notable efforts with a strong recreational focus, but which also protect ecological processes, are taking place in San Francisco, where the Bay Trail and the Bay Area Ridge Trail trace concentric rings around San Francisco Bay; along the Chattanooga River in Chattanooga, Tennessee; from New York City to Albany and beyond along the Hudson River; and in Boston, where the Bay Circuit Trail encircles the metropolitan area much as Frederick Law Olmsted's Emerald Necklace encircled the inner city more than a century ago.

Many coordinated urban greenway networks are now underway that stress both recreation and conservation in cities such as Boulder, Colorado; Davis, California; and Raleigh, North Carolina. The state of Maryland has a statewide greenways program that seeks to combine water resource and habitat protection. Other examples abound, some of which are quite important ecologically.

Establishment of River Greenways

Although much of the historical development of greenways has been led by planners and landscape architects, efforts in river and stream conservation have also resulted in the protection of many riparian greenways. Especially since the 1960s, when the problem of water pollution from sewage and industrial waste was raised in the public consciousness, restoring water quality and aquatic habitat has been a priority for government agencies and many nonprofit conservation organizations. Previously strong national support for dams and other large federal water projects also came to be tempered by concerns, articulated largely by national environmental groups, about the environmental damage and lost recreational opportunities caused by damming the nation's remaining free-flowing rivers.[71]

With passage of the National Wild and Scenic Rivers Act in 1968, protecting rivers became a component of national environmental policy. As of 2002, this legislation had been used to protect 176 rivers or river segments, totaling 11,338 miles (18247 km), from dams and impoundments.[72] Many of these designations have resulted in increased protection of riverside lands through federal land purchases, improved management of existing public lands, or increased local regulation of development and land use. Many states have implemented river protection programs that complement the federal wild and scenic river system by protecting additional waterways.[73]

Another piece of federal legislation that has fostered the establishment of riparian greenways is Section 404 of the Clean Water Act, which offers significant protection to many of the nation's wetlands. Also important, although not water-related, has been the National Trails System Act, which was designed to spur the creation of a national system of hiking trails. The act has been used to purchase land along extensive stretches of the Appalachian Trail and to support planning and management efforts by numerous volunteer trail groups, who sponsor eight National Scenic Trails with a combined length of more than 14,000 miles (22,531 km).[74]

Land-use regulations have also been used systematically by states and municipalities to protect streamside corridors across large areas. For instance, Maine's Shoreland Zoning Act requires municipalities to designate protection standards for zones 250 feet (76 m) wide around lakes and ponds and 75 feet (23 m) wide along streams.[75] In similar fashion, Maryland requires towns to limit development along streams and rivers that drain into Chesapeake Bay, where reduced water quality threatens the estuary's health and productivity.[76] Although these and other regulatory programs do not usually lead to officially designated greenways, they have offered at least partial protection to thousands of miles of waterways.

The Challenge of Environmental Justice

Beginning in the 1980s, the environmental justice movement presented an important challenge to mainstream environmentalism. Since its inception in the 19th century, resource conservation and nature preservation—the broad movement that we now call environmentalism—has tended to be a middle and upper class social movement focused disproportionately on the "wise use" of resources for industrial purposes and on the protection of scenic, recreational spaces in landscapes distant from urban centers. Although attention to air and water pollution was always relevant to all social groups, it was not until the 1980s that grassroots activism drew attention to the fact that the greatest share of environmental hazards—especially toxic contaminants—are often borne most heavily by low-income and minority communities.[77] Toxic nightmares like Love Canal and Times Beach made it clear that existing initiatives did not point toward a clean environment for all Americans, as is often suggested, but rather that environmental quality and good health are often unjustly related to one's economic or ethnic status.

Although tension between the old guard of mainstream environmentalism and the new, more strident justice advocates still exists, environmental justice has been embraced, at least in principle and often in deed, by virtually all environmental agencies and nonprofit organizations. Most recently, concerns about the distribution of environmental benefits in the form of access to greenspace and to productive natural resources have been added to the environmental justice agenda.[78] Just as wealth and ethnicity are often related to environmental risks, in many places the existence and quality of greenspace and recreational resources may be lacking in low-income areas. As we will see in chapter 5, these issues are now beginning to be taken up by innovative greenway projects.

Genesis of Green Infrastructure and Ecological Network Movements

In recent years there has been a logical progression from planning individual greenways to networks of greenways, which in Europe are called ecological networks, and at times in North America, green infrastructure. Green infrastructure has a somewhat utilitarian outlook, and is often presented in terms of services (e.g., flood control and water quality protection) these systems of greenspace provide. The concept advocates that these services should be considered as carefully as gray infrastructure, such as roads and utility lines.

An ecological network is "a framework of ecological components, e.g., core areas, corridors, and buffer zones, which provides the physical conditions necessary for ecosystems and species populations to survive in a human-dominated landscape."[79]

Greenway Examples

The following examples demonstrate some of the diversity of greenways today.

Southeastern Wisconsin Environmental Corridors

For more than thirty years the Southeastern Wisconsin Regional Planning Commission and its constituent local governments have made systematic efforts to delineate and protect greenways, which they call environmental corridors (figure 1.17). The result of these efforts is an extensive network of greenspace in locations ranging from urban to suburban to rural. By applying an innovative combination of land-use regulation and land acquisition to the highest priority corridors, the seven counties have achieved what may be the most comprehensive regional system of greenways in North America today.

Corridor protection in the seven-county, southeastern region of Wisconsin dates from the 1920s, when a system of parkways was initiated in Milwaukee County. In the 1960s, the concept was further promoted by Professor Phillip Lewis, Jr., of the University of Wisconsin at Madison. Lewis, a landscape architect, recognized the concentration of important natural resources along waterways and ridgelines and recom-

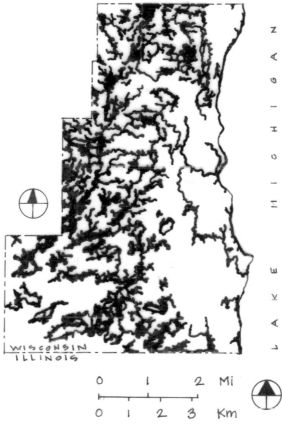

FIGURE 1.17

Primary environmental corridors in the seven-county southeastern Wisconsin region have been protected from most forms of development through land acquisition or a combination of local, state, and federal regulations.

(After Southeastern Wisconsin Regional Planning Commission 1985.)

mended their protection by the state for both recreation and conservation. Lewis's recommendations were adopted by the regional planning commission as part of its regional land-use plan in 1966.[80] Since then, corridor protection has been one of the commission's primary goals in this rolling, glacially sculpted terrain west of Lake Michigan.

The commission has identified primary and secondary environmental corridors, as well as isolated natural resource areas. These areas contain one or more of these key features: lakes, rivers, and streams; undeveloped shorelands and floodlands; wetlands; woodlands; prairie remnants; wildlife habitat; rugged terrain and steep slopes; unique landforms or geological formations; unfarmed, poorly drained, and organic soil; existing outdoor recreation sites; potential outdoor recreation sites; significant open spaces; historic sites and structures; and outstanding scenic areas and vistas.

Primary environmental corridors have concentrations of these natural and cultural resources. They are at least 400 acres (162 ha) in size, at least two miles (3.2 km) long, and at least 200 feet (61 m) wide. Secondary environmental corridors have smaller concentrations of resources. They are at least 100 acres (41 ha) in size and at least one mile (1.6 km) long, unless they link primary corridors. Isolated natural resource areas contain significant remaining resources apart from environmental corridors. They are at least five acres (2 ha) in size and at least 200 feet (61 m) wide.[81]

Bogotá, Colombia

A mayor of Bogotá, Colombia, made impressive strides in implementing urban greenways as a means of promoting social equity and community. In three years in office (1998–2001) the administration of Enrique Peñalosa began creating bikeways, greenways, parks, and other public facilities as part of his plan, *Por la Bogotá que Queremos* (For the Bogotá We Want), for what was then a city of 6.5 million people.[82]

Rather than considering public pedestrian spaces as irrelevant or frivolous in the face of considerable poverty, Peñalosa viewed these public facilities as important places where people of all socioeconomic classes could encounter each other as equals. Greenways and other public places became vehicles to "generate a profound change in how citizens live, recovering the confidence in their capacity both to build a better future and to dynamize their social, economic and cultural development."[83] An underlying principle of the plan was to improve people's quality of life, helping individuals, families, and society achieve well-being and happiness. Four of the plan's priorities were (1) reducing marginalization, (2) increasing social interaction, (3) enhancing the human scale of the city, and (4) improving mobility.

In recent years, Bogotá had grown in population, size, and density, with many new squatters settling at the urban fringe, generally in high-risk areas with steep slopes. Accordingly, much of the city's growth had been unplanned, and many neighborhoods lacked basic public services.

In an unusual process for the city, local communities were seen as collaborators, not merely recipients of services. Physical infrastructure was seen as a vehicle for social action, not an end in itself. Access to services by every citizen was viewed as very important, no matter where he or she lived. Greenways—some with very wide and separate paths for those on bicycles and those

FIGURE 1.19

The High Line Canal, here in Littleton, Colorado, snakes through the Denver metropolitan area, and in parts creates a linear oasis.

(Photo by Richard H. Johnson/Denver Water.)

walking—were developed in areas where the government wanted to direct development and thereby more effectively provide infrastructure.

The goals, among several, were to create pedestrian paths and bikeways that crossed the city in every direction, with bikeways physically separated from car traffic on all major roads, and abundant parks, plazas, and pedestrian public space. The effort, one of the largest physical infrastructure projects in the recent history of the city, resulted in 1,200 new or rejuvenated parks; 217 miles (349 km) of bikeways; schools, libraries, and a new bus system (figure 1.18).

High Line Canal, Denver

A prime example of a multiple-use corridor, providing water conveyance, trail-based recreation, and wildlife habitat, is Denver Water's 66-mile (106 km) High Line Canal (figure 1.19). It was built in 1879 as part of a scheme to irrigate the dry plains around the city. Today five recreation management agencies provide all maintenance and capital improvements for the recreational facilities, while Denver Water manages for water delivery. There are more than sixty miles (97 km) of continuous trail through the corridor, and thousands enjoy it each day, including bicycle commuters. Giant cottonwoods and other trees line much of the canal's length, making it attractive to wildlife and people alike.

But change is coming to the canal in 2010, when Denver Water will no longer need the lower 22 miles (35 km) of the canal for water distribution. Such an unlined canal is an inefficient way to convey water, because vegetation, evaporation, and seepage remove a considerable percentage of the flow. Citizens have expressed concern for the future of the corridor if there are not to be regular deliveries of water and the corridor's current vegetation does not survive.

Through collaborative planning, Denver Water and other agencies have developed a plan for sustaining the corridor's resources into the future.[84] The plan doesn't resolve all the issues that may affect the corridor after water conveyance has finished, but it does offer many innovative approaches, including:

- Changing policy to allow historic stormwater inflows to continue discharging into the canal, which could help provide water to the corridor's vegetation.
- Diverting new sources of storm drainage into the lower part of the canal, while metering and managing these flows to avoid overtopping or subsequent damage to the canal.
- Selectively lining the canal to reduce seepage.
- Introducing excess reuse (recycled) water as a drought protection supply in early spring and late fall when the canal is not operating.

Major Contributions Can Flow from Carefully Designed Greenways

These three examples of greenways and greenway networks—one statewide, one citywide, and one a single corridor—just barely begin to suggest the tremendous diversity and potential of greenways today. The southeastern Wisconsin environmental corridors illustrate the contribution a regional greenspace framework can make to recreation and conservation for millions of people. From Bogotá we learn how greenways can address environmental equity and contribute to economic well-being for some of a region's neediest citizens. The multiple purposes of the High Line Canal corridor and its possible demunition remind us that we have inherited unintentional greenways that may need special attention to be sustained. These are some of the topics to be presented in subsequent chapters.

Notes

[1] A 2000 article pointed out that the National Recreation and Park Association included limited information on greenways in their planning and design guidelines, including them as merely one park resource among many traditional types (such as neighborhood and community parks). The authors go on to demonstrate the considerable diversity of functions performed by greenways. Shafer, C. S., and D. Scott, et al. (2000). "A greenway classification system: Defining the function and character of greenways in urban areas." *Journal of Park and Recreation Administration* 18(2): 88–106.

[2] This definition is based in part on one proposed by landscape architect Jack Ahern: "greenways are networks of land that are planned, designed and managed for multiple purposes including ecological, recreational, cultural, aesthetic, or other purposes compatible with the concept of sustainable land use." Ahern, J. (1996). "Greenways as a planning strategy." p. 131–155, in *Greenways: The Beginning of an International Movement*, J. Fabos and J. Ahern, ed. Amsterdam, Elsevier.

[3] Little, C. (1990). *Greenways for America*. Baltimore, MD, Johns Hopkins University Press.

[4] Randolph, J. (2004). *Environmental Land Use Planning and Management*. Washington, DC, Island Press, p. 98. Also see (http://www.greeninfrastructure.net).

[5] Jongman, R. H. G., M. Külvik, et al. (2004). "European ecological networks and greenways." *Landscape and Urban Planning* 68(2–3): 305–319.

[6] Planner Alex Krieger wrote, "Ban the term 'open space.' When a development touts that 'forty percent of the land is devoted to open space,' it is likely that forty percent of the land has been insufficiently considered. We actually have more trash-strewn setbacks, scraggly buffer strips, fetid retainage basins, and purposeless asphalted acreage—all 'open space'—than we know what to do with. What we can use is more parks, natural preserves, tot lots, recreational areas, baseball fields, and football fields. If space on a development plan is labeled only open space, you don't want it." Krieger, A. (2002). "Rules for designing cities." p. 105–111, in *The Mayors' Institute Excellence in City Design*, J. S. Russell, ed. Washington, DC, National Endowment for the Arts, p. 110.

[7] Odum, W. E. (1982). Environmental degradation and the tyranny of small decisions. *Bioscience* 32: 728–729.

[8] Thompson, I. H. (2000). *Ecology, Community, and Delight: Sources of Values in Landscape Architecture*. New York, E & FN Spon. Thompson adapts these three terms from the triad of the famous Roman planner, Vitruvius: economy, commodity, and delight.

[9] Noss, R. F. (1995). "Ecological integrity and sustainability: Buzzwords in conflict?" p. 60–76, in *Perspectives on Ecological Integrity*. L. Westra and J. Lemons, ed. Boston, Kluwer Academic Publishers.

[10] Forman, R. T. T. (1995). *Land Mosaics: The Ecology of Landscapes and Regions*. New York, Cambridge University Press.

[11] Leopold, A. (1933). *Game Management*. Madison, University of Wisconsin Press, p. xxxii.

[12] Ahern, J. (2002). *Greenways as Strategic Landscape Planning: Theory and Application*. Ph.D. dissertation. Wageningen, Netherlands, Wageningen University.

[13] Forman, R. T. T., (1995), *Land Mosaics*; Noss, chapter 3, this volume.

[14] Soulé, M. and M. E. Gilpin (1991). "The theory of wildlife corridor capability." p. 3–8 in *Nature Conservation 2: The Role of Corridors*. D. A. Saunders and R. J. Hobbs, ed. Chipping Norton, NSW, Australia, Surrey Beatty & Sons.

[15] Shu, J. K. (2003). "The role of understanding urban ecosystems in community development." p. 39–45, in *Understanding Urban Ecosystems: A New Frontier for Science and Education*. A. R. Berkowitz, C. H. Nilon, and K. S. Hollweg, ed. New York, Springer-Verlag, Inc., p. 40.

[16] National Park Service Rivers Trails and Conservation Assistance. (1995). *Economic Impacts of Protecting Rivers, Trails, and Greenway Corridors: A Resource Book*. Washington, DC, National Park Service.

[17] See, for example, Headington, L. (2003). *The Other Tragedy of the Commons: Redevelopment of Denver's South Platte River and the Homeless*. Ph.D. dissertation. Boulder, CO, University of Colorado.

[18] U.S. Department of Agriculture, Natural Resources Conservation Service. (2001). *National Resources Inventory: Summary*. (http://www.nrcs.usda.gov/technical/NRI/). Non-Federal forest land is the dominant land type being developed.

[19] Forman, R. T. T., and M. Godron. (1986). *Landscape Ecology*. New York, John Wiley & Sons; Lowrance, R., R. Leonard, et al. (1985). "Managing riparian ecosystems to control nonpoint pollution." *Journal of Soil and Water Conservation* 40: 87–91.

[20] Wilcove, D. S., C. H. McLellan, et al. (1986). "Habitat fragmentation in the temperate zone," p. 237–256, in *Conservation Biology: The Science of Scarcity and Diversity*. M. E. Soulé, ed. Sunderland, MA, Sinauer Associates; Wilcox, B. A., and D. D. Murphy. (1985). "Conservation strategy: The effects of fragmentation on extinction." *American Naturalist* 125: 879–887; Noss, chapter 3, this volume.

[21] Mitchell, W. J. (2002). "The Internet, new urban patterns, and conservation." p. 50–60, in *Conservation in the Internet Age: Threats and Opportunities*. J. N. Levitt, ed. Washington, DC, Island Press.

[22] Ibid.

[23] Ibid, p. 59.

[24] Dr. Larry Harris, professor emeritus, Department of Wildlife Ecology and Conservation, University of Florida, Gainesville. personal communication.

[25] Forman and Godron, (1986), *Landscape Ecology*.

[26] Spirn, A. W. (1984). *The Granite Garden: Urban Nature and Human Design*. New York, Basic Books.

[27] Grey, G. W., and F. J. Deneke. (1986). *Urban Forestry*. New York, John Wiley and Sons.

[28] Forman and Godron, (1986), *Landscape Ecology*.

[29] For examples, see Harris, L. (1985). *Conservation Corridors: A Highway System for Wildlife*. ENFO. Winter Park, FL, Environmental Information Center of the Florida Conservation Foundation, Inc.; Forman and Godron, (1986), *Landscape Ecology*; Noss, R. F. (1987). "Corridors in real landscapes: A reply to Simberloff and Cox." *Conservation Biology* 1: 159–164.

[30] Wegner, J., and G. Merriam. (1979). "Movement by birds and small mammals between a wood and adjoining farmland habitats." *Journal of Applied Ecology* 16: 349–357; Merriam, G., and A. Lanoue. (1990). "Corridor use by small mammals: Field measurements for three experimental types of *Peromyscus leucopus*." *Landscape Ecology* 4: 123–131; Maehr, D. S. (1990). "The Florida panther and private lands." *Conservation Biology* 4: 167–170.

[31] Bennett, A. (1990). "Habitat corridors and the conservation of small mammals in a fragmented forest environment." *Landscape Ecology* 4: 109–122.

[32] Johnson, W. C., and C. S. Adkisson. (1985). "Dispersal of beech nuts by blue jays in fragmented landscapes."

American Midland Naturalist 113(2): 319–324; Dmowski, K., and M. Kozakiewicz. (1990). "Influence of shrub corridor on movements of passerine birds to a lake littoral zone." *Landscape Ecology* 4: 99–108.

[33] Harris, (1985), *Conservation Corridors*, p. 4.

[34] *Terminator 2: Judgment Day*, 1992. *Repo Man*, 1984. *Grease*, 1978.

[35] City of San José. (2002). *Guadalupe River Park Master Plan*. San José, California, City of San José Redevelopment Agency, Santa Clara Valley Water District, United States Army Corps of Engineers.

[36] Louv, R. (2005). *Last Child in the Woods: Saving Our Children from Nature-Deficit Disorder*, Chapel Hill, NC, Algonquin Books; Nabhan, G., and S. Trimble. (1994). *The Geography of Childhood: Why Children Need Wild Places*. Boston, Beacon Press.

[37] Nelson, A. C., R. Pendall, et al. (2002). "The link between growth management and housing affordability: The academic evidence." The Brookings Institution Center on Urban and Metropolitan Policy.

[38] Nelson, A. C. (1988). "An empirical note on how regional urban containment policy influences an interaction between greenbelt and ex-urban land markets." *Journal of the American Planning Association* 54: 178–184.

[39] National Park Service Rivers Trails and Conservation Assistance (1995). *Economic Impacts of Protecting Rivers, Trails, and Greenway Corridors: A Resource Book*. Washington, DC, National Park Service.

[40] Harnik, P. (2005). "History of the Rail-Trail Movement." Retrieved April 15, 2005, (http://www.railtrails.org/about/history.asp).

[41] Collins, T. (2000). "Interventions in the Rust-Belt, The art and ecology of post-industrial public space." *British Urban Geography Journal, Ecumene* 7(4): 461–467.

[42] Koh, J. (2004). "Ecological reasoning and architectural imagination." Inaugural address of Prof. Dr. Jusuck Koh, Wageningen, Netherlands.

[43] Ahern, (2002), *Greenways as Strategic Landscape Planning*.

[44] Landscape architects Jusuck Koh and Anemone Beck, partners in the firm Oikos Design, speak of master "principles" rather than master "plans." They find plans frequently to be static, but principles more adaptable. Personal communication, 2005.

[45] Fisher, I. D. (1986). *Frederick Law Olmsted and the City Planning Movement in the United States*. Ann Arbor, MI, University of Michigan Research Press; Little, (1990), *Greenways for America*.

[46] Little, (1990), *Greenways for America*.

[47] Zaitzevsky, C. (1982). *Frederick Law Olmsted and the Boston Park System*. Cambridge, MA, Harvard University Press.

[48] Steiner, F., G. Young, et al. (1988). "Ecological planning: Retrospect and prospect." *Landscape Journal* 7(1): 31–39.

[49] Little, (1990), *Greenways for America*.

[50] Newton, N. T. (1971). *Design on the Land*. Cambridge, MA, The Belknap Press of Harvard University Press; Little, (1990), *Greenways for America*.

[51] Little, (1990), *Greenways for America*; E. Carr, personal communication.

[52] Howard, E. (1902). *Garden Cities of Tomorrow*. London, Swan Sonnenschein and Company. Originally published in 1898 as *Tomorrow: A Peaceful Path to Real Reform*, p. 24.

[53] Ibid.

[54] Newton, (1971), *Design on the Land*.

[55] Whyte, W. (1968). *The Last Landscape*. Garden City, NY, Doubleday.

[56] Steiner, Young, et al., (1988), "Ecological planning: Retrospect and prospect"; Newton, (1971), *Design on the Land*; Little, (1990), *Greenways for America*.

[57] MacKaye, B. (1928). *The New Exploration: A Philosophy of Regional Planning*. New York, Harcourt Brace, p. 179.

[58] Lewis, P. H. (1964). "Quality corridors for Wisconsin." *Landscape Architecture Quarterly* 54: 100–107; Wisconsin Department of Resource Development. (1962). *Recreation in Wisconsin*. Madison, WI.

[59] Wisconsin Department of Resource Development, (1962), *Recreation in Wisconsin*.

[60] McHarg, I. (1969). *Design with Nature*. p. 65.

[61] Steinitz, C., P. Parker, et al. (1976). "Hand-drawn overlays: Their history and prospective uses," *Landscape Architecture* 66: 444–455.

[62] Steiner, Young, et al., (1988), "Ecological planning: Retrospect and prospect."

[63] Taking a landscape ecological perspective, Richard Forman warned of a potential shortcoming of overlay processes. An overlay analysis may put too much emphasis on the internal characteristics of a site, rather than its more important context. Such an analysis may also miss broader movements and flows over the whole landscape, which are fundamental in determining uses of the land. A simple overlay process will likely miss important aspects of landscape change, which are best considered from the perspective of a mosaic over time. Forman, (1995), *Land Mosaics*.

[64] MacArthur, R. H., and E. O. Wilson. (1967). *The Theory of Island Biogeography*. Princeton, Princeton University Press.

[65] Little, (1990), *Greenways for America*.

[66] The success rate was 83 percent, with 64 of 77 local and state measures passing. Trust for Public Land. (2003). "Americans vote for open space—again." Retrieved December 15, 2005, (http://www.tpl.org/tier3_cd.cfm?content_item_id=13145&folder_id=1487).

[67] President's Commission on Americans Outdoors. (1987). *Americans Outdoors: The Legacy, the Challenge, with Case Studies*. Washington, DC, Island Press.

[68] Ibid.

[69] Scenic Hudson, Inc. and National Park Service. (1989). "Building greenways in the Hudson River Valley: A guide for action." Privately printed report.

[70] PKF Consulting. (1994). "Analysis of economic impacts of the Northern Central Rail Trail." Annapolis, MD, Maryland Greenways Commission, Maryland Department of Natural Resources.

[71] Palmer, T. (1986). *Endangered Rivers and the Conservation Movement*. Berkeley, CA, University of California Press.

[72] National Park Service. (2002). "River mileage classifications for components of the National Wild & Scenic Rivers System." Retrieved December 17, 2005, (http://www.nps.gov/rivers/wildriverstable.html).

[73] Palmer, (1986), *Endangered Rivers and the Conservation Movement*; Stokes, S. N., A. E. Watson, et al. (1989). *Saving America's Countryside: A Guide to Rural Conservation*. Baltimore, MD, The Johns Hopkins University Press.

[74] Stokes, Watson, et al., (1989), *Saving America's Countryside*.

[75] Maine Revised Statutes, 38 M.R.S.A. sec. 435-449 (Article 2-B: Mandatory Shoreland Zoning).

[76] Rome, A. (1991). "Protecting natural areas through the planning process: The Chesapeake Bay example." *Natural Areas Journal* 11(4): 199–202.

[77] Bullard, R. (1994). *Dumping in Dixie: Race, class, and environmental quality*. Boulder, CO, Westview; Dowie, M. (1995). *Losing Ground: American Environmentalism at the Close of the Twentieth Century*. Cambridge, MA, MIT Press.

[78] Mutz, K. M., G. C. Bryner, et al., eds. (2002). *Justice and Natural Resources*. Washington, DC, Island Press; Headington, L. (2003). *The Other Tragedy of the Commons*.

[79] Jongman, R. H. G., and G. Pungetti (2004). "Introduction: ecological networks and greenways," p. 1–6, in *Ecological Networks and Greenways: Concept, Design, Implementation*. R. H. G. Jongman and G. Pungetti, ed. Cambridge, Cambridge University Press.

[80] Rubin, B. P., and J. G. Emmerich. (1981). "Redefining the delineation of environmental corridors in southeastern Wisconsin." Southeastern Wisconsin Regional Planning Commission Technical Record, 4; Southeastern Wisconsin Regional Planning Commission. (1985). "Twenty-five years of regional planning." Waukesha, WI.

[81] University of Wisconsin-Extension. (2004). "Environmental corridors: Lifelines of the natural resource base." *Plan on It*.

[82] Alcaldia Mayor de Bogotá (1998). Plan de Desarrollo Económico, Social y de Obras Públicas para Santafé de Bogotá, D.C. 1998–2001. "Por la Bogotá que Queremos," Bogotá, Colombia, Imprenta Distrital. Quoted in Espinosa, J. C. (2004). Enrique Peñalosa's Plan for Bogotá: Bridging the Gap between Two Distinctive Planning Paradigms. New Haven, CT, Yale University School of Forestry and Environmental Studies; Peñalosa, E. (2004). personal communication.

[83] Translated from the Spanish by Espinosa, J. C. (2004). Enrique Peñalosa's Plan for Bogotá.

[84] Wenk Associates, Inc. (2002). *High Line Canal Future Management Study*. Denver, Denver Water.

CHAPTER 2

GREENWAY ECOLOGY AND THE INTEGRITY OF LANDSCAPES: AN ILLUSTRATED PRIMER

Picture two members of a greenway design committee who are arguing. One is an activist, the other an ecologist. The activist proposes many exciting steps to protect a proposed greenway. To him, there is no time to lose because of numerous threats to the corridor they both seek to conserve. The other committee member seems to be resisting his proposals, questioning aspects of each suggestion. She wonders if any greenway route will be able to accomplish the laundry list of objectives the first member touts as inevitable benefits. As a trained scientist, she proposes that research be conducted to determine the specific species of wildlife the corridor will accommodate and other investigations. "But, it depends," is her oft-repeated response to her colleague's blanket statements of how things will work ecologically. At times the two seem to be using the same terms in very different ways. For example, he speaks of *biodiversity* as a target and believes it must be something that is easily measured. She asks what kind of biodiversity he is concerned with and wonders out loud why they should be protecting species such as raccoons and skunks that generally need no encouragement. They share the same overall goal, but can't agree on how to proceed.[1]

"Emotional citizen planners can be exasperating," thinks the ecologist. "Scientists can throw up roadblocks in the face of obvious threats and once-in-a-lifetime opportunities," the activist concludes.

Bringing Together Diverse Perspectives

If you are not a scientist it may be easy to conclude that science can slow down a greenway project when there isn't time to spare. If you are a scientist, you may decide a lot more scientific rigor should inform decisions in designing greenways, given the tremendous investment they represent, both at the outset and ever after. Clearly both perspectives can be right, sometimes even at the same time, when there is no single correct answer in the face of uncertainty.

In chapter 3 of this book, Reed Noss observes that greenways, although conspicuous components of many land-use plans in recent years, are "often designed without clear reference to biological knowledge." Conversely, the 1992 Rio Declaration on Environment and Development (the "Earth Summit") suggests the importance of subscribing to a "precautionary principle"—taking conservation steps even without full scientific certainty, if resources may be lost in the absence of quick action.[2] It can be infuriating that "ecologists often say the first law of ecology is 'It depends.'"[3]

Greenway designers, whether scientists, activists, or regular citizens, are frequently confronted by this balancing act, wanting to expand the scientific basis of decision making and meet other community goals, while still being responsive to the urgency of developing and implementing a plan. Given that multiple stakeholders and perspectives are typically part of greenway design, it is important to build communication bridges between participants.

One capability frequently missing among participant teams is the shared vocabulary to understand and talk about the elements of the landscape and how they function. The study of landscape ecology can help.

A Willingness to Communicate beyond Narrow Limits

Greenway projects need conceptual bridge builders and visionaries. If you adequately understand the individual contributions of team members and how the issues can fit together, you can play the role of integrator and visionary. This larger role has often been turned over to one or more focused specialists, who may not easily find the broader perspective. Massachusetts Institute of Technology professor Anne Spirn noted that professionals who concentrate on certain parts of the landscape often fail to understand the landscape as a continuous whole.[4]

American artist and greenway designer Timothy Collins warned, "We are a culture that has fractured the complex experiences and understanding of life into specific disciplines and independent specialties."[5] He added that "the quantitative evaluation of experts has taken precedence over the layman's ability to use experience and general qualitative analysis as a method of making decisions." From this inclusive standpoint, even nonscientists have an important role to play in greenway design.

To talk effectively about the landscape all participants need a basic shared vocabulary, which landscape ecology can provide. But, in addition to vocabulary, participants also need to appreciate that although science-informed decisions are important, there are other significant factors that will affect greenway design, such as politics and economics.

Landscape Ecology a Boon to Greenway Design

Professionals in a range of scientific disciplines, including wildlife biology, conservation biology, aquatic ecology, and environmental sociology, have knowledge or can help raise questions relevant to greenway design and connectivity. Other disciplines also focus on natural resources, such as botany, ecosystem ecology, and ecosystem management, and may aid the greenway designer. Less well known, but especially helpful is the newer field of landscape ecology.

Landscape ecology examines the patterns of landscapes and the relationships of those patterns to ecological processes. In this book, we argue that landscape ecology can also incorporate social-ecological processes—relationships in the landscape that affect the well-being of particular social groups and society as a whole. Because it is fundamentally spatial, landscape ecology can be a very useful tool in landscape planning.[6] It can help greenway designers understand how landscapes function, as well as how they might function in the future once a greenway is created and being managed.[7]

"Landscape ecology is a curious mix of subjects," observed scientists Frank Golley and J. Bellot.[8] And so it is. The basic concepts of landscape ecology relate to landscape structure, function, and change[9]—that is, the significance of shape and pattern, ecological and social process, and the changes over time and space that are part of the landscape.

Although the term "landscape ecology" was coined in 1939 by Carl Troll, a German geographer, only in the last few decades has interest in the subject in North America mushroomed. Landscape ecology has developed with two main schools or approaches, one European and the other North American, although each is represented in places beyond those suggested by the names.

The older, European school, has emphasized landscape typology, classification, and nomenclature, and largely has focused on human-dominated landscapes. This approach has been popular with landscape ecologists in Europe, as well as landscape architects, planners, and other designers in Europe and North America. The North American school has primarily examined natural or seminatural landscapes and has more typically focused on developing theories and models (with mathematical formulae).

Landscape Ecology as an Inclusive Perspective

The Dutch ecologist I. S. Zonneveld offered a very inclusive definition of who can be a landscape ecologist: "Any geographer, geomorphologist, soil scientist, hydrologist, climatologist, sociologist, anthropologist, economist, landscape architect, agriculturalist, regional planner, civil engineer—even general, cardinal, minister, or president, if you like—who has the 'attitude' to approach our environment . . . as a coherent system, as a kind of whole that cannot be really understood from its separate components only, is a landscape ecologist."[10] Zonneveld described landscape ecology as a holistic attitude or perspective, one to which any person can adhere.

Although North American greenway designers might feel more comfortable with the European school and appreciate its inclusiveness, most of the professional landscape ecologists who assist them will probably be of the North American school. Both perspectives are valuable and relevant to greenway design because of the complementary emphases on human-dominated landscapes of the one and models of the other.[11]

BOX 2.1 Supplemental Sources

This chapter provides an effective way for a person to understand the landscape and to be able to communicate more effectively about it.

For a generalized overview of landscape ecology see the slim, but well illustrated guide, *Landscape Ecology Principles in Landscape Architecture and Land-Use Planning*, by Wenche Dramstad, James Olson, and Richard Forman.[1] For a more detailed treatment with a similar approach, see Richard Forman's *Land Mosaics*.[2] A more comprehensive introduction to the subject (with a North American perspective) is offered in *Landscape Ecology in Theory and Practice: Pattern and Process*, by Monica Turner, Robert Gardner, and Robert O'Neill.[3]

[1]Dramstad, W. E., J. D. Olson, et al. (1996). *Landscape Ecology Principles in Landscape Architecture and Land-Use Planning*. Washington, DC, Island Press.

[2]Forman, R. T. T. (1995). *Land Mosaics: the Ecology of Landscapes and Regions*. New York, Cambridge University Press.

[3]Turner, M. G., R. H. Gardner, et al. (2001). *Landscape Ecology in Theory and Practice: Pattern and Process*. New York, Springer.

Taking the Broader View

Taking the "landscape" perspective in planning and design implies considering places within their larger spatial and temporal contexts. It's an approach inherently concerned with at least some aspects of sustainability.

There is disagreement about just what a landscape exactly is, or how big it is. An early landscape ecology definition of *landscape* is "a heterogeneous land area composed of a cluster of interacting ecosystems that is repeated in similar form throughout."[12] Key to this definition is the concept of the mosaic containing repeating patterns, whose composition and configuration define the extent of the landscape. Also part of this perspective is the notion that a landscape can range in size down to a few kilometers or miles in diameter. Defining landscape this way has a certain intuitive appeal to greenway designers and others because it relates to the scale and manner in which people perceive the landscape.

More recently, the term "landscape" has been defined much more generically, as an "area that is spatially heterogeneous [or patchy] in at least one factor of interest."[13] With this definition, the size of a landscape relates to the life history of a wildlife species; the functioning of an ecological process, such as erosion; or some other object of interest. This approach is useful because it moves away from a predefined, fundamentally anthropocentric definition of landscape to a concept that is explicitly related to whatever is being studied. One team of scientists put it this way: "If we consider how organisms other than humans may see their landscape, our own sense of landscape may be broadened to encompass components relevant to a honey bee, beetle, vole, or bison."[14] The importance of viewing the landscape from nonhuman perspectives is one that we will return to in many places throughout this book.

Getting to Know a Landscape at a Human Scale

Although a more detailed, specific, nonhuman view of the landscape is vital as part of most projects, it can still be helpful to start with a more broad-brush examination of a landscape, such as is described later in this chapter. It is important and useful for nonscientist greenway designers to know their landscapes firsthand, as a precursor and complement to interacting with scientists who will have more detailed information. It is important, however, not to let this typically anthropocentric framework mistakenly be used as if it explained how nonhuman users might perceive a landscape. In most cases, the requirements of nonhuman uses will be something quite different.

An Illustrated Primer: The Language of Landscape Integrity

Planner Chris Duerksen and his colleagues put it bluntly when they wrote, "all models are wrong, some are useful."[15] Scientists develop and debate and refine, and accept or reject, representations of the landscape, some of which are models relevant to greenway design. All of these are "wrong," to some degree, because they can't fully represent all aspects of complex systems, especially landscapes. Many of these models are still helpful. Models, in fact, are very much part of the way everyday people deal with the world's complexity.

Presented here are models—ways of looking at the landscape—that should prove helpful for greenway designers. Such models must be used carefully, because some will be oversimplifications or may be irrelevant in landscapes other than where they were developed. These models and terms should prove useful, first in understanding how landscapes function and change and later in envisioning, implementing, and managing greenways sustainably, and in ways that contribute to landscape integrity.

Landscape Elements: Patches, Corridors, Matrix

According to at least one approach to landscape ecology, any landscape anywhere in the world can be described as

FIGURE 2.1

A landscape can be described as a mosaic of repeating patterns of patches and corridors, and the matrix within which these elements sit. Here there is a grassland matrix with patches of trees and shrubs and vegetated corridors along the streams. (Drawing by Joe McGrane.)

a mosaic of repeating patterns of patches and corridors, and the matrix within which these elements sit (figures 2.1 and 2.2).[16] Other approaches, less concerned with differentiating and categorizing these landscape elements, instead consider the landscape as a surface perceived variably by different organisms. The simpler, patch-corridor-matrix approach provides a good starting point for analyzing a landscape and getting a sense of the lay of the land through which a greenway might pass. A more species-specific approach will also be important at other points in the process of designing a greenway.

The following definitions are fundamental to this approach:

A *patch* is a relatively homogenous nonlinear area that differs from its surroundings.[17] Human-dominated patches may include housing, commerce, industry, and public space surrounded by different land uses or land cover. Examples of undeveloped patches include a woody area in a savanna, a meadow in a forest, and a wetland in a shrubland.

A *corridor* is a strip of land of a particular type that differs from adjacent land on either side.[18] With an eye specifically toward wildlife connectivity, Reed Noss (chapter 3) defines a corridor as "a strip or band through which nondomesticated organisms may move, especially between areas of habitat."

Corridors, at least according to the first, broader definition, include riparian (i.e., river bank) forests and highway verges, roads and trails, streams, and utility rights-of-way. Also under this more generic definition, corridors may serve other functions beyond being conduits for movement, such as providing habitat.

A *matrix* is the most extensive and best connected element—the land use or land cover that predominates—in a landscape. The matrix plays the dominant role in how the landscape functions.[19] In agricultural areas the matrix is farmland. It is woodland in forested areas, grasslands in prairie, and urban development in a city. When a person is in "the middle of nowhere," suggested ecologist Richard Forman, that person is probably located in that landscape's matrix.[20] Historically, in many parts of eastern North America or northern Europe, the matrix was forest. On the prairies of the midwestern United States, the cerrado of Brazil, or the savannas of Africa, the matrix is, or at least was, often grassland. The conditions in a landscape's matrix will vary, and except in the

FIGURE 2.2

Two major landscapes are shown in this illustration: a hilly, mostly undeveloped landscape to the left and a flatter, mostly agricultural landscape to the right. The hilly landscape is predominately forested—this is its matrix (M1)—but has patches of grasses (P1a), isolated houses (P1b), and small-scale agriculture (P1c). The matrix is also interrupted by stream (C1a) and road (C1b) corridors. The agricultural landscape to the right is much more dominated by people. While its matrix is agricultural (M2), it also includes a large urbanized patch (P2a) that is the city center, suburban patches (P2b) of varying size, and patches that are heavily industrialized, such as the sand and gravel operation next to the river (P2c). This landscape has an extensive network of stream (C2a) and transportation (C2b) corridors. (Drawing by Joe McGrane.)

FIGURE 2.3

The matrix is the background of the landscape and frequently the source of the landscape's generalized name. (a) In this grassland matrix in Northern California the expanse of grasses is interrupted by individual trees and small to large patches of trees. (Photo by Lynn Betts.) *(b) In this northeast Iowa agricultural scene, the contour strip-cropped matrix is punctuated by farmsteads and bisected by roads and stream corridors.* (Photo by Lynn Betts.) *(c) Homes and roads are the major elements of the matrix of this suburban landscape in Las Vegas. Tiny patches of vegetation are associated with those homes and some neighborhoods are broken up by relatively large patches of irrigated vegetation, such as the golf course in the lower right.* (Photo by Lynn Betts.) *(d) Two matrices are visible in this photograph of Jefferson City, Missouri. The area to the left of the Missouri River has a matrix of urban forest, buildings, and streets. To the right is a large-field agricultural matrix with few obvious patches.* (Photo by Sarah Minor.) (Photos courtesy of U.S. Department of Agriculture—Natural Resources Conservation Service.)

most developed of landscapes, typically should not necessarily be thought of as a uniform, hostile "ocean" inhospitable to wildlife (figure 2.3).[21]

Whether an elongated patch is more appropriately classified as a patch or a corridor depends on the focus of your investigation or project. These classifications of landscape elements are flexible, practical tools, not unequivocal judgments. Such tools let us talk about and begin to understand the functioning of what might otherwise appear to be a landscape's inscrutable complexity.

The Patch-Corridor-Matrix Paradigm May Portray Spatial Patterns of Social Phenomena

A city has patches, corridors, and matrices, even if they are defined primarily by the built environment and by social, instead of natural, processes. An urban grid filled with row houses, apartment buildings, and office towers constitutes a form of landscape matrix—one in which there are also distinct patches, such as shopping centers, vacant lots, or neighborhood parks, as well as corridors in the form of roads, sidewalks, and urban greenways. Patches may also be related to wealth and class, as low- or high-income neighborhoods that often occur in discrete locations (figure 2.4). Sometimes these patches are directly related to environmental conditions, as when low-income groups occupy residences adjacent to highways, industrial zones, or contaminated lands. At the other end of the spectrum, high-amenity areas adjacent to waterfronts, parks, and greenways may over time come to be dominated by wealthy residents.

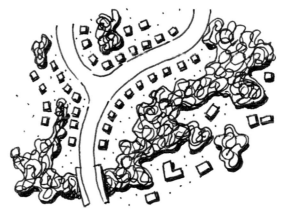

FIGURE 2.4

Patches may be defined by wealth and class. Here, more expensive homes are nestled in the woods, while less expensive ones are along the roads.

(Drawing by Joe McGrane.)

These examples point to the close relationship between physical landscape structure and overlapping features of *social structure*. Just as discrete patches and corridors are distinguishable by their difference from one another, human social groups have distinctive features related to race, ethnicity, gender, age, and class that set them apart. Because those variables are often related to territory and resources (wealth), there is often a close relationship between social structure and landscape structure.

Landscape Structure Consists of Composition, Configuration, and Connectivity

According to ecologist Gray Merriam, landscape structure is best thought of in terms of its three C's: composition, configuration, and connectivity.[22]

The variety and relative abundance of patch and corridor types represented in a landscape define that landscape's *composition* (figure 2.5). For example, a landscape may be composed of separate patches of aspen and ponderosa pine, with more pine patches than aspen. Typically, landscape composition is summarized with indices that measure diversity of patch types.

The *configuration* of a landscape's elements is the spatial arrangement, position, or orientation of those elements or the irregularity of their shape (figure 2.6).[23]

FIGURE 2.5

FIGURE 2.5

Landscape composition is defined by the variety and relative abundance of patch and corridor types represented in that landscape. Patches shown here at the bottom (left to right) are dominated by trees, shrubs, or grasses.

(Drawing by Joe McGrane.)

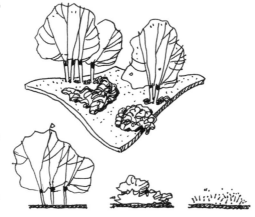

Landscape *connectivity* is the degree to which the landscape makes it easier or more difficult to move among resource patches[24] (figure 2.7). Merriam described landscape connectivity as the functional inverse of isolation. Especially important to note is that connectivity depends on the needs and preferences of specific organisms or other users—that is, it is not a generic condition of the landscape. It isn't meaningful to say a landscape has good connectivity without specifying for what species or uses. An urban landscape may have high functional connectivity for people and squirrels but not for most other wildlife species. Likewise, Georgia's Okefenokee Swamp has high connectivity for native wildlife but is extremely isolating for all but the most adventurous and skilled outdoors-people.

This functional connectivity is what really matters in greenway design. It is a measure of how well a landscape and its elements function for a specific species or particular use. When possible, using the whole landscape to facilitate wildlife movement is better than depending on just a few landscape elements. For nature conservation, for example, it is best if the landscape as a whole—patches, corridors, and matrix—can be managed for connectivity. If not, then corridors and stepping-stones (patches) should be so managed.[25]

FIGURE 2.6

The spatial arrangement, position, or orientation of landscape elements or the irregularity of their shape defines configuration. The arrangement of the various lobes and patches of this landscape determine its configuration.

(Drawing by Joe McGrane.)

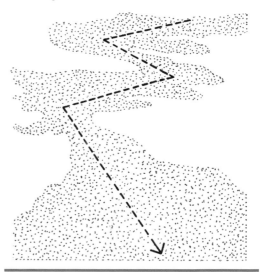

FIGURE 2.7

Functional connectivity is the flow of individuals and their genes among habitats and populations. It is determined by the ease with which an organism can move through the landscape. Functional connectivity interests conservation biologists more than simply corridors, per se.

Origin and Function of Landscape Elements

Origins and Longevities Differ

Various processes may be responsible for creating or sustaining a patch or corridor, and these landscape elements may persist for varying lengths of time.

A patch or a corridor may:

- have resulted from a *disturbance* to the landscape, such as wildfire, insect infestation, or severe winds that changed an area of vegetation without changing its surroundings.
- have *regenerated* after an area was disturbed, such as when grasses and wildflowers revegetate an area that previously burned.
- be a *remnant* left intact while surrounding areas were disturbed, such as when a lengthy drought kills exposed vegetation but leaves remnants of vegetation on more moist, north-facing slopes.
- be caused by localized *environmental conditions*, such as where groundwater close to the ground's surface sustains a wetland.
- be *introduced* by humans, such as when an agricultural field is cleared from the forest, a tree plantation is planted, or a parking lot is paved.

Knowing the origin of a landscape element can help you understand how it might function as part of a greenway. One patch, such as a remnant wooded area that is gradually losing species, is a very different resource for a greenway than another patch, which may exist because of long-term environmental conditions, such as a wetland.

Landscape Elements Perform Multiple Functions

Landscape elements—corridors, patches, and background matrix—function in a range of ways. For example, although you may think of a specific element as a corridor, being a conduit may be just one of the ways it functions (figure 2.8).

Landscape elements may serve as *habitat*, such as a patch of cottonwood and willow trees where herons roost or a neighborhood where people live.

They may serve as *conduits*, as when wildlife move through a patch, vectors (such as wind or water) carry contaminants, or tree species move down a slope gradient (over thousands of years). Corridors or other landscape elements may also be conduits for things deemed harmful to greenway management or broader conservation objectives. Some disturbances that may be facilitated by corridors, such as diseases, predators, invasive exotic species, and fire, may threaten the usefulness of a greenway or even the health of its broader landscape.

Landscape elements may serve as *barriers,* such as a grassland matrix that is impenetrable by species that require more extensive cover and that consistently remain in wooded patches or corridors. A road can be a significant barrier to salamanders if it separates habitat they use seasonally. A freeway or extensive developed patch may be a barrier when it precludes human access to a nearby natural area. A greenway may become a barrier to foot travel in areas where high crime rates discourage people from using the greenway, especially at night.

FIGURE 2.8

Six basic functions of corridors and other landscape elements: (a) habitat; (b) conduit; (c) barrier; (d) filter; (e) source; and (f) sink.

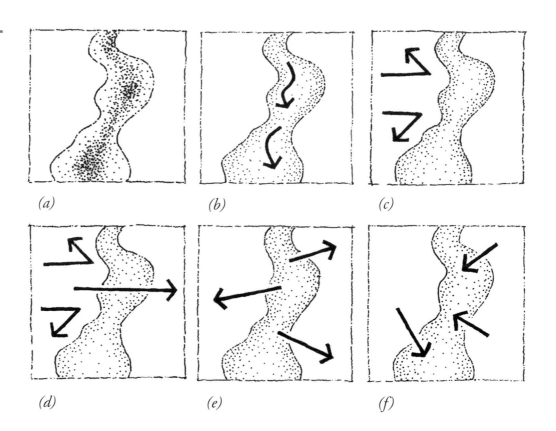

Landscape elements may serve as *filters*, as when streamside vegetation filters out some of the nutrient- and pesticide-rich runoff from an agricultural field.

Landscape elements may serve as *sources*, as when:

- young of a wildlife species disperse from one part of the landscape to another to establish home ranges away from their parents and siblings;
- an outfall pipe from a sewage treatment facility sends nutrient-rich effluent into a river;
- one area of a city is the source of visitors to a greenway;
- a greenway is a source of attractive scenery for people, or a source of community pride or identity; or
- efforts to develop and manage a greenway increase social interaction and social capital.

Landscape elements may serve as *sinks*—traps or places of accumulation—such as when animals are killed when they venture into a busy highway corridor, when sediments eroding from a construction site are trapped by an adjacent wetland, or when people leave trash in a remote corner of a greenway.

Greenway corridors also have social functions that are less clearly tied to these spatial categories. Greenways that run through diverse city neighborhoods may increase social interaction in positive ways. Especially where greenways are a focus of grassroots activism or management they can foster civic participation and collaboration within and between neighborhoods, and expand people's sense of community. Greenways can affect local economies by increasing commercial activity and real estate values (which in turn raises complex questions about how benefits should be distributed), or by providing places for community gardens and forests. Finally, greenways function as places for recreation, enjoyment, and education.

Species Use the Landscape in Different Ways

Evaluating a landscape's connectivity requires understanding its composition and configuration.[26] More importantly, it requires selecting appropriate organisms as lenses through which to evaluate the likelihood of movement through that landscape.[27] The connectivity of a landscape for a deer mouse is likely to be very different from that of a mule deer or other wide-ranging mammal (figure 2.9). The requirements for a tree species to be able to migrate over millennia may have little in common with what is needed to provide an integrated, seamless recreational experience for hikers or bikers. One scientist suggested, for example, "There is little evidence that forest-dwelling vertebrates perceive old growth stands as distinctly as we do."[28]

FIGURE 2.9

The connectivity of a landscape for a deer mouse is likely to be very different from that of a mule deer or other wide-ranging mammals. These and other species, as well as other uses, can serve as specific l enses through which to view and understand the landscape.

(Drawing by Joe McGrane.)

Preference for Edge Versus Interior

Some species, such as Cooper's hawk, bobcat, and red-eyed vireo, are referred to as *interior species* because they prefer that kind of habitat, away from the perimeter of patches and corridors. *Edge species* are just the opposite, more frequently found at edges (figure 2.10). Of course there is much variability to this, with changes based on the stage in life history and geography. Typically, edge conditions dominate narrow corridors, and at times completely preclude any interior conditions and the species that require them.

FIGURE 2.10

Although habitat needs vary over life history and geography, some species prefer interior habitat, away from perimeters, while others may be frequently found at edges.

(Drawing by Joe McGrane.)

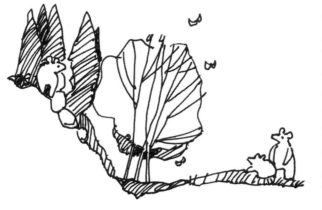

Generalist Versus Specialist Species

Species vary in their habitat niche breadth. *Generalists species* are those that tolerate frequent disturbance, use a wide range of habitats in different ways, and often adapt well to humans. White-tailed deer and coyote are generalist species. *Specialist species*, such as the prairie-loving regal fritillary butterfly and the bamboo-eating panda, use specific habitats in specific ways. Generalists and specialists differ in their habitat and connectivity requirements (figure 2.11). Some generalists don't need greenways at all, while some specialists won't use greenways because they are (typically) too narrow. Greenways are designed for species with requirements between these two.

Species May Persist Even after Major Alterations

Long-lived vertebrate species may persist in an altered landscape for some time after the alteration, even though their long-term survival and reproduction are unlikely.[29] These species, still found in an area where their habitat needs are no longer met, make up what has been called a landscape's extinction debt.[30] People may note the presence of such species and mistakenly conclude that habitat conditions are better than they actually are.

Wildlife Move through the Landscape for Different Reasons

Animals move through the landscape in three ways: within a home range, in dispersal, and in migration.[31] Animals feed and carry out their other daily activities within a *home range*. A raccoon's home range will depend on the quality of habitat, and may overlap with that of other raccoons. *Dispersal* is the one-time movement of an individual to find a new home range, where it might breed. For example, young red foxes may move away from the family group in which they were born. When animals *migrate* seasonally, they move between separate areas where they find resources during different times of the year. Some elk in the Rocky Mountains of Colorado spend their winters at low altitudes, but summer in high-altitude meadows.

Landscape Connectivity Is Fundamental to Greenway Design

Greenways are fundamentally about connections, either between nodes of interest or along a line that has special qualities itself. Landscape ecology helps us understand what connectivity is for a particular species or use and in a specific landscape. But connections as viewed by people may be quite different from what wildlife need in a greenway, for example.

In figure 2.2, even though the landscape on the right side in the illustration has been extensively developed for agriculture, there is a network of remnant wooded stream corridors and patches. If a wildlife species can make use of such a network, this part of the landscape may be judged to

(a)   *(b)*   *(c)*   *(d)*   *(e)*   *(f)*

have good connectivity. However, another species with need for wider corridors, allowing greater separation from disturbing noises, may find the network and that part of the landscape not conducive to movement.

As landscape connectivity is lost, habitat can become *fragmented* and species may not be able to move between the habitat fragments to access the resources they need to survive. Habitat fragmentation is rampant in many parts of the world, and some evidence suggests it to be the greatest threat to biodiversity today.[32] The problems associated with fragmentation are multiple and sometimes confounding (figure 2.12), such as:[33]

- the size and number of habitat patches may decrease,
- the distance between habitat patches may increase,
- the distribution of prey animals may change,
- the productivity of habitat patches may increase,
- the quality of habitat patches may decrease,
- the importance of edge effects may increase, and
- two or more of these processes may work in concert.

These impacts are not related linearly to the extent of original habitat, so one patch half the size of another may be less than half as suitable for a given species. For example, it may be completely unsuitable if there is insufficient interior habitat.[34]

The transformation of the forested areas in Cadiz Township, Wisconsin (figure 1.3), from 1831 to 1950, shows how humans change the landscape in general and patches in particular. As forests were cleared and patches created, the curved edges resulting from natural processes were replaced by straight lines. The straight lines were often based on property boundaries. Over time, as more forest was cleared, the overall amount of forest continued to decline and patches became smaller and more isolated. Species for which the open landscape is not passable may be restricted to the patches. Over time some or all patches may become too small to be hospitable for certain species that will then be lost from the area.

FIGURE 2.12

The problems associated with fragmentation are multiple. For example, a) the size of patches may decrease, b) between-patch distance may increase, c) distribution of prey may change, d) productivity may increase (because of increased light penetration), e) habitat quality may decrease, and f) the importance of edge effects may increase. These conditions may also confound one another.

(Drawing by Joe McGrane.)

FIGURE 2.13

Whether wildlife will cross a gap in a corridor depends on the range of conditions found in the gap.

(Drawing by Joe McGrane.)

Corridors, Gaps, and Stepping-Stones

The width of a corridor (or greenway) can dramatically affect how it functions.

- *Line* corridors are narrow and for most uses/users have no interior habitat conditions. A hedgerow, a fence, and a path are all examples of line corridors.
- *Strip* corridors are wider than line corridors, with enough width to have interior conditions.
- *Landscape linkages* are broad, several-mile-wide connections, such as the Pinhook Swamp in Florida. Such

linkages are wide enough to contain substantial areas with interior conditions and to constitute major habitat reserves in their own right.

Gaps Can Disrupt Corridor Functions

Gaps in corridors disrupt movement, especially for interior-dwelling species. Whether an individual will cross a gap in a corridor (figure 2.13) depends on:

- that individual's tolerance for edge conditions,
- its movement and dispersal characteristics,
- the length of the gap, and
- the amount of contrast between the corridor and the gap.

Connectivity without Corridors

Over the last few decades, some have suggested, conservation planners may have found connectivity through corridors so intuitively appealing that corridor protection has outpaced scientific understanding and the collection of empirical data on the requirements for species movement through such linkages.[35] The emphasis should be on connectivity more generally, rather than corridors specifically, because of the matrix's potential role in movement and the ways stepping-stone patches can contribute to connectivity.

For instance, in the upper right-hand corner of figure 2.2, there are wooded corridors that run right to left and several large wooded patches. Some species may be able to move perpendicular to the corridors if they can use the patches as stepping-stones.

A greenway project may depend on stepping-stones to provide connectivity for certain species or uses in landscapes with discontinuous habitat. A good example of this is the Green Links effort in Vancouver and the lower mainland, Canada. The primary activity of this project is to strengthen connectivity by planting native vegetation in utility corridors, parks, and even backyards. This is being done in an attempt to increase biodiversity by improving functional connectivity in strategic areas between parks and other green spaces.[36]

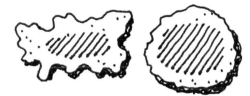

FIGURE 2.14

The rounder a patch (right), the more interior habitat it will have and the less edge habitat compared to a less round patch (left).

Patches

Patch shape affects the amounts of edge and interior habitat. The more deeply convoluted the edge of a patch, the less interior habitat there is. The closer patch shape is to round, the more interior habitat is maximized (figure 2.14).

Richard Forman proposed a useful shape for a patch, the "ecologically optimized" patch (figure 2.15).[37] It combines a central roundness (for maximizing interior habitat) with octopus tentacle-like corridors extending out. These corridors are meant to facilitate movement in and out of the patch.

When patches become more isolated, some natural processes within them can be greatly disrupted. For example, the seeds of plants may no longer be able to reach suitable habitat, and the plants' pollinators may not be able to find them in the isolated patch where they are growing. Predator-prey relationships can also be disrupted, as when a patch's isolation keeps prey and predators apart. Some of these disruptions, such as slowing the movement of disease, may be seen as desirable goals, but many other disruptions can reduce the ecological integrity of a landscape.

FIGURE 2.15

An "ecologically optimized" patch might have enough roundness to ensure interior habitat, and with its attached corridors, it may facilitate movement in and out of the patch.

Matrices Are Not Always Inhospitable

Some scientists have criticized as an oversimplification the island biogeographic perspective of landscape structure in which patches and corridors sit within an "inhospitable matrix" (figure 2.16).[38] The matrix may not actually be inhospitable to all species and is likely to have a range of conditions. Although this adds to the complexity of conceptualizing the landscape, it also adds realism. Certainly there are landscapes in which the matrix may be very inhospitable to most wildlife, such as in some very urban settings.

Boundaries and the Edge Effect

Early wildlife managers were very aware that certain game birds and mammals were attracted to edges.[39] By increasing the amount of edge, they sought to increase the numbers of these species for hunting. They weren't aware of the potential negative effects of these actions on species that prefer interior conditions. *Edge effects* occur along greenway boundaries. They include humidity, light exposure, wind exposure, and other aspects of microclimate, as well as species composition and habitat conditions created at the boundaries (figure 2.17). These effects vary in how deeply they penetrate in from the edge.

Microclimate changes near edges have been found to extend one to three tree heights into forests, depending on the aspect and the variable being observed. The largest effect on biological organisms occurs within 164 feet (50 m) of the edge, but some effects can extend considerably

FIGURE 2.16

Depending on the species involved and the conditions found in the matrix, the matrix may or may not be inhospitable for use by patch dwellers. Backyards, for example, might have enough tree cover to encourage between-patch movement by some birds.

(Drawing by Joe McGrane.)

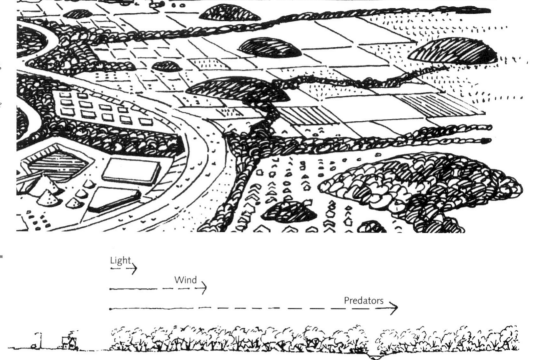

FIGURE 2.17

Edge effects along greenway boundaries will vary in how deeply they penetrate into the greenway. Light, shade-intolerant vegetation, wind, and edge-adapted predators will penetrate progressively greater distances in forested environments.

(Drawing by Jane Shoplick.)

farther. One review of studies of edge effects, however, found that some negative edge effects, such as increased predation and parasitism, documented in the eastern or midwestern United States, were not found in the Pacific Northwest.[40]

Horizontal Shape Affects Greenway Function

Landscape edges created by humans tend to be straight and abrupt (figure 2.18). Typically there is less flow of wildlife and wind across such edges and more flow along them. Nature's edges, however, tend to be curvier, which accommodates greater cross-boundary movement. Undulating boundaries create variable conditions for flows. For instance, at a lobe (e.g., a peninsula that juts out from an edge) concentrations of wildlife may exit and enter a corridor or patch because the lobe may function as a kind of corridor itself, with conditions more conducive to entering and exiting the corridor than adjacent coves or straight edges. Wind-borne seeds and dust, on the other hand, may be funneled by patch lobes and primarily enter at coves, which are indentations along an edge.

Boundary Abruptness Affects Movement

An abrupt edge may stand between the forest interior on one side and an

FIGURE 2.18

Human-created boundaries (left) tend to be straight, while nature's edges are often more curved. This has important ecological implications.

(Drawing by Joe McGrane.)

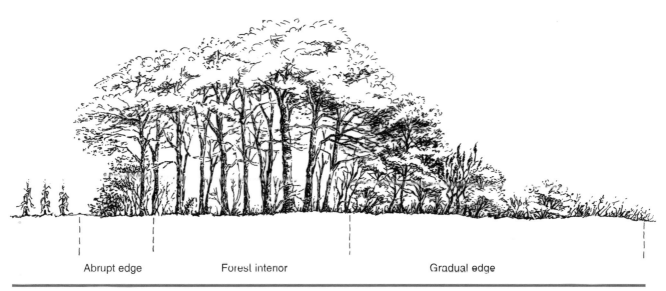

Abrupt edge   Forest interior   Gradual edge

FIGURE 2.19

An abrupt, maintained edge (left) contrasts strongly with a gradual, advancing edge (right). The gradual edge is a more highly structured buffer between the forest interior and an abandoned field. (Edge and interior dimensions are not shown to scale.) (Drawing by Jane Shoplick.)

adjacent agricultural or other open matrix on the other (figure 2.19). Microclimates at such edges can differ greatly from those in more gradually advancing edges. Edge effects become greater with increasing contrast between adjacent habitats, such as a forested corridor in a grassland matrix.[41]

Some Edge Effects Are Not Pronounced

It is much easier to see the pronounced edges between forested and agricultural landscapes, for example, than the edges common in more open landscapes. Edges between grasslands and shrublands are not as crisp nor are habitat patches as easily defined. Many of the early studies of habitat fragmentation took place in landscapes with crisp edges, places such as England and eastern North America. Such studies may translate poorly to forests in western North America.[42]

Importance of Vertical Layering of Vegetation

The vertical structure (understory and canopy) of a corridor's vegetation (figure 2.20), which may vary widely through the length of a greenway, can be very important to birds and other wildlife. This characteristic may be overlooked if a greenway is being planned only on paper in plan view, where it is possible

FIGURE 2.20

Greenway designers should consider the vertical structure (understory and canopy) of a corridor's vegetation, which may vary widely through the length of a greenway. The area on the left has little understory, while the area on the right has a more developed vertical structure.

(Drawing by Joe McGrane.)

FIGURE 2.21

Diagram of landscape function, showing solar energy, the hydrologic cycle, erosion, and human activity. Other components of landscape function include the growth and movement of plants and animals and other types of energy and material flows.

(Drawing by Jane Shoplick.)

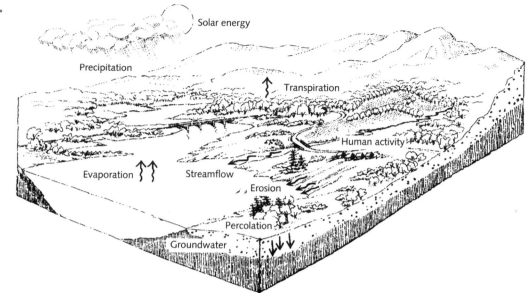

to consider only horizontal dimensions, not vertical, or without information about the vegetation layers. Vertical structure will have significant implications for future states of vegetation and overall management.

Interrelationship between Landscape Structure and Function

Ecological processes or functions that take place in a landscape influence that landscape's structure (patches, corridors, and matrix) and are influenced by it (figure 2.21). For example, an open area formed in a forested landscape after a large tree blows down (i.e., a patch) may alter the wind velocity locally, which may then cause additional trees to fall and thus further alter the pattern of the forest. Some species may require such dynamics to create the conditions they need to survive, but in a plantation such blow down may be very disruptive to management objectives.

Wind and other disturbances and consequent shifts in vegetation types are the principal agents of change in corridor vegetation.[43] Thus, landscape structure and processes can change over time and influence each other in a continuous dynamic. Understanding this dynamic, which has not always been considered in greenway design, is crucial to designing and managing a greenway because there may be a temptation to consider landscape structure as if it were static.

BOX 2.2

Flooding is a disturbance required for cottonwood regeneration. Before they were channelized and dammed, New Mexico rivers would flood more frequently, clearing sandbars where there would be enough moisture and sunlight for cottonwood seedlings to establish. In places such as Albuquerque, New Mexico, the Rio Grande River has been completely confined by dikes, and natural cottonwood regeneration has not occurred since the 1940s when the dikes were constructed.[1]

[1]Cleverly, J. (1999). "The Rio Grande Cottonwood, *Populus deltoids* spp. *wislizenii* (Salicaceae)." Retrieved September 3, 2004, (http://sevilleta.unm.edu/~cleverly/cw.html).

Change Is Inevitable and Some Disturbances Occur Naturally

Change is a constant in any landscape and any greenway. Plants and animals, water and wind, eroding soil, and glaciers move across the landscape. To survive, biological components of these systems must adapt to their surroundings.

Disturbances play important roles in maintaining the structure and processes of landscapes; they are forces with which native organisms have had to evolve. A disturbance can be defined as "any relatively discrete event in space and time that disrupts ecosystem, community, or population structure and changes resources, substrate, or the physical environment."[44] That a disturbance is discrete distinguishes it from chronic stress or background environmental variability that may be present in the landscape.

A landscape's disturbance regime is a kind of summary of the dynamics of disturbances in that landscape over a long period of time.[45] The regime includes the frequency, intensity, postdisturbance residuals (such as downed trees), return interval, rotation period, severity, and size of disturbances.

Humans affect natural disturbance regimes, often intentionally. They can make natural disturbances smaller or larger, less or more frequent, and less or more intense. For instance, the effects of otherwise naturally occurring floods may be intensified as more of a watershed is developed with houses, roads, and other impervious surfaces. Humans also introduce previously unknown disturbances or chronic stresses and tend to homogenize natural landscape patterns.

Importance of Greenways' Surroundings

The matrix is the landscape element that exerts the most influence over landscape process and change, and a greenway will be heavily subject to its environs. This is because linear habitats are particularly vulnerable to edge effects, with outside conditions influencing what happens at the edge of the greenway. The narrower a corridor, the greater the potential edge effects and the less the area of interior conditions (figure 2.22). For example, at the edge of a greenway, solar radiation, incident light, humidity, temperature and wind speed may vary considerably from the greenway's interior and in ways that are not supportive of greenway functions, such as needed interior habitat. Similarly, narrow stream corridors and the quality of a stream's waters may be very vulnerable to upland matrix conditions.

FIGURE 2.22

The narrower a corridor, the less the area of interior conditions within that corridor and the more likely edge conditions are to overwhelm it.

Greenways Must Adapt to Natural Disturbances

Natural disturbances, such as wind, fire, and insects, are part of the landscape and processes that help shape the patterns of landscapes. For instance, in a landscape that has frequent forest fires or other disturbances that create patches, the minimum width of a greenway might be set to be larger than the average width of a typical disturbance patch. Also, streams and other elements that are the focus of a greenway may be very dynamic, for example, cutting new channels or flooding. To the degree possible, greenway design should accommodate these disturbances and changes.

Succession as a Form of Landscape Change

Succession is the process through which communities of plant and animal species in a particular area are replaced over time by a series of different and usually more complex communities. For example, after agricultural land is abandoned in humid climates there are progressive stages of vegetation that may culminate in old-growth forest (figure 2.23). The transition from grasses to young forest can occur over the course of a few decades, whereas several centuries are required for old-growth forest to regenerate. Understanding these potential stages can help in planning for changes in a greenway.

Historically many scientists believed that succession culminated in a climax vegetation state (e.g., old-growth forest) that was nearly at equilibrium. Today most scientists instead think of landscapes as much more dynamic or not at equilibrium. This is another example where an appealing, but simplistic model (in this case climax equilibrium) belies the complexity of a natural system (here, succession).

Human Impacts Form a Gradient across the Landscape

The traditional sense of nature as something wild and separate from people misses the fact that, at least to some degree, people shape most of our planet's landscapes, and that even in cities there are elements of nature.[46] A useful model of this relationship is the landscape modification gradient (figure 2.24).[47]

Because the intensity of human use varies across the landscape, different ecological goals may be appropriate in different places. For instance, the goal of achieving major habitat connectivity within an urban area may not make sense, because targeted species may have little chance of surviving there.

The landscape modification gradient concept is very useful in understanding relative levels of human modification in a landscape and what they might mean for greenway goals. For example, in figure 2.24, conditions change dramatically along the stream that starts in the foreground and

FIGURE 2.23

The progression of successional stages following abandonment of agricultural land in a humid climate, culminating in old-growth forest.

(Drawing by Jane Shoplick.)

grasses   herbs   shrubs   young forest   mature forest   old-growth forest

FIGURE 2.24

Recognizing a modification gradient across the landscape makes it clear that different ecological goals may be appropriate in different places. From urban (at the top of the drawing) through suburban, cultivated, and managed to more unmanaged (at bottom), the gradient shown here sweeps through very different ecological conditions and calls for different greenway objectives in each zone. (Drawing by Joe McGrane.)

then flows into the river below and onward through the city. At the highest elevations there may be little or no development—hiking trails perhaps—and little impacts on the stream's water quality. By the time the stream reaches the area shown in the foreground of the drawing, there are adjoining roads, buildings, and some agriculture. Although the dominant factors characterizing this area are mostly natural processes, human activities have a greater impact here, as water quality is degraded by runoff and riparian habitat is fragmented by development. When the river reaches the city, natural processes are severely constrained and transformed by the extensive development. Certainly nature is found in the city, but it is in a special partnership with human factors. In this urban setting, nature can still help make the city more habitable for people and be a token of more pristine nature now at a distance.

Although historically there has often been a distinct dichotomy between nature and city in both our minds and on the ground, that doesn't have to be in either case. Even within cities, natural processes are present and can play a role in humanizing places. At the other extreme, even in places remote from the city, there is almost certainly going to be some evidence of people, even if it is only air pollution or the fact that frequently these places have become the playgrounds for city dwellers.

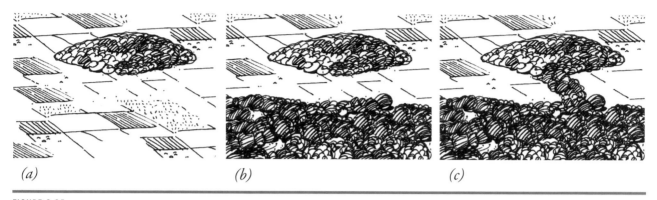

(a)   *(b)*   *(c)*

FIGURE 2.25

Based on island biogeographic theory, conservationists developed recommendations for patch characteristics that might indicate species richness. The least desirable situation would be an isolated patch (a). Better for sustaining species richness is a patch near a potential source of recolonization (b). Better yet is a patch that is not only near, but directly connected to a recolonization source (c).

Although quite helpful, the landscape modification gradient model may be misleading in some ways because it oversimplifies. In presenting a continuum that varies between developed and undeveloped, it ignores the discontinuities and complexities of real landscapes. It also may further an unhelpful nature/culture dichotomy, ignoring the interwoven nature of people and nature in the landscape. The gradient concept may be misleading in that it ignores the possibility that urban development may be less disruptive (and more appropriate) than far-flung and scattered exurban development. It also implies that lands that have been heavily modified biologically, such as farms or managed forests, can be assumed, simply because they are rural, to be less human-dominated than, say, an urban natural area.

Island Biogeography

Although its influence has waned over the years, island biogeography has been historically significant in the development of landscape ecology and conservation biology. It still frames the way many conservation strategies are described.

Robert MacArthur and Edward Wilson, the originators of island biogeography, theorized that islands and their species richness/diversity across geologic time depended on several characteristics, such as the size of the island, the distance of the island from the mainland (and the potential for recolonization), and the length of geologic time the island had been separated from the mainland.[48]

Conservationists took island biogeographic theory and applied it, not to islands surrounded by ocean, but to habitat patches in a "sea" (i.e., matrix) of other land cover. Conservationists suggested that species richness would be greater if conservation areas were (figure 2.25):

- big rather than small,
- one large rather than several smaller patches with the same total area,
- near rather than far,
- connected rather than isolated, and
- newer islands rather than older ones.

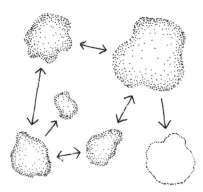

FIGURE 2.26

A greenway that supports wildlife may play a role in preserving metapopulation connections and contribute to the survival of the metapopulation. Metapopulations are systems of local populations linked by occasional dispersal, where local populations go extinct periodically, "winking" off and on over time. Here arrows indicate the direction of movement of individuals between their source and destination patches. There was a local extinction in the lower-right patch and the arrow coming toward it indicates recolonization.

Separated Populations May Function as a Unified Metapopulation

In articulating their theory of island biogeography, MacArthur and Wilson were describing an early metapopulation model. Metapopulation models have largely replaced island bio-geographic models as the theoretical framework within which issues of habitat fragmentation are considered.[49]

A metapopulation is a set of local populations connected by migrating individuals. It is a population of populations.[50] Preserving the metapopulations' connections across the matrix or through corridors is crucial to the survival of the metapopulations and may be an important role for a greenway (figure 2.26). Roads can divide some wildlife populations, creating separate populations or subpopulations (figure 2.27).

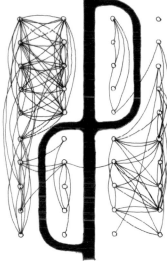

FIGURE 2.27

Roads can be major barriers for some species, creating separate populations, or if the barriers are not totally impenetrable, separate subpopulations of a metapopulation. The lines show the movement paths of beetles that were marked and recaptured.

(Redrawn from Mader, H.-J. [1984]. "Animal habitat isolation by roads and agricultural fields." *Biological Conservation* 29: 81-96. Used with permission of Elsevier.)

Endangered populations in isolated patches are more likely to be "rescued" by dispersing individuals from other patches if the patches are close together or otherwise connected.[51] Patches are said to "wink on and off," as they are recolonized or suffer local extinction.

Understanding Spatial Scale Is Crucial

Landscape patterns are scale dependent. This means that patterns can change—or be observable—depending on how close the observer is to the landscape (figure 2.28). What looks like a broad corridor from an airplane, for instance, may seem like a series of small patches on the ground. Similarly, using maps of different scale to measure such things as landscape patchiness may yield very different results for the same landscape.

How connected a landscape is for an organism is influenced by the scale at which the organism perceives the landscape relative to the structure (the scale and pattern of patchiness) of the landscape.[52]

Two important aspects characterize spatial scale: extent and grain (figure 2.29). Extent is how

(a)

FIGURE 2.29

Extent and grain are two important aspects of spatial scale. Extent (a) refers to the breadth of the view, while grain (b) is the amount of detail within a view. (Drawings by Joe McGrane.)

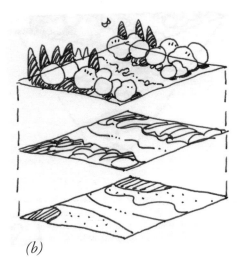

(b)

FIGURE 2.28

How landscape patterns are distinguished depends on the scale at which they are examined. What looks like a broad corridor from an airplane, for instance, may seem like a series of small patches on the ground. (Drawing by Joe McGrane.)

expansive the map or area of study is. Grain relates to how much detail there is within the extent. With geographic information systems, for example, two different kinds of data may be gathered for the same extent, but with different resolutions (e.g., 2.5 acres vs. 25 acres [1 ha vs. 10 ha]). Data of different resolutions may suggest different patterns for the same area.[53]

The Importance of Broader Time Scales

Another important dimension of scale is temporal—how length of time influences one's perspective on the landscape. A one-day visit in a landscape may give a very different impression from what that landscape is like the rest of the year, let alone what it was like 100 years ago. The space-time principle suggests that the larger an area studied, the longer the relevant time scale.[54] This temporal perspective is crucial in understanding how parts of a greenway may change.

Guiding a Fragmenting Landscape toward Connectivity

Landscape ecology can be an especially useful guide in aiming for the process William Laurance and Claude Gascon have called creative landscape fragmentation.[55] With this approach, greenway designers would identify and conserve the core structure of a landscape as a greenway network, so that it continues to support critical functions even as the rest of the landscape is radically transformed. Without such an approach, fragmented habitat is likely to be scattered. This is one of the underlying strategies of the Chatfield Basin Conservation Network in its work in southwestern suburban Denver. With the likelihood of considerable new development in this area of substantial natural resources, project collaborators are identifying a skeletal system of green infrastructure in advance of more development (see chapter 6).

Is Spatial Pattern Always Crucial?

It is especially important to plan with landscape pattern in mind when target habitat is rare or fragmented. Both theory and empirical data suggest that spatial pattern has a strong influence when habitat suitable for some species occupies less than 20–30 percent of a landscape. Spatial pattern is also important if edge effects are significant parts of the process being studied or if there are limits on dispersal between patches and metapopulation dynamics may affect habitat use.

With an understanding of the concepts presented in this primer a greenway designer should be better prepared to discuss important greenway issues with scientists of many types. As you gain familiarity with these terms you are becoming more conversant in the rich language of greenspace, and especially greenways, which should enhance your ability to design a successful greenway project.

Notes

[1] For a similar discussion that actually took place in a New England town, see Pollan, M. (1991). *Second Nature: A Gardener's Education*. New York, Dell Publishing.

[2] Principle 15 of the Rio Declaration states: "In order to protect the environment, the precautionary approach shall be widely applied by States according to their capabilities. Where there are threats of serious or irreversible damage, lack of full scientific certainty shall not be used as a reason for postponing cost-effective measures to prevent environmental degradation." See: (http://www.unep.org/Documents.multilingual/Default.asp?DocumentID=78&ArticleID=1163).

[3] Perlman, D. L., and J. C. Milder. (2004). *Practical Ecology for Planners, Developers, and Citizens*. Washington, DC, Island Press, p. 12.

[4] Spirn, A. W. (1998). *The Language of Landscape*. New Haven, CT, Yale University Press.

[5] Collins, T. (2000). Interventions in the Rust-Belt, The art and ecology of post-industrial public space. *British Urban Geography Journal, Ecumene* 7(4):461–467, p. 464.

[6] Ndubisi, F. (2002). *Ecological Planning: A Historical and Comparative Synthesis*. Baltimore, Johns Hopkins University Press.

[7] Ahern, J. F. (2002). "Greenways as strategic landscape planning: Theory and application." Ph.D. Dissertation. Wageningen, Netherlands, Wageningen University.

[8] Golley, F. B., and J. Bellot (1991). "Interaction of landscape ecology, planning, and design." *Landscape and Urban Planning* 21: 3–11.

[9] Ndubisi, (2002), *Ecological Planning*.

[10] Zonneveld, I. S. (1982). "Presidential address." *International Association for Landscape Ecology Bulletin* 1, p. 1.

[11] Cook, E. A., and H. N. van Lier, eds. (1994). *Landscape Planning and Ecological Networks*. Amsterdam, Elsevier.

[12] Forman, R. T. T., and M. Godron. (1986). *Landscape Ecology*. New York, John Wiley & Sons.

[13] Turner, M. G., R. H. Gardner, et al. (2001). *Landscape Ecology in Theory and Practice*. New York, Springer.

[14] Ibid.

[15] Duerksen, C. J. (1997). *Habitat Protection Planning: Where the Wild Things Are*. Chicago, IL, American Planning Association.

[16] Forman, R. T. T. (1995). *Land Mosaics: The Ecology of Landscapes and Regions*. New York, Cambridge University Press.

[17] Ibid.

[18] Ibid.

[19] Forman and Godron, (1986), *Landscape Ecology*.

[20] Forman, (1995), *Land Mosaics*.

[21] Jules, E. S., and P. Shahani. (2003). "A broader ecological context to habitat fragmentation: Why matrix habitat is more important than we thought." *Journal of Vegetation Science* 14: 459–464.

[22] Merriam, G. (1995). Movement in spatially divided populations: Responses to landscape structure, pp. 64–77, in *Landscape Approaches in Mammalian Ecology and Conservation*. J. William Z. Lidicker, ed. Minneapolis, University of Minnesota Press.

[23] O'Neill, R. V., J. R. Krummel, et al. (1988). "Indices of landscape pattern." *Landscape Ecology* 1: 153–162.

[24] Taylor, P. D., L. Fahrig, et al. (1993). "Connectivity is a vital element of landscape structure." *Oikos* 68: 571–73.

[25] Bennett, A. (1999). *Linkages in the Landscape: The Role of Corridors and Connectivity in Wildlife Conservation.* Gland, Switzerland, IUCN.

[26] Interestingly, the word "landscape" can be traced back to its Dutch root (*landschap*), which meant "a place on the land where a community had formed." J. Albers. (2000). *Hands on the Land; A History of the Vermont Landscape*, Cambridge, MA, MIT Press, p. 12. Later the word came to describe a picture of a scene, rather than the scene itself. This perceptual sense of the word may be useful if we turn it around and accept a wide range of species, in addition to humans, as possible perceivers of the landscape. The key here is that functions associated with landscape pattern need to be evaluated for specific species and uses, and certainly not solely in some generic or anthropocentric way.

[27] Stamps, J., M. Buechner, et al. (1987). "The effect of edge permeability and habitat geometry on emigration from patches of habitat." *American Naturalist* 129: 533-552; Taylor and Fahrig, (1993), "Connectivity is a vital element of landscape structure."

[28] Bunnell, F. L. (1999). "What habitat is an island?" pp. 1–31, in *Forest Fragmentation: Wildlife and Management Implications.* J. A. Rochelle, L. A. Lehmann, and J. Wisniewski, ed. Leiden, Netherlands, Brill.

[29] Doak, D. F. (1995). "Source-sink models and the problem of habitat degradation: general models and applications to the Yellowstone grizzly bear." *Conservation Biology* 9: 1370–1379.

[30] Tilman, D., R. M. May, et al. (1994). "Habitat destruction and the extinction debt." *Nature* 371(6492): 65–66.

[31] Swingland, I. R., and P. J. Greenwood, ed. (1983). *The Ecology of Animal Movement.* Oxford, Clarendon Press.

[32] Ferraz, G., G. J. Russell, et al. (2003). "Rates of species loss from Amazonian forest fragments." *Proceedings of the National Academy of Sciences* (PNAS Online). (http://www.pnas.org/cgi/content/full/100/24/14069).

[33] Oksanen, T., and M. Schneider. (1995). "The influence of habitat heterogeneity on predator-prey dynamics." pp. 122–150, in *Landscape Approaches in Mammalian Ecology and Conservation.* W. Z. J. Lidicker, ed. Minneapolis, University of Minnesota; Johnson, C. W. (1999). "Conservation corridor planning at the landscape level: Managing for wildlife habitat." *USDA National Biology Handbook*, Part 614.4. 190-vi-NBH.

[34] Johnson, C. W. (1999). "Conservation corridor planning at the landscape level."

[35] Bennett, A. (1999). *Linkages in the Landscape: The Role of Corridors and Connectivity in Wildlife Conservation.*

[36] Rudd, H. (2004). "Green links." Retrieved March 14, 2004, (http://www.stewardshipcentre.bc.ca/caseStudies/cs_builder.asp?request_no=132).

[37] Forman, (1995), *Land Mosaics.*

[38] With, K. A. (1999). "Is landscape connectivity necessary and sufficient for wildlife management?" pp. 97–115, in *Forest Fragmentation: Wildlife and Management Implications.* J. A. Rochelle, L. A. Lehmann, and J. Wisniewski, ed. Leiden, Netherlands, Brill. p. 99.

[39] Leopold, A. (1933). *Game Management.* Madison, University of Wisconsin Press.

[40] Kremsater, L., and F. L. Bunnell. (1999). "Edge effects: Theory, evidence and implications to management of western North American forests," pp. 117–153, in *Forest Fragmentation: Wildlife and Management Implications.* J. A. Rochelle, L. A. Lehmann, and J. Wisniewski, ed. Leiden, Netherlands, Brill. This supports the observation of Rochelle et al. that fragmentation may be a useful conceptual tool, but may have limited value as a generalizable phenomenon. Rochelle, J. A., L. A. Lehmann, et al., eds. (1999). *Forest Fragmentation.*

[41] Harris, L. D. (1988). "Edge effects and the conservation of biotic diversity." *Conservation Biology* 2: 330–332.

[42] Flaspohler, D. J. (2000). "Simple concepts, elusive clarity." *Conservation Biology* 14(4): 1216–1217; Rochelle, Lehmann, et al., eds. (1999). *Forest Fragmentation.*

[43] Johnson, C. W. (1999). "Conservation corridor planning at the landscape level."

[44] White, P. S., and S. T. A. Pickett. (1985). "Natural disturbance and patch dynamics: An introduction," pp. 3–13, in *The Ecology of Natural Disturbance and Patch Dynamics.* S. T. A. Pickett and P. S. White, eds. Orlando, Academic Press.

[45] Turner, M. G., R. H. Gardner, et al. (2001). *Landscape Ecology in Theory and Practice.*

[46] Swafield, S. (2003). "New urbanism, old nature? Transforming cities in Australia and New Zealand." Auckland, New Zealand, Urbanism Downunder 2003, 2nd Australasian Congress for New Urbanism, NZ Institute of Landscape Architects 2003 Conference; Spirn, A. W. (1984). *The Granite Garden: Urban Nature and Human Design.* New York, Basic Books.

[47] Forman, (1995), *Land Mosaics.*

[48] MacArthur, R. H., and E. O. Wilson. (1967). *The Theory of Island Biogeography.* Princeton, NJ, Princeton University Press.

[49] Turner, M. G., R. H. Gardner, et al. (2001). *Landscape Ecology in Theory and Practice*.

[50] Lidicker, W. Z. J. (1995). "The landscape concept: Something old, something new." pp. 3–19, in *Landscape Approaches in Mammalian Ecology and Conservation*. W. Z. J. Lidicker, ed. Minneapolis, University of Minnesota Press.

[51] Brown, J. H., and A. Kodric-Brown. (1977). "Turnover rates in insular biogeography: Effect of immigration on extinction." *Ecology* 58(2): 445–449. But this is not always the case. Michael Soulé (1991). "Conservation: Tactics for a constant crisis." *Science* 253: 744–750. Soulé found in studying isolated chaparral fragments in San Diego, California, that the distance between patches didn't matter because chaparral-requiring bird species dispersed poorly, if at all, through nonnative habitat and that recolonization following local extirpations appeared to be rare. He found a slight benefit of patch proximity for rodents, rabbits, and hares. For most nonflying animals in most places, however, he concluded that proximity of habitat remnants will not slow the loss of species unless there are corridor connections to other patches.

[52] With, K. A. (1999). "Is landscape connectivity necessary and sufficient for wildlife management?"

[53] Turner, Gardner, et al., (2001), *Landscape Ecology in Theory and Practice*.

[54] Forman, (1995), *Land Mosaics*.

[55] Laurance, W. F., and C. Gascon. (1997). "How to creatively fragment a landscape." *Conservation Biology* 11(2): 577–579.

CHAPTER 3

GREENWAYS AS WILDLIFE CORRIDORS

Reed F. Noss

While academic biologists debate the costs and benefits of habitat corridors for wildlife, land-use planners around the world are eagerly incorporating corridors into their designs. Sometimes they do so based on detailed scientific studies, but other times they do so with little thought as to which species might use the corridors and which might not. Greenways have been conspicuous components of many land-use plans in recent years, but they are often designed without clear reference to biological knowledge. For example, some kinds of corridors, such as utility rights-of-way, are touted as beneficial greenways for wildlife, but are more likely to have negative effects, at least on forest species.[1] As noted by Bennett "in many ways, the acceptance of corridors as a concept for biodiversity conservation has outpaced scientific understanding and the collection of empirical data. . . . "[2]

Are corridors and greenways just a fad? Do they contribute to conservation goals, or could they potentially do more harm than good for wildlife? These are some of the overarching questions to be addressed in this chapter. Other pressing questions in land-use planning for connectivity include the following:

- What conditions are required for a given species to use a corridor?
- Which species are likely to benefit from a specific kind of corridor and which will not?
- Is a narrow corridor, dominated by "weedy" species or with abundant human use, better than no corridor at all?
- Are there species important enough to a region so that wherever they occur, corridors should be planned to accommodate them?

These and other issues must be addressed if we are to design greenways that contribute to broad conservation goals, in addition to serving people.

Like many biologists, I believe that the loss of *biodiversity*—which includes not only the extinction of species, but also the loss of distinct populations and genes and the decline and degradation

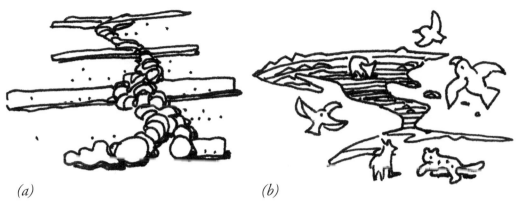

(a)   *(b)*

FIGURE 3.1

Although both are corridors, an English hedgerow (a) and the Isthmus of Panama (b) function very differently for wildlife.

of ecosystems—is the most serious crisis of our time. If we are to halt massive biological impoverishment of the earth, we need to reform our land-use planning dramatically to ensure that native species can maintain viable populations in landscapes dominated by humans, as well as in wilderness. Because most of the remaining natural areas in human-dominated landscapes are becoming increasingly fragmented (i.e., smaller and more isolated from one another), it makes sense to provide opportunities for animals and plants to move among areas, and by so doing, maintain larger interbreeding populations. However, the devil is in the details.

What interests conservation biologists is not corridors per se, but rather *functional connectivity*, which involves the flow of individuals and their genes among habitats and populations.[3] This connectivity can be measured by the degree to which the landscape facilitates or impedes movement of organisms among habitat patches.[4] Connectivity is determined by both a species's behavior and other life history characteristics, as well as the structure of the landscape. Hence, connectivity is both species- and landscape-specific.[5]

Well-designed studies generally show that corridors provide connectivity for the species being studied.[6] Nevertheless, a specific greenway may or may not provide functional connectivity for all species concerned given the structure of the corridor. A corridor to one species may be a barrier to another.

Corridors can be discrete linear landscape features such as hedgerows or *riparian* (streamside) strips, or broad, internally heterogeneous zones that permit movement of species between habitat patches, landscapes, or—over long periods of time—even regions.[7]

Wildlife traditionally refers to animals, especially vertebrates, but recent definitions encompass "all forms of life that are wild"[8] and are closely linked to the concept of biodiversity: the variety of life on earth. A *wildlife corridor* is defined here as a strip or band through which nondomesticated organisms may move, especially between areas of habitat. Because relatively few studies have addressed the value of corridors for plants,[9] most of the examples given in this chapter are for animals.

Spatial and temporal scales are important to consider in any discussion of wildlife corridors. Although both are corridors, an English hedgerow and the Isthmus of Panama function very differently for wildlife (figure 3.1). In this chapter, I discuss corridor functions mostly at the spatial scale at which greenways are planned (that is, within landscapes and regions ranging from hundreds to millions of acres) and at an ecological time scale of days to decades. This chapter presents an overview of important concepts related to wildlife corridors and movement. It addresses how corridors function as habitat and for daily, seasonal, and dispersal movement of wildlife, and the roles of corridors in population persistence and long-distance range shifts. I discuss potential problems and design issues and provide recommendations of how wildlife movement should be considered in designing greenways. Any and all of the points discussed in this chapter will have to be reviewed for their relevance to the local conditions of specific greenway projects. Although biological conservation is arguably the most valuable potential function of greenways and of land-use planning in general, economic, recreational, and aesthetic values of corridors are important to people and, when carefully planned, can be compatible with conservation.[10]

Wildlife Movement and the Role for Corridors

To better understand and plan for wildlife movement, conservationists have developed a number of models of how landscapes work. Corridors can be especially effective in accommodating movement, but so can other landscape elements.

Wildlife Movement Is Fundamental

The movement of organisms across landscapes is one of the most fundamental ecological processes. It affects the persistence of populations, distributions of species and genes, composition of biological communities, spread of disturbances, and other ecological phenomena.[11] Many species of animals use distinct travel routes, often identifiable as habitat corridors, or a string of stepping-stone habitat patches distinct from the surrounding matrix.[12] The latter may be especially true in landscapes altered by human activities, but may also be the case in wilderness areas.

Corridors Are Especially Effective for Functional Connectivity

As noted by Bennett,[13] habitat corridors may be among the best means for providing functional connectivity under certain conditions, such as when (1) much of the landscape is modified by human activity and inhospitable to native species; (2) the species in question are *habitat specialists* or depend on undisturbed habitat; (3) the species in question are unable to travel the distances between remaining patches of natural habitat, so must be able to dwell and breed in corridors; (4) the goal is to maintain continuity of populations among habitat patches, rather than just to allow infrequent movements; (5) the goal is to maintain continuity of entire faunal communities; or (6) maintenance of key ecological processes requires habitat continuity.

Wildlife managers have long been aware of the value of movement corridors for particular game mammals and birds, such as squirrels and quail.[14] Corridors have been invoked as tools for the conservation of biodiversity since the mid-1970s, when conservation biologists produced a series of influential papers on design principles for nature reserves.[15] More recently, in North America, corridors and connectivity have been major topics of research and discussion in landscape ecology and metapopulation theory.[16] (See chapter 2 for background discussion.)

Corridors Were Included in Island Biogeographic Theory

The reserve-design recommendations, including wildlife corridors, of conservation biologists in the 1970s and for some time thereafter were based largely on the equilibrium theory of *island biogeography*.[17] Island biogeographic theory predicts that small, isolated islands (or patches of habitat that resemble islands) will experience higher extinction rates and lower immigration rates of species than large islands closer to a species' source. Corridors were suggested as a means to increase species immigration to nature reserves and other habitat islands in fragmented landscapes, thus maintaining species richness (figure 2.25).[18]

Beyond Island Biogeography

The limitations of island biogeographic theory have become clear, however, as data from empirical studies have accumulated and our understanding of landscape ecology has matured. Habitat patches are not truly islands in a homogenous sea. Rather, the matrix that surrounds habitat patches is a source of species (often invasive weeds) that may colonize patches, and the habitat structure of the matrix influences the ability of species to move across it. For example, a landscape with a high density of roads (especially busy highways) will be impermeable to species that hesitate to cross roads or that get killed trying.[19]

Island biogeographic theory was important because it spurred conservationists to think about patch size and isolation, which are central considerations in conservation planning. In a number of cases, the area and isolation of habitat fragments have proven to be the best predictors of species distribution and abundance (e.g., mammalian carnivores in southern California).[20] Nevertheless, landscape ecologists now take the more realistic view of landscapes as heterogeneous mosaics. A given landscape will be permeable to some species but not to others. For some wide-ranging species, an area of farms, managed forests, or ranches may function as a corridor. This is most evident when considered on a regional scale where, for example, a wolf disperses from one wilderness area to another and crosses many miles of human-altered habitat along the way, while avoiding the most heavily developed areas.

Even Narrow Corridors Useful

Even narrow corridors of vegetation may be used by some species for traveling about the landscape in relative safety. Blue jays, for example, may travel several miles in the fall to cache acorns and beechnuts for later use. When making these movements in Wisconsin, jays show a strong tendency to fly immediately above wooded fencerows. If a hawk (especially a migrating accipiter, such as a sharp-shinned or Cooper's hawk) approaches, a jay dives into the cover of the fencerow.[21] Wegner and Merriam found that several bird species preferred to fly along fencerows rather than cross open fields.[22] Well-vegetated corridors likely often provide cover for escape from predators to animals that travel about the landscape.

Corridors Serve Many Functions

The scientific literature on wildlife corridors focuses primarily on how corridors function as conduits, allowing individuals of a target species to move from point A to point B. But a corridor in a real landscape will have myriad functions, affecting a large number of species. Although a particular target species may be the primary concern in some situations, the net effect of alternative corridor designs on a whole suite of species and ecological processes should be considered for comprehensive land-use planning. The two overarching potential benefits of wildlife corridors in biological conservation are (1) providing dwelling and breeding habitat for plants and animals, and (2) serving as a conduit for movement (see chapter 2).

The conduit role can be further subdivided into several functions: (1) permitting daily and seasonal movements of animals; (2) facilitating dispersal, consequent gene flow between populations, and rescue of small populations from extinction; and (3) allowing long-distance range shifts of species, such as in response to climate change. An additional role of corridors, not considered in depth in this chapter, is maintaining flows of such ecological processes as fire, wind, and floods (and associated transport of materials and organisms). Flooding and related issues are discussed in chapter 4.

Corridors as Habitat

Corridors, even narrow ones, provide habitat in which some kinds of organisms will live and reproduce. In many landscapes, most of the natural vegetation has been removed, and remnants are distributed either as isolated patches or as linear features between agricultural fields or along rivers, railroads, highways, power lines, or other rights-of-way. For some species, such as cottontail rabbits in a midwestern American hedgerow, the value of these corridors is greater as habitat than as travelway. In fact, the habitat and conduit functions can work together for even greater benefit. The most effective movement corridors are likely those that contain resident, reproducing populations of the species of interest (see discussion of dispersal later).[23]

Riparian Greenways Important for Native Biota

Streamside (or riparian) forests are naturally linear or sinuous features whose habitat values for wildlife are well known. In many regions of the world, these forests constitute linear remnants of native vegetation in a human-dominated landscape. The biological richness of riparian forests stems from several factors: (1) they are structurally complex because they lie at the dynamic interface between aquatic and terrestrial ecosystems; (2) they offer in close proximity both aquatic and terrestrial habitats, the adjacency of which is important to species such as aquatic insects, amphibians, and wetland birds, whose life cycles include use of both; and (3) their rich soils and dependable supply of water lead to high biological productivity.[24]

Bottomland hardwood forests of the southern United States exemplify these characteristics. These corridors have rich alluvial soils, high productivity, microclimates moderated by the year-round presence of water, an abundance of insects and plant foods, and numerous tree cavities to serve as homes or nests for birds and mammals.[25] Although the extent of bottomland hardwood forests has declined significantly, these forests have partially been protected by default because, in the absence of dams, regular flooding makes them unsuitable for development.[26]

Undammed coastal-plain rivers, such as the Suwannee and its tributaries in Florida, often have broad riparian corridors that contrast sharply with adjacent agricultural uplands.

Vertebrate densities are usually high in riparian forests. In Iowa, for example, floodplain forests have been found to support an average of 506 breeding pairs of birds per 100 acres (40 ha), compared to 339 pairs in the same area of upland forest.[27] Also, many species of plants and animals are found only in riparian zones, and these areas often contain more species than other terrestrial habitat types.[28] Forested riparian zones also provide many

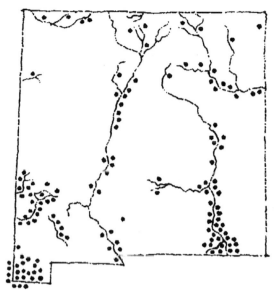

FIGURE 3.2

Map of New Mexico showing the distribution of rare vertebrates that occur in riparian habitats. Each dot represents a known location of a federally listed threatened or endangered species. Of ninety-four rare vertebrates in the state, sixty-nine are associated with or depend on riparian habitat.

(After A. S. Johnson. [1989]. "The thin green line: Riparian corridors and endangered species in Arizona and New Mexico," pp. 34–36, in *Preserving Communities and Corridors.* G. Mackintosh, ed. Washington DC, Defenders of Wildlife.)

benefits to adjacent aquatic communities. They may help maintain water quality, contribute woody debris and leaves that provide food and habitat for aquatic organisms, moderate water temperature through shading, and ameliorate the effects of flooding.

In many countries, states, and provinces, forest regulations require retaining vegetated strips along streams (especially fish-bearing streams) in logged landscapes. Although typically the primary purpose of preserving these riparian strips is to maintain water quality, they also function as dwelling and movement habitat for wildlife, especially when surrounding uplands are altered by human activities.

In Newfoundland, before an area was clear-cut, tracks of five mammal species—the endangered Newfoundland marten, short-tailed weasel, red fox, red squirrel, and snowshoe hare—were more abundant in forest interior than in riparian habitats.[29] Following clear-cutting, however, riparian buffers were used by these species more than clear-cut or other open areas. This was especially true for the marten, which is known from other studies to avoid clear-cuts.[30] Thus for some species, in human-disturbed landscapes, riparian corridors appear to function as *refugia*—places where organisms can avoid life-threatening or otherwise undesirable disturbances.

The values of riparian corridors are particularly evident in the arid and semiarid western United States, where they may constitute the only low-elevation areas with trees or tall shrubs. Southwestern riparian zones are literally "linear oases."[31] Some 80 percent of all vertebrate species in Arizona and New Mexico depend on riparian habitat for at least a portion of their life cycles.[32] Although only about 2 percent of the Southwest was occupied by riparian ecosystems before settlement, Arizona and New Mexico are estimated to have lost 90 percent of these rare ecosystems over the last century.[33] Thus, it is not surprising that 70 percent of Arizona's and 73 percent of New Mexico's threatened vertebrates are either closely associated with, or completely dependent on, riparian habitat (figure 3.2). Cottonwood-dominated riparian vegetation in the Southwest reportedly has the highest density of breeding birds in North America.[34]

If riparian corridors are conserved and adjacent upland areas are ecologically restored, it may be possible to reestablish a full gradient of habitat supporting riparian and upland communities.

A similar affinity of vertebrates for riparian zones occurs in less arid parts of the American West. In the Blue Mountains in eastern Oregon and Washington, 285 (75 percent) of the 378 species of terrestrial vertebrates either depend on, or strongly prefer, riparian habitats.[35] Riparian greenways thus have the potential to support a large portion of the native biota in some landscapes.

For a more complete discussion of riparian corridors and their functions, see chapter 4.

Upland Habitats Also Important

In some landscapes, many species of conservation concern are associated with upland habitats and do not occur in riparian zones. This is true in Florida, where upland longleaf pine and scrub communities contain many of the state's most characteristic, endemic, and threatened species.[36] The degree to which riparian greenways can encompass the range of native species will depend on the nature of species distribution in particular landscapes. A valid conservation strategy might be to start protection with riparian corridors and then widen them by ecologically restoring upland areas (figure 3.3). This may reestablish a full gradient of habitat supporting riparian and upland communities.

Edge Conditions in Agricultural Areas

In agricultural landscapes, fencerows, hedgerows, shelterbelts, and even roadsides with native or seminative vegetation stand in marked contrast to the monotony of cultivated fields (figure 3.4). In Iowa, Best found the greatest number of bird species in fencerows with continuous trees and shrubs.[37]

Hedgerows may offer the only wooded habitat in many agricultural landscapes.

Although the fencerows were considered valuable for maintaining bird populations in Iowa's agricultural landscape, the most common birds in fencerow habitats were weedy species tolerant of human habitat modification, such as the brown-headed cowbird, house sparrow, northern flicker, mourning dove, and American robin. These birds are known as edge species (in contrast to interior species) because they inhabit the interfaces between contrasting habitats, such as between forest and field.

Not only are such corridors typically home to edge species, but they also may serve as conduits for nonnative animals. Likewise, they may also make it easier for opportunistic predators to move through the landscape and prey on nests.

Edges are generally drier and brighter than forest interiors; a fencerow or hedgerow is entirely edge habitat. North American hedgerows are typically dominated by forest-edge plants, including many nonnative species.[38] Pollard referred to British hedgerows as woodland edges without the woods.[39] Edge species often increase in abundance as landscapes are fragmented by human activity. Thus, on the one hand the value of fencerows, hedgerows, and other narrow corridors for conservation of native species is limited. On the other hand, in landscapes where large blocks of natural habitat no longer exist, narrow corridors add biodiversity to an otherwise monotonous countryside. Some edge birds may also help control insect pests. Field margins and hedgerows also may provide critical habitats for predatory invertebrates, including beetles and spiders, which may help control agricultural pests.[40] Lewis found more species of insects in an English hedgerow than in adjacent bean fields and pastures.[41]

Hedgerow ecology has been particularly well studied in Europe, where it has been conclusively shown that many animals characteristic of agricultural landscapes are dependent, at least at some point of their life cycle, on hedgerows.[42] Without hedgerows or well-vegetated fencerows, many agricultural landscapes around the world would be far poorer in species and far less interesting to naturalists (figure 3.5).

FIGURE 3.5

Without hedgerows or well-vegetated fencerows, many agricultural landscapes around the world would be far poorer in species. (a) A midwestern agricultural landscape with few connecting hedgerows. (b) A photo simulation of the same landscape with hedgerows added.

(Courtesy of U.S. Department of Agriculture—Natural Resources Conservation Society.)

FIGURE 3.6

Generally, power-line corridors introduce common edge species into forested landscapes, but a greater variety of birds may be found when the power-line corridor contains a high density of shrubs such as blackberries.

(Photo courtesy of USDA.)

Farmstead shelterbelts in Minnesota, although planted primarily to protect humans and their property from high winds and snow, also provide nesting and feeding habitat for birds.[43] Once again, however, the species that benefit are generally common edge species. Power-line corridors introduce a similar set of species into forested landscapes[44]; the greatest variety of birds is found when the power-line corridor contains a high density of shrubs such as blackberries (figure 3.6).[45] A shrubby, structurally diverse power-line right-of-way in Rhode Island, free of herbicide treatments for seven years, supported a richer bird community than a nearby park-like residential area.[46] Although such edge-dominated corridors are not as valuable as wide greenways composed of mature vegetation, they clearly contain more biodiversity than many other land uses in urban and suburban landscapes.

Some Species Avoid Edges and Narrow Corridors

Forest-interior birds, which often avoid habitat edges, require wide, forested corridors. In a study of bird use of remnant hardwood strips in pine plantations in Virginia,[47] interior species usually occurred only in corridors at least 165 feet wide (50 m). Acadian flycatchers were seldom found in corridors less than 165 feet wide, hairy woodpeckers and pileated woodpeckers required minimum strip widths of 165–200 feet (50–61 m), and the northern parula was generally restricted to strips 265 feet (81 m) or wider. We can assume that wider strips would be needed if the adjacent habitats were all clear-cuts rather than pine plantations, because edge effects become greater with increasing contrast between adjacent habitats.[48]

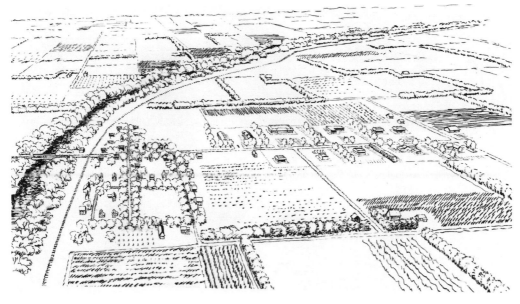

FIGURE 3.7

*In the eastern Great
Plains and midwestern
United States, many
of the highest-quality
remnants of native
tallgrass prairie occur
along old railroad lines.
These areas were never
plowed and sparks
from coal-fired steam
engines replicated the
frequent fires with
which prairies evolved.*
(Drawing by Jane Shoplick.)

Narrow Corridors Increase Predation

Human hunters and other predators may learn to concentrate their activity along animal move-ment routes. Thus, narrow corridors in particular may become mortality *sinks*.[49] For example, predators have been reported hunting in constructed wildlife crossings under roads.[50] Although further research is needed, the existing evidence suggests that highway crossings and other corri-dors designed for wildlife seldom function as *prey-traps*.[51] More generally, greenways and wildlife crossings in developed landscapes should be designed and managed to provide adequate cover for wide-ranging species and to discourage human uses that might result in harassment. In wilder land-scapes, intact roadless corridors should be maintained, and, where possible, roads should be closed to minimize conflicts between humans and wildlife by reducing human access.

Narrow Corridors May Conserve Important Plant Communities

In the eastern Great Plains and midwestern United States, many of the highest quality remnants of native tallgrass prairie occur along old railroad lines, because these areas were never plowed and because sparks from coal-fired steam engines replicated the frequent fires with which prairies evolved (figure 3.7). In these areas prairie restoration and management may be quite feasible for greenways established as part of a rails-to-trails program.[52] In such cases, prescribed burning, rein-troduction of extirpated prairie plants, and other restorative management should be applied.[53] Although, in narrow greenways of this sort, the animal component of these prairie communities can be expected to be very incomplete, plant populations may thrive with diligent stewardship.

How wide a corridor must be to achieve interior conditions depends on a number of complex variables. Fencerows through agricultural fields may sustain populations of some plants native to the presettlement forest. In most cases, however, the high light levels and dry conditions of these habitats favor shade-intolerant species characteristic of forest edges rather than forest-interior

FIGURE 3.8

*Line corridors, which
are entirely edge habitat,
and strip corridors,
which contain both
edge and interior habi-
tat, can be either forested
or open, depending on
the type of surrounding
matrix.* (After R. T. T.
Forman. [1983]. "Corridors in
a landscape: Their ecological
structure and function,"
Ekologia 2:375–387.)

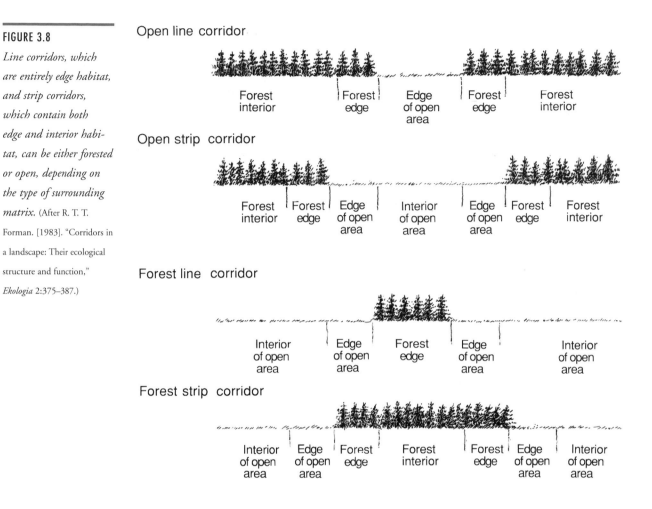

species. Hence, in southeastern Wisconsin, narrow forest corridors are dominated by shade-intolerant trees such as hawthorns, oaks, hickories, yellow birch, buckthorn, willows, quaking aspen, butternut, hop hornbeam, and black cherry. Corridor widths may have to exceed 330 feet (100 m) to sustain populations of beech and 100 feet (30 m) to sustain sugar maple.[54] Both of these tree species are shade-tolerant and depend on relatively moist conditions.

The difference in species composition between narrow and wide corridors led Forman and Godron[55] to distinguish between line corridors, composed entirely of edge habitat, and strip corridors that contain true interior habitat (figure 3.8). In fragmented landscapes, strip corridors are more valuable than line corridors in conserving most native species of concern.

Road Edges Benefit Wildlife, Although Roads Represent a Tremendous Threat

Although roads represent one of the greatest threats to biodiversity worldwide,[56] (see later in this chapter), often remnant vegetation along their verges can benefit some native wildlife. Viles and Rosier[57] suggested that the overall road network in New Zealand be used to maintain wildlife habitat and partially mitigate the adverse effects of the roads themselves.

FIGURE 3.9

Lessons from the ecology of hedgerows, roadsides, and other narrow corridors may apply to greenway design and management because greenways in urban and suburban landscapes are also often narrow and dominated by edge habitat.

(© Regents of the University of Minnesota. Used with permission of Metropolitan Design Center.)

The conservation value of Australian roadside remnants is particularly well documented.[58] In the wheatbelt region of Western Australia, remnants of native vegetation are confined mostly to small patches and narrow (16–165 feet [5–50 m]) strips along roadways.[59] A high proportion of the region's birds use these habitats. In southeastern Australia, eighteen species of mammals, representing 78 percent of the total mammalian fauna (excluding bats), inhabit roadside strips.[60] Although such linear roadside remnants may currently contain stable, high-density populations of particular species, such as the squirrel glider, the long-term viability of populations in these remnants is questionable because the remnants are narrow, easily fragmented, and subject to ongoing degradation.[61]

In Great Britain, road verges have been documented as breeding habitat for 20 of the country's 50 species of mammals, 40 of the 200 bird species, all 6 reptiles, 5 of the 6 amphibian species, and 25 of the 60 species of butterflies.[62] Roadside strips in Iowa also provide valuable habitat for butterflies. However, roadsides restored to native prairie contained twice the number of habitat-sensitive butterfly species and five times greater abundance of butterflies than grassy and weedy roadsides dominated by exotic plants.[63] More detailed demographic studies are needed, however, to determine whether roadsides may be acting as sink habitat (i.e., where mortality exceeds reproduction) for some species.

In southern California, remnant strips of vegetation and revegetated highway rights-of-way were used by fragmentation-tolerant bird species and a number of native rodents, but the highway rights-of-way were seldom used by fragmentation-sensitive species.[64] Whether or not these sites were sinks was not established.

Landscape Context Important in Appraising Conservation Value

The studies summarized above point to the value of linear habitats in heavily disturbed landscapes, but also indicate problems related to corridor narrowness and associated edge effects. Landscape context (including the composition of the regional species pool, the surrounding habitat matrix, the habitat quality of patches being connected, and the source-sink dynamics of sensitive species) is a vital consideration for appraising the conservation value of corridors as well as habitat patches.[65] Because greenways in urban and suburban landscapes are often narrow and dominated by edge habitat, useful lessons from the ecology of hedgerows, roadsides, and other narrow corridors will often apply to greenway design and management (figure 3.9).

Effectiveness of Urban Greenways Rarely Studied

Relatively few studies have directly evaluated the capability of urban greenways to sustain native species. However, a recent study in Sweden found seven red-listed—that is, assessed to be extirpated, endangered, or threatened—forest bird species breeding in urban "green space corridors."[66] The authors recommended that mature and decaying trees and patches of moist deciduous forest be retained in these corridors to benefit sensitive species, and that the corridors be linked into a network that includes large areas of natural vegetation.

Corridors in Daily and Seasonal Wildlife Movements

Another function of corridors is to allow animals to move safely across a landscape, either on a daily or seasonal basis, to find food, water, cover, or mates. A fox in a suburban landscape, for example, may use rows of shrubbery for nocturnal travels through its home range, whereas large mammals in a wilder setting use corridors in seasonal movements between summering and wintering areas.

Elk often make seasonal movements in response to forage conditions.[67] During migration, as well as on summer and winter ranges, hiding or escape cover can be important to elk.[68] Forested travel lanes adjacent to open meadows enable Rocky Mountain elk to make efficient use of the vegetation mosaic.[69] In the Blue Mountains in Oregon, forested corridors enable elk to cross from one canyon to another in continuous cover.[70] Maintaining safe travel opportunities for elk is largely a matter of protecting them from human predation, which is often related to road access. Many other large herbivores make regular seasonal migrations along established routes. Protecting travel corridors for such species should be a conservation priority. In southeastern Alaska, Schoen and Kirchoff[71] recommended that old-growth forest be retained in large swaths extending from sea level to the subalpine zone to allow Sitka black-tailed deer to make elevational movements in response to changing snow conditions. Wide swaths of continuous, unfragmented natural habitat are probably the optimal corridors for large mammals that are sensitive to human persecution or disturbance. Although developed regions no longer have this option, wildlands currently undergoing development or resource extraction should be managed to retain broad corridors.

Providing Connectivity Means Circumventing Barriers

Providing connectivity for wide-ranging mammals is largely a matter of circumventing barriers to movement, such as highways and developed areas, and minimizing human-caused mortality, such as from hunting, trapping, and vehicle collisions. Large predators have much to gain from preservation of secure movement corridors, because their large body size and food requirements demand that they travel widely.[72] For these species, corridors with limited access to humans are needed to provide safe movement between large blocks of habitat.[73] Year-round home ranges of puma (sometimes called mountain lions or cougars) vary from about 12,500 to 500,000 acres (5,059–202,343 ha), and it is not unusual for puma to travel 75–100 miles (121–161 km) in linear distance.[74] When moving between mountains and across plains and valleys, puma usually follow watercourses, seeking cover in the riparian vegetation.[75]

In southern California, even in highly developed landscapes, puma use riparian corridors and other strips of remnant vegetation to meet their requirements.[76] In this region, the puma is the carnivore species most sensitive to habitat fragmentation and the best indicator of functional, landscape-level connectivity. The bobcat is intermediate in its sensitivity, and therefore a good indicator in more fragmented landscapes, whereas coyotes and mesopredators (predators that are also the prey of other predators, e.g., opossums, domestic cats) are least sensitive.[77]

Bobcats are also known to follow natural riparian corridors. River otters may require several miles of linear riverine and riparian habitat (which, in some cases, may constitute their entire home range). Black bears in Florida use riparian corridors, in part, for their daily and seasonal movements.[78] These movements are extensive, as male bears typically have home ranges of 50–120 square miles (130–311 km²); female ranges generally are 10–25 square miles (26–65 km²).[79] Grizzly bears forage for widely dispersed food items and track seasonal changes along elevational gradients. Subadult males may disperse far out of the maternal range. Travel corridors most commonly used by grizzlies are ridgetops, saddles, and creek bottoms.[80]

Nearly All Species Need Various Habitat Types

In addition to large predators and animals that make regular seasonal migrations between different habitats, many nonmigratory species depend upon multiple habitat patches in the landscape. Species that are usually considered either upland or wetland wildlife commonly require different habitats from time to time to fulfill dietary requirements, escape flooding, breed, or hibernate. Examples of such species include the raccoon, white-tailed deer, river otter, swamp rabbit, bobcat, gray fox, and turkey.[81] Many turtles inhabit aquatic habitats but require sandy upland sites, sometimes several hundred yards from a river, to lay eggs. Conversely, in times of drought, a number of upland animals move downslope to riparian areas, a function of corridors that may be particularly critical in arid landscapes. Many vertebrates periodically depend on water sources that, at least seasonally, are some distance from their territory or nest site. In fragmented landscapes, the various habitats needed by animals on a daily or seasonal basis are often disjunct. Corridors can be retained or restored to connect these patches.

Habitat for many species is dispersed across numerous patches over the landscape. For instance, the pileated woodpecker in eastern North America is no longer restricted to large tracts of mature forest but has developed the behavior of incorporating several woodlots into its home range. Wooded fencerows may be important linkages followed by these woodpeckers in their movements.[82] Large predators and large fruit eaters often range widely to meet dietary requirements. In Western Australia, Carnaby's cockatoo requires woodlands for nesting cavities and heathland or

FIGURE 3.10

*There are three ways
in which corridors may
facilitate dispersal of
individual animals and
genes between habitat
patches: (a) direct, long-
distance movement by a
single individual; (b)
periodic movement by a
single animal, punctuat-
ed by pauses; and (c)
gene flow through a
reproducing population
resident in the corridor.*

(From A. F. Bennett. [1990].
*Habitat Corridors: Their Role
in Wildlife Management and
Conservation.* Melbourne,
Australia: Arthur Rylah
Institute for Environmental
Research, Department of
Conservation and
Environment.)

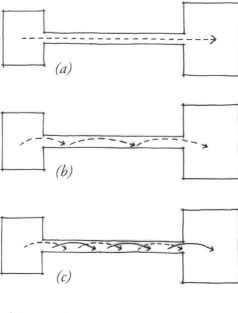

mallee for seed foraging.[83] Broad strips of roadside vegetation help cockatoos move between vegetation patches in the landscape.[84] When corridors are incomplete or of poor quality, nestling growth rates and fledging success of these birds are reduced.

Corridors and Other Landscape Elements in Dispersal

Dispersal—the movement of organisms away from their place of origin[85]—is one of the most critical of all biological processes.[86] A corridor can promote dispersal if individual animals or plant seeds travel from one population to another by means of the corridor, or if resident populations in the corridor allow the gradual flow of genes from one end to another[87] (figure 3.10).

Natural selection exerts strong pressure on an animal or plant to disperse. Staying too near a parent can result in competition between parents and offspring, and exploring new territory is often advantageous in an ever-changing environment. Because dispersal of young birds and mammals is usually sex-biased (one sex disperses farther than the other), dispersal reduces the chances of mating between close relatives and allows genes to travel from one population to another. At regional and continental scales, dispersal helps explain how species are distributed geographically. By understanding previous dispersal patterns it may be possible to predict future distributions that respond to global trends, such as climate change.

Dispersal is an endangered process in fragmented landscapes. In such landscapes, the scattered patches of natural habitat separated by unsuitable habitat are not by themselves sufficient to maintain populations of many dispersal-limited species in the long run. A small woodlot may be mostly edge habitat and thus support only very small numbers of a forest-interior bird, such as many warblers.[88] For interior species restricted to remnant patches, movement of individuals among patches must be great enough to balance extirpation from local patches, or the regional population will eventually become extinct.[89] Problems of population persistence in fragmented landscapes and the role of corridors in promoting persistence are discussed later in this chapter.

Many Methods of Plant Dispersal

Plants may be dispersed by wind, water, or animals. All of these mechanisms are passive, but the last of these obviously depends on active animals. Fruits of many plants, including tick trefoil, beggar's-ticks, and ragweed, become attached to the fur of mammals, whereas fleshy fruits, such as those of cherries, blackberries, and junipers, are designed to be eaten and passed through the gut

of animals. Nutty fruits of trees, such as oaks, hickories, and beech, are gathered by squirrels, jays,
and other seed predators, but many of the cached
nuts are never eaten and later germinate. Hence, as
animals move across a landscape, the plants they
carry also move.

Animal-Dispersed Plants Benefit from Corridors

Animal-dispersed plants benefit from corridors to
the extent that their animal dispersers do. Grizzlies
and black bears are among the mammals that
disperse the seeds of fleshy fruits and that often use corridors such as riparian forests in their movements.[90] Birds are also important dispersal agents. Even in highly fragmented landscapes, beechnuts dispersed 1–2 miles (1.6–3.2 km) by blue jays should be able to reach most forest patches,
with blue jays often following wooded fencerows in making these movements.[91] The long distances
over which blue jays disperse beechnuts and acorns may explain the finding of Davis that heavy-
seeded oaks and beech sometimes dispersed northward after the Pleistocene faster than trees such
as spruce, which have light, windblown seeds (figure 3.11).[92]

Movement of terrestrial animals and their plant associates may be maintained or enhanced by
well planned greenways or other corridors. A compelling experimental demonstration of the value
of corridors in promoting multiple species was provided by Tewksbury et al.[93] In this study seeds of
two large fruiting shrubs were dispersed by birds much more effectively when habitat patches were
connected by corridors than when they were not. Moreover, movement of butterflies preferentially
through corridors resulted in dramatic increases in movement of pollen. As a result, a significantly
higher proportion of flowers produced fruit in connected patches than in unconnected patches.[94]

Not all species depend on corridors for dispersal, of course. Wind-dispersed plants, ballooning spiders, and some open-country birds are examples of species that don't. The cabbage butterfly disperses
long distances in apparently random directions and does not detect suitable habitat patches from afar.[95]
However, corridors do increase movement rates among patches for many other species of butterflies.[96]

Landscape Matrix May Provide Connectivity

Functional connectivity need not depend on distinct linear corridors. At the regional scale at which
the conservation of many species is now being discussed, that portion of the landscape matrix that
lies between two or more large habitat patches may provide functional connectivity by allowing
movement of organisms between patches (figure 3.12). As noted earlier, conserving large carnivores
requires considering vast regions in which core areas may be separated by areas that have variable
permeability to movement.[97] As Wiens[98] points out, the probability that dispersal can occur
between fragments and forestall extinction of sensitive species on a regional scale is influenced by
the configuration of the fragments and the landscape mosaic in which they are embedded.

An experiment involving three species of amphibians showed that although small-mouthed

FIGURE 3.11

*Plants with seeds
dispersed by animals
benefit from corridors
to the extent that their
animal dispersers do.
For example, blue jays
can disperse beechnuts
and acorns over long
distances, which may
explain why heavy-seed-
ed oaks (left) and beech
sometimes dispersed
northward after the
Pleistocene faster than
trees with light, wind-
blown seeds, such as
spruce (right).*

(Drawing by Joe McGrane.)

FIGURE 3.12

Functional connectivity need not depend on distinct linear corridors. At the regional scale at which the conservation of many species is now being discussed, the portion of the landscape matrix that lies between two or more large habitat patches may provide functional connectivity. Embedded in this suburban land-scape are patches of vegetation that may func-tion in just such a way for some species.

(© Regents of the University of Minnesota. Used with permission of Metropolitan Design Center.)

salamanders apparently moved randomly away from ponds, juvenile American toads and spotted salamanders avoided open-canopy habitat and moved several times farther into forests than into fields.[99] Forest fragmentation by agriculture could thus affect the long-term viability of these species. Fragmentation experiments in Amazonia have confirmed the important influence of the landscape matrix on the connectivity and functioning of forest fragments.[100]

Discouraging the Dispersal of Some Species

The goal of a landscape connectivity strategy should not be to encourage dispersal of all species. Indeed, there are a number of organisms (such as introduced weeds and diseases) whose dispersal must be actively thwarted to maintain native species composition in any given region. Whereas habi-tat modification by humans has imposed new barriers and has restricted movement of many species, it has facilitated movement of other species far beyond their native ranges. Introduced species are among the greatest threats to biotic integrity, both within nature reserves and across the landscape as a whole.[101] Widespread mixing of faunas and floras results in biotic homogenization, through which regions lose their distinctive character and many endemic species are outcompeted to extinction.

Roads Support Biological Invasions

One common type of corridor in human-dominated landscapes—roads and roadsides—has fos-tered many biological invasions.[102] Many nonnative plants, insect pests, and fungal diseases of trees are known to disperse and invade natural habitats via roads and vehicles.[103] Disturbed roadsides with high light levels harbor many weeds, which disperse along the route of the road and often invade adjacent forests and other habitats. Vehicles using the road transport seeds and spores long distances, sometimes hundreds of miles. Other edge-dominated corridors, including fencerows and hedgerows, may also favor the spread of opportunistic species (both those native to North America, such as the brown-headed cowbird, and exotics, such as the European starling) at the expense of sensitive species.[104] Any corridor in the landscape should be evaluated for which species are most likely to benefit and which may be harmed.

The Role of Dispersal Corridors in Population Persistence

The preceding section discussed dispersal in heterogeneous landscapes and the role of corridors in supporting dispersal. This section discusses how dispersal and interchange of individuals among populations may reduce the risk of extinction, both through demographic (population process-related) and genetic effects.

Corridors Influence Demographics

A *population* is a group of individuals of the same species living within a geographic area restricted enough so that any member of the population can potentially mate with any other member of the opposite sex. At least some species are distributed as *metapopulations*, that is, as systems of local populations linked by occasional dispersal.[105] It is the fate of local populations in these systems to go extinct periodically, or to "wink" off and on over time (figure 2.26). Local extinctions may be caused by apparently random (stochastic) demographic effects, such as chance variation in sex ratios or birth and death rates in very small populations. More commonly, small local populations are eliminated by disturbances (including those caused by humans), extreme weather, or other environmental factors.

With dispersal of individuals across the landscape, and subsequent colonization of vacated or other suitable habitats, the metapopulation as a whole can persist despite local extinctions (figure 2.26). If this dispersal is interrupted, as may happen when habitats are fragmented by development, the probability of persistence diminishes. A small, isolated habitat patch is expected to have a smaller population of a given species of interest and less opportunity to be rescued demographically or genetically by individuals moving in from surrounding populations.[106] An unoccupied but isolated patch of suitable habitat also is less likely to be colonized or recolonized by a species.

If enough connections between suitable habitat patches are severed, the metapopulation as a whole is destabilized and less likely to persist. Extinctions of local populations under these circumstances signal bit-by-bit extinction of the metapopulation or the species as a whole.[107] Thus the survival of metapopulations depends, in large part, on both the rate of local extinctions in habitat patches and the rate at which organisms move among patches, which in turn is affected by connectivity between patches.[108] In some cases, however, patch area and isolation are not the main factors that control metapopulation dynamics. For example, Fleishman et al. found that measures of the quality of habitat were better predictors of which patches were occupied by the Nokomis fritillary butterfly and how often those populations turned over.[109] This finding is especially relevant in systems that are highly variable, either naturally or because of human disturbance.

Corridors May Help Prevent Local Extinctions

Corridors can lower the chances of extinction for small, local populations by augmenting population size and by increasing population growth rates.[110] White-footed mouse populations in Ontario woodlots suffer high rates of overwinter extinction. Dispersal and resulting higher population growth rates in woodlots connected by fencerows ensure that populations begin the winter with more individuals and have a better chance of lasting until spring.[111]

By helping recolonize vacated patches, corridors may also increase the likelihood that local extinctions can be reversed. This, in turn, increases the chances that the entire metapopulation will survive. Decades ago, Baumgartner[112] noted that fencerows in Ohio served as travel lanes for fox squirrels, allowing them to recolonize woodlots that had been "shot out" by hunters. Similarly, in Ontario landscapes where woodlots are well connected by fencerows, local chipmunk extinctions are rapidly reversed as individuals recolonize from other patches.[113] In such landscapes, population dynamics in individual woodlots are of only local importance. One must look to the entire landscape mosaic to plan workable conservation strategies.

A recent study of the blue-breasted fairy wren in western Australia provides one of the best demonstrations of the value of corridors in helping populations persist in fragmented landscapes. The study determined that whether a population persisted largely depended on the mortality rate of dispersing yearling birds. Dispersal mortality can be as high as 18 percent in an area of poorly connected habitat remnants and as low as 4 percent in well connected remnants.[114] The authors concluded that "failure to maintain an adequate corridor network may . . . be one of the most important factors contributing to the species' decline in fragmented habitats."

Corridors May Help Some Bird Populations Persist

It might seem that the power of flight would free birds from any need for corridors, but in fact, many birds have relatively poor dispersal abilities. For instance, the agricultural landscape surrounding woodlots in the Netherlands has a significant isolating effect on birds, to the point that immigration may not keep up with extinction.[115] The number of species of forest-interior birds inhabiting a woodlot is positively associated with the density of corridors connecting to that woodlot. A similar situation exists in Australia.[116] In southern California, chaparral-dependent birds in habitat patches surrounded by development suffer high rates of extinction due to the birds' reluctance to cross even narrow strips of unsuitable habitat. For some species, movement corridors, even as narrow as 3–33 feet (1–10 m), appear to offer the best prospects for maintaining populations of these species.[117]

Genetics Important to Persistence

Especially when one considers the fate of populations over longer time spans, genetics may be as important to persistence as is demographics. In fact, in some cases genetic deterioration can occur quite rapidly after isolation.[118] Small, isolated populations are prone to two kinds of detrimental genetic effects: inbreeding depression and random genetic drift.

Without Dispersal, Inbreeding May Occur

Inbreeding depression is a result of mating between close relatives in species where a certain proportion of individuals normally breed with individuals from other populations. It occurs in isolated populations when individuals are unable to disperse and find mates in other populations. By reducing genetic diversity and allowing harmful recessive genes to be expressed, inbreeding can raise mortality rates (especially among juveniles) and reduce health, vigor, and fertility. Although once discounted as a largely theoretical concern in wild populations, data from recent studies confirm that inbred populations often experience reduced growth and increased rates of extinction.[119]

Immigrating Individuals Aid Genetic Diversity

Random genetic drift is a change in gene frequencies in a population due to chance. In large populations, the effects of drift are insignificant. But in small populations, genetic drift leads to the loss of genetic diversity. Not only do genetically impoverished populations often show reduced viability and fertility (the effects of drift and inbreeding may be difficult to disentangle), but in the long run they will be less able to adapt to changing environmental conditions. The process of evolution itself is threatened by genetic impoverishment.[120]

Until recently there was little empirical evidence that immigrants contribute much to genetic variation in small populations. Indirect evidence and mathematical models, however, suggest that some level of immigration and gene flow will help populations maintain genetic diversity and will reduce the expression of harmful recessive genes through inbreeding. Allendorf predicted that an average exchange of one reproductively successful migrant between populations per generation is sufficient to avoid the loss of gene types through drift.[121] He also suggested this exchange would still allow populations to diverge as a result of adaptation to local environments through natural selection. This suggestion has been reasonably well supported by recent studies. Population models suggest that the decrease in population viability becomes much higher when the number of migrants is less than one per generation.[122]

Even a single immigrant can sometimes contribute substantially to the genetic diversity of a population and reduce its risk of extinction.[123] If a population is inbred, mating with immigrants can lead to "hybrid vigor," which in turn can increase gene flow through increasing migration rate, as recently demonstrated experimentally for water fleas.[124] To the extent that corridors facilitate an exchange of individuals among populations, they will help maintain genetically viable populations. Bennett[125] has suggested that gene flow between populations will be enhanced if there are resident individuals of the target species within the corridor. Thus, the roles of corridors as habitat and as conduit may be complementary.

Undesirable Genetic Variation

Some have expressed concern about the desirability of corridor-facilitated genetic exchange and the effect it might have on genetically distinct populations and local adaptation.[126] There are essentially two forms of genetic variation within species, namely, the variety of genetic material among individuals within a population and variation among different populations. Gene flow between two populations, which occurs when individuals disperse from one population to another, will favor the retention of genetic variation within each population, but it will also make the two populations more similar genetically, reducing the between-population component of genetic variation. If enough genetic material is exchanged, the two populations may eventually become one and the same population. Some biologists maintain that the loss of genetically distinct populations within species is a problem that is at least as important as the loss of entire species.[127]

Local populations, particularly those near the periphery of their species's range, may have adapted through natural selection to local environmental conditions, or they may differ genetically only as a result of random factors, such as genetic drift or mutation. A genetically distinct population may be in the early phases of forming a new species. Increased gene flow could disrupt this process by increasing genetic similarity between populations. Outbreeding depression—the tendency to have reduced fitness in offspring that are the product of two very different genetic backgrounds—becomes more of a concern with increasing genetic distance between populations.[128]

Seek to Maintain or Restore Naturally Occurring Connectivity

The prudent course in the face of uncertainty about genetic and ecological effects of connecting populations is to maintain or restore natural kinds and levels of landscape connectivity but to avoid creating connections where none existed before. For instance, maintaining a continuous network of forest would be a sensible strategy for a region that was originally forested, whereas maintaining a continuous network of weed-dominated roadsides (which, for example, might connect patches of grassland that were originally isolated) would not contribute to conservation goals in that same region.

The Role of Corridors in Facilitating Long-Distance Range Shifts

A glaring deficiency in the conservation movement to date has been our failure to recognize and to accommodate change in nature. Conservation strategists have implicitly assumed that natural communities are unchanging, stable entities.[129] Hence, we are not prepared for change. We seek to freeze in time snapshots of scenic splendor for future generations, to "preserve" forests that naturally burn or blow down, and to maintain collections of species that have been apart for longer periods of their evolutionary histories than they have been together. Preservation is a noble idea, but we have been too concerned with static pattern and not enough with dynamic process.

Community Composition Changes Continuously over Space and Time

Current plant communities over much of North America have developed only within the last 4,000–8,000 years.[130] Before this time, many of the species now found together were separated geographically; many of the communities we see today did not exist anywhere. In some regions, modern vegetation and flora have become established only over the past few centuries, for example, about 430 years ago in southwestern Wisconsin[131] and 300 years ago in southcentral Minnesota.[132] Since the Pleistocene (Ice Age) ended 10,000 years ago, the ranges of many plant species have shifted by more than 620 miles (1,000 km). Because species migrated northward at different rates and by different routes, community composition has changed continuously over space and time.[133] The response of animal species to climate change has also been individualistic; Ice Age species associations were far different from those observed today.[134]

Climate Change May Outstrip Species' Abilities to Respond

Migration, often over amazingly long distances, is the primary way that species responded to past climate changes.[135] Hence, our present system of mostly isolated nature reserves may be incapable of maintaining biodiversity during the current period of global warming.[136] Reserves that were set aside to protect a certain set of species will no longer be suitable for those species under a new climatic regime. Even natural rates of change pose significant challenges to species confined to reserves surrounded by inhospitable habitat. The increased rates of change projected to occur with greenhouse warming may eliminate all but the most mobile species. Less mobile species may fail to track shifting climatic conditions.

In addition to the natural barriers to migration at regional and continental scales, such as mountain ranges, desert basins, lakes, and rivers, human activities have superimposed an entirely new set of barriers in the form of cities, highways, fields, and clear-cuts. The impacts of these barriers will be cumulative, as successful long-distance dispersal becomes less likely with each additional barrier.

Broad-Scale Biogeographic Corridors Important during Past Climate Change

Can wildlife corridors function at regional and continental scales and allow species to adjust their distributions to new climates? We know that broad-scale biogeographic corridors have been important during past climate changes. During the Pleistocene, several major dispersal corridors existed along North American rivers, in particular the Mississippi valley.[137] The northeast-to-southwest–trending Appalachian Mountains did not present a major obstacle to species moving south in advance of the glaciers and cooler climates. In Europe, however, dispersal was blocked by the east-to-west–trending ranges of the Alps and Pyrenees. As a consequence of the enormous difference in migration opportunities, eastern North America is much richer today than Europe in plant species, despite the fact that the two subcontinents had similar levels of diversity before the Pleistocene. The Smoky Mountains alone contain as many species of trees as all of Europe.[138]

Continental-Scale Greenways May Inadequately Address Rapidly Changing Climate

Unfortunately, historical evidence of corridor functions during past climate changes cannot assure us that corridors will provide for species migration during global warming. The rate of warming during the next half century is projected to be at least ten times greater than average rates over the last 100,000 years. According to global circulation models, suitable habitat for beech could shift northward by 435–560 miles (700–900 km) during the next century. Yet historical rates of beech migration averaged only 12 miles (19 km) a century (but were sometimes faster, probably due to dispersal by jays). The highest migration rate known for any tree is for spruce, at 124 miles (200 km) a century, although rare long-distance dispersal events may be substantially greater. Migration rates for many types of animals, such as forest invertebrates with limited dispersal abilities, are expected to be slow. Whereas other animal species may be theoretically capable of migrating quickly enough to adapt to global warming, their dependence on particular plants may prevent them from doing so. The inescapable conclusion is that if estimated rates of global warming for the next century are accurate, north-to-south–oriented corridors will be of little utility for most species. The only species able to keep pace with rapid warming may be weedy plants and animals that do not require corridors of natural habitat to disperse—the same species that conservationists do not need to worry about protecting.[139]

Although Untested, Corridors Are a Conservation Strategy

If the global warming models are overly pessimistic and the rate of warming in coming decades is similar to past climate changes, broad corridors may be effective in maintaining biodiversity. Even if the warming is faster than most past changes, corridors may work in mountainous regions, where necessary dispersal distances are much shorter. A rise in temperature of 3° C translates to a latitudinal range shift of roughly 155 miles (249 km) but to an elevational range shift of only 1,640 feet (500 m). During the warm period of the mid-Holocene, about 4,000 years ago, eastern hemlock and white pine were found 1,150 feet (351 m) higher on mountains than they are today. Future responses to climate change could be facilitated by retaining upslope corridors, as well as well connected, heterogeneous landscapes with abundant microhabitats.[140]

Uncertainty is the dominant theme in all climatic projections. The only certainty is that climates will change, in some direction and at some rate. Maintaining habitat connectivity to allow species migration is a prudent strategy under any climate change scenario. A general rule is that wide, continuous corridors parallel to existing climatic gradients (elevational and latitudinal) will best promote migration of species with climate change. Although the utility of corridors in conserving species in a rapidly changing climate is not proven, "their incorporation into a strategy for dealing with the effects of climate change adds an option to what is otherwise a rather sparse repertoire."[141]

Key Greenway Design Issues

It is not a simple task to design greenways that will contribute to wildlife conservation while providing recreational, aesthetic, and other benefits to humans. Two broad questions are useful in framing a discussion of wildlife corridor design. First, what is the relative value of sensitive native species versus exotic or opportunistic species? Second, should corridors focus on one or several target species or on entire communities? We cannot assume that a particular greenway will be unequivocally good for native biodiversity. Habitats represented in the greenway will meet the living and dispersal requirements of some species but not of others. In some cases, species that benefit from the greenway may be opportunistic or weedy species that prosper at the expense of more sensitive species. Corridor quality must be assessed relative to the needs of the latter. Vegetation in corridors may need to be managed to reduce the degree of interaction between the corridor and surrounding disturbed habitats, such as roadsides and farmland.[142]

Diamond remarked that "conservation should not treat all species as equal but must focus on species and habitats threatened by human activities."[143] Although certainly appropriate on a global or regional scale, this rule must be considered in context. Where it is feasible to maintain or restore large blocks of roadless, natural habitat connected by broad corridors and thus maintain large carnivores and sensitive forest-interior species, this strategy should be pursued. But in many agricultural and urban landscapes, disturbed habitats (for example, hedgerows or roadsides) and weedy species may be the only remnants of nature. Such remnants are preferable to a landscape where nothing natural remains and should be managed with the goal of maintaining or restoring natural qualities and native species richness.[144]

Whether focused on particular species or entire communities, greenways and other corridors potentially provide a broad range of habitat structures and will have quite different effects on the many species that use them. Even when a corridor is designed with a particular species in mind, planners must consider potential effects on other species and ecological functions, or unanticipated negative impacts are likely. In designing greenways, planners should seek to provide a safe corridor for the native species actually or potentially present, especially those that are most sensitive to human activities.

Habitat Quality Is Fundamentally Important

Habitat quality within corridors is a fundamental consideration in any landscape and for any species. A poor-quality corridor can indeed be worse than no corridor at all if it lures animals into conditions that threaten their survival. A computer model by Henein and Merriam showed that corridors can be a drain on metapopulations of white-footed mice if they are sites of high mortality.[145] In contrast, high-quality corridors in simulation allowed metapopulations to grow and stabilize at larger sizes than at which they began. Corridors with dense, structurally complex vegetation are preferred by white-footed mice, apparently because dense cover reduces the risk that mice will be captured by predators. Although there is no empirical documentation of corridors designed for conservation purposes having net negative effects on wildlife, such effects become more likely as corridors become narrower and more surrounded by intensive human land-uses.

Corridor Width Is Crucial

A central consideration in greenway design is width. The corridor width issue has been troublesome because empirical studies are almost entirely lacking. When asked by planners how wide a corridor should be, conservation biologists may have little recourse but to reply "the wider, the better." Soulé and Gilpin, however, warned against wide corridors.[146] They argued that a wide corridor will permit relatively unconstrained movement of organisms from side to side, slowing the rate of movement toward their goal. This suggestion was based on a model assuming "stupid dispersers" with little sense of direction and probably underestimates the knowledge that many vertebrates have about the landscape in which they live. A migrating elk or dispersing bear is unlikely to waste time wandering from side to side when driven by changing seasons or flowing sex hormones. It knows instinctively where to go. Wide corridors offer protection to these species, not diversion.

Benefits of Wider Corridors

Wider corridors can be beneficial in three main ways—by (1) reducing edge effects on a corridor and increasing interior conditions within the corridor; (2) incorporating a larger area and, therefore, a greater diversity and abundance of habitats and species; and (3) increasing the probability that the corridor will be used by area-demanding species, which are often the species most sensitive to habitat fragmentation.[147]

Penetration of Edge Effects Is Crucial

The penetration of edge effects may be the overriding consideration in many corridor designs. Narrow corridors, such as fencerows and many greenways, are entirely edge habitat and can be expected to produce high rates of mortality for sensitive species. Opportunistic, medium-sized predators (mesopredators) such as jays, crows, opossums, raccoons, foxes, skunks, and domestic dogs and cats may abound in such corridors and reduce populations of low-nesting birds.[148]

Many weedy species increase in edge habitat at the expense of sensitive species. Robbins warned that corridors connecting a number of small woodlots to a larger forest might entice forest birds into the edge-dominated woodlots, where they could fail reproductively because of increased nest predation, parasitism, or competition with edge species. Conversely, narrow corridors might act as funnels, drawing opportunistic edge birds such as the common grackle (a nest predator) and brown-headed cowbird (a brood parasite) into a forest. These suggestions raise many questions as yet unanswered by scientific research and argue, in the meantime, for careful consideration of corridor options in particular cases.[149]

Edge effects can extend anywhere from several yards to several hundred yards, depending on the type of forest and the variables measured (figure 2.17). Of particular importance is the difference between physical, microclimatic effects (increased light, wind, and dryness) and resulting changes in vegetation, and farther-reaching penetration of opportunistic edge species of birds and mammals. Edge vegetation, growing with increased light and dryness, typically occupies a fairly narrow band. In Wisconsin hardwood forests, Ranney et al. found that significant differences in the composition and structure of vegetation extended between 33 and 100 feet (10–30 m) from the forest edge.[150] Increased frequency of blowdown typically extends two to three tree heights into a forest. Therefore, in old-growth Douglas fir forests in Oregon, where canopy trees are commonly 265 feet (81 m) tall, corridors would need to be at least one-third of a mile (0.5 km) wide to maintain a modest 656-foot–wide (200 m) interior strip. In eastern North American forests, most trees are less than half this tall, so corridors on the order of 1,150 feet (351 m) wide may suffice to minimize blowdown problems.[151]

Research in eastern deciduous forests, however, has shown that predation of nests may be significantly increased up to 2,000 feet (607 m) from a forest edge over interior areas of the forest.[152] Because nest predation and parasitism are among the most serious threats to forest-interior bird species, a forested greenway in this environment would need to be 0.9 miles (1.5 km) wide to maintain a 656-foot–wide (200 m) strip of safe interior habitat. There appears to be no practical way to fight most of the problems associated with edge effects in narrow corridors, beyond the obvious strategy of widening corridors. In some cases, planting a dense buffer (such as conifers) along the edges of a corridor may ameliorate microclimatic effects and thereby discourage colonization by some edge species.[153] In lieu of a more dependable solution, site-specific analysis and interpretation within the context of local, regional, and broader conservation goals are needed to determine whether the anticipated benefits of narrow or otherwise poor-quality corridors outweigh the potential costs. It is absolutely critical that greenway planners consult with professional ecologists about these matters.

Narrow Corridors May Not Suffice for Larger Animals

Although larger animals may not suffer directly from physical or biological edge effects (indeed, large predators may benefit from more abundant prey), those that are shy and sensitive to human influence may require wide corridors for adequate cover and seclusion. Exactly how wide depends on the habitat structure and quality within the corridor, the nature of the surrounding habitat, the patterns of human use, the length of the corridor, and the particular species expected to use the corridor.[154]

Corridors may have to be several miles wide to protect large mammals from human predation or harassment where the landscape matrix is developed and has many roads and corridor edges are readily accessible to humans.[155] If trails or other recreational facilities occur within a corridor, as they generally do within greenways, the corridor should be wide enough so that the most sensitive animals using the corridor are not disturbed by human activity.

Miles-Wide Greenways Needed?

When long corridors are used to link natural areas at a regional scale, they should ideally be wide enough to encompass resident populations of target species. Gene flow can then occur sequentially through reproducing resident populations instead of relying on individuals making the full journey from one end of the corridor to the other (figure 3.10). Harris and Scheck suggested that "when the movement of entire assemblages of species is being considered, and/or when little is known about the biology of the species involved, and/or if the faunal dispersal corridor is expected to function over decades, then the appropriate width must be measured in kilometers."[156]

An example of a corridor potentially wide enough to fulfill these functions is the Pinhook Swamp

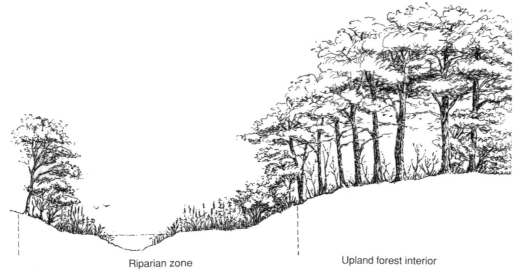

Riparian zone   Upland forest interior

FIGURE 3.13

Riparian corridors should ideally extend upslope to include an area of upland interior habitat.

FIGURE 3.14

Options for corridor and network structure. The most basic concerns are avoiding breaks (a) and establishing a continuous linkage (b). Redundancy (c) provides alternative movement corridors, whereas nodes (d) provide dwelling habitat at intervals along a corridor. Redundant links and nodes can be combined to form a habitat network (e), whereas broad strip corridors (f) are the most effective at protecting habitat and movement routes.

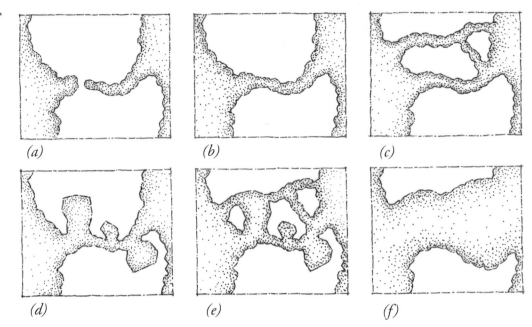

(a)   (b)   (c)

(d)   (e)   (f)

corridor, parts of which have been purchased by the U.S. Forest Service to link Osceola National Forest in northern Florida with Okefenokee National Wildlife Refuge in southern Georgia. The purchase was made to provide habitat for Florida panthers (which, however, have yet to be introduced because of the objections of local politicians and special interest groups). The Pinhook Swamp corridor is more than 22,000 acres (8,903 ha),[157] about 3–6 miles (4.8–10 km) wide, and about twice as long.

One way to ensure that corridors are wide enough is to center them on rivers and extend their protection up one or both slopes so that the entire slope with its vegetation is included. A narrow riparian corridor may not be useful to many upland species and may eventually flood to the point of forcing terrestrial wildlife into unsuitable adjacent upland areas. Forman[158] recommended that "the stream corridor should cover the floodplain, both banks, and an area of upland, at least on one side, which is wider than an edge effect" (figure 3.13).

Corridor Networks May Be Needed for Diversity

When development has precluded opportunities for wide and internally diverse corridors, and near-term restoration is unlikely, a network of multiple corridors may be the best means of collectively encompassing an area's range of habitat types (figure 3.14). Networks also provide redundancy, or multiple movement pathways, and thereby reduce the impact of the destruction of any single corridor by catastrophic disturbance.[159]

In recommending that a diversity of habitats be represented in corridors, I refer to vegetation types native to the landscape, which are, of course, dynamic and constantly changing. Planting vegetation foreign to the landscape, such as exotic fruiting trees introduced by wildlife managers or horticulturists, is generally not recommended because of its potential to spread and displace native vegetation. Planting foreign vegetation may be justified, however, in emergency efforts for an

FIGURE 3.15

Planners should expand their view of what constitutes connectivity for species beyond the basic notion of distinct linear corridors. Connectivity for many species may be provided, for example, by a system of "stepping-stone" habitats, such as shown here. (© Regents of the University of Minnesota. Used with permission of Metropolitan Design Center.)

endangered species. As Knopf[160] showed, bird species native to the Great Plains have not benefited from riparian vegetation that has grown along streams as a result of the interruption of the natural flood-drought cycle. Instead this new vegetation has allowed birds from eastern forests to invade.

"Stepping-Stones" of Habitat May Support Movement

Planners would do well to expand their view of what constitutes connectivity for species beyond the basic notion of distinct linear corridors. Connectivity for many species may be provided, for example, by a system of "stepping-stone" habitats (figure 3.15). Stepping stones are most likely to be useful in cases where animals (1) can detect a stepping-stone from a core area or other source; (2) are not constrained or directed by habitat boundaries; (3) are unwilling to enter corridors that are dominated by edge habitat; or (4) experience high levels of predation within corridors.[161]

A recent study of red squirrels in northern England and Scotland showed that squirrels can move considerable distances through a fragmented landscape by traveling through a series of stepping-stone forest patches.[162] Recent enlargement of these stepping-stones through conifer plantings has defragmented the landscape (from the perspective of the squirrels) and allowed substantial genetic mixing across a distance of approximately 62 miles (100 km). Because originally the squirrels at either end of this restored linkage zone were genetically well mixed through interbreeding, this new mixing is returning the squirrel population to its original genetic structure. The literature documenting stepping-stone dispersal in various species suggests that distinct, continuous corridors are not always necessary to provide for wildlife movement. Yet, from a broader spatial perspective, the linkage provided by stepping-stones in close proximity serves as a kind of corridor.

FIGURE 3.16

Greenways that cross roads can be designed to maintain connectivity and to reduce road kills by incorporating tunnels, underpasses, land bridges, or other crossing structures for animal movement. (a) This road underpass was built near Salzwedel, Germany, to provide safe passage to otters traveling along the Iron Curtain Green Band (greenway). (Photo by P. Hellmund.) *(b) In the Netherlands a number of wildlife overpasses or ecoducts have been built across major highways.* (Photo by Edgar van der Grift.)

Roads May Be the Greatest Threat to Wildlife Movement

Roads slice through many areas of otherwise contiguous habitat and may be the single most destructive element of human land use among many. Trombulak and Frissell listed seven general effects of roads that are documented in the literature: (1) mortality from road construction, (2) mortality from collision with vehicles, (3) modification of animal behavior, (4) alteration of the physical environment, (5) alteration of the chemical environment, (6) spread of exotics, and (7) increased use of areas by humans.[163]

Animal behavior may be modified when roads create barriers to animal movement, which is a direct form of fragmentation.[164] Some animals simply do not cross roads, or do so only rarely. Therefore, a greenway that intersects roads, without proper wildlife crossings, may not function for certain wildlife.

When individual animals hesitate to cross roads, roads may be fragmenting populations into smaller demographic units that are more vulnerable to extinction (figure 2.27). Many studies have shown that roads—especially wide, paved roads, but also sometimes narrow, unpaved tracks—are barriers to movement of rodents. In Germany, several species of carabid beetles and two species of forest rodents rarely or never crossed two-lane roads. Even a narrow, unpaved forest road, closed to public traffic, was a barrier.[165]

Roads in a forested landscape in Maine had little effect on the use of habitat and movements of frogs and toads. Salamanders, however, were much less abundant near roads and seldom crossed roads. Many other studies have documented the barrier effects of roads, even for animals as large as black bears and as seemingly mobile as birds. When animals do attempt to cross roads, they often die. Roads are among the largest sources of mortality for many vertebrates and have been implicated in widespread amphibian declines as traffic volume has increased in many regions. The current road network in the northeastern, southeastern, and central regions of the United States may be limiting populations of land turtles and, to a lesser extent, large-bodied pond turtles.[166]

Road Crossings Need Special Attention

Roads should be a major concern to greenway planners; roads intersect many greenways, sometimes at frequent intervals. A greenway interrupted by roads will fail to promote movement of some species and therefore is seriously compromised in its conservation functions. Nevertheless, greenways that cross roads can be designed to maintain connectivity and to reduce road kills by incorporating tunnels, underpasses, land bridges, or other crossing structures for animal movement (figure 3.16).

In Colorado and other western states, migrating mule deer are often killed trying to cross highways. Collisions between deer and vehicles also injure motorists. In 1970, the Colorado Division of Highways constructed a 10- by 10-foot (3-m by 3-m) concrete tunnel under Interstate 70 west of Vail for use by mule deer. They constructed fences to keep deer away from the road and to funnel them down to the underpass. A study by the Colorado Division of Wildlife confirmed that hundreds of migrating mule deer used the tunnel, but also suggested that larger and more open underpasses would be more appealing and result in greater rates of deer movement.[167]

Since the Colorado experiment, wildlife underpasses have been used successfully in many cases worldwide. In Australia, a funnel-shaped rocky corridor and two tunnels beneath a road restored natural movements of the imperiled mountain pygmy-possum. Small "toad tunnels" have been used in several European countries, and increasingly in the United States, to help migrating amphibians avoid the hazards of road crossings. The most useful sites for such highway crossing structures can be pinpointed with such information as habitat suitability models in geographic information systems, data on roadkill locations, radio-telemetry points, remote camera photos, known migratory paths, and animal signs such as tracks and scats.[168]

Greenways should incorporate well-tested designs for wildlife crossings, tailored to the species expected to use them, when greenways intersect roads that cannot feasibly be closed.

The International Conference on Ecology and Transportation is an important source of information on wildlife road-crossing issues. Proceedings from the conferences are available at www.icoet.net.

Conclusion

Landscapes are naturally dynamic, heterogeneous mosaics of differing habitat types. But within these mosaics, most habitats are fundamentally interconnected. As humans modify a landscape, its connectivity declines and natural habitats become more like islands.[168] Greenways that function as wildlife corridors are one tool that land-use planners and managers can use to maintain or restore habitat connectivity in human-modified landscapes.

Notes

[1] Hay, K. G. (1994). *Greenways: Wildlife and Natural Gas Pipeline Corridors. New Partnerships for Multiple Use.* Arlington, VA, The Conservation Fund.

[2] Bennett, A. F. (1999). *Linkages in the Landscape: The Role of Corridors and Connectivity in Wildlife Conservation.* Cambridge, UK, IUCN.

[3] Noss, R. F., and A. Cooperrider. (1994). *Saving Nature's Legacy: Protecting and Restoring Biodiversity.* Washington, DC, Defenders of Wildlife and Island Press; Beier, P., and R. F. Noss. (1998). "Do habitat corridors provide connectivity?" *Conservation Biology* 12:1241–1252; Bennett, (1999), *Linkages.*

[4] Tischendorf, L., and L. Fahrig. (2000). "On the usage and measurement of landscape connectivity," *Oikos* 90:7-19.

[5] Bennett, (1999), *Linkages*.

[6] Beier and Noss, (1998), "Habitat corridors."

[7] Brown, J. H., and M. V. Lomolino. (1998). *Biogeography*, 2nd ed. Sunderland, MA, Sinauer; Bennett, (1999), *Linkages*.

[8] Hunter, Jr., M. L. (1990). *Wildlife, Forests, and Forestry*. Englewood Cliffs, NJ, Prentice Hall.

[9] But see Tewksbury, J. J., et al. (2002). "Corridors affect plants, animals, and their interactions in fragmented landscapes," *Proceedings of the National Academy of Sciences USA* 99:12923–12926; Kirchner, F., et al. (2003). "Role of corridors in plant dispersal: An example with the endangered *Ranunculus nodiflorus*," *Conservation Biology* 17: 401–410.

[10] For example, Florida Greenways Commission. (1994). *Creating a Statewide Greenways System*. Tallahassee, FL, Report to the Governor.

[11] Wiens, J. A., et al. (1993). "Ecological mechanisms and landscape ecology," *Oikos* 66: 369–380; Ims, R. A. (1995). "Movement patterns related to spatial structures," *Mosaic Landscapes and Ecological Processes*. London, Chapman and Hall.

[12] Forman. R. T. T. (1995) *Land Mosaics: The Ecology of Landscapes and Regions*. Cambridge: Cambridge University Press; Bennett, (1999), *Linkages*.

[13] Bennett, (1999), *Linkages*.

[14] Sumner, E. (1936). *A Life History of the California Quail, with Recommendations for Conservation and Management*. Sacramento, California State Printing Office; Allen, D. (1943). "Michigan fox squirrel management," *Game Division Publication* 100. Lansing, Department of Conservation; L. Baumgartner. (1943). "Fox squirrels in Ohio," *Journal of Wildlife Management* 7: 193–202; for a review, see Harris, L. D., and K. Atkins. (1991). "Faunal movement corridors, with emphasis on Florida," pp. 117–134, in W. Hudson, ed. *Landscape Linkages and Biodiversity: A Strategy for Survival*. Washington, DC, Island Press.

[15] Willis, E. O. (1974). "Populations and local extinctions of birds on Barro Colorado Island, Panama," *Ecological Monographs* 44: 153–169; Diamond, J. M. (1975). "The island dilemma: Lessons of modern biogeographic studies for the design of natural preserves," *Biological Conservation* 7: 129–146; Sullivan, A. L., and M. L. Shaffer. (1975). "Biogeography of the megazoo," *Science* 189: 13–17; Wilson, E. O., and E. O. Willis (1975). "Applied biogeography," pp. 522–534, in M. Cody and J. Diamond, ed. *Ecology and Evolution of Communities*. Cambridge, MA, Belknap Press of Harvard University Press; Diamond, J. M., and R. M. May. (1976). "Island biogeography and the design of natural reserves," pp. 163–186, in R. M. May, ed. *Theoretical Ecology: Principles and Applications*. Philadelphia, W. B. Saunders.

[16] Forman, R. T. T., and M. Godron. (1983). "Corridors in a landscape: Their ecological structure and function," *Ekologia* 2: 375–387; Forman, R. T. T., and M. Godron. (1986). *Landscape Ecology*. New York, John Wiley and Sons; Forman, R. T. T., and M. Godron. (1981). "Patches and structural components for a landscape ecology," *BioScience* 31: 733–740; Forman, (1995), *Land Mosaics*; Noss, R. F. (1982). "A regional landscape approach to maintain diversity," *BioScience* 33: 700–706; Fahrig Hansson, L. L., and G. Merriam. (1995). *Mosaic Landscapes and Ecological Processes*. London, Chapman and Hall; Hanski, I. (1999). *Metapopulation Ecology*. Oxford, UK, Oxford University Press.

[17] MacArthur, R. H., and E. O. Wilson. (1967). *The Theory of Island Biogeography*. Princeton, NJ, Princeton University Press.

[18] Harris, L. D. (1994). *The Fragmented Forest*. Chicago, University of Chicago Press; Noss and Cooperrider, (1994), *Saving Nature's Legacy*.

[19] Trombulak, S. C., and C. A. Frissell. (2000). "Review of ecological effects of roads on terrestrial and aquatic communities," *Conservation Biology* 14: 18–30; Forman et al. (2003). *Road Ecology: Science and Solutions*. Washington, DC, Island Press.

[20] Crooks, K. R. (2002). "Relative sensitivities of mammalian carnivores to habitat fragmentation," *Conservation Biology* 16: 488–502.

[21] Johnson, W. C., and C. S. Adkisson. (1985). "Dispersal of beechnuts by blue jays in fragmented landscapes," *American Midland Naturalist* 113: 319–324.

[22] Wegner, J. F., and G. Merriam. (1979). "Movements of birds and small mammals between a wood and adjoining farmland habitat," *Journal of Applied Ecology* 16: 349–357.

[23] Bennett, A. F. (1990). *Habitat Corridors: Their Role in Wildlife Management and Conservation*. Melbourne, Australia, Arthur Rylah Institute for Environmental Research, Department of Conservation and Environment; Noss and Cooperrider, (1994), *Saving Nature's Legacy*.

[24] Bennett, (1999), *Linkages*.

[25] Harris, L. D. (1984). *Bottomland Hardwoods: Valuable, Vanishing, Vulnerable*. University of Florida Cooperative

Extension Service, University of Florida Special Publication 28: 1–20; Harris, L. D., "The faunal significance of fragmentation of southeastern bottomland forests," in Proceedings of the Symposium: *The Forested Wetlands of the Southern United States*, General Technical Report SE-50, D. D. Hook and R. Lea, ed. Asheville, NC, USDA Forest Service, Southeastern Forest Experiment Station.

[26] Korte, P. A., and L. H. Frederickson. (1987). "Loss of Missouri's lowland hardwood ecosystem," Transactions of the North American Wildlife and Natural Resources Conference 42: 31–41; Harris, (1984), *Bottomland Hardwoods*.

[27] Stauffer, D. A., and L. B. Best. (1980). "Habitat selection by birds of riparian communities: Evaluating effects of habitat alterations," *Journal of Wildlife Management* 44: 1–15.

[28] Harris, (1984), *The Fragmented Forest*.

[29] Forsey, S. E., and E. M. Baggs. (2001). "Winter activity of mammals in riparian zones and adjacent forests prior to and following clear-cutting at Copper Lake, Newfoundland, Canada," *Forest Ecology and Management* 145: 163–171.

[30] Potvin, F., L. Belanger, and K. Lowell. (2000). "Marten habitat selection in a clearcut boreal landscape," *Conservation Biology* 14: 844–857.

[31] Johnson, A. S. (1989). "The thin green line: Riparian corridors and endangered species in Arizona and New Mexico," pp. 34–36, in *Preserving Communities and Corridors*. G. Mackintosh, ed. Washington, DC, Defenders of Wildlife.

[32] Ibid.

[33] Ibid.

[34] Strong, T. R., and C. E. Bock. (1990). "Bird species distribution patterns in riparian habitats in southeastern Arizona," *Condor* 92: 866–885.

[35] Thomas, J. W., C. Maser, and J. F. Rodiek. 1979. "Riparian zones," pp. 40–47, in *Wildlife Habitats in Managed Forests: the Blue Mountains of Oregon and Washington*. J. W. Thomas, ed. Washington, DC, USDA Forest Service Agricultural Handbook No. 553.

[36] Noss, R. F. (1988). "The longleaf pine landscape of the Southeast: Almost gone and almost forgotten," *Endangered Species Update* 5: 1–8.

[37] Best, L. B. (1983). "Bird use of fencerows: Implications of contemporary fencerow management practices," *Wildlife Society Bulletin* 11: 343–347.

[38] Forman, R. T. T., and J. Baudry. (1984). "Hedgerows and hedgerow networks in landscape ecology," *Environmental Management* 8: 495–510.

[39] Pollard, E., M. D. Hooper, and N. W. Moore. (1974). *Hedges*. London, W. Collins Sons.

[40] Bennett, (1999), *Linkages*.

[41] Lewis, T. (1969). "The diversity of the insect fauna in a hedgerow and neighboring fields," *Journal of Applied Ecology* 6: 453–458.

[42] Bennett, (1999), *Linkages*.

[43] Yahner. R. H. (1982). "Avian use of vertical strata and plantings in farmstead shelterbelts," *Journal of Wildlife Management* 46: 50–60.

[44] Anderson, S. H., K. Mann, and H. H. Shugart. (1977). "The effect of transmission-line corridors on bird populations," *American Midland Naturalist* 97: 216–221.

[45] Kroodsma, R. L. (1982). "Bird community ecology on power-line corridors in east Tennessee," *Biological Conservation* 23: 79–94.

[46] Geibert, E. H. (1980). "Songbird diversity along an urban powerline right-of-way in Rhode Island," *Environmental Management* 4: 205–213.

[47] Tassone, J. F. (1981). "Utility of hardwood leave strips for breeding birds in Virginia's Central Piedmont," Master's thesis. Blacksburg, Virginia Polytechnic Institute and State College.

[48] Harris, L. D. (1988). "Edge effects and the conservation of biotic diversity," *Conservation Biology* 2: 330–332.

[49] Simberloff, D., and J. Cox. (1987). "Consequences and costs of conservation corridors," *Conservation Biology* 1: 63–71.

[50] Foster, M. L. and S. R. Humphrey. (1995). "Use of highway underpasses by Florida panthers and other wildlife," *Wildlife Society Bulletin* 23: 95–100.

[51] Beier and Noss, (1998), "Do Habitat Corridors Provide Connectivity?"; Little, S. J., R. G. Harcourt, and A. P. Clevenger. (2002). "Do wildlife passages act as prey-traps?" *Biological Conservation* 107: 135–145.

52 Grove, N. (1990). "Greenways: Paths to the future," *National Geographic*, June: 77–99.

53 Jordan, W. R., R. L. Peters, and E. B. Allen. (1988). "Ecological restoration as a strategy for conserving biological diversity," *Environmental Management* 12: 55–72.

54 Ranney, J. W., M. C. Bruner, and J. B. Levenson. (1981). "The importance of edge in the structure and dynamics of forest islands," pp. 67–95, in *Forest Island Dynamics in Man-Dominated Landscapes*. R. L. Burgess and D. M. Sharpe, ed. New York, Springer-Verlag, 1981.

55 Forman and Godron, (1981), "Patches and structural components for a landscape ecology"; Forman and Godron, (1986), *Landscape Ecology*.

56 Noss and Cooperrider, (1994), *Saving Nature's Legacy*; Trombulak and Frissell, (2000), "On the usage and measurement of landscape connectivity."

57 Viles, R. L., and D. J. Rosier. (2001). "How to use roads in the creation of greenways: case studies in three New Zealand landscapes," *Landscape and Urban Planning* 55: 15–27.

58 Bennett, (1999), "Linkages in the Landscape."

59 Saunders, D. A., and J. A. Ingram. (1987). "Factors affecting survival of breeding populations of Carnaby's cockatoo *Calyptorhynchus funereus latirostris* in remnants of native vegetation," pp. 249–258, in *Nature Conservation: The Role of Remnants of Native Vegetation*. D. A. Saunders, G. W. Arnold, A. A. Burbridge, and A. J. M. Hopkins, ed. New South Wales, Australia, Surrey Beatty and Sons.

60 Bennett, A. F. (1988). "Roadside vegetation: A habitat for mammals at Naringal, south-western Victoria," *Victorian Naturalist* 105: 106–113.

61 Van der Ree, R. (2002). "The population ecology of the squirrel glider (*Petaurus norfolcensis*) within a network of remnant linear habitats," *Wildlife Research* 29: 329–340.

62 Way, J. M. (1977). "Roadside verges and conservation in Britain: A review," *Biological Conservation* 12: 65–74.

63 Ries, L. D. M. Debinski, and M. L. Wieland. (2001). "Conservation value of roadside prairie restoration to butterfly communities," *Conservation Biology* 15: 401–411.

64 Bolger, D. T., T. A. Scott, and J. T. Rotenberry. (2001). "Use of corridor-like landscape structures by bird and small mammal species," *Biological Conservation* 102: 213–224.

65 Noss, R. F., and L. D. Harris. (1986). "Nodes, networks, and MUMs: Preserving diversity at all scales," *Environmental Management* 10: 299–309.

66 Mortberg, U., and H.G. Wallentinus. (2000). "Red-listed forest bird species in an urban environment: Assessment of green space corridors," *Landscape and Urban Planning* 50: 215–226.

67 Adams, A. W. (1982). "Migration," pp. 301–321, in *Elk of North America: Ecology and Management*. J. W. Thomas and D. E. Toweill, Harrisburg, PA, Stackpole Books.

68 Skovlin, J. M. (1982). "Habitat requirements and evaluations," pp. 369–413, in *Elk of North America: Ecology and Management*. J. W. Thomas and D. E. Toweill, Harrisburg, PA, Stackpole Books.

69 Winn, D. S. (1976). "Terrestrial vertebrate fauna and selected coniferous habitat types on the north slope of the Uinta Mountains," Wasatch National Forest Special Report. Salt Lake City, UT, USDA Forest Service.

70 Pederson, R. J., and A. W. Adams. (1976). "Rocky Mountain elk research project progress report," Project No. W-70-R-6. Portland, Oregon Department of Fish and Wildlife.

71 Schoen and Kirchoff, (1990), "Seasonal Habitat Use."

72 McNab, B. K. (1963). "Bioenergetics and the determination of home range size," *American Naturalist* 97: 133–140.

73 Noss, R. F., H. B. Quigley, M. G. Hornocker, T. Merrill, and P. C. Paquet. (1996). "Conservation biology and carnivore conservation in the Rocky Mountains," *Conservation Biology* 10: 949–963.

74 Anderson, A. E. (1983). "A critical review of literature on puma (*Felis concolor*)," Special Report No. 54. Denver, Colorado Division of Wildlife.

75 Young, S. P. (1946). "History, life habits, economic status, and control, Part 1," pp. 1–173, in *The Puma, Mysterious American Cat*. S. P. Young and E. A. Goldman, ed. Washington, DC, The American Wildlife Institute.

76 Beier, P. (1993). "Determining minimum habitat areas and habitat corridors for cougars," *Conservation Biology* 7: 94–108; P. Beier. (1995). "Dispersal of juvenile cougars in fragmented habitat," *Journal of Wildlife Management* 59: 228–237.

77 Crooks, (2002), "Relative sensitivities."

78 Harris, L. D. (1985). "Conservation corridors: A highway system for wildlife," *ENFO Report*. Winter Park, Florida Conservation Foundation.

79 Florida Fish and Wildlife Conservation Commission, unpublished.

80 LeFranc, M. N., M. B. Moss, K. A. Patnode, and W. C. Sugg, ed. (1987). *Grizzly Bear Compendium*. Washington, DC, National Wildlife Federation and Interagency Grizzly Bear Committee.

81 Frederickson, L. H. (1978). "Lowland hardwood wetlands: Current status and habitat values for wildlife," pp. 296–306, in *Wetland Functions and Values: The State of Our Understanding*. Proceedings of the National Symposium on Wetlands. P. E. Greeson, J. R. Clark, and J. E. Clark, ed., Minneapolis, American Water Resources Association.

82 Merriam, G. (1991). "Corridors and connectivity: Animal population in heterogeneous environments," pp. 133–142, in *Nature Conservation: The Role of Corridors*. D. A. Saunder and R. J. Hobbs, ed. New South Wales, Australia, Surrey Beatty and Sons.

83 Saunders, D. A. (1990). "Problems of survival in an extensively cultivated landscape: The case of Carnaby's cockatoo (*Calyptorhynchus funereus latirostris*)," *Biological Conservation* 54: 111–124.

84 Saunders, D. A., and J. A. Ingram. (1987). "Factors affecting survival of breeding populations of Carnaby's cockatoo *Calyptorhynchus funereus latirostris* in remnants of native vegetation," pp. 249–258, in *Nature Conservation: The Role of Remnants of Native Vegetation*. D. A. Saunders, G. W. Arnold, A. A. Burbridge, and A. J. M. Hopkins, ed., New South Wales, Australia, Surrey Beatty and Sons.

85 Brown and Lomolino, (1998), *Biogeography*.

86 Bullock, J. M., R. E. Kenward, and R. S. Hails, ed. (2002). *Dispersal Ecology*. Oxford, UK, Blackwell Science.

87 Bennett, (1990), "Habitat corridors: Their role."

88 Whitcomb, R. F., et al. (1981). "Effects of forest fragmentation on avifauna of the eastern deciduous forest," pp. 125–205, in *Forest Island Dynamics in Man-Dominated Landscapes*. R. L. Burgess and D. M. Sharpe, ed. New York, Springer-Verlag.

89 Wiens, J. A. (1989). *The Ecology of Bird Communities, Vol. 2, Processes and Variations*. New York, Cambridge University Press.

90 LeFranc et al., (1987), *Grizzly Bear Compendium*; Harris, L. D., and P. B. Gallagher. (1989). "New initiatives for wildlife conservation: The need for movement corridors," pp. 11–34, in *Preserving Communities and Corridors*. G. Mackintosh, ed. Washington, DC, Defenders of Wildlife.

91 Johnson and Adkisson, (1985), "Dispersal of beechnuts."

92 Davis, M. B. (1981). "Quaternary history and the stability of forest communities," pp. 132–153, in *Forest Succession*. D. C. West, H. H. Shugart, and D. B. Botkin, ed. New York, Springer-Verlag.

93 Tewksbury et al., (2002), "Corridors affect."

94 Ibid.

95 Fahrig, L., and J. Paloheimo. (1988). "Effect of spatial arrangement of habitat patches on local population size," *Ecology* 69: 468–475.

96 Haddad, N. M. (1999). "Corridor and distance effects on interpatch movements: A landscape experiment with butterflies,"*Ecological Applications* 9: 612–622.

97 Singleton, P., W. Gaines, and J. Lehmkuhl. (2002). *Landscape Permeability for Large Carnivores in Washington: A Geographic Information System Weighted-Distance and Least-Cost Corridor Assessment*. Research Paper PNW-RP-549. Portland, OR, USDA Forest Service, Pacific Northwest Research Station; Carroll, C., R. F. Noss, P. C. Paquet, and N. H. Schumaker. 2004. "Extinction debt of protected areas in developing landscapes." *Conservation Biology* 18(4): 1110–1120.

98 Wiens, (1989), "Ecology of bird communities."

99 Rothermel, B. B., and R. D. Semlitsch. (2002). "An experimental investigation of landscape resistance of forest versus old-field habitats to emigrating juvenile amphibians," *Conservation Biology* 16: 1324–1332.

100 Laurance, W. F., T. E. Lovejoy, et al. (2002). "Ecosystem decay of Amazonian forest fragments: A 22-year investigation," *Conservation Biology* 16: 605–618.

101 Elton. C. S., (1958). *The Ecology of Invasions by Animals and Plants*. London, Methuen.; Mooney, H. A., and J. Drake, ed. (1986). *The Ecology of Biological Invasions of North America and Hawaii*. New York, Springer-Verlag; Usher, M. B. (1988). "Biological invasions of nature reserves: A search for generalizations,"*Biological Conservation* 44: 119–135.

102 Huey, L. M. (1941). "Mammalian invasion via the highway," *Journal of Mammalogy* 22: 383–385; Getz, L. L., F. R.

Cole, and D. L. Gates. (1978). "Interstate roadsides as dispersal routes for *Microtus pennsylvanicus*," *Journal of Mammalogy* 59: 208–212.

[103] Schowalter, T. D. (1988). "Forest pest management: A synopsis," *Northwest Environmental Journal* 4: 313–318; Wilcox, D. A. (1989). "Migration and control of purple loosestrife (Lythrium salicaria) along highway corridors," *Environmental Management* 13: 365–370; Tyser, R. W., and C. A. Worley. (1992). "Alien flora in grasslands adjacent to road and trail corridors in Glacier National Park, Montana (USA)," *Conservation Biology* 6: 253–262.; Wilson, J. B., G. L. Rapson, M. T. Sykes, A. J. Watkins, and P. A. Williams. (1992). "Distributions and climatic correlations of some exotic species along roadsides in South Island, New Zealand," *Journal of Biogeography* 19: 183–193; Lonsdale, W. M., and A. M. Lane. (1994). "Tourist vehicles as vectors of weed seeds in Kakuda National Park, northern Australia," *Biological Conservation* 69: 277–283; Parendesm, L. A. and J. A. Jones. (2000). "Role of light availability and dispersal in exotic plant invasion along roads and streams in the H.J. Andrews Experimental Forest, Oregon," *Conservation Biology* 14: 64–75.

[104] Ambuel, B., and S. A. Temple. (1983). "Area-dependent changes in the bird communities and vegetation of southern Wisconsin forests," *Ecology* 64: 1057–1068; Simberloff and Cox, (1987), "Consequences and costs."

[105] Levins, R. (1970). "Extinction," pp. 77–107, in *Some Mathematical Questions in Biology: Lectures on Mathematics in the Life Sciences*, Vol. 2. M. Gerstenhaber, ed. Providence, RI, American Mathematical Society; Gilpin, M. E., and I. Hanski, ed. (1991). Metapopulation Dynamics: Empirical and Theoretical Investigations. London, Linnaean Society of London and Academic Press; Hanski, 1999, *Metapopulation Ecology*.

[106] Brown, J. H., and A. Kodric-Brown, (1977), "Turnover rates in insular biogeography: Effect of immigration on extinction," *Ecology* 58: 445–449.

[107] Harrison, S. (1994). "Metapopulations and conservation," pp. 111–128, in *Large-Scale Ecology and Conservation Biology*. P. J. Edwards, R. M. May, and N. R. Webb, ed. Oxford, UK, Blackwell Science.

[108] den Boer, P. J. (1981). "On the survival of populations in a heterogeneous and variable environment," *Oecologia* 50: 39–53.

[109] Fleishman, E., C. Ray, P. Sjögren-Gulve, C. L. Boggs, and D. D. Murphy. (2002). "Assessing the roles of patch quality, area, and isolation in predicting metapopulation dynamics," *Conservation Biology* 706–716.

[110] Merriam, G. (1988). "Landscape dynamics in farmland," *Trends in Ecology and Evolution* 3: 16–20.

[111] Fahrig, L., and G. Merriam. (1985). "Habitat patch connectivity and population survival," *Ecology* 66: 1762–1768.

[112] Baumgartner, (1943), "Fox squirrels."

[113] Henderson, M. T., G. Merriam, and J. Wegner. (1985). "Patchy environments and species survival: Chipmunks in an agricultural mosaic," *Biological Conservation* 31: 95–105.

[114] Brooker, L., and M. Brooker. (2002). "Dispersal and population dynamics of the blue-breasted fairy-wren, *Malurus pulcherrimus*, in fragmented habitat in the Western Australian wheatbelt," *Wildlife Research* 29: 225–233.

[115] Opdam, P., G. Rijsdijk, and F. Hustings. (1985). "Bird communities in small woods in an agricultural landscape: Effects of area and isolation," *Biological Conservation* 34: 333–352; Van Dorp, D., and P. F. M. Opdam. (1987). "Effects of patch size, isolation and regional abundance on forest bird communities," *Ecology* 1: 59–73.

[116] Saunders, D. A., and C. P. de Rebeira. (1991). "Values of corridors to avian populations in a fragmented landscape," pp. 221–240, in *Nature Conservation: The Role of Corridors*. D. A. Saunders and R. J. Hobbs, ed. New South Wales, Australia, Surrey Beatty and Sons.

[117] Soulé, M. E., D. T. Bolger, A. C. Alberts, J. Wright, M. Sorice, and S. Hill. (1988). "Reconstructed dynamics of rapid extinction of chaparral-requiring birds in urban habitat islands," *Conservation Biology* 2: 75–92.

[118] Gerlach, G., and K. Musolf. (2000). "Fragmentation of landscape as a cause for genetic subdivision in bank voles," *Conservation Biology* 14: 1066–1074; Williams, B. L., J. D. Brawn, and K. N. Paige. (2003). "Landscape scale genetic effects of habitat fragmentation on a high gene flow species: *Speyeria idalia (Nymphalidae)*," *Molecular Ecology* 12: 11–20.

[119] Keller, L. F., and D. M. Waller. (2002). "Inbreeding effects in wild populations," *Trends in Ecology and Evolution* 17: 230.

[120] Frankel, O. H., and M. E. Soulé. (1981). *Conservation and Evolution*. Cambridge, UK, Cambridge University Press; Schonewald-Cox, C. M., S. M. Chambers, B. MacBryde, and W. L. Thomas, ed. (1983). *Genetics and Conservation: A Reference for Managing Wild Animal and Plant Populations*. Menlo Park, CA, Benjamin/Cummings.

[121] Allendorf, F. W. (1983). "Isolation, gene flow, and genetic differentiation among populations," in *Genetics and Conservation: A Reference for Managing Wild Animal and Plant Populations*. C. M. Schonewald-Cox et al., ed. Menlo Park, CA, Benjamin/Cummings.

[122] Couvet, D. (2002). "Deleterious effects of restricted gene flow in fragmented populations," *Conservation Biology* 16: 369–376.

123 Ingvarsson, P. K. (2002). "Lone wolf to the rescue," *Nature* 420: 472.

124 Ebert, D., C. Haag, M. Kirkpatrick, M. Riek, J.W. Hottinger, and V.I. Pajunen. (2002). "A selective advantage to immigrant genes in a Daphnia metapopulation," *Science* 295: 485–488.

125 Bennett, (1990), "Habitat corridors: Their role."; Bennett, A. F. (1990). "Habitat corridors and the conservation of small mammals in a fragmented forest environment," *Landscape Ecology* 4: 109–122.

126 Simberloff, D., and J. Cox. (1987). "Consequences and costs of conservation corridors," *Conservation Biology* 1: 63–71; Noss, R F. (1987). "Corridors in real landscapes: A reply to Simberloff and Cox," *Conservation Biology* 1: 159–164.

127 Ehrlich, P. R. (1988). "The loss of diversity: Causes and consequences," pp. 21–27, in *Biodiversity*. E. O. Wilson, ed. Washington, DC, National Academy Press.

128 Edmands, S., and C. C. Timmerman. (2003). "Modeling factors affecting the severity of outbreeding depression," *Conservation Biology* 17: 883–892.

129 Hunter, Jr., M. L., G. L. Jacobson, and T. Webb. (1988). "Paleoecology and the coarse-filter approach to maintaining biological diversity," *Conservation Biology* 2: 375–385.

130 Davis, (1981), "Quaternary history."; Webb III, T. (1987). "The appearance and disappearance of major vegetational assemblages: Long-term vegetational dynamics in eastern North America," *Vegetatio* 69: 177–187.

131 Kline, V. M , and G. Cottam. (1979). "Vegetation response to climate and fire in the driftless area of Wisconsin," *Ecology* 60: 861 68.

132 Grimm, E. C. (1984). "Fire and other factors controlling the Big Woods vegetation of Minnesota in the mid-nineteenth century," *Ecological Monographs* 54: 291–311.

133 Davis, (1981), "Quaternary history."

134 Graham, R. W. (1986). "Response of mammalian communities to environmental changes during the Late Quaternary," pp. 300–313, in *Community Ecology*. J. Diamond and T. J. Case, ed. New York, Harper and Row.

135 Coope, G. R. (1979). "Late Cenozoic fossil Coleoptera: Evolution, biogeography, and ecology," *Annual Review of Ecology and Systematics* 10: 247–267; Prothero, D. R., and T. H. Heaton. (1996). "Faunal stability during the early Oligocene climatic crash," *Palaeogeography Palaeoclimatology Palaeoecology* 127: 257–283.

136 Peters, R.L., and J. D. S. Darling. (1985). "The greenhouse effect and nature reserves," *BioScience* 35: 707–717; Peters, R. L. (1988). "Effects of global warming on species and habitats: An overview," *Endangered Species Update* 5 (7): 1 8.

137 Delcourt, H. R., and P. A. Delcourt. (1984). "Ice Age haven for hardwoods," *Natural History*, Sept.: 22–28.

138 Whittaker, R. H. (1972). "Evolution and measurement of species diversity," *Taxon* 21: 213–251.

139 Peters, (1988), "Effects of global warming"; L. Roberts. (1989). "How fast can trees migrate?" *Science* 243: 735–737; Clark, J. S. (1998). "Why trees migrate so fast: Confounding theory with dispersal biology and the paleorecord," *American Naturalist* 152: 204–224; Mader, J. H. (1984). "Animal habitat isolation by roads and agricultural fields," *Biological Conservation* 29: 81–96.

140 Peters, (1988), "Effects of global warming"; R. H. MacArthur. (1972). *Geographical Ecology: Patterns in the Distribution of Species*. Princeton, NJ, Princeton University Press; M. B. Davis. (1983). "Holocene vegetational history of the eastern United States," in *Late-Quaternary Environments of the United States: Vol. 2, The Holocene*. H. E. Wright, ed. Minneapolis, University of Minnesota Press; Noss, R. F. (2001). "Beyond Kyoto: Forest management in a time of rapid climate change," *Conservation Biology* 15: 578–590.

141 Hobbs, R. J., and A. J. M. Hopkins. (1991). "The role of conservation corridors in a changing climate," pp. 281–290, in *Nature Conservation: The Role of Corridors*. D. A. Saunders and R. J. Hobbs, ed. New South Wales, Australia, Surrey Beatty and Sons; Noss, (2001), "Beyond Kyoto."

142 Panetta, F. D., and A. J. M. Hopkins. (1991). "Weeds in corridors: Invasion and management," pp. 341–351, in *Nature Conservation: The Role of Corridors*. D. A. Saunders and R. J. Hobbs, ed. New South Wales, Australia, Surrey Beatty and Sons.

143 Diamond, J. M. (1976). "Island biogeography and conservation: Strategy and limitations," *Science* 3: 1027–1029.

144 Ibid.

145 Henein, K., and G. Merriam. (1990). "The elements of connectivity where corridor quality is variable," *Landscape Ecology* 4: 157–170; Merriam, G., and A. Lanoue. (1990). "Corridor use by small mammals: Field measurement for three experimental types of *Peromyscus leucopus*," *Landscape Ecology* 4: 123–131; Beier and Noss, (1998), "Do habitat corridors provide."

146 Noss, R. F., (1987), "Corridors in real landscapes"; Hunter, 1990, *Wildlife, Forests, and Forestry*; Soulé, M. E., and M. E. Gilpin. (1991). "The theory of wildlife corridor capability," pp. 3–8, in *Nature Conservation: The Role of Corridors*. D. A. Saunders and R. J. Hobbs, ed. New South Wales, Australia, Surrey Beatty and Sons; M.E. Soulé, personal communication.

147 Bennett, (1999), *Linkages*.

148 Wilcove, D. S., C. H. McLellan, and A. P. Dobson. (1986). "Habitat fragmentation in the temperate zone," pp. 237–256, in *Conservation Biology: The Science of Scarcity and Diversity*. M. E. Soulé, ed. Sunderland, MA, Sinauer Associates; Soulé et al., (1988), "Reconstructed dynamics"; Crooks, K., and M. E. Soulé. (1999). "Mesopredator release and avifaunal extinctions in a fragmented system," *Nature* 400: 563–566.

149 Robbins, C. S. (1979). "Effect of forest fragmentation on bird populations," pp. 198–212, in *Management of North Central and Northeastern Forests for Nongame Birds*. R. M. DeGraaf and K. E. Evans, ed. Washington, DC, USDA Forest Service General Technical Report NC-51; Ambuel and Temple, (1983), "Area-dependent changes."

150 Ranney et al., (1981), "The importance of edge."

151 Harris, (1984), *The Fragmented Forest*.

152 Wilcove, D. S. (1985). "Forest fragmentation and the decline of migratory songbirds," Ph.D. dissertation. Princeton, NJ, Princeton University.

153 Ranney et al., (1981), "The importance of edge."

154 Noss, (1987), "Corridors in real landscapes"; Bennett, (1990), "Habitat corridors: Their role"; Bennett, 1999, *Linkages*.

155 Noss, (1987), "Corridors in real landscapes"; R. F. Noss. (1992). "The Wildlands Project: Land conservation strategy," *Wild Earth*, Special Issue: 10–25.

156 Noss and Cooperrider, (1994), *Saving Nature's Legacy*; Bennett, (1990), "Habitat corridors: Their role"; A. F. Bennett, (1990), "Habitat corridors and the conservation of small mammals in a fragmented forest environment," *Landscape Ecology* 4: 109–122; Harris, L. D., and J. Scheck. (1991). "From implications to applications: The dispersal corridor principle applied to the conservation of biological diversity," pp. 189–200, in *Nature Conservation: The Role of Corridors*. D. A. Saunders and R. J. Hobbs, ed. New South Wales, Australia, Surrey Beatty and Sons.

157 Nature Conservancy. (1990). "Florida: Corporations make a trio of bargain sales," *Nature Conservancy*, May/June, 25.

158 Forman, (1983), "Corridors in a landscape."

159 Ibid.

160 Knopf, F. L. (1986). "Changing landscapes and cosmopolitism of the eastern Colorado avifauna," *Wildlife Society Bulletin* 14: 132–142.

161 Haddad, N. (2000). "Corridor length and patch colonization by a butterfly, *Junonia coenia*," *Conservation Biology* 14: 738–745.

162 Hale, M. L., et al. (2001). "Impact of landscape management on the genetic structure of red squirrel populations," *Science* 293: 2246–2248.

163 Noss and Cooperrider, (1984), *Saving Nature's Legacy*; Bennett, A. F., "Roads, roadsides, and wildlife conservation: A review," pp. 99–118, in *Nature Conservation: The Role of Corridors*. D. A. Saunders and R. J. Hobbs, ed. New South Wales, Australia, Surrey Beatty and Sons; Trombulak and Frissell, (2000), "Review of ecological effects"; Forman et al., (2003), *Road Ecology*.

164 Noss, R. F., and B. Csuti. (1997). "Habitat fragmentation," pp. 269–304, in *Principles of Conservation Biology, 2nd ed.* G. K. Meffe and R. C. Carroll, ed. Sunderland, MA: Sinauer Associates; Baker, W. L., and R. L. Knight. (2000). "Roads and forest fragmentation in the Southern Rocky Mountains," pp. 97–122, in *Forest Fragmentation in the Southern Rocky Mountains*. R. L. Knight, F. W. Smith, S. W. Buskirk, W. H. Romme, and W. L. Baker, ed. Boulder, CO, University Press of Colorado.

165 Oxley, D. J., M. B. Fenton, and G. R. Carmody. (1974). "The effects of roads on populations of small mammals," *Journal of Applied Ecology* 11: 51–59; Wilkins, K. T. 1982. "Highways as barriers to rodent dispersal," *Southwestern Naturalist* 27: 459–460; Adams, L. W., and A. D. Geis. (1983). "Effects of roads on small mammals," *Journal of Applied Ecology* 20: 403–415; Garland, T., and W. G. Bradley. (1984). "Effects of a highway on Mojave Desert rodent populations," *American Midland Naturalist* 111: 47–56; Swihart, R. K., and N. A. Slade. (1984). "Road crossing in *Sigmodon hispidus* and *Microtus ochrogaster*," *Journal of Mammalogy* 65: 357–360; Gerlach and Musolf, (2000), "Fragmentation of landscape"; Mader, (1984), "Animal habitat isolation."

166 deMaynadier, P. G., and M. L. Hunter, Jr. (2000). "Road effects on amphibian movements in a forested landscape," *Natural Areas Journal* 20: 56–65; A. J. Brody and M. P. Pelton. (1989). "Effects of roads on black bear movements in western North Carolina," *Wildlife Society Bulletin* 17: 5–10; Develey, P. F., and P. C. Stouffer. (2001). "Effects of roads on movements by understory birds in mixed-species flocks in central Amazonian Brazil," *Conservation Biology* 15: 1416–1422; Lalo, J. (1987). "The problem of road kill," *American Forests*, Sept./Oct.: 50–53, 72; Baker and Knight, (2000), "Roads and forest fragmentation"; Fahrig et al., 1995, "Habitat patch connectivity"; Gibbs, J. P., and W. G. Shriver. (2002). "Estimating the effects of road mortality on turtle populations," *Conservation Biology* 16: 1647–1652.

167 Reed, D. F., T. N. Woodard, and T. M. Pojar. (1975). "Behavioral response of mule deer to a highway underpass," *Journal of Wildlife Management* 39: 361–367.

168 Mansergh, L. M., and D. J. Scotts. (1989). "Habitat continuity and social organization of the mountain pygmy-possum." *Journal of Wildlife Management* 53: 701–707; Langton, T., ed. (1989). *Amphibians and Roads*. Shefford, UK, ACO Polymer Products; Singer, F. J., and J. L. Doherty. (1985). "Managing mountain goats at a highway crossing," *Wildlife Society Bulletin* 13: 469–477; Foster and Humphrey, (1995), "Use of highway underpasses"; Scheick, B., and M. Jones. (1999). "Locating wildlife underpasses prior to expansion of highway 64 in North Carolina," pp. 247–250, in *Proceedings of the Third International Conference on Wildlife Ecology and Transportation*. FL-ER-73-99. Tallahassee, Florida Department of Transportation; Clevenger, A. P., and N. Waltho. (2000). "Factors influencing the effectiveness of wildlife underpasses in Banff National Park, Alberta, Canada," *Conservation Biology* 14: 47–56; Clevenger et al. (2002). "GIS-generated, expert-based models for identifying wildlife habitat linkages and planning mitigation passages," *Conservation Biology* 16: 503–514; Henke, R. K., P. Cawood Hellmund, and T. Sprunk. (2002). "Habitat connectivity study of the I-25 and US-85 corridors, Colorado," *Proceedings of the International Conference on Ecology and Transportation*. Raleigh, NC, Center for Transportation and the Environment; Lyren, L. M., and K. R. Crooks. (2002). "Factors influencing the movement, spatial patterns and wildlife underpass use of coyotes and bobcats along State Route 71 in Southern California," *Proceedings of the International Conference on Ecology and Transportation*. Raleigh, NC, Center for Transportation and the Environment.

169 Godron, M., and R. T. T. Forman. (1983). "Landscape modification and changing ecological characteristics," pp. 12–28, in *Disturbance and Ecosystems*. H. A. Mooney and M. Godron, ed. Berlin, Springer-Verlag.

CHAPTER 4

RIPARIAN GREENWAYS AND WATER RESOURCES

Michael W. Binford and Richard J. Karty

Corridors of streamside plant communities, called riparian forests, shadow streams as they run through the landscape. These corridors with running water, moist and fertile soils, and well-developed vegetation are dynamic environments that have complex and multilayered functions. Of the many kinds of corridors in the landscape, riparian ecosystems are especially important for both conservation and human use.

The ecological integrity of a stream is largely affected by its response to sediment, nutrients, and other materials coming from uphill areas. Riparian ecosystems, which constitute the interface between land and water, intercept these materials from above. They also supply vital materials to streams, including nutrients and organic debris. Therefore, natural areas located between a stream and degraded sections of the landscape can lessen the effects of upland disturbances and maintain healthy aquatic processes.

Riparian corridors also moderate in-stream flow and thereby influence water availability and the magnitude of floods. Streamside vegetation reduces bank and floodplain erosion by slowing the stream and reducing its erosive energy. Trees and shrubs produce shade and control water temperature, which can be a critical variable for many aquatic organisms. The capability of riparian systems to stabilize, buffer, or control all of these processes, and in turn to improve water quality, is essential for healthy landscape function. Finally, riparian vegetation is vitally important to wildlife (both aquatic and terrestrial), which is typically most abundant and most diverse in these habitats.

Riparian corridors are very attractive for a variety of human uses. They are often used for transportation and agriculture. Many waterways are used for disposal of municipal and industrial waste or are channelized and dammed for flood control and power production. Water is diverted for agricultural and urban needs, resulting in the decline of riparian forests and aquatic habitat. Streamside environments are also highly valued recreational areas.

When human uses extend to the edge of a stream, they cause fragmentation of the riparian corridor and can thus diminish its function as a connecting element within the landscape. Some animals may not cross gaps in streamside vegetation. Aquatic ecosystems are also degraded along and downstream from bare stretches. Water quality at a given location may be only as good as the most degraded reaches upstream allow. Thus, the health of a particular stream segment is dependent on the integrity of the entire riparian network.

Protecting and restoring streamside vegetation are increasingly used as strategies for maintaining or improving water quality. The challenge for planning and design professionals is to use specific knowledge of the characteristics of riparian ecosystems to create greenways that help achieve water-quality goals. Although the same basic ecological processes operate everywhere, the details of each ecosystem are unique. Factors that control nutrient and sediment flow, hydrologic regime, and wildlife use for a given riparian system must be understood in detail in order to establish effective greenway designs. This understanding will also show that riparian corridors are rarely a complete buffer between upland development and streams. Each system has its own limitations, which must be respected by designing and managing upland activities and developments so that they will not overtax streamside corridors.

This chapter describes how riparian greenways help maintain high-quality water resources and discusses how these corridors can be designed, managed, or restored. We describe the ecological structure, function, and context of riparian corridors in some detail because these complex systems must be understood before they can be modified or managed properly. We then discuss specific design issues and suggest guidelines for the design, management, and restoration of riparian greenways.

Structure of Riparian Corridors and Their Associated Watersheds

Riparian corridors are ecosystems: they consist of interacting living and nonliving components in an area defined in space and time. All ecosystems have functional connections with neighboring ecosystems, are elements of the landscape, and are composed of smaller ecosystems. This hierarchical and interconnected organization requires that the larger system of which riparian corridors are a part be understood and considered if greenway design is to be successful. This section provides an overview of watershed geomorphology and stream processes. We define several widely used terms and describe the processes that control stream and watershed shape and ecological function.

Watersheds and Stream Networks

A watershed, sometimes called a catchment, is an area of landscape that drains into a stream or other body of water; a watershed is the next ecosystem larger than a riparian corridor. Topographic divides form the boundaries between watersheds (in Europe, it is these divides that are called watersheds) (figure 4.1). The amount, movement, and characteristics of many substances and phenomena can be measured and described within this unit, including energy, water, nutrients, biomass, patterns of biological diversity, human activities, and habitat patches and corridors. Watershed ecosystems are therefore useful for ecological study and for landscape design and management. (Unfortunately, basin divides seldom coincide with political boundaries. Streams often mark

FIGURE 4.1

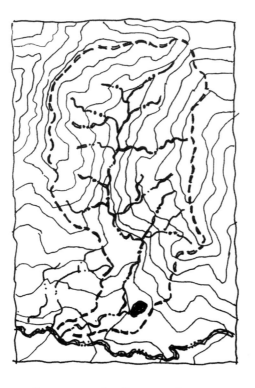

Map of Hubbard Brook watershed in the White Mountains of New Hampshire, showing the watershed's topographic boundaries and stream network. As part of the Hubbard Brook Experimental Forest, several of the subwatersheds shown have been sites of long-term ecosystem studies.

FIGURE 4.2

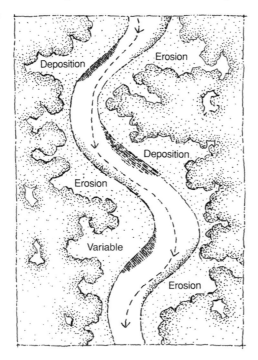

Bank erosion and sediment deposition, caused by variable speed and direction of flow in different parts of a stream channel, result in a dynamic and changing stream environment.

political divisions, and their basins are typically divided between two or more jurisdictions. For design or management to be successful in a basin, political coordination is often crucial.)

Although every watershed is unique in detail, geologists have defined a set of general, quantitative characteristics useful for describing and comparing characteristics of watershed shape (table 4.1). These characteristics are related to one another, and each affects functional aspects of the system.[1] For example, within a given climatic and topographic region, streams in larger watersheds have greater length and sinuosity, higher discharge, and more channel cross-sectional area than streams in smaller watersheds, but have lower average slope. The amounts of water and sediment that come from a watershed are controlled by watershed area, length, shape, and relief. Large, flat watersheds produce a smaller output of sediment and water per square mile than do small, steep watersheds because there is more area with mild slope for deposition before sediment is delivered to the stream. Sediment yields are influenced further by existing vegetation and land uses.

The evolution of the shape of watersheds is a natural process governed by physical, chemical, and biological factors. Climate and bedrock are the master controls, and interactions between precipitation and temperature on the one hand and soils and vegetation on the other determine the form of all watersheds. A dynamic balance is established between rock weathering, soil erosion, and the subsequent transport and deposition of eroded material. Sediment moves downslope through floodplains and channels and eventually into ponds, lakes, reservoirs, and the ocean. Along the way, the stream channel meanders by eroding material on the outside of bends and depositing it on the inside of downstream bends (figure 4.2).

Within a watershed, stream discharge varies throughout the year, and the periods of high and

TABLE 4.1 Morphological characteristics of watersheds and stream channels.

CHARACTERISTIC	UNITS	RELATIONSHIPS
Watersheds		
Area (A)	m^2	Measured[1]
Perimeter (p)	km	Measured
Watershed length		
Channel length (CL)	km	Measured
Valley length (VL)	km	Measured (midvalley line)
Air length (AL)	km	Measured (shortest distance between mouth and source of stream)
Total length of all channels in watershed (L)	km	Measured
Elevation (e)	m	Measured
Relief (R)	m	$e_{high} - e_{low}$
Slope (between point x and point y)	m/m	$(e_x - e_y)/CL_{x-y}$
Shape		
Form factor (F)	N/A	A/L^2
Watershed circularity	N/A	$4\,^{\circ}A/p^2$
Watershed elongation (E)	N/A	$2\sqrt{(A/p)}/CL$
Channel density (Dd)	$m\,m^{-2}$	L/A
Storage area (lakes and wetlands)	m^2	Measured
Stream channels		
Channel length (CL)	km	Measured (map scale-dependent)
Channel area (AC)	m^2	Measured cross-section (field study)
Channel volume (VC)	m^3	$L\,A_C$
Channel sinuosity[2]		
Total sinuosity (CI)	N/A	CL/AL
Topographic sinuosity (VI)	N/A	VL/AL
Hydraulic sinuosity (HSI)	%	$(CI-VI)/(CI-1) \times 100\%$

[1] All measured variables are scale-dependent, which means that they vary depending on the scale of measurement. For example, watershed perimeter would be less if measured at 1:25,000 than if measured at 1:200 because more curves are visible at 1:200. It should be obvious then that any variable derived from these measurements is also dependent on the scale. The variables are useful for comparisons between watersheds or between different times in the same watershed.

[2] Note that sinuosity can also be described qualitatively. Schumm has defined five categories to describe increasing sinuosity: straight, transitional, regular, irregular, and tortuous (Schumm, S. A. [1963]. "A tentative classification of river channels." U.S. Geological Survey Circular 477) .

Source: From Gregory, K. J., and D. E. Walling. (1973). *Watershed Form and Process.* New York, John Wiley and Sons.

low flows are different in different regions of North America.[2] In Rocky Mountain snowmelt streams and eastern perennial streams, discharge is usually highest in spring and lowest in early to midautumn. On the West Coast, discharge is highest during wet seasons that extend from fall through spring and is lowest in summer. In the southwestern part of the United States, high discharges can occur in virtually any season, depending on the elevation and geographical location of the watershed. In desert watersheds, however, summer is often the season of highest discharge. Periods of high discharge are also periods of maximum erosion, and much sediment can be deposited on the floodplain during floods.

The relative size of perennial streams and watersheds can be described with a stream order classification. According to the leading scheme, headwaters with no tributaries are first-order streams.[3] Where two first-order streams join, a second-order stream is formed, and so on (figure 4.3).

FIGURE 4.3

Stream order designation. Two first-order streams join to form a second-order stream, two second-order streams join to form a third-order stream, and so on. (After Strahler, A. N. [1964].

"Quantitative geomorphology of watersheds and channel networks." in *Handbook of Applied Hydrology*, V. T. Chow, ed. New York, McGraw-Hill.)

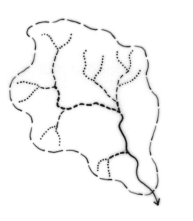

.... 1st order
----- 2nd order
--- 3rd order
—— 4th order

Higher-order streams are formed only by the joining of two streams of the same lower order. Thus, a second-order stream that joins a first-order stream does not make a third-order stream, but two converging second-order streams do. Cascading mountain streams are usually first- or second-order streams. Large, navigable rivers, like the Hudson or the Missouri, are likely to be sixth-, seventh-, or eighth-order waterways. Stream order designations are not as useful for larger, navigable streams and major rivers because the differences between adjacent orders are not so pronounced. For example, although there are important hydrological and ecological differences between first- and second-order streams, ninth- and tenth-order streams are usually quite similar.

All of the characteristics in table 4.1 are correlated with stream order. Higher-order streams have watersheds with larger areas, longer lengths, wider and deeper channels, greater relief, and less slope. Some variables, such as stream network density and relative relief, vary inversely with stream order and consequently with watershed area.[4]

Physical gradients (gradual changes in physical characteristics) along streams and rivers from headwaters to lower reaches result in a continuum of structural and functional characteristics of biotic communities. A description of stream ecology based on these gradients, known as the river continuum concept (RCC), is a useful way to view both the structure and function of waterways.[5]

The continuum concept indicates that headwaters have fast-moving water, steep slopes, shaded channels, low temperature, and minimal organic matter stored in sediments. Because water temperature is low and dissolved oxygen concentrations are usually high, oxygen-dependent species such as trout can thrive. Stream-water chemistry is determined predominantly by the chemistry of rainfall and bedrock. Stream organisms use energy from organic material produced outside the stream, usually coarse particulate leaf litter from riparian vegetation.

At the other end of the continuum, large lowland rivers have sluggish flow, mild slopes, channels open to the sky, and a large proportion of organic-rich sediments. These sediments are produced both by upstream biological processing of terrestrial litter (shredding by insects, etc.) and by primary production of aquatic algae and higher plants. Dissolved oxygen concentration is lower because large water bodies have relatively less surface exposure to atmospheric oxygen and because abundant plants and animals use more oxygen than the aquatic plants produce. Intermediate stream reaches have intermediate characteristics, depending on the relative position between headwaters and mouth.

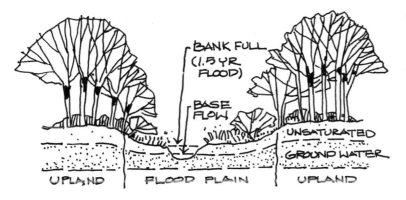

FIGURE 4.4

Cross-section of a riparian forest, showing characteristics of the stream channel, floodplain, and uplands.

(Drawing by Joe McGrane.)

Of course, this simple description is a generalization that will differ from case to case. The manner in which the system changes along the gradient depends on regional and local climate, geology, and the nature of tributaries and long-term human activities.[6] For example, one of the basic premises of the RCC is that the overall influence of the riparian zone decreases as the stream becomes larger and therefore as the volume of water relative to the area covered by riparian vegetation becomes larger. For greenway design, this premise suggests that, in general, a high level of protection for lower-order streams will yield the greatest benefit for the stream network as a whole.

However, this generalization does not hold true universally. For instance, along rivers that have broad floodplains in their lower reaches, riparian forests can be a major source of dissolved organic matter, which is critical to the stream's metabolism. This effect has been documented on the Ogeechee River in the coastal plain of Georgia, where the influence of the riparian forest on metabolic processes increases along downstream reaches.[7] Thus, designers and managers who wish to compare a specific stream with the generalized predictions of the RCC should understand where their case fits into the original theory, as modified by more recent research on specific stream types.

Defining Riparian Corridors

Defining the precise extent of a riparian corridor is not a simple procedure. Each stream system is the result of a combination of many physical, climatic, geological, and biological processes, and no two cases exist in which all the variables are identical. Nor are all variables likely to coincide exactly for a given system; there are no simple lines to be drawn. General principles must be adapted to individual situations to develop accurate descriptions of the systems and to allow formulation of valid design and management proposals.

Defining riparian corridors begins with identifying the corridor's basic geological unit, the floodplain. The floodplain is the area adjacent to the stream channel that is periodically inundated with water (figure 4.4). Although this definition seems simple, there are at least three ways that floodplains are defined in the United States. First, the geomorphic floodplain is the area within which a stream meanders over decades to centuries and is limited by uplands or terraces on either side of the stream. Second, the recurrence-interval floodplain can be defined as the area covered by floods of a certain magnitude likely to recur over the course of a given interval of time (e.g., the 100-year floodplain). Third, a legal floodplain is defined arbitrarily by experience, law, custom, or insurance companies as a riparian area that might be flooded. This last designation may or may not coincide with either geomorphic or recurrence-interval floodplains. The geomorphic definition of floodplain is the most appropriate for designers and environmental managers because it describes the physical extent of the channel, and any structures built in the geomorphic floodplain risk eventual loss (over periods of decades to centuries) due to river meandering and flooding.

At the least, the riparian environment extends from the stream and the floodplain in which it meanders, up the banks of the floodplain and into the transitional area where upland slopes and vegetation begin. Riparian ecosystems have two essential characteristics: laterally flowing water that rises and falls at least once within a growing season and a high degree of connectedness with aquatic and upland ecosystems.[8] The common combination of rich alluvial soils deposited in the riparian zone by floodwaters and a readily available water supply explains the existence of rich vegetation. Riparian ecosystems are subject to constant physical changes as the stream meanders in response to cycles of water flow, bank erosion, and sediment deposition. Not coincidentally, streamside trees have historically provided productive stands for harvesting fuel wood, especially in arid regions, where they might be the only trees in the landscape.

Riparian corridors usually include wetlands, which have characteristic hydrologic properties and vegetation. Because geomorphic floodplains have saturated soils at least part of the year, wetlands tend to form along stream channels. Water and other materials moving from the uplands must traverse these wetlands before entering the stream. True wetlands exist along a moisture gradient from shallow ponds to seasonal standing water to wetland forests that lack standing water but have high water tables.[9] All riparian wetlands carry out to some extent the functions described for riparian corridors in the next section, and all are valuable for maintaining the quality of stream resources.

Riparian Corridor Functions

Defining Water Quality

Water quality is a description of the suitability of water for its intended use, whether by biological communities or by people. It can be expressed quantitatively by physical variables (temperature, velocity, flow regime), chemical variables (pH, alkalinity, and dissolved materials, including nutrients and nonnutrient elements), and biological variables (diversity, abundance and health of organisms, biological productivity, and the presence of pathogenic organisms). The amount, concentration, or magnitude of each variable helps determine overall water quality. Historically, water quality has been defined strictly by physical and chemical characteristics. Although these are important descriptors, they are insufficient to fully describe and understand the ability of water resources to support living systems, including humans. For many purposes, especially biological ones, high-quality water resources are characterized by stable and natural temperature, high oxygen but low nutrient concentrations, pH within a natural range determined by bedrock and soil weathering, and diverse biological communities, including abundant organisms with narrow environmental tolerances (i.e., pollution-sensitive species). Each of these properties is influenced by riparian corridors, which moderate the influence of external factors.

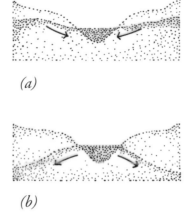

(a)

(b)

FIGURE 4.5

Within a riparian corridor and beyond, the hydrologic relationship between streams and groundwater depends largely on climate. In humid regions or during wet seasons (a) groundwater recharges streams and maintains base flow. In arid environments or during dry seasons (b) stream flow recharges groundwater.

This section outlines the major functions of riparian greenways that relate directly or indirectly to water quality, including hydrologic regulation, filtration of sediment and dissolved nutrients, sediment and erosion control, nutrient removal, regulation of water temperature, and provision of aquatic habitat.

Hydrologic Regulation

Hydrologic regimes—the quantity and timing of stream flow—depend largely on climate and precipitation patterns (figure 4.5). Vegetation also helps control hydrology in several ways. Vegetation throughout a watershed passes moisture to the atmosphere through transpiration. Wetlands and floodplains also provide natural floodwater storage, and their vegetation physically slows the velocity of floodwaters.[10]

The litter and soil associated with riparian vegetation act as sponges to hold water for slow release, creating a stable water supply and aquatic environment. Vegetation retards runoff and increases the rate at which water infiltrates soil. Water then seeps slowly through the soil to the stream to maintain base flow (streamflow during the driest time of the year) and to attenuate peak flows. Without riparian vegetation, the temporary increase in runoff from a watershed during a storm causes a spike in streamflow quantity and velocity, which erodes the channel bank and streambed. However, when riparian vegetation is present it slows the rate at which runoff enters the stream and reduces or prevents such erosion. This process moderates both floods and droughts and is especially important in arid regions, where base flow may depend completely on water stored in the soil profile.[11] The magnitude of moderating effects is directly related to the proportion of watershed covered by, and consequently to the width of, the riparian corridor.

Riparian wetlands perform an especially important role in reducing flood flows because they allow floodwater to spread horizontally, to infiltrate soils, and to be released slowly. After a devastating flood in the greater Boston area in 1968, the U.S. Army Corps of Engineers declared that wetlands in the Charles River watershed should be protected as a nonstructural flood-control alternative (figure 4.6).[12] According to the corps' calculations at the time, if 40 percent of the watershed's wetlands were drained, dikes and dams costing as much as $100 million would have to be built to protect Boston, Cambridge, and other towns along the lower reaches of the Charles.[13] Buying or otherwise protecting the wetlands was estimated to be much less expensive.

Flow in a stream with a riparian forest is more constant but may have lower total annual discharge than one without, because some soil moisture is taken up by vegetation and transpired to

FIGURE 4.6

Wetlands along the Charles River during (a) a period of normal stream flow and (b) after spring flooding. The wetlands were found to be highly effective for flood storage. (Photos courtesy of U.S. Army Corps of Engineers.)

the atmosphere. By retarding flow, vegetation and the litter layer also allow a higher proportion of the water to evaporate than if the runoff were to enter the stream directly.

All of these effects differ greatly between humid and arid areas. In arid landscapes, elimination of woody riparian vegetation and debris may result in the eventual loss of summer streamflow because the water storage capacity of soils is reduced.[14] The age of riparian vegetation can affect hydrologic characteristics of streams in arid areas. Recent studies in Utah have shown that whereas young trees with shallower roots use water that would otherwise support streamflow, mature trees use water from below the active streamflow zone.[15] If this observation holds true in general, newly restored riparian corridors may temporarily reduce stream discharge, but as the vegetation matures, discharge should not only return to the higher levels but also be more constant seasonally because of improved litter and soil conditions.

In humid areas, widespread deforestation around intermittent streams can cause them to become perennial because of the increased water yield during growing seasons; this can increase sediment transport.[16] Greenways in humid regions, however, may have minimal effects on the overall amount of water reaching a stream because riparian vegetation transpires a small percentage of the total groundwater flow. In drier climates, where there is much less groundwater, vegetation along a stream may have a significant effect, even though arid-region plants use little water per unit of biomass.[17]

Sediment and Nutrient Filtration

In many instances, the greatest threats to water quality are excessive inputs of sediment and nutrients from adjacent lands. These and other contaminants can be filtered by vegetative buffers, which can also help to stabilize and reduce erosion of stream banks.

Although all stream segments will benefit from such buffers, protecting greenways along low-order streams may offer the greatest benefits for the stream network as a whole. Human activity in headwaters has a disproportionate influence on downstream areas for several reasons. Because networks of first- to third-order streams comprise about 85 percent of the total length of running waters, they obviously make up the bulk of the stream miles in a given watershed.[18] Because riparian corridors are narrower along headwater streams, upland disturbances are usually closer to the stream. Consequently, the input of contaminants per unit area of the corridor is apt to be greater than in higher-order streams. When contaminated headwater drainage moves downstream, it will inevitably affect lower reaches. If pollutants can be filtered out along headwaters, water-quality benefits for the network as a whole will be substantial.

Sediment and Erosion Control

Upland erosion occurs naturally, but in an undisturbed landscape equilibrium is established between sediment production on the one hand and sediment transport to streams and out of the watershed on the other hand. When upland disturbances cause an excessive amount of material to enter a stream network, sediment can carry excess nutrients to the waterway and smother rocky or gravelly streambeds with silt. Excessive sedimentation blankets the gravel beds in which eggs and young fish develop and destroys habitats for aquatic invertebrates such as insects, crustaceans, and shellfish. Sediment deposited in lakes and reservoirs can degrade water quality and decrease water storage capacity.

Riparian vegetation often filters out upland sediment moving toward streams. The amount of material trapped in the riparian zone can be substantial. For example, the riparian forest of the Little River in Georgia trapped nearly all of the annual sediment yield from an agricultural watershed.[19] Reports of rates of sediment removal as high as 80 or 90 percent are not uncommon (table 4.2), although the distinctly wide range of results indicates that these figures are highly site-specific. Sufficient data have not yet been reported to allow for generalizations.

Most sediment eroded from cultivated fields in a coastal-plain watershed in Maryland was deposited in the forested buffer strip, but significant deposition extended 265 feet (81 m) from the forest-field edge.[20] A much smaller amount of sediment was deposited closer to the stream,

TABLE 4.2 Sediment removal effectiveness of riparian buffer zones.

LOCATION	BUFFER VEGETATION	BUFFER WIDTH (M)	SLOPE (%)	PERCENT REDUCTION[1]	REFERENCE
Pennsylvania	Oats	6	14	76 (by mass)	Hall et al. (1983)
Nebraska	Grass and grass + woody plants	7.5–15.0	6–7	12–82 (by mass) 40–81 (by concentration)	Schmitt et al. (1999)
Connecticut	Grass + woody plants Orchardgrass Grass	30 4.6–9.1 4.6–9.1	5 11–16 3.5	92 11–16 } (by concentration) 66–82	Clausen et al. (2000) Dillaha et al. (1988, 1989) Magette et al. (1989)
Oregon	Not specified	30	Not specified		Moring (1982)
Rocky Mountains	Primary coniferous forest	9	35-55	Nearly all	Haupt (1965)
Maryland	Mixed hardwood forest	265 ft (81m)	2-5	"most"	Lowrance (1988)
North Carolina	Not specified	330 ft (101m)	up to 20	50	Cooper (1987)

[1]Pollutant reduction attributable to buffers is expressed as percent of the pollutant leaving cultivated fields.

Adapted from Wenger, S. (1999). "A review of the scientific literature on riparian buffer width, extent and vegetation." Athens, Office of Public Service and Outreach, Institute of Ecology, University of Georgia; and from Dosskey, M. G. (2001). "Toward quantifying water pollution abatement in response to installing buffers on crop land." *Environmental Management* 28: 577–598, with additions (Moring 1982, Haupt 1965).

suggesting that 265 feet (81 m) would constitute an effective buffer in this case. The surface drainage area of the field was only about 11.4 acres with an average slope of 2–5 percent, and the field was managed with moderate erosion-reduction practices.

In a similar study on the coastal plain of North Carolina, slopes of cultivated fields varied from 0 to 7 percent, and slopes of an uncultivated upland buffer adjacent to the floodplain ranged up to 20 percent. In this case, slightly more than 50 percent of the total sediment was deposited within 330 feet (101 m) of the field-forest boundary.[21] Another 25 percent of the sediment was deposited in a floodplain swamp lateral to the stream channel at various distances from the field-forest boundary.

As a sediment sink, riparian vegetation can be effective for a very long time. In another watershed on the coastal plain of Georgia, the riparian zone has trapped all the sediment eroded from adjacent agricultural fields, plus additional sediment derived from upstream areas, since 1880.[22]

Although riparian wetlands trap sediment, they may retain this material on a time scale of only decades or less.[23] Trapped sediment may eventually be added to streams when floodplains are eroded by moving floodwater, in which case the sediment will be deposited downstream in riparian areas when floods recede. Over tens or hundreds of years, sediment trapped by wetlands is thus removed by the stream at a rate specific to the channel's shape and meander pattern and the stream's discharge and flooding characteristics.

Bank erosion and channel scour (erosion from the stream bottom) are minor sources of sediment when the stream is stable, but they can be important sediment sources where the stream's bottom or banks are unstable.[24] Maintaining stability is largely a matter of maintaining streamside vegetation, of which roots, stems, and foliage are important. Stems and foliage reduce flow velocity, and roots and rhizomes reinforce the soil, particularly the nutrient-rich clays commonly found along stream banks.[25] Riparian vegetation and debris also increase channel roughness and thereby reduce flow velocity and potential energy during periods of elevated discharge.

Invasive Plant Species and Erosion

These crucial functions, however, can be lost when stream banks are colonized by certain invasive species whose presence is harmful to bank structural integrity. One species that is notoriously troublesome almost worldwide—including most of the United States—is Japanese knotweed (*Polygonum cuspidatum* or *Reynoutria japonica*). This extraordinarily fast-spreading weed is adept at colonizing riparian zones (within its climatic range) and displacing the existing vegetation. Its dense growth, both above and below ground, crowds out whatever was growing previously at a site and prevents new vegetation from becoming established. However—and this is where its harm extends beyond the displacement of native species—despite their great density, the rhizomes (roots that can sprout) provide poor erosion control. A typical sight at the waterline of a stream bank covered by knotweed is a mass of sturdy rhizomes in "midair," projecting out over a near-vertical highly eroded bank of bare soil, the rest having been washed away (figure 4.7).

Japanese knotweed can easily colonize new areas vegetatively. That is, a portion of a stem, rhizome, or root can itself grow into a new plant, circumventing the normal process of sexual

FIGURE 4.7

Japanese knotweed, an invasive species, forms dense clumps of vegetation in riparian corridors but actually causes increased erosion because of its sparse root network.

(Photo by D. Smith)

reproduction. A stem or rhizome fragment as small as 0.39 inches (1 cm) long develops into a plant that is a clone of the original plant. This individual is then fully capable of spreading to form an entire colony in a remarkably short time.

It is very easy for Japanese knotweed to spread downstream when such fragments are transported by water. This ability to spread quickly and easily is typical of invasive species, whether they can reproduce vegetatively or not. Like virtually all invasive nonnative species, Japanese knotweed is not harmful in its native range (East Asia), where it is held in check by highly complex, subtle, and little-understood interactions of natural predators, nonlethal pathogens, soil, and climate factors.

Although considerable effort has been expended on the search for methods of controlling Japanese knotweed, no truly feasible method has yet been found, nor is one likely for many years. Mechanical removal (cutting, mowing, hand-pulling) is almost never feasible because it must be done with a frequency far beyond the capacity of any land management team, while the herbicides known to be effective are highly toxic and for the most part banned by federal law for use near bodies of water. Research into biological controls such as natural insect predators is only in its infancy. Still, along the Sandy River in Oregon, a team of Nature Conservancy employees dedicated specifically to weed management has successfully eradicated knotweed through labor-intensive manual and chemical methods. The team has also conducted community outreach and education, led volunteer and youth work parties, and trained local land managers about the threat and management of invasive species in the region.[26]

The Sandy River example demonstrates what those involved in combating invasive species have come to recognize in recent years: that the future of invasive species management, given its enormous cost and logistical difficulties, lies in coordination among agencies and stakeholders, many of which are not normally associated with one another. To this end, the National Invasive

Species Council was created by an Executive Order of President Clinton in 1999 with the purpose of coordinating invasive species activities among a wide range of federal agencies.

It should be pointed out that stream-bank erosion is not the only type of harm that waterside invasives can cause. The harm caused by one of the most prominent invaders of wetlands, *Phragmites communis*, is not erosion, but rather the filling-in of wetlands, especially estuarine, and associated loss of habitat and consequent far-reaching ecosystem effects.

There are scores of harmful invasive species in North America but not all are harmful everywhere on the continent, nor are all invasive species nonnative. Phragmites, for example, is native to North America, but closely related subspecies have been introduced from overseas, and these subspecies are believed to be the aggressive invaders in the northeastern United States.

Some non-native species have been introduced along watercourses specifically for the purpose of preventing erosion. Yet in some cases these have spread to other sites where they harmed ecosystems in other ways. Thus, species may be valuable for bio-remediation in one site while being an unforeseen invader in other sites.

The connectivity provided by a stream and its corridor, then, is not always a good thing. In fact, stream corridors are, in general, major vectors for the spread of invasive plant species.[27] In this way, invasive species can reach relatively undisturbed areas: they are first introduced by humans to disturbed sites, where they easily establish, and from there they can spread downstream to less-disturbed areas—a prime example of an indirect effect that anthropogenic development can have beyond just the development site itself.

Removal of Nutrients and Pollutants

To understand how riparian vegetation filters out excess nutrients, it is first important to consider the ways in which nutrients move through biological systems, known as nutrient cycling. Six elements—carbon, hydrogen, oxygen, nitrogen, phosphorus, and sulfur—comprise about 95 percent of all living biomass and as such are essential nutrients for life. Because they are so important and occur in such large quantities, they are called macronutrients. Many other elements, including calcium, potassium, and iron, are also essential for life processes but are needed in smaller amounts; these are called micronutrients.

All nutrient elements cycle through living and nonliving components of ecosystems. Inorganic, mineral forms are necessary for plant growth and are used to create organic compounds that are the basis for all living tissue in plants and animals. Nutrients in excreted organic waste and dead organic matter must be converted back to mineral forms (mineralized) before they are available again to plants. Microorganisms execute the important chemical transformations of decomposition and mineralization, converting biologically unavailable forms of nutrients to available forms. If there is an inadequate supply of any one of these essential elements for a particular organism, its growth and health will be limited. Thus, the biological production of entire ecosystems, beginning with photosynthetic plants, can be limited by the lack of availability of a specific element. In particular, the availability of nitrogen and phosphorus has been shown to limit primary production in most ecosystems. Phosphorus is often a limiting nutrient in freshwater systems in northern temperate areas, and both phosphorus and nitrogen limit production in terrestrial and marine ecosystems. Many freshwater systems in midlatitude and subtropical areas, in more arid regions such as prairies and deserts, and at high altitudes are nitrogen-limited, at least for part of the year.[28] Phosphorus is generally the least available of all the macronutrients because it has no gaseous component in its cycle but is added to ecosystems only from rock and soil weathering or from human sources. Phosphorus control is also less expensive than nitrogen control and has been the focus of most eutrophication modeling and abatement planning.[29]

Ecosystems can be damaged by excess levels of nutrients, too—even the so-called "limiting" nutrients that are usually in short supply. There can be too much of a good thing. For example, cultural eutrophication is a common problem marked by the enrichment of water bodies by increased nutrient input from human activities. Eutrophication causes unfavorable changes in the composition of aquatic plant communities, reduction of the diversity of the aquatic biota, unpleasant odors and tastes, and even human health problems. Eutrophication is usually the result of excessive nitrogen or phosphorus input from sewage disposal, agricultural fertilizers, or erosion. To reduce cultural eutrophication, nutrient input to the water body must be limited.

The manipulation of ecosystem production by controlling production-limiting elements is often an objective of environmental management. If the goal is to preserve clean water, then biological production should be maintained at natural levels by reducing the excess, anthropogenic input of limiting nutrients. The natural rate of production, and its controls, can be determined by research on each system that is subject to management.

Nutrient elements occur in both particulate and dissolved forms. Inorganic silt and clay particles have large surface areas on which nutrient molecules attach, and water is a strong solvent for many nutrient-bearing compounds. Nutrients may enter a riparian zone by any of four main pathways: bound to sediment particles that are suspended in water flowing from upland, dissolved in water (that is, not bound to sediment particles), directly from the atmosphere, or from plant and animal matter that physically moves into the riparian zone, such as leaf litter or animal droppings. The quantity of nutrients in the bound and dissolved forms in most cases is greater, and poses greater threats to stream ecosystem health, than do the nutrients from the atmosphere and plant/animal matter.

Once nutrients have entered the riparian corridor, they may undergo any one of four possible fates. They may (1) flow directly into the stream or (2) be converted into their gaseous form and released into the atmosphere through the metabolic activity of soil microorganisms. If they are to remain in the buffer zone, the nutrients must either (3) bind to soil particles, in the process known as sorption, and be taken up by roots and incorporated into plant biomass, or (4) along with the sediment particles that carried them there, settle out of the water that flowed into the riparian zone. Of these four pathways, release into the atmosphere is in principle the most desirable, because within the scale of a given riparian ecosystem, the atmosphere can be considered a bottomless sink: it is capable of absorbing all the nutrients soil microorganisms can convert to gaseous form. This is in contrast to the other three processes, all of which can reach saturation points beyond which no more nutrients will be removed from the runoff. In practice, however, of the two nutrients that are of greatest concern in runoff, nitrogen can be converted to its gaseous form by soil microorganisms, but phosphorus cannot.

In most cases where careful measurements have been made, nearly all phosphorus and much nitrogen in surface runoff are attached to sediment, especially clays.[30] Substantial amounts of nutrients in surface runoff can therefore be removed by slowing down surface runoff with riparian vegetation, which allows the sediment to settle out of the runoff. Vegetation and soil can filter as much as 99 percent of total phosphorus mass and 10–60 percent of total nitrogen.[31] Denitrification, the process by which bacteria convert belowground nitrogen to its gaseous form and release it to the atmosphere, is another important mechanism for nutrient filtering that can increase the total percentage of nitrogen removed from groundwater.[32] This process requires anaerobic conditions (i.e., a lack of free, molecular oxygen) and occurs most efficiently in soils that undergo periodic flooding and drying, such as in riparian areas.[33] The exact percentage of nutrients removed by a buffer shows considerable variation, depending on the site slope, buffer width, type and density of vegetation and soil microorganisms, soil chemical and physical properties, and runoff velocity (table 4.3).

Riparian vegetation, especially woody trees and shrubs, also removes nutrients from shallow groundwater flow.[34] Nitrogen dissolved in groundwater can be a major input to streams.[35] Nitrogen can be controlled either by reducing inputs from upland sources or by maintaining riparian vegetation. Uptake by vegetation is especially important in watersheds that have permeable soils overlying impermeable material (subsoil or bedrock) because groundwater will remain in or near the zone where roots can absorb nutrients. This situation exists in the Little River in Georgia,[36] where woody vegetation removed six times as much nitrogen as was exported to the stream.

In a coastal-plain agricultural watershed in Maryland, 61 percent of the nitrogen input to a riparian forest was via groundwater.[37] Eighty-nine percent of the groundwater nitrogen (54 percent of the total input) was removed by the riparian forest. One-third of this amount was retained by vegetation, and two-thirds was lost to the atmosphere by denitrification. Because most phosphorus occurs in particulate form, 94 percent of the phosphorus input to the forest was through surface runoff, of which the riparian vegetation retained 80 percent (or 75 percent of the total input). Other studies in the coastal plain of the southeastern United States have demonstrated that similar proportions of nutrients leaving cropland areas were removed in riparian areas.[38]

Wetlands can also filter out excess nutrients but are much more variable in this respect than riparian forests. Although wetlands almost always function as sediment sinks, at least over fairly short time scales (years or decades), they can serve as either sources or sinks of nitrogen, phosphorus, and other nutrients. Even when soil-bound phosphorus is retained in wetland sediments, it may later be released in soluble forms. The filtration capacity of wetlands will depend on their particular hydrological, chemical, and biological characteristics; determinations should therefore be made case by case.

Riparian forests retain other nutrients and contaminants such as calcium, potassium, magnesium, and lead.[39] When pollutants such as these enter a stream not from a single location such as an industrial plant but from the runoff of pavement, lawns, and agriculture, they are known as *nonpoint source pollutants.* Field studies in northern Virginia showed that 85–95 percent of the lead in nonpoint urban runoff is trapped with bulk sediment in riparian zones.[40] Riparian vegetation can also filter oils and other pollutants such as pesticides and herbicides.

TABLE 4.3 Nutrient and pollutant removal effectiveness of riparian buffer zones.

COMPONENT	LOCATION	VEGETATION	BUFFER WIDTH (M)	SLOPE (%)	SOIL TEXTURE[2]	REDUCTION BY MASS (%)[3]	REDUCTION BY CONCENTRATIONS (%)	REFERENCE
N[1]	various	various	4.6–60	various	various	0–99		various
P[1]	various	various	4.6–30	various	various	0–79		various
bromide	northeast US	grass and grass + woody plants	7.5–15.9	6–16	SiL-SiCl	0–25	0–14	Schmitt et al. (1999)
chloride	Finland	grass and grass + woody plants	10	>10	C-CL		50	Uusi-Kämppä et al. (2000), Uusi-Kämppä and Yläranta (1996)
herbicide	various	various	6–15.7	6–14	various	0–91		various
pesticide	northeast US	grass and grass + woody plants	7.5–15.8	6–15	SiL-SiCl	0–80	25-73	Schmitt et al. (1999)

[1] Values represent the ranges of approximately 55 published studies of either N or P removal. Various forms of N and P have different ecosystem functions and reveal different aspects of ecosystem health. Therefore, the table should be understood primarily as an indication that nutrient and pollutant removal has been documented and not as a source of generalizable results. N was assessed in one or more of the following forms: total N, nitrate (in soil pore water, in groundwater, or not specified), total Kjeldahl N, ammonium, or particulate organic N. P was assessed in one or more of the following forms: total P, bioavailable P, or dissolved P. Buffer width, slope, soil type, and vegetation varied considerably among the studies.

[2] Soil texture classes: SiCL = silty clay loam; SiL = silt loam; CL = clay loam; C = clay.

[3] These authors also reported instances where buffered streams had *more* of the nutrient or pollutant than did non-buffered streams. This is believed to have been caused by pollutants that were trapped by the buffers in the past, before the respective studies were conducted, and then released by the buffer into the stream during rainfall*. This time lag highlights the importance of long-term stream buffer research that incorporates measures taken at various intervals instead of 'single-snapshot' studies.

*Coyne, M. S., R. A. Gilfillen, A. Vallalba, Z. Zhang, R. Rhodes, L. Dunn, and R. L. Blevins. 1998. Fecal bacteria trapping by grass filter strips during simulated rain. *Journal of Soil and Water Conservation* 53:140–145; Magette, W. L., R. B. Brinsfield, R. E. Palmer, and J. D. Wood. 1989. Nutrient and sediment removal by vegetated filter strips. *Transactions, American Society of Agricultural Engineers* 32:663–667.

Sources: Adapted from Dosskey, M. G. (2001). "Toward quantifying water pollution abatement in response to installing buffers on crop land." *Environmental Management* 28: 577–598; Hickey, M. B. C., and B. Doran. (2004). "A review of the efficiency of buffer strips for the maintenance and enhancement of riparian ecosystems." *Water Quality Research Journal of Canada* 39: 311–317; and Wenger, S. (1999). "A review of the scientific literature on riparian buffer width, extent and vegetation." Athens, Office of Public Service and Outreach, Institute of Ecology, University of Georgia.

Recent research has shown that riparian buffers are capable of removing a substantial portion of such contaminants, frequently more than 50 percent and in some cases as much as 90 percent, by either containing them in the soil or sequestering them in plant tissue.[41] The plants themselves are not harmed because the compounds are diluted to nontoxic concentrations, bound to sites in plant tissues where they cause no further harm, chemically detoxified by enzymes or other means, or diffused into the atmosphere.[42]

The effectiveness of riparian buffers in removing pollutants depends on a host of factors, foremost among them the chemical characteristics of the compound, soil properties, buffer width, and runoff rate. The body of published research on the effectiveness of riparian buffers in removing particular contaminants is rather smaller than that for nitrogen, phosphorus, and sediment, because there is a great variety of pesticides and herbicides, all with different properties, and these chemicals are found in acutely high quantity only in agricultural runoff, whereas nitrogen and phosphorus are ubiquitous and can pose problems in any ecosystem affected by human activity.

Seasonal growth patterns of riparian vegetation in the temperate zone can control the timing, composition, and concentration of the input of excessive nutrients and sediment to waterways. Nitrogen is taken up by riparian forests in summer and released in the fall and early spring, rather than during the peak summer growing season.[43] In addition to any net retention of nutrients, the release of nutrients after the growing season means that primary production in the stream may not increase appreciably. Instead, excess nutrients flow downstream and will thus affect receiving water bodies, but not the stream segment in question.

Although the information in this section is complex, it is clear that riparian forests can be effective filters for most sediment and nutrients that flow from uphill land uses. The filtration capacity is determined both by the slope and width of the floodplain and by the nature of the riparian vegetation, including density, successional stage, and seasonal variation of growth and senescence. Wider, denser riparian forests filter better than narrow, sparse ones, and fast-growing, early successional vegetation will absorb more nutrients than mature forests.

Regulation of Water Temperature

Temperature is an important water-quality characteristic. Higher water temperature reduces the capacity of water to carry oxygen and, in turn, to decompose organic material and waste and to support aquatic organisms. Many desirable game fish, especially most species of trout, require cool water

FIGURE 4.8

Streamside forests help maintain low water temperatures by producing shade.

(Photo by D. Smith.)

temperatures and are excluded from streams that are too warm. Higher temperatures also increase the release rate of nutrients from accumulated sediment. For example, slight increases in temperature above 59°F produce substantial increases in the release of sedimentary phosphorus.[44]

Riparian vegetation, especially when directly adjacent to the stream channel, prevents temperature extremes by shading the water surface in summer[45] (see figure 4.8). Thus, in the northern hemisphere, vegetation on the southern bank of a stream is more important for this purpose than vegetation on the northern bank.[46] Within and beyond the riparian corridor, vegetation also increases infiltration and the water storage capacity of soils, which help keep water temperature in streams lower in warm seasons.

Because of their increased infiltration and storage capacity, wider greenways will usually maintain lower water temperatures than narrower corridors. When groundwater input forms a significant amount of stream discharge, water temperatures will be more stable because

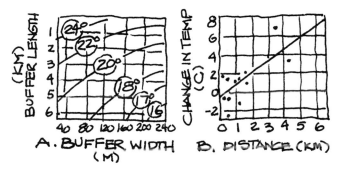

FIGURE 4.9

(a) Relationships among buffer width, buffer length, and stream water temperature from an empirical model based on data from southern Ontario streams. (b) Relationship between stream water temperature and distance below intact riparian forest. (Redrawn from Barton, D. R., W. D. Taylor, and R. M. Biette. [1985]. "Dimensions of riparian buffer strips required to maintain trout habitat in southern Ontario streams." *North American Journal of Fisheries Management* 5: 364–378, with permission of American Fisheries Society.)

groundwater temperature is often constant and equal to the annual mean air temperature.[47] This temperature stability may be especially present in small streams, whose lowest flows are sustained solely by groundwater (base flow). In all streams, the distance that a protected corridor extends upstream will have a major influence on water temperature at a particular location.

Because of their low water volume, temperatures of small headwater streams are also greatly influenced by changes in solar radiation.[48] Headwater temperatures are thus easy to control with streamside vegetation.[49] Larger, wider streams, although they have proportionally smaller shaded areas, are usually less affected by solar radiation because greater water flow and volume offset surface temperature increases.[50] Low-gradient streams are exceptions to this generalization because water residence time in the channel is longer and the daily variation of water temperature can be substantial.[51]

For very small streams, the density of vegetation, and thus its ability to produce shade, is the only characteristic of the riparian vegetation important in its ability to control temperature.[52] In these cases only, the overall width of riparian corridors is not important for temperature control as long as the density of vegetation is high.

However, along larger streams (second- and third-order) near Toronto, Ontario, both the length and width of riparian corridors influenced summer water temperature to the extent that important fish species were excluded from streams with narrow or fragmented corridors.[53] Brook, brown, and rainbow trout do not occur in the Ontario streams with an average summer temperature higher than 72°F. Thus, maintenance of low water temperature is an important management objective. Figure 4.9a, a contour plot of stream temperatures in this case, indicates that narrower buffers must extend farther upstream to maintain stream water temperature at a desired level. As figure 4.9b shows, where downstream areas are exposed, water temperature rises about 1.5°C per kilometer downstream from the end of the riparian forest. When width and extension upstream are considered together, a linear extrapolation of stream water temperature may present a guide for determining the minimum width of a riparian forest: "An unbroken buffer extending 3 km upstream of a site need only be 10 m wide to produce a maximum weekly temperature of less than 22°C."[54]

The authors of the study caution that the extrapolation may not be appropriate beyond their study site or to other environments and that it is valid only if stream water temperature less than 72°F is the sole management objective. Furthermore, fish distribution in other parts of the world may be constrained by temperatures that are lower or higher than 72°F. Nonetheless, this study indicates the sort of useful guidelines that can be derived from local or regional research programs.

TABLE 4.4 Effectiveness of riparian buffer zones for protection of floral and faunal community structure.
The first section refers to studies that compared riparian zones in which clearing or timber harvest was conducted up to the stream against control sites in which there was no clearing/harvest either streamside or upland. In the second section, buffer zones that were protected from adjacent clearing/harvest are compared against undisturbed control sites.

LOCATION	UPLAND TREATMENT	BUFFER WIDTH	INDICATOR	PERCENT OF INDICATOR REMAINING AFTER REMOVAL OF RIPARIAN COVER, AS COMPARED TO UNDISTURBED SITE	EFFECTIVENESS OF BUFFER (PERCENT OF INDICATOR REMAINING IN BUFFER PROTECTED FROM ADJACENT CLEARING/TIMBER HARVEST, AS COMPARED TO UNDISTURBED CONTROL SITES)	COMMENTS	REFERENCE
\multicolumn{8}{Comparisons between riparian zones subjected to clearing/timber harvesting and undisturbed control sites}
Ontario	Timber harvest	No buffer; all riparian cover removed	Small woody debris	10%			France et al. (1996)
Washington	Timber harvest	No buffer; all riparian cover removed	Small woody debris	~10%			Bilby and Bisson (1992)
Alaska	Timber harvest	No buffer; all riparian cover removed	Small woody debris	~10%			Duncan and Brusven (1985)
British Columbia	Timber harvest	No buffer; all riparian cover removed	Fish density	25%		Population recovered after streamside revegetation	Young et al. (1999)
\multicolumn{8}{Comparisons between protected riparian buffer zones adjacent to clearing/timber harvesting and buffer zones adjacent to undisturbed control sites}
Pacific Northwest	NA; does not affect LWD	1 tree length	Large woody debris		"Most"	Most LWD came from within 1 tree length of stream	Robinson and Beschta (1990)
Cascade Mountains, Oregon	NA; does not affect LWD	1 tree length	Large woody debris		"Most"	Most LWD came from within 1 tree length of stream	Van Sickle and Gregory (1990)
Washington and Oregon	NA	30 m	Large woody debris		85%		McDade et al. (1990)
Washington and Oregon	NA	30 m	Large woody debris		<50%		McDade et al. (1990)
Alberta	None	40 m	Vegetation community		Nearly all		Harper and MacDonald (2001)
Maine	Timber harvest	80 m	Shrub density		Shrub density greater in buffer than in control		Johnson and Brown (1990)
Maine	Timber harvest	80 m	Tree and snag density		Tree & snag density lower in buffer than in control		Johnson and Brown (1990)
Quebec, mature balsam fir forest	Timber harvest	20 m, 40 m	Shrub stem density		Shrub density greater in buffer than in control	20-m buffer had higher shrub density than 40-m buffer	Darveau et al. (1995)

		35–80 m	Stream shading		60–80%		Brazier and Brown (1973)
		75–125 m	Stream shading		60–80%		Steinblums et al. (1984)
Wyoming	Not tested	Not a study of buffer width	Fish abundance		See comment	Density of bank cover correlated with fish population	Wesche et al. (1987)
Maine	Timber harvest	80 m	Bird density and richness		Bird density lower in buffer than in control		Johnson and Brown (1990)
Newfoundland, balsam fir forest	Timber harvest	20-50 m	Bird abundance		Disturbance-tolerant species more abundant; disturbance-sensitive species less abundant		Whitaker and Montevecchi (1999)
Quebec, balsam fir forest	Timber harvest	20 m	Bird density: ubiquitous species		No change		Darveau et al. (1995)
Quebec, balsam fir forest	Timber harvest	60 m	Bird density: forest-interior species		Little change		Darveau et al. (1995)
Ontario, game preserve	Timber harvest	60 m	Moose density		> 100%	In winter, moose preferred harvest adjacent buffers over natural areas. No preference in summer.	Brusnyk and Gilbert (1983)
Quebec, balsam fir forest	Timber harvest	20, 40, 60 m	Small mammal abundance		No difference among the widths		Darveau et al. (1995)

NA = not available. LWD = large woody debris.

Riparian Corridors and Aquatic Habitat

Many structural, hydrologic, and water-quality processes that are influenced by riparian vegetation have, in turn, a direct influence on stream organisms and communities (table 4.4). Streamside vegetation is essential to aquatic life because, in addition to the functions described earlier, it stabilizes and contributes to the diversity of stream habitat. Fallen trees, branches, and root masses that come from the riparian area establish pools, waterfalls, and riffles (figure 4.10), and standing trees stabilize banks.[55] Diverse habitats produced by the debris give rise to greater diversity of aquatic organisms.[56] Material that falls into streams and vegetation along the bank provides a diversity of cover. Most aquatic insects are directly or indirectly dependent on riparian vegetation at some stage in their life cycle.[57] Removal of streamside vegetation, though, is not synonymous with destruction of habitat for macroinvertebrates: Carlson et al.[58] and Noel et al.[59] found population densities to be higher in logged than in unlogged riparian areas, presumably due to increased light availability. Newbold et al. found no difference in densities of macroinvertebrate populations in buffers more than 98 feet (30 m) wide, but species diversity decreased in buffers less than 98 feet.[60]

In addition, the more a stream meanders, the more diverse are the aquatic habitats available

FIGURE 4.10

Pools and riffles created by fallen trees are crucial to establishing diverse aquatic habitats.

(Photo by D. Smith.)

to stream organisms.[61] As the diversity of bottom types, water depths, and water velocity increases, fish diversity increases.[62]

Forests adjacent to streams are also a major source of food energy for aquatic organisms. In forested watersheds, more than 99 percent of the energy in the stream food web may originate in the forest adjacent to streams.[63] Along headwater streams, riparian vegetation is especially critical as an energy source. Large, woody debris from riparian forests forms dams that impede downstream movement of organic matter in both headwater and higher-order streams, thereby providing a reliable, year-round food supply.[64] Young et al. reported that fish abundance along streams whose riparian zones were harvested for timber decreased 75 percent but recovered when the vegetative cover returned.

A rich and diverse population of aquatic organisms develops when there is a diversity of food sources in the riparian vegetation.[65] Herbaceous ground cover is high in nutrient content and is consumed by organisms as soon as it falls into the stream. Leaves from deciduous shrubs and trees are higher in fiber content and take 60–90 days after entering the stream to be used fully by the organisms. Coniferous leaves take 180–200 days to be processed. Stems and trunks that enter the stream constitute a long-term nutrient reserve for a stream's food chain. Healthy and diverse riparian vegetation thus provides a dependable supply of food throughout the year. Research has shown, though, that these functions will be compromised if buffer width is reduced. For example, in Washington and Oregon streams studied by McDade et al., quantities of large woody debris entering streams with buffers of 98 feet (30 m) were 85 percent those of intact streams, while buffers less than 33 feet (10 m) had less than 50 percent of control levels of large woody debris.[66]

Habitat fragmentation, the focus of much attention for terrestrial species, can also be a major threat to the integrity of aquatic ecosystems. Through the impacts described earlier, excessive alteration of uplands and riparian vegetation can reduce the movement of fish and other aquatic organisms upstream and downstream. Extreme changes in water quality caused by urban and agricultural development have been shown to isolate populations in stream networks.[67] Like terrestrial animals, some aquatic species cannot tolerate these changes, whereas others can. In addition to providing habitat, intact and continuous riparian corridors maintain connectivity and movement pathways for aquatic organisms.

Factors Influencing Buffer Effectiveness

A host of factors influences the effectiveness of buffers for sediment, nutrient, and pollutant abatement (table 4.5). In broad terms, these factors may be properties of the geography and topography of the landscape and buffer zone, the hydrologic dynamics, the runoff itself, the soil, or the biota. As discussed earlier, floodplain width is a crucial factor, since a buffer narrower than the floodplain will not be able to contain the water of severe floods.

With steep slopes in either the watershed as a whole or the riparian corridor, the runoff travels through the riparian zone with higher velocity and there is less time for sediment to settle out and for nutrients to bind to soil particles and be assimilated by roots. Thus the sediment and nutrients are more likely to enter the stream channel.

Land use in the watershed also affects runoff speed and timing, because rain water runs quickly off pavement and buildings—known collectively as impervious surfaces—instead of being absorbed and slowly released by vegetated soils. In this regard, lawns are not much better for stream ecosystem health than impervious surface: the rate at which rainwater infiltrates lawns is low, so there is considerable runoff, which usually contains herbicides, pesticides, and fertilizers.

Watershed size is sometimes believed to affect the nutrient and sediment load on riparian buffers, but this has not been conclusively proven. Although it may seem intuitively logical that larger watersheds would create larger inputs, there is evidence to refute this. It has been observed that in large watersheds, nutrients and sediment from distant sources do not necessarily reach the riparian zone.[68]

Buffer width is of prime importance to buffer effectiveness, as seen throughout this section in the discussions of empirical research that relates buffer width to ecosystem function. We will discuss the question of how to determine the necessary width for any particular riparian greenway later in this chapter.

Hydrologic processes affect buffer effectiveness in that erosion and sedimentation are directly controlled by runoff velocity, which is a function of slope and surface roughness. Faster runoff has higher erosive energy and carries more sediment; a wider buffer is therefore required to effectively filter the runoff. Furthermore, flow intensity is subject to spatial and temporal variation. Filtration and storage capacity of riparian corridors is greatest where runoff is spread evenly in sheet flow. Most surface runoff (and sediment), however, is routed through swales, gullies, and rills, where flow is concentrated during rainstorms.[69] Flow concentration is even more likely in arid regions

TABLE 4.5 Summary of factors that determine buffer effectiveness.

FACTOR	ECOSYSTEM COMPONENT OF WHICH IT IS A PROPERTY
Sediment, nutrient, and pollutant input rate	Runoff
Sediment, nutrient, and pollutant concentration	Runoff
Sediment particle size	Runoff
Vegetation type	Biotic community
Rainfall, amount and intensity	Climate
Overland flow intensity, speed, or volume	Hydrology
Infiltration rate (permeability)	Soil
Soil moisture content; water holding capacity	Soil
Soil: other (redox potential, pH, temperature)	Soil
Soil adsorption capacity	Soil
Slope of contributing area	Topography
Floodplain width	Topography
Catchment size	Topography
Land use	Human activity

and in rough terrain, where uncommon but severe storms are the norm and where the landscape is especially susceptible to uneven erosional patterns.[70]

Characteristics of the substances in the runoff also influence buffer effectiveness. The overland distance required for sediment to be deposited from runoff varies according to particle-size distribution. As water velocity slows, larger particles drop from suspension before smaller particles. Consequently, narrow riparian corridors may be able to trap sand but not silts or clays. Floodplain swamps provide the best opportunity for clay deposition because water velocity slows to nearly zero and water is resident in the swamp long enough for the fine clay particles to settle out of suspension.[71]

The effectiveness of a buffer depends in great measure on the chemical and physical characteristics of its soil. The permeability, or rate at which water infiltrates the soil, is quantified in terms of the *saturated hydraulic conductivity*. *Water holding capacity* determines how much moisture the soil is able to contain. The capacity of a soil for binding compounds and thereby removing them from the runoff is measured by the *adsorption capacity*. Other chemical properties, such as temperature, pH, and *redox potential* (the affinity of a substance for negative electrical charges; in practical terms, a measure of the degree of aeration), can be used to predict a soil's ability to bind compounds and support reactions such as denitrification.

Finally, the vegetation is another determinant of buffer effectiveness. Different species or communities will take up different nutrients at different rates. Their ability to retard flow rates depends on the nature of above- and belowground structures—the quantity and size of roots and stems.

Vegetation reduces flow velocity and therefore enhances sediment filtration as long as the vegetation is tall enough not to be submerged or bent in the current.[72] Riparian areas can be effective sediment filters over long periods of time because of natural changes in the plant community from year to year. For example, in experimental riparian areas in the White Mountains in New Hampshire, sediments do not clog loose surface litter, nor do they decrease filtration efficiency, because leaf fall forms a fresh litter surface annually.[73] Some species are capable of sequestering or detoxifying pollutants, while others are damaged by the contaminants. The vegetation that traps contaminants before they reach streams may eventually be compromised by its own effectiveness if too great a quantity of contaminants accumulates. The most obvious problem is that riparian vegetation may be damaged by sediment that contains salts, heavy metals, and other hazardous chemicals. An enormous body of literature exists on the effects of pollutants on plants. Although little of the research has consisted specifically of in situ trials of plants in riparian zones, it is likely that plants are harmed, biological productivity is impaired, and trapping efficiency is consequently reduced in areas where pollutant concentrations are high.

In principle, the capacity of riparian corridor vegetation to block nutrients from reaching the stream by incorporating them into biomass could be limited by the amount of biomass the buffer zone is physically capable of supporting.[74] Before that limit is reached, the plants continue to incorporate incoming nutrients into increasing quantities of biomass. But when that limit is reached, there will be no net nutrient uptake until disturbance—whether natural, as in the form of tree mortality due to hurricanes, or human, as in tree removal—allows for new biomass to be produced.

Over many years, intercepted nutrients eventually find their way into the stream through groundwater or are washed downstream by bank erosion.[75] Much of this nutrient input, however, will be in the form of organic debris, which serves as food for many aquatic organisms and is less likely to cause eutrophication than dissolved inorganic nutrients, which are readily available to plants.

Riparian forests may be seasonally ineffective at filtering materials when plant growth does not coincide with pulses of runoff-borne pollution. For example, road salting occurs in northern temperate climates in the winter and contributes significant material to streams. When combined with snowmelt, large storm events result in elevated runoff and stream discharges in early spring before riparian forests have begun to take up nutrients. As noted previously, although early spring discharge does not coincide with periods of aquatic growth, these nutrients could still affect downstream reaches later in the season.

Some of these problems can be solved by management strategies designed to remove accumulated materials. Selective tree harvesting and sediment removal in areas of concentrated deposition have effectively mitigated these problems in several cases, mostly in the southeastern United States.[76] These practices removed nutrients in several watersheds in the Atlantic coastal plain for at least twenty-three years of similar land use and cropping patterns.[77] Harvesting should be carefully timed and executed to avoid adverse effect on the riparian zone's capability to control nonpoint source pollution. Only mature trees should be harvested, and this should be done during dry periods to minimize soil disturbance. If vegetation remains in an active growth phase and the composition of the trapped sediment is not toxic, then the riparian forest should be a sustainable, effective nutrient and sediment filter.

Effects of Human Activities on Riparian Corridors

Waterways and riparian ecosystems have been critical resources for nearly every culture in the world, past and present.[78] Just as predictable as the location of human activity along rivers have been the effects of this activity on aquatic ecosystems. The major human activities that affect water quality and the ecological integrity of riparian corridors are agriculture, urbanization, forestry, transportation, recreation, flood control, and withdrawals for water supply. Each activity has a characteristic set of negative consequences, some of which may be ameliorated by maintaining or restoring natural riparian vegetation.

The flow of materials into streams can either be concentrated at a single spot (point source) or be spread across a wide area (nonpoint source). Discharges from sewage treatment plants, storm sewers, and waste pipes are examples of the former. These point sources of contaminants can be controlled with engineering solutions, but riparian vegetation does not have much effect on them. Some authorities believe that half of the pollution of surface waters in the United States comes from point sources.[79] Most human activities also provide nonpoint sources of contaminants. These sources are much more difficult to control because there are no single points at which they enter streams. The best method of nonpoint source control is to eliminate contaminants at their source through effective land-use planning in upland areas. But where the sources do exist, a buffer of intact riparian vegetation can be a very effective second line of defense.

Agriculture

The federal Clean Water Act of 1972, along with more recent amendments, has resulted in enormous investments in cleaning up the nation's waterways. Most of the effort has been spent on controlling municipal and industrial effluents, which are usually point sources. These programs have success stories, such as the restoration of Lake Erie[80] and Lake Washington in Seattle.[81] But despite three decades of action, most of the surface waters of the nation continue to suffer from degraded water quality. Although atmospheric deposition, deforestation, and increasing human and domestic animal populations all contribute to nonpoint nutrient loading of aquatic systems, agriculture probably has the greatest influence of all human activities.[82]

Agricultural practices remove natural vegetation, manipulate and transport soils, introduce fertilizers and toxic chemicals as insecticides and herbicides, and generally change the structure and processes of both terrestrial and aquatic communities. Nutrients in fertilizers applied to the land and not taken up by crops eventually end up in surface-water runoff or in groundwater. Moist and fertile soil conditions have made riparian corridors productive areas for agriculture. Consequently, once continuous corridors are often fragmented by croplands. When bottomland areas are converted to agriculture, a twofold detrimental impact occurs downstream. Sediment and nutrient inputs from the surrounding landscape are increased, and the filtering capability of the remaining riparian forest is diminished because of clearing.[83]

Livestock

In the arid West, riparian corridors often provide the only oases for livestock in an otherwise inhospitable landscape. They offer a reliable supply of water, plentiful vegetation, and more shelter than surrounding dry areas. However, livestock congregate in riparian areas for extended periods, trampling stream banks and often eating most of the vegetation.[84] Stream banks and floodplains erode rapidly when trampled and stripped of vegetation, and this erosion in turn degrades the stream's ecological integrity by the processes described earlier. Degraded riparian vegetation is unable to trap sediments and nutrients in runoff and is unable to diffuse flood energy, which leads to still more erosion. The stream then deposits more sediment into receiving lakes and reservoirs. Lacking healthy vegetation and stream structure, the corridor loses its capacity to hold water, and the local water table is lowered. In arid areas, a stream may then change from perennial to intermittent, and the stream may dry completely in the summer months. Livestock in both arid and humid regions also add additional waste and thus excess nutrients to the stream. The composite effect can be devastating to the stream, its water quality, biota, and terrestrial wildlife as well as to ecosystems and land uses downstream.[85]

Channelization

Flood-control programs during the past century resulted in the channelization (straightening and deepening) of many streams in the United States, with the objective of facilitating runoff and lowering groundwater levels. The question of whether channelization has yielded flood-control benefits is controversial, but the consensus among biologists is that channelization is an ecological disaster.[86] Channelization reduces the length of streams and the area covered by riparian vegetation. The effects of upstream channelization can ultimately neutralize many efforts to filter sediment, showing the importance of comprehensive watershed management.

One of the best documented examples of channelization effects is Florida's Kissimmee River. J. R. Karr described the primary effects of channelization as follows:[87]

- Transformation of the river from a 103-mile (166-km) meandering channel to 56 miles (90 km) of wide, deep channel that is almost useless as a biological system.
- Lowering of the water table because of increased drainage and the consequent loss of water to most of the floodplain wetlands.
- Degradation of the remaining wetlands because seasonal flow no longer floods previously wet areas.
- Alteration of high and low seasonal flow patterns so that during periods of low flow the channelized system acts more like a reservoir than a river.
- Reduced complexity of both terrestrial and wetland plant communities and thus diminished habitat for both terrestrial animals and fish.

Stream channelization, including the removal of riparian forests, has potent effects on nonpoint source pollution. Nitrogen and phosphorus levels in a channelized stream in a North Carolina coastal-plain watershed were significantly higher than in undisturbed streams.[88] Nitrogen inputs increased because lowered groundwater levels allowed riparian wetlands, which previously trapped nutrients, to be converted to agriculture. Lowering the level of groundwater also reduced groundwater discharge to the river so that flow from upstream areas, which contained a significant concentration of nitrogen, made up the bulk of streamflow. Phosphorus concentrations also increased as a result of greater erosion in the cropland and on steepened channel banks.

Diversion and Groundwater Extraction

Streams, reservoirs, and groundwater are all used as water sources. In each case, water quality and the integrity of riparian vegetation can be degraded. D. C. Erman and E. M. Hawthorne showed that lowered water levels caused by headwater diversion are especially devastating to fish that use these waters for spawning and as hatcheries because of diminished discharge. Decreased in-stream flow also degrades water quality by concentrating contaminants.[89]

As in many other riparian corridors across the West, groundwater extraction lowered the water table in the Carmel River valley in California and caused the decline of riparian vegetation and subsequent increases in bank erosion.[90] This conflict between groundwater extraction and maintaining the water table often exists because soils in floodplain aquifers are generally excellent sources of groundwater, especially in arid areas.[91]

Transportation and Utility Corridors

The corridors that rivers and streams have carved into the landscape often provide convenient locations for transportation and utility facilities because they have gentle topography and easily worked soils. Roads, especially, can have a major impact on stream environments. When salt and other chemicals from roads are washed into the system, vegetation can be damaged and the ability of the riparian corridor to trap these pollutants can be overwhelmed. Erosion is also accelerated by increased runoff from impermeable surfaces of roads, buildings, and parking lots.

Recreation

In recent years, riparian corridors have become magnets for recreational use. This attraction is a result of the variety of recreational opportunities and settings that riparian corridors provide and of the affinity people have for running waters. Effects of recreation on riparian corridors can include the loss of vegetation and litter layer from trampling, compaction, and reduced soil permeability and subsequent increases in runoff, erosion, and sedimentation.[92] The presence of human beings and their pets disturbs animals that use the corridor.

Urbanization

When urbanization covers the landscape with impermeable surfaces, water cannot infiltrate the soil and so runs off much more rapidly than it would otherwise. Drainage is altered, and contaminants enter streams readily and in more concentrated forms. This situation is especially likely during construction because freshly disturbed and devegetated soils are highly susceptible to erosion.

Much of the runoff from urban systems goes into storm drains, through storm sewers, and then into receiving streams. Storm-sewer effluent contains high concentrations of sediment, nutrients, and toxic materials that are washed off roads and parking lots. Sometimes, storm runoff is conducted through on-site retention or detention basins, which permit sedimentation.[93] Riparian vegetation usually has little influence on these point sources. In some cases, however, point sources have been diverted to constructed wetlands where filtration can occur.

Most sanitary sewage from urban areas in the United States and Canada is now treated to some degree at central facilities and thus becomes a point source that flows directly into waterways. In some suburban and rural areas, however, sewage is disposed of in septic systems and community leaching fields. These practices add contaminants, mostly nutrients, to groundwater, which can then be taken up by vegetation.

Applications in Design and Management

There is little doubt that intact, healthy riparian corridors protect water quality and aquatic habitat. Conversely, altering or removing riparian vegetation from the margins of streams can set off a chain reaction of undesirable results. In many greenway projects, however, a disproportionate effort goes to the process of land acquisition rather than to the design of the most appropriate corridor dimensions and configuration. As many of the examples discussed in this book illustrate, simply protecting an arbitrary swath of land is unlikely to be the most effective course; the specific design of a corridor will largely determine how well a greenway functions.

This section examines the principal issues in the ecological design of riparian greenways for the purpose of maintaining high-quality water resources. The section explains the need for measuring ecological health and understanding the context of riparian corridors and discusses specific issues such as corridor width, the elements that should be included in a riparian greenway, riparian corridor management, and ecological restoration.

It is important to recognize that research on the specific capacities and limitations of riparian corridors is in its early stages. Very little is known about the more complex ways that many processes work in riparian corridors and about how these ecosystems interact with uplands and streams. Although the trend toward maintaining riparian corridors as greenways is encouraging, there is a danger that riparian corridors might be considered a panacea for protecting water resources. The solution is clearly not that simple.

Leaving a strip of riparian vegetation to mitigate the effects of a forest clear cut or an urbanizing upland is not an adequate measure on its own, because too much pressure from upland activities can overwhelm and degrade the riparian ecosystem. Although riparian forests play a vital role in ameliorating the effects of erosion, both the health and growth rates of riparian vegetation can change because of increased inputs of sediment, associated nutrients, and toxic chemicals.[94] How these changes ultimately manifest themselves is unknown. Care must be taken to design agricultural, suburban, and urban development so that greenway functions will not be compromised by upland disturbances.

Measuring Ecological Health

Although maintaining ecological health or integrity is the objective of much environmental legislation, the concept has not often been well defined. According to one recent definition, a healthy biological system is one that realizes its inherent potential, is stable, has the capacity for self-repair when perturbed, and requires minimal maintenance.[95]

Included in the idea of inherent potential is a biotic community that possesses healthy individuals and community structure, a high level of native biodiversity, and natural levels of productivity.

Because change is an inherent condition in nature even where human disturbance is minimal, it is unlikely that strictly defined baseline conditions representing ecological health can be identified for a given ecosystem. Still, it is possible to identify and measure generalized conditions that indicate the degree of ecological integrity for a given system.

For designers and managers, identifying healthy conditions when they exist—or predicting their potential when they are degraded—will often be crucial in setting objectives for maintaining or restoring the quality of water resources. Measurement will also be important in gauging the relative success of a project over time. Although ecological health can be estimated qualitatively in a very rough way, a scientific approach is more effective and provides an objective description of healthy conditions. The next section outlines one such approach, the index of biotic integrity, which is a method for assessing the ecological health of streams through direct sampling of aquatic communities.

The Index of Biotic Integrity

The index of biotic integrity (IBI) is a relatively simple and easily learned method for assessing the ecological health of aquatic systems based on the diversity, productivity, and health of fish communities.[96] For a given site, the IBI is the sum of scores assigned to twelve different biological characteristics (determined by sampling the aquatic community) compared with the sum of scores for a similar site in an undisturbed condition. Although the specific characteristics studied may differ from region to region, they include measurements of species richness and composition (total number of species, number and kind of sensitive bottom-dwelling species, water-column species, long-lived species, pollution-intolerant species, and pollution-tolerant species), trophic composition (percentages of omnivores, insectivores, and top carnivores), and the abundance and condition of individuals (for example, the total number of individual fish in samples at a site, the percentage of hybrid individuals, and the percentage of diseased or deformed individuals).

Each characteristic is checked against the same characteristic at a similar but undisturbed site. The degree of correspondence with values expected at undisturbed sites determines the score for a given characteristic, each of which is assigned a score of 1 for poor, 3 for moderate, or 5 for good correspondence. A perfect score of 60 (5 multiplied by the 12 characteristics) defines an undisturbed site, whereas lower scores indicate some degree of ecological degradation.

It is particularly important that the potential scores for criteria of this index are scaled regionally. For example, streams in the coastal drainages of the middle-Atlantic states naturally have higher fish species diversity than Rocky Mountain streams. Thus, the index values for total number of fish species are scaled relative to a local, undisturbed situation.

The costs of measuring the IBI were reported in 1989 to be $740 per sample for the fish community and $824 for the macroinvertebrate community (insects, crustaceans, and shellfish). Each sample is used to measure the twelve characteristics. These costs were provided to Karr[97] by the Ohio Environmental Protection Agency and may be different in other parts of the country. Also, the number of samples needed and the frequency of sampling will depend on careful specification of the objectives of the study and on the size and extent of the area in question. It is therefore impossible here to accurately estimate the cost of the IBI. However, an investment of $10,000 to $50,000 (in 1989 dollars) would probably be sufficient for determining the IBI of a typical stream or stream segment in most cases.

The significance of the IBI as a method of measuring ecological health becomes evident when one compares watersheds with different levels of urbanization and riparian forests. IBI scores for ten watersheds in southern Ontario were very strongly related to the proportion of urban land use and the percentage of remaining riparian forest (figure 4.11).[98] These watersheds were near Toronto, where climate, stream ecology, and human activities are similar to those in the upper midwestern and northeastern United States.

Understanding the Context of the Riparian Ecosystem

When designing a greenway for a portion of a riparian network, understanding how that portion functions within the network is essential. The location of the corridor, for instance, in the headwaters or middle reaches of the network and its condition in comparison to the other reaches should be factors in design and management practices. Recall that removing riparian vegetation alters headwater streams more than high-order streams and that a corridor's width, length, and extension upstream from a site are important for maintenance of water temperature. On the one hand, within a relatively healthy network, a stretch that stands out as degraded might be a priority for restoration and protection. On the other hand, if a watershed is highly industrialized, maintaining the health of a few undisturbed headwater segments may be a more realistic goal and will prevent further degradation of water that will eventually affect downstream reaches.

Special emphasis should be given to greenways that connect a variety of habitats and thus aid in the preservation of biodiversity over a broad area. For example, riparian greenways often include

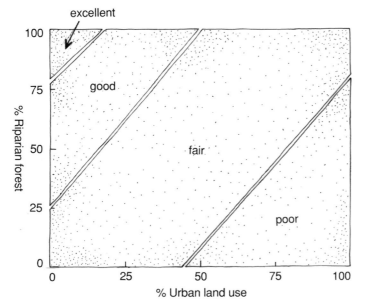

FIGURE 4.11

Contour plot of index of biotic integrity (IBI) ratings in southern Ontario streams as a function of urbanization and riparian forest. IBI is expressed qualitatively within regions that have given proportions of urban land and of remaining riparian forest. For example, if 25 percent of a watershed is in urban land use, then at least 50 percent of the riparian forest should be preserved along the stream to maintain a "good" IBI.

(Redrawn from Steedman, R. J. [1988]. "Modification and assessment of an index of biotic integrity to quantify stream quality in southern Ontario." *Canadian Journal of Fisheries and Aquatic Sciences* 45: 492–501.)

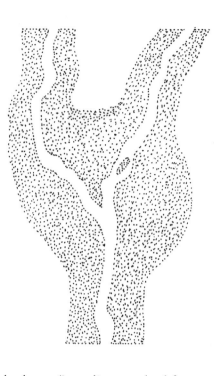

areas where two or more streams converge. These sites are nodes in the larger network, and they connect numerous areas that would otherwise be separated. If a break in a greenway occurs at a node, then the loss of greenway function may be more than doubled compared to the loss from a break in a single section, because at least two corridors are interrupted by one disturbance. A break at a node prevents organisms that use the greenway from moving among the various segments and may also allow material that would otherwise be filtered to pass into two channels. Thus, nodes should be recognized and protected both by increasing the width of the corridor and by restricting use of the banks (figure 4.12).

It is important to understand a corridor within the context of its surroundings. Through what sort of landscape does a river flow, and how does the corridor function in relation to the other components of the landscape (i.e., adjacent upland forest, grassland, agriculture, or suburbs; figure 4.13)? Is the corridor important for wildlife movement? How does the corridor segment affect, and how is it affected by, other segments upstream and downstream? The condition of the surrounding landscape should be surveyed, including the extent to which it has been modified by human activities and the character of the nonpoint source pollution entering the riparian corridor. This assessment includes defining the mixture, intensity, and configuration of the land use adjacent to the stream and understanding how various land uses—forestry, agriculture, suburbs, or urban development—influence the corridor.

Designers and planners can gain an understanding of the ecological characteristics of the greenway and its surroundings by consulting with local ecologists, agronomists, foresters, or other land-use experts. Many components and processes should be investigated, including soils, nutrient cycles, vegetation and animal communities, the physical structure of the stream, the nature and frequency of natural disturbances, and changes in the stream and its corridor over time. The hydrologic regime—flood stages and frequencies, low-flow characteristics, groundwater discharge and recharge periods, and stream water velocity—must be determined. Government agencies, such as local offices of the U.S. Geological Survey or state water resources agencies, often have data or empirical models useful for predicting streamflow. Stream ecologists affiliated with universities or environmental consulting firms can provide data and expert opinions if asked the right questions, which should be possible after one has carefully read this chapter.

Ideally, these questions should be investigated through original, site-specific research. A sample design for a preimplementation study followed by monitoring during management is given in table 4.6. The study measures sediment and nutrient fluxes (via surface runoff and shallow

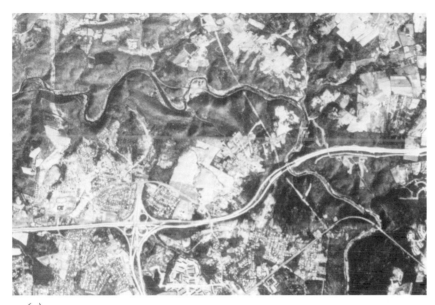

(a)

FIGURE 4.13

A riparian corridor's context within the landscape will be crucial to its design and the way it functions. (a) The Patapsco River Greenway extends from the riparian ecosystem into forested uplands in a mixed landscape of farms and suburbs outside of Baltimore. (b) Rock Creek Park is a narrower, urban greenway in Washington, D.C. In each of these settings, greenways will have different design requirements and functions.

(Photos courtesy of U.S. Geological Survey.)

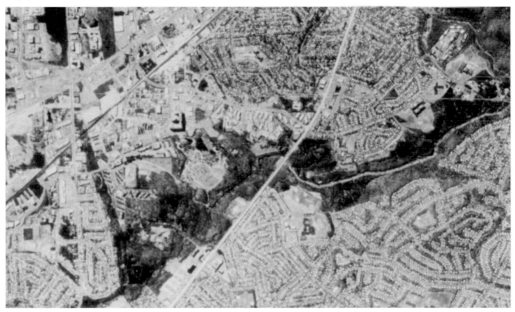

(b)

groundwater) from upland areas to the riparian zone and to the stream itself, as well as nutrient cycling processes within the riparian forest. Such a study is quite comprehensive and should cost (in 1990 dollars) about $90,000 in the first year and $40,000 per year thereafter for monitoring. Proposed greenways with more modest objectives than complete nutrient and sediment control will be less expensive because the full range of variables will not require measurement. Depending on the particular case, a useful study might be accomplished for much less than these amounts.

TABLE 4.6 Tasks and budget for pre-implementation study of a particular riparian greenway with objective of preserving water quality in stream. (In order to develop models for making broader generalizations on the buffer width required to protect stream health in a given area or watershed, it would be necessary to conduct mutiple studies in order to obtain baseline data from which width recommendations for other streams could be inferred (see discussion on pp. 143-144).)

MEASUREMENT[1]	METHOD	ESTIMATED COST (1990 DOLLARS)
Bulk precipitation	Continuous gauge (tipping bucket).	5,000 (installation)
Stream discharge	Gauging station with continuous stage recorder, established rating curve.	5,000 (installation) 5,000 per year (monitoring)
Groundwater discharge	Well nests, piezometers.	20,000 (installation)
Water and sediment chemistry (precipitation, runoff, stream, and groundwater)	Precipitation collector, flow-weighted sampler, grab samples, sampling from wells.	10,000 (installation) 5,000 per year (sampling)
Laboratory analyses	NO_3, total Kjeldahl N, ammonium-N, total P, orthophosphate-P, organic matter conc., exchangeable ammonium-N, exchangeable orthophosphate-P, total suspended particulates, and organic matter concentrations as bio-chemical oxygen demand (BOD).	15,000 per year (about $1.00 per analysis per sample)
Vegetation	Point-quarter, quadrat, or other technique for trees. Increment cores in trees for standing bio-mass and age distribution analysis.	10,000 (first year only)
Upland land uses: crops, suburbs, golf courses, etc.	Data on fertilizer applications from farmers, homeowners, greenskeepers, etc.	5,000 per year
Data analysis, computer modeling, etc.	Mass-balance description of system, analyzed as mass of nutrient or other material per m^2 per year input, output, change in storage in each component of ecosystem.	10,000 per year
Total cost	First year Second and subsequent years	90,000 40,000

[1]The objective of the study is to measure the movements and transformation of waterborne nutrients (N, P, and C) as they move into an ecosystem, then through the watershed to the stream in surface runoff and shallow groundwater. The measurements result in quantitative estimates for the mass of nutrients imported by precipitation and from upland areas, the rates of nutrient uptake and loss in riparian vegetation, and the amount of material that is transported to the stream under different riparian conditions. Ideally, the study should last for a minimum of two years before implementing the greenway. Subsequent years of monitoring should give information about the influence of variable weather, changes of land use, and so on. These costs assume that the stream is first- through fourth-order with a watershed of less than 40 square miles or that the proposed greenway extends less than 6 miles along a higher-order stream.

Source: After Peterjohn, W. T., and D. L. Correll. (1984). "Nutrient dynamics in an agricultural watershed—observations on the role of a riparian forest." *Ecology* 65: 1466–1475.

Other materials such as pesticides, heavy metals, or road salt could also be measured with the same field methods at some increase of laboratory expense. Observation stations, including wells and discharge gauges, can be maintained for long-term monitoring. A study of temperature regulation modeled after the Ontario streams work by D. R. Barton and colleagues mentioned earlier could be accomplished even more inexpensively.[99]

Riparian and stream ecosystems are different at each location. Such differences should provide the basis for formulating greenway designs and should thus be thoroughly investigated. A proper study may seem expensive, and some organizations will simply not have the resources to pay for one. However, to put it in a different light, a description of a riparian ecosystem sufficient for design and management purposes can be established in two to three years, whereas greenway management may occur for the next century or more. A moderate investment at the beginning of a project followed by relatively inexpensive monitoring is likely to be a sound, long-term investment. If funding is not available, knowledge from local experts and consultants may have to suffice. Part of the job for designers and managers is to advise decision makers about the information requirements for certain decisions; advocacy of ecosystem studies or other consultations is often an important part of that advice.

We wish to point out the similarities between product research and development carried out by industry and these preimplementation studies, as well as the similarities between quality assurance and quality control programs in manufacturing and monitoring during environmental management. Industries allocate a certain portion of their resources to both activities, and we believe that environmental management programs deserve the same sort of investment.

Corridor Design

Although a riparian greenway may have many intended uses, protection of water resources and environmental integrity should always be a primary goal. Toward this end, several core components should always be included in a greenway: the geomorphic, hydrological, and vegetational components of the original, natural riparian zone. At a minimum, the greenway should contain the following features (note that there is often a great deal of spatial overlap among these components):

- the natural meandering span of the stream, which we have defined as its geomorphic floodplain;
- the riparian forest; and
- the area over the stream's shallow groundwater system, including any significant groundwater recharge areas in uplands outside the floodplain and riparian forest (the water table near streams is both a source and a sink for stream water, depending on the time of year and recent weather).

Together, these elements make up the riparian ecosystem and are thus essential to its healthy functioning. Beyond these core components, additional area should usually be added to the greenway if it is to function optimally. Two questions about the physical form of the greenway must be answered. First, what will be the most effective width at various locations along the greenway? Second, what additional critical areas beyond this width should be included in the corridor, and what critical areas within the boundaries should receive special management attention?

These questions can be answered and the core components defined most effectively by using the information from the studies described in the previous section and by consulting with local experts. Appropriate greenway dimensions and configuration differ regionally according to climate and physiography, as well as locally among the streams of a watershed, along stretches of a particular stream,

A greenway with an arbitrary width (a) may be too narrow to filter sediment from an agricultural field and may fail to fully protect significant natural features. A greenway in the same location that has a flexible width (b) can be widened at appropriate locations.

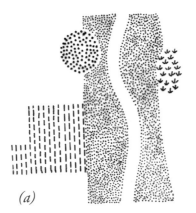

(a)

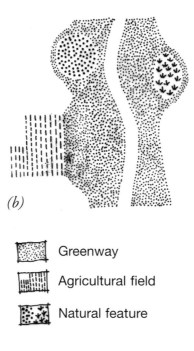

(b)

Greenway

Agricultural field

Natural feature

and according to land use and other variables. The structure and function of the landscape through which the stream passes therefore provide the most appropriate guides to designing the greenway.

Determining Width

Along a greenway, variable widths will often be needed to filter sediments and nutrients, to help maintain natural flow regimes, and to protect significant natural features. The width of a riparian corridor should not be defined arbitrarily. The width of a riparian buffer should increase in direct proportion to (1) the size of the area contributing runoff, sediment, and nutrients; (2) the steepness of both the adjacent slope and the riparian zone; and (3) the intensity of cultural activities and disturbances in the uplands, such as agriculture, forestry, or suburban or urban development. Less width may be needed when there is greater complexity, density, and roughness of corridor vegetation and microtopography.[100] The fixed widths typically set by statute as part of stream protection programs are straightforward and easily measurable for making and implementing policy. However, an arbitrary distance from the stream typically results from compromises among ecological, economic, and political interests. In most cases, an arbitrary width will not reflect the highly variable circumstances found along the length of any given corridor. A set width may be too narrow in some places and unnecessarily wide in others (figure 4.14).

Numerous studies and regulations have tried to generalize effective widths for streams in a given area, watershed, or region, but no consensus or magic number has emerged. Ideally, widths should be determined by consideration of the attributes of the specific watershed and stream corridor but a number of quantitative methods for making broader generalizations, with varying degrees of complexity, have been proposed. All are, essentially, equations that calculate the appropriate width by using quantitative measures of various watershed and stream properties. Some use only one such measure, such as the method of Nieswand et al., which uses only slope, although in their model the relation between width and slope is not a simple linear one.[101] In more complex models, width is a function of several factors, such as overland flow; specific area (a ratio that compares watershed size to stream length); so-called roughness coefficients that describe the irregularity, shape, and obstructions of a stream channel infiltration rate; and soil properties such as adsorption capacity or moisture storage capacity.[102] Sophisticated algorithms taking full advantage of computing and remote-sensing capabilities have also been proposed, although their details are beyond the scope of this chapter.[103] At the more comprehensive end of the spectrum is the Riparian Ecosystem Management Model of Lowrance et al., a computer simulation that models the water quality impacts of buffer systems of different widths, slopes, soils, and vegetation.[104]

However, collecting the data to be entered into any of these models for width determination can be expensive, more because of labor costs rather than any requirements for highly specialized scientific methods or equipment. To date, few of the parties involved in watershed planning have the financial resources that these models require for data collection and implementation. At the time of this writing, none of the methods is in widespread use or has even been widely tested. Clearly, the scientific determination of buffer width is still in its early stages.

Currently, buffer width guidelines in the United States and Canada are based on far simpler criteria. The guidelines have been compared and summarized by Lee et al.,[105] who reported that the jurisdictions (American states and Canadian provinces and territories) based their recommended or required widths on various criteria such as watershed slope, watershed area, whether the water body is a lake or stream, whether it contains fish, whether it is used for drinking water, and so forth. Twenty-two percent of the jurisdictions surveyed based width on only one of these factors, while 44 percent of the jurisdictions used three or more. These factors, though, are used in a rough checklist fashion, instead of quantitative ecological models, and the formulae are not primarily derived from empirical data. This situation is, if not desirable, then at least understandable given

TABLE 4.7 Mean recommended buffer widths in meters for jurisdictions in Canada (provinces and territories) and the United States (states), combined and separately for each country.

These are the average buffer widths currently recommended by state and provincial authorities. They are based primarily on estimates (often scientifically informed, but ultimately intuitive) of the width necesssary to achieve stream protection and not on scientific determinations, for which the necessary research does not yet exist. To the extent possible, width determinations should be based on local stream studies.

WATERBODY CLASSES	COMBINED ($N = 60$)	CANADA ($N = 12$)	UNITED STATES ($N = 48$)
Large permanent streams	28.1	43.8 [1]	24.2 [2]
Small permanent streams	21.8	29.6 [1]	19.9 [2]
Intermittent streams	15.1	13.8 [1]	15.5 [1]
Small lakes	27.6	47.1 [2]	22.9 [2]
Large lakes	29.0	54.6 [1]	22.7 [2]

[1]The differences between these values are not statistically significant.
[2]The differences between these values are not statistically significant.

Adapted from Lee et al. (2004).

the legal complexities involved in such land-use regulations and the dearth of published information that quantifies buffer width functions. The average corridor width recommended for a small permanent stream is 71.5 feet (22 m)[106] for each stream bank (table 4.7); in the 78 percent of jurisdictions using more than one factor to calculate width, this figure would be modified according to each stream's particular characteristics.

As an alternative to expensive but sophisticated modeling techniques on the one hand, and the overly crude methods currently in place for determining buffer widths on the other, Budd and colleagues developed a practical method for subjectively determining stream-corridor width by using simple field survey methods on selected reaches of a stream.[107] With this method, a riparian corridor's potential for sediment filtration and temperature control is assessed qualitatively, as are terrestrial and aquatic habitat and vegetation's contribution to stream structure. Characteristics surveyed include stream type, slope of the streambed, soil class, runoff and erosion potential, water capacity of the soil, vegetation cover, temperature control, stream structure, sedimentation control, and wildlife habitat. All these factors are used by the evaluator to estimate necessary corridor width, an estimate based as much on intuition and experience as on objective criteria. An example was provided of a study of a stream in King County, Washington, in which all corridor widths were recommended to be 50 feet (15 m) or less. Those determinations are probably significant underestimates that were based more on existing land use than on any ecological principles.

The approach of Budd et al. may be appropriate where no resources are available to support the studies that help determine corridor widths objectively. Nonetheless, it is problematic on several counts. First, being qualitative, the approach is subjective and not replicable and is therefore difficult to defend in legal or scientific terms. If several different evaluators, each with a different bias, were to examine the streams, they would probably recommend several different widths, and a commission or judge would still not know with any certainty which width would be adequate. One particular perspective, whether that of developers, foresters, environmentalists, or some other interested party, could prevail without respect to ecosystem properties. Second, this particular method is unclear and incomplete as described. The authors do not state how soils, slopes, vegetation, and other characteristics are to be used in the determination but only state that they are important criteria. Third, the method depends on having relatively undisturbed reaches of the stream available for analyses. If no segment of the stream remains undisturbed, then a recommendation cannot be made. Nonetheless, this or other qualitative methods, if conducted by well-trained, experienced, and—it should be emphasized—disinterested resource professionals, are likely to be the next best alternatives when complete scientific studies cannot be undertaken.

Critical Areas to Include

Several types of critical areas, both adjacent to and beyond the main corridor, should be included as part of a greenway and given special management attention. Intermittent tributaries, gullies, and swales draining into the stream are critical areas because large quantities of sediment and runoff collect in them before entering the stream. The physical structure and natural vegetation in and along the side slopes of these minor drainages should be maintained. Vegetation in these areas has naturally dense growth because of good soil and moisture conditions and thus provides excellent sediment and nutrient filtration capacity. Natural vegetation left in minor and intermittent drainage ways promotes channel stability in the main stream by slowing flow during storms and decreasing erosion in swales.[108] Keeping these areas undisturbed and vegetated is very important, especially in arid lands, where most watercourses are intermittent.

Another kind of critical area includes potential and actual areas of erosion or deposition in contact with the stream. These areas include steep slopes, unstable soil areas, lateral wetlands, undercut banks (especially on the outside of stream bends), bridge crossings, path or boat ramp accesses, and other locations vulnerable to increased disturbance and erosion or having potential to act as sediment sinks.[109]

Other critical areas that may or may not be in direct contact with a stream have an important influence on sediment input and must be considered when designating a protected riparian corridor. Development sites, areas of intensive forest cutting, pastures or paddocks subject to overgrazing, and cultivated fields near streams are examples of critical watershed areas.[110] The existence of such areas requires wider riparian corridors because of the need to sequester a greater volume of eroded sediment.

Aquifer recharge or discharge zones that help maintain year-round streamflow should also be protected. These areas are not often easily discovered by simple, qualitative field methods; only hydrogeological studies are capable of proving that an area is a discharge or recharge zone. Some simple rules of thumb, however, can be applied to indicate whether further studies are necessary. If a wetland or seasonally wet soils occur uphill from a stream, then they are probably groundwater recharge areas. Outcrops of bedrock known to be aquifers are also important recharge areas. Springs laterally uphill from streams are discharge areas for the aquifer and may be recharge areas for the stream. Finally, nearly all of the geomorphic floodplain is either a recharge or discharge area for stream water.

One last critical area is the zone just above the point of topographic leveling of floodplain banks, or the shoulder of the hill (figure 4.15). If this zone remains undisturbed, it can be a highly effective sediment filter because of its gradual slope compared to the banks below. This upland area will be a stable, long-term sink for sediment and nutrients, whereas wetlands and riparian areas may eventually be disturbed by bank erosion and stream-channel meander.

The edge of some floodplains consists of multiple terraces caused by very large floods in the past that deposited huge amounts of sediment. In these cases, the protected corridor should ideally extend beyond the last terrace, because this marks the point beyond which the stream is unlikely to meander in the future.

Site Design, Vegetation Management, and Alternative Planting

Once a greenway's boundaries have been determined, there remains the task of designing elements within the corridor itself at the site scale. The most important areas for attention are along the greenway's edges where intensive land uses such as agriculture or urbanization are immediately

adjacent to the riparian buffer. If the disturbance is severe and sediment inputs are great, additional efforts may be required to prevent contaminants from overwhelming the riparian corridor. For example, detention or retention basins are required below developments in many states as a best management practice, and much literature describing the function of these structures has been published.[111] Alternatively, a combination of berms and dense vegetation at the forest edge may be necessary to provide additional barriers to the agricultural runoff.[112]

After a greenway has been designed and implemented, riparian forests must often be managed on an ongoing basis so their function of protecting water resources can be maintained. As described earlier in this chapter, selective harvesting of trees will remove accumulated nutrients from the riparian system and promote continued nutrient uptake and forest growth. In areas with very high levels of sediment deposition, periodically removing sediment can prevent the corridor vegetation from being damaged over the long term.

Native vegetation is usually the most effective for maintaining water quality and requires little or no maintenance. A diverse vertical stratification with trees, a shrub layer, and herbaceous ground cover should be encouraged within the corridor.

Alder, which is a native species in many riparian communities, can be effective for long-term bank protection because its roots are water-tolerant and support the bank by penetrating deeply into the soil.[113] However, alder roots bear nodules that contain nitrogen-fixing microorganisms and may supply biologically available nitrogen compounds to the stream.[114] If nitrogen is a limiting nutrient for the stream, alders may increase productivity and contribute to eutrophication, although the significance of this effect is not well studied. Where excess nitrogen is not a concern, alder should make an excellent stream-bank planting. Even

FIGURE 4.16

Mowed grass or other low vegetation will usually make a poor filter of sediments carried by surface water and should be avoided.

(Photo by D. Smith.)

where nitrogen is a problem, alder may safely be used in a limited way to stabilize streams at points where banks are particularly vulnerable. Other native species, like willow and cottonwood, will also be effective in specific situations; appropriate species should be identified by consulting with local botanists or horticulturalists.

However, if human activities make natural vegetation impossible to maintain, alternative plantings may be more durable and quite effective. In one instance, a 1,000-foot (305-m) strip of planted coastal Bermuda grass removed 99 percent of the sediment from runoff with an initial concentration of 5,000 parts per million—a moderately high level.[115] Although this species will not be appropriate in many landscapes, other plants may function in a similar manner. In general, plants used for sediment filtration should have deep and vigorous root systems to resist scouring in swift currents, dense, well-branched top growth, and an ability to recover after being inundated with sediment. Aggressive plants that might spread to other areas and compete with native vegetation should be avoided.

Riparian greenways with trails are sometimes landscaped with closely cut grass (figure 4.16). When grasses are clipped and flow rates are high enough to submerge the sod, filtering efficiency can be lost entirely.[116] Therefore, mowing streamside vegetation should be discouraged, especially during periods when storms or high flows are likely.

Corridor Restoration

Restoring stream corridors can be a cost-effective means of controlling nonpoint source pollution.[117] As we have emphasized, the primary objective of stream restoration should be to re-create the natural habitat, not just to plant a species that is hardy, attractive, or easy to maintain.[118] Restoration efforts should therefore be guided by the structure of the original riparian vegetation

FIGURE 4.17

A segment of the Kissimmee River, before (a) and after (b) restoration. Returning diverted flow to the original river course has helped flush out accumulated sediments and aquatic growth and has enhanced wildlife habitat and fisheries.
(Courtesy of Southwest Florida Water Management District.)

as well as by the original structure of the stream and its hydrologic processes. Restoration should establish an appropriate structure within which natural processes can operate so that the system can be sustainable and capable of recovery following natural disturbances.

The first requirement in a restoration project is to restore the stream's original flow regime because naturally fluctuating flows are essential to riparian communities. The second step is to restore the stream's ability to attain its appropriate meander pattern and riffle-pool structure (the alteration of still pools and faster flowing riffles) and to stabilize the banks to prevent further erosion.[119] The most laborious and costly measure is the removal of dams and channel levees.[120] This action may be the one needed if seed sources of the original riparian vegetation exist nearby or upstream. In this case revegetation and physical changes to the stream channel will occur by themselves over time. Direct methods of stabilizing and revegetating banks include the placement of coarse woody debris—that is, logs and large branches—in the stream channel such that they will slow the streamflow and alter its pattern, in turn reducing bank erosion and allowing the bank to consolidate and ultimately revegetate. Banks also can be stabilized by mats known as geotextiles, which may be either synthetic or natural and biodegradable, as in the case of sisal. "Whips," typically of willow or other native species such as hawthorn that have the necessary properties, can be laid on the ground and bound or woven together in any of various grid formations. The whips will physically stabilize the soil and simultaneously root, sprout, and grow into trees. If erosion has been severe, regrading will be necessary before any of the above measures is implemented.

In one of the best contemporary examples of stream restoration, degraded areas along the Kissimmee River in southern Florida have recovered dramatically following the diversion of channelized flow back into the old river course.[121] In only a few years, habitat complexity and diversity increased. Connections between the stream and riparian habitat have been enhanced, resulting in increased input of insects to the river and its food chain, flushing of floating plants and sediment that had accumulated in the channel, and growth of fish and waterfowl populations (figure 4.17).

Still, as recently as 2003, unequivocal and quantitative proof of overall, multifactor riparian ecosystem recovery as a result of buffers has proved elusive. Parkyn et al. compared several stream rehabilitation projects within a single ecosystem that aimed to improve conditions but not necessarily recreate the pristine state.[122] They found that only visual water clarity and channel stability were linked to buffer size in all cases. Their results also pointed to a chain of causation in which age of buffer and type of vegetation (closed tree canopy) create shade, which, if the buffer is sufficiently long, reduces water temperature. The lower temperature in turn is favorable to invertebrate animal communities. Apart from these results, though, it appears that the multiplicity of interacting feedback pathways in ecosystem functioning still poses an obstacle to making confident generalizations about buffer size.

If the stream's channel or hydrology has been irreversibly altered, complete restoration may not be possible.[123] The most common examples of permanent changes are large dams, which prevent flooding downstream, and flood-control levies that protect towns and cities by restricting floodwaters. In such cases, expectations will have to be lowered. Instead of full restoration, other important objectives, such as maintenance of clean water or special kinds of fisheries, may be attainable.

Riparian ecosystems damaged by livestock often recover naturally if grazing is eliminated or restricted.[124] Cottonwood, alder, sycamore, and willow grow prolifically after livestock exclusion, assuming there are no other ongoing stresses to the system.[125] Successful solutions depend both on the specific characteristics of the degraded corridor and on the alternatives for modifying ranching operations. For example, in the Coronado Forest in southern Arizona, completely fencing out livestock was the only method that ensured adequate protection and improvement of riparian systems.[126] But complete exclusion may not be necessary in other cases. In a damaged riparian zone in the Rocky Mountains a combination of seasonal exclusion and lowering the number of grazing animals resulted in intermediate levels of stream protection.[127] Whether complete or partial exclusion is needed will depend on many local variables, including the type and health of vegetation and soils, the degree of aridity, and rainfall patterns.

A restoration technique that holds promise for some areas is the reintroduction of beaver. In Wyoming, a combination of livestock exclusion and beaver reintroduction was instrumental in improving degraded riparian corridors.[128] Beaver dams reduced streamflow velocities, erosive potential, and capacity to carry sediment and increased both sediment deposition and the level of the corridor's water table. The combination of beaver activity and livestock exclusion allowed willows to become reestablished, and the riparian plant community became self-sustaining after three years. Beaver introductions may cause problems in some situations because new ponds and wetlands may not be appreciated by landowners and ornamental plants are often considered delicacies by hungry beavers. In these cases the maintenance of at least a partially natural habitat by adjacent landowners may be essential but not always easy to achieve. Educational programs, original development covenants, compensation for conservation easements, and clever landscape design[129] can all help create the essential goodwill.

Finally, several technical problems are common in any restoration or enhancement project and must be avoided.[130] Water ponding and damage to some plants are a consequence of clayey soils often found in subsoils or fill material. Exotic weeds colonize newly created riparian habitat to the detriment of intended plantings. Groundwater depth determines whether planted riparian vegetation survives and should be a key issue in selecting enhancement sites. In addition, soil microorganisms important for nutrient uptake by newly planted vegetation should be introduced by spreading leaf litter collected from nearby mature riparian communities following planting.

This list is not exhaustive and actually only begins to describe all the issues and problems that might be encountered with restoration projects. Designers and managers should recognize that scientists understand ecosystems in a general way but do not usually know enough about the structure and function of specific riparian ecosystems to specify effective management or restoration methods without detailed investigations.

Conclusion

Greenways will be most effective when designers, planners, and managers have gained a thorough knowledge of the ecosystem in question and its context in the landscape. Occasionally, this knowledge may already exist in sufficiently detailed form. But in most cases, original research will be well advised. A comprehensive study can answer most if not all of the pertinent design questions. However, it may not always be within a project's budget. Fortunately, there are alternatives that, although much less effective, are more affordable. Many scientists in colleges, universities, or environmental consulting firms have experience with local stream systems and may be willing to work with designers and managers to establish more specific recommendations for corridor configuration and composition.

For example, the index of biotic integrity (IBI) depends on a knowledge of regional fish ecology. Universities with an ichthyologist on the faculty probably have collections of samples from local streams and lakes, some of which may be considered undisturbed localities for baseline determinations and others which may be the streams of interest to the designer or manager. A reasonable estimate of the IBI can be determined from archived collections or unpublished data with the assistance of the biologist. If recent map or aerial photographs are available, the spatial relationships among land use, riparian forests, and stream water quality can easily be determined. In any event, local ecological knowledge will always be useful. It is the designers' and managers' responsibility to be educated sufficiently to ask the right questions of scientists and the scientists' responsibility to answer the questions in ways that are useful to designers and managers.

If we as a society believe that protecting clean water and biological diversity is important, the preservation or restoration of riparian vegetation can go far toward achieving this goal. Ecosystem and environmental scientists must study sediment and nutrient flows from uplands through riparian zones to streams. Stream ecologists must collaborate with terrestrial ecologists to understand the relationships among land use, the configuration and composition of riparian vegetation, and stream water quality and biotic integrity. Environmental designers, planners, and managers must become educated about the ecological function of these systems, must learn how to ask appropriate questions of scientists and consultants, and then must understand their answers well enough to implement effective programs. Perhaps even more important, ecologists should become more involved in applying their knowledge to the practical problems and be willing to help practitioners ask appropriate questions, to argue strongly for suitable studies, and to provide useful answers.

Table References

Bilby, R.E., and P. A. Bisson. (1992). "Allochthonous versus autochthonous organic matter contributions to the trophic support of fish populations in clear-cut and old growth forested streams." *Canadian Journal of Fisheries and Aquatic Sciences* 49: 540–551.

Brazier J. R., and G. W. Brown. (1973). *Buffer Strips for Stream Temperature Control.* Research Paper No. 15. Corvallis, OR, Oregon State University, Forest Research Laboratory.

Brusnyk, L. M., and F. F. Gilbert. (1983). "Use of shoreline timber reserves by moose." *Journal of Wildlife Management* 47: 673–685.

Cooper, J. R., J. W. Gilliam, R. B. Daniels, and W. P. Robarge. (1987). "Riparian areas as filters for agricultural sediment." *Soil Science Society of America Journal* 51:416–420.

Clausen, J. C., K. Guillard, C. M. Sigmund, and K. Martin Dors. (2000). "Water quality changes from riparian buffer restoration in Connecticut." *Journal of Environmental Quality* 29: 1751–1761.

Darveau, M., P. Beauchesne, L. Belanger, J. Huot, and P. LaRue. (1995). "Riparian forest strips as habitat for breeding birds in boreal forest." *Journal of Wildlife Management* 59: 67–78.

Dillaha, T. A., R. B. Reneau, S. Mostaghimi, and D. Lee. (1989). "Vegetative filter strips for agricultural nonpoint source pollution control." *Transactions of the ASAE* 32(2): 513–519. (Annual Report). Athens, GA, University of Georgia.

Dillaha, T. A., J. H. Sherrard, D. Lee, S. Mostaghimi, and V.O. Shanholtz. (1988). "Evaluation of vegetative filter strips as a best management practice for feed lots." *Journal of the Water Pollution Control Federation* 60(7): 1231–1238.

Duncan, W. F. A., and M. A. Brusven. (1985). "Energy dynamics of three low-order southeast Alaska USA streams: allochthonous processes." *Journal of Freshwater Ecology* 3. 233–248.

France, R., H. Culbert, and R. Peters. (1996). "Decreased carbon and nutrient input to boreal lakes from particulate organic matter following riparian clear-cutting." *Environmental Management* 20: 579–583.

Hall, J. K., N. L. Hartwig, and L. D. Hoffman. (1983). "Application mode and alternative cropping effects on atrazine losses from a hillside." *Journal of Environmental Quality* 12: 336–340.

Harper, K. A., and S. E. MacDonald. (2001). "Structure and composition of riparian boreal forest: New methods for analyzing edge influence." *Ecology* 82: 649–659.

Haupt, H. F., W. J. Kidd. (1965). "Good logging practices reduce sedimentation in central Idaho." *Journal of Forestry* 63, 664–670.

Johnson, W. N. J., and P. W. Brown. (1990). "Avian use of a lakeshore buffer strip and an undisturbed lakeshore in Maine USA." *Northern Journal of Applied Forestry* 7: 114–117.

Lowrance, R., S. McIntyre, and C. Lance. (1988). "Erosion and deposition in a field forest system estimated using cesium-137 activity." *Journal of Soil and Water Conservation* 43:195–199.

Lee, P., Smith, C., and Boutin, S. (2004) "Quantitative review of riparian buffer width guidelines from Canada and the United States." *Journal of Environmental Management* 70: 165–180.

Magette, W. L., R. B. Brinsfield, R. E. Palmer, and J. D. Wood. (1989). "Nutrient and sediment removal by vegetated filter strips." *Transactions of the ASAE* 32(2): 663–667.

McDade, M. H., F. J. Swanson, W. A. McKee, J. F. Franklin, J. Van Sickle. (1990). "Source distances for coarse woody debris entering small streams in western Oregon and Washington." *Canadian Journal of Forestry* 20: 326–330.

Moring, J. R., (1982). "Decrease in stream gravel permeability after clear-cut logging: An indication of intragravel conditions for developing salmonid eggs and aleevins." *Hydrobiologia* 88, 295–298.

Robinson, E.G., and R. L. Beschta. (1990). "Identifying trees in riparian areas that can provide coarse woody debris to streams." *Forest Science* 36: 790–801.

Schmitt, T. J., M. G. Dosskey, and K. D. Hoagland. (1999). "Filter strip performance and processes for different vegetation, widths, and contaminants." *Journal of Environmental Quality* 28: 1479–1489.

Steinblums, I.J., H.A. Froehlich, and J.K. Lyons. (1984). "Designing stable buffer strips for stream protection." *Journal of Forestry* 82: 49–52.

Uusi-Kämppä, J., B. Braskerud, H. Jansson, N. Syversen, and R. Uusitalo. (2000). "Buffer zones and constructed wetlands as filters for agricultural phosphorus." *Journal of Environmental Quality* 29: 151–158.

Uusi-Kämppä, J., and T. Yläranta. (1996). "Effect of buffer strips on controlling soil erosion and nutrient losses in southern Finland." pp. 221–235, in G. Mulamoottil et al. (ed.). *Wetlands: Environmental Gradients, Boundaries, and Buffers*. Boca Raton, FL, CRC Press, Lewis Publishers.

Van Sickle, J., and S. V. Gregory. (1990). "Modeling inputs of large woody debris to streams from falling trees." *Canadian Journal of Forest Research* 20: 1593–1601.

Wesche, T. A., C. M. Goertler, and C. B. Frye. (1987). "Contribution of riparian vegetation to trout cover in small streams." *North American Journal of Fisheries Management* 7: 151–153.

Whitaker, D. M., and W. A. Montevecchi. (1999). "Breeding bird assemblages inhabiting riparian buffer strips in Newfoundland, Canada." *Journal of Wildlife Management* 63: 167–179.

Young, K., S. Hinch, and T. Northcote. (1999). "Status of resident coastal cutthroat trout and their habitat." *North American Journal of Fisheries Management* 19: 901–911.

Notes

[1] Gregory, K. J., and D. E. Walling. (1973). *Watershed Form and Process*. New York, John Wiley and Sons.

[2] Poff, N. L., and J. V. Ward. (1989). "Implications of streamflow variability and predictability for lotic community structure—regional analysis of streamflow patterns." *Canadian Journal of Fisheries and Aquatic Sciences* 46: 1805–1818.

[3] Strahler, A. N. (1964). "Quantitative geomorphology of watersheds and channel networks." in *Handbook of Applied Hydrology*, V. T. Chow, ed. New York, McGraw-Hill.

[4] Gregory and Walling, (1973), *Watershed Form and Process*.

[5] Vannote, R. L., G. W. Minshall, K. W. Cummins, J. R. Sedell, and C. E. Cushing. (1980). "River continuum concept." *Canadian Journal of Fisheries and Aquatic Sciences* 37: 130–137; Cummins, K. W., G. W. Minshall, J. R. Sedell, C. E. Cushing, and R. C. Petersen. (1984). "Stream ecosystem theory." *Verhandlungen Internationale Vereinigung für Limnologie* 22: 631–641.

[6] Minshall, G. W., K. W. Cummins, R. C. Petersen, C. E. Cushing, D. A. Bruns, J. R. Sedell, and R. L. Vannote. (1985). "Developments in stream ecosystem theory." *Canadian Journal of Fisheries and Aquatic Sciences* 42: 1045–1055.

[7] Meyer, J. L., and R. T. Edwards. (1990). "Ecosystem metabolism and turnover of organic-carbon along a blackwater river continuum." *Ecology* 71: 668–677.

[8] Ewel, K. C. (1978). "Riparian ecosystems: Conservation of their unique characteristics." p. 56–62, in *Strategies for Protection and Management of Floodplain Wetlands and Other Riparian Ecosystems: Proceedings of the Symposium*. U.S. Government Printing Office, Washington, DC.

[9] Mitsch, W. J., and J. G. Gosselink. (1986). *Wetlands*. New York, Van Nostrand Reinhold.

[10] Stabler, F. (1985). "Increasing summer flow in small streams through management of riparian areas and adjacent vegetation: A synthesis." p. 206–210, in *Riparian Ecosystems and Their Management: Reconciling Conflicting Uses*. R. R. Johnson, C. D. Ziebell, D. R. Paton, P. F. Ffolliott, and R. H. Hamre, ed. USDA Forest Service.

[11] Lowrance, R., R. Leonard, and J. Sheridan. (1985). "Managing riparian ecosystems to control nonpoint pollution." *Journal of Soil and Water Conservation* 40: 87–91.

[12] U.S. Army Corps of Engineers, N.E.D. (1968). "Charles River watershed study." in *Meeting of the Coordinating Committee for the Charles River Watershed*, Waltham, MA, February 15, 1968.

[13] U.S. Army Corps of Engineers, N.E.D. (1976). Natural valley storage: A partnership with nature. Public information fact sheet. Waltham, MA, USACOE.

[14] Stabler, (1985), "Increasing summer flow."

[15] Dawson, T. E., and J. R. Ehleringer. (1991). "Streamside trees that do not use stream water." *Nature* 350: 335–337.

[16] Corbett, E. S., and J. A. Lynch. (1985). "Management of streamside zones on municipal watersheds." in *Riparian Ecosystems and Their Management: Reconciling Conflicting Uses*. R. R. Johnson, C. D. Ziebell, D. R. Paton, P. F. Ffolliott, and R. H. Hamre, ed. USDA Forest Service.

[17] Forman, R. T. T., and M. Godron. (1986). *Landscape Ecology*. New York, John Wiley and Sons.

[18] Leopold, L. B., M. G. Wolman, and J. P. Miller. (1964). *Fluvial processes in geomorphology*. San Francisco, Freeman.

[19] Lowrance, Leonard, and Sheridan, (1985), "Managing riparian ecosystems."

[20] Lowrance, R., S. Mcintyre, and C. Lance. (1988). "Erosion and deposition in a field forest system estimated using cesium-137 activity." *Journal of Soil and Water Conservation* 43: 195–199.

[21] Cooper, J. R., J. W. Gilliam, R. B. Daniels, and W. P. Robarge. (1987). "Riparian areas as filters for agricultural sediment." *Soil Science Society of America Journal* 51: 416–420.

[22] Lowrance, R., J. K. Sharpe, and J. M. Sheridan. (1986). "Long-term sediment deposition in the riparian zone of a coastal-plain watershed." *Journal of Soil and Water Conservation* 41: 266–271.

[23] Phillips, J. D. (1989). "Fluvial sediment storage in wetlands." *Water Resources Bulletin* 25: 867–873.

[24] Schlosser, I. J., and J. R. Karr. (1981). "Riparian vegetation and channel morphology impact on spatial patterns of water quality in agricultural watersheds." *Environmental Management* 5: 233–243.

[25] Ibid; Bache, D. H., and I. A. Macaskill. (1981). "Vegetation in coastal and stream-bank protection." *Landscape Plan* 8: 363–385; Forman and Godron, (1986), *Landscape Ecology*.

[26] Tu, M., and J. Soll. (2004). Knotweed eradication at a watershed scale in the Pacific Northwest. The Nature Conservancy. Retrieved December 15, 2005, (http://tncweeds.ucdavis.edu/success/or002.html).

[27] Pysek, P. S., and K. Prach. (1994). "How important are rivers for supporting plant invasions?" pp. 19–26, in *Ecology and Management of Invasive Riverside Plants*. L. C. de Waal, L. E. Child, C. P. M. Wade, and J. H. Brock, ed. New York, Chichester, John Wiley and Sons, Ltd.; Staniforth, R. J., and P. B. Cavers. (1976). "An experimental study of water dispersal in *Polygonum* spp." *Canadian Journal of Botany* 54: 2587–2596.

[28] Brenner, M., M. W. Binford, and E. S. Deevey. (1990). "Lakes." pp. 364–391, in "Ecosystems of Florida." R. L. Myers and J. J. Ewel, ed. Gainesville, University of Florida Press; Goldman, C. R. (1981). "Lake Tahoe: Two decades of change in a nitrogen-deficient oligotrophic lake." *Verhandlungen Internationale Vereinigung für Limnologie* 21: 45–70.

[29] Reckhow, K. H., and S. C. Chapra. (1981). *Engineering Approaches for Lake Management*. Ann Arbor, MI, Ann Arbor Science.

[30] Karr, J. R., and I. J. Schlosser. (1977). "Impact of nearstream vegetation and stream morphology on water quality and stream biota." U.S. Environmental Protection Agency, Ecological Research Series. EPA-600/3-77-097; Delwiche, L. L. D., and D. A. Haith. (1983). "Loading functions for predicting nutrient losses from complex watersheds." *Water Resources Bulletin* 19: 951–959; Cooper, Gilliam, Daniels, and Robarge, (1987), "Riparian areas as filters for agricultural sediment."

[31] Karr and Schlosser, (1977), "Impact of nearstream vegetation."

[32] Lowrance, Leonard, and Sheridan, (1985), "Managing riparian ecosystems to control nonpoint pollution."

[33] Patrick, W. H., and K. R. Reddy. (1976). "Nitrification-denitrification reactions in flooded soils and water bottoms—dependence on oxygen-supply and ammonium diffusion." *Journal of Environmental Quality* 5: 469–472.

[34] Lowrance, R., R. Todd, J. Fail, O. Hendrickson, R. Leonard, and L. Asmussen. (1984). "Riparian forests as nutrient filters in agricultural watersheds." *Bioscience* 34: 374–377; Lowrance, Leonard, and Sheridan, (1985), "Managing riparian ecosystems to control nonpoint pollution."

[35] Peterjohn, W. T., and D. L. Correll. (1984). "Nutrient dynamics in an agricultural watershed—observations on the role of a riparian forest." *Ecology* 65: 1466–1475.

[36] Lowrance, Leonard, and Sheridan, (1985), "Managing riparian ecosystems to control nonpoint pollution."

[37] Peterjohn and Correll, (1984), "Nutrient dynamics in an agricultural watershed."

[38] Yates, P., and J. M. Sheridan. (1983). "Estimating the effectiveness of vegetated floodplains wetlands as nitrate-nitrite and orthophosphorus filters." *Agriculture, Ecosystems and Environment* 9: 303–314.

[39] Lowrance, Leonard, and Sheridan, (1985), "Managing riparian ecosystems to control nonpoint pollution."

[40] Hartigan, J. P., B. Douglas, D. J. Biggers, T. J. Wessel, and D. Stroh. (1979). "Areawide and local frameworks for urban nonpoint pollution management in northern Virginia." in *National Conference on Stormwater Management Alternatives*, Wilmington, Del., October 3–5, 1979.

[41] Reviewed in Wenger, S. (1999). "A review of the scientific literature on riparian buffer width, extent and vegetation." Athens, Office of Public Service and Outreach, Institute of Ecology, University of Georgia; Dosskey, M. G. (2001). "Toward quantifying water pollution abatement in response to installing buffers on crop land." *Environmental Management* 28: 577–598; Hickey, M. B. C., and B. Doran. (2004). "A review of the efficiency of buffer strips for

the maintenance and enhancement of riparian ecosystems." *Water Quality Research Journal of Canada* 39: 311—317; Karthikeyan, R., L. C. Davis, L. E. Erickson, K. Al-Khatib, P. A. Kulakow, P. L. Barnes, S. L. Hutchinson, and A. A. Nurzhanova. (2004). "Potential for plant-based remediation of pesticide-contaminated soil and water using nontarget plants such as trees, shrubs, and grasses." *Critical Reviews in Plant Science* 23: 91–101; Also see Borin, M., E. Bigon, G. Zanin, and L. Fava. (2004). "Performance of a narrow buffer strip in abating agricultural pollutants in the shallow subsurface water flux." *Environmental Pollution* 131: 313–321.

[42] Karthikeyan, R., et al., (2004), "Potential for plant-based remediation."

[43] Kibby, H. V. (1978). "Effects of wetlands on water quality." pp. 289–297, in *Strategies for Protection and Management of Floodplain Wetlands and Other Riparian Ecosystems: Proceedings of the Symposium.* Washington, DC, Government Printing Office.

[44] Karr, J. R., and I. J. Schlosser. (1978). "Water-resources and land-water interface." *Science* 201: 229–234.

[45] Johnson, S. L., and J. A. Jones. (2000). "Stream temperature responses to forest harvest and debris flows in western Cascades, Oregon." *Canadian Journal of Fisheries and Aquatic Sciences* 57: 30–39.

[46] Budd, W. W., P. L. Cohen, P. R. Saunders, and F. R. Steiner. (1987). "Stream corridor management in the Pacific-Northwest. 1. Determination of stream-corridor widths." *Environmental Management* 11: 587–597.

[47] Ibid.

[48] Brown, G. W., and J. T. Krygier. (1970). "Effects of clear-cutting on stream temperature." *Water Resources Research* 6: 1133.

[49] Karr and Schlosser, (1978), "Water-resources and land-water interface."

[50] Everest, F. H., N. B. Armantrout, S. M. Keller, W. D. Parante, J. R. Sedell, T. E. Nickelson, J. M. Johnston, and G. N. Haugen. (1982). Salmonids westside forest—wildlife habitat relationship handbook. Portland, OR, U.S. Forest Service, Pacific Northwest Forest and Range Experiment Station.

[51] J. Meyer, personal communication.

[52] Karr and Schlosser, (1978), "Water-resources and land-water interface."

[53] Barton, D. R., W. D. Taylor, and R. M. Biette. (1985). "Dimensions of riparian buffer strips required to maintain trout habitat in southern Ontario streams." *North American Journal of Fisheries Management* 5: 364–378.

[54] Ibid.

[55] Budd, Cohen, Saunders, and Steiner, (1987), "Stream corridor management in the Pacific-Northwest."

[56] Benke, A. C., T. C. Vanarsdall, D. M. Gillespie, and F. K. Parrish. (1984). "Invertebrate productivity in a sub-tropical blackwater river—the importance of habitat and life-history." *Ecological Monographs* 54: 25–63; Angermeier, P. L., and J. R. Karr. (1984). "Relationships between woody debris and fish habitat in a small warmwater stream." *Transactions American Fisheries Society* 113: 716–726.

[57] Erman, N. A. (1981). "The use of riparian systems by aquatic insects." in *Riparian Forests in California: Their Ecology and Conservation.* A. Sands, ed. University of California, Davis, Institute of Ecology Publication No. 15.

[58] Carlson, J. Y., C. W. Andrus, and H. A. Froehlich. (1990). "Woody debris, channel features, and macroinvertebrates of streams with logged and undisturbed riparian timber in northeastern Oregon, USA." *Canadian Journal of Fisheries and Aquatic Sciences* 47: 1103–1111.

[59] Noel, D. S., C. W. Martin, and C. A. Federer. (1986). "Effects of forest clearcutting in New England on stream macroinvertebrates and periphyton." *Environmental Management.* 10: 661–670.

[60] Newbold, J. D., D. C. Erman, and K. B. Roby. (1980). "Effects of logging on macroinvertebrates in streams with and without buffer strips." *Canadian Journal of Fisheries and Aquatic Sciences* 37: 1076–1085.

[61] Karr and Schlosser, (1977), "Impact of nearstream vegetation."

[62] Gorman, O. T., and J. R. Karr. (1978). "Habitat structure and stream fish communities." *Ecology* 59: 507–515.

[63] Budd, Cohen, Saunders, and Steiner, (1987), "Stream corridor management in the Pacific-Northwest"; Likens, G. E., F. H. Bormann, N. M. Johnson, D. W. Fisher, and R.S. Pierce. (1970). "Effects of forest cutting and herbicide treatment on nutrient budgets in Hubbard Brook watershed-ecosystem." *Ecological Monographs* 40: 23; Bormann, F. H., and G. E. Likens. (1969). "The watershed: Ecosystem concepts and studies of nutrient cycles." in *The Ecosystem Concept in Natural Resource Management.* G. M. Van Dyne, ed. New York, Academic Press.

[64] Angermeier and Karr, (1984), "Relationships between woody debris and fish habitat in a small warmwater stream."

[65] Meehan, W. R., F. J. Swanson, and J. R. Sedell. (1977). "Influences of riparian vegetation on aquatic ecosystems with

particular reference to salmonid fishes and their food supply." pp. 137–145, in *Importance, Preservation, and Management of Riparian Habitat: A Symposium*. R. R. Johnson and D. A. Jones, ed. USDA Forest Service.

[66] McDade, M. H., F. J. Swanson, W. A. McKee, J. F. Franklin, J. Van Sickle. (1990). "Source distances for coarse woody debris entering small streams in western Oregon and Washington." *Canadian Journal of Forestry* 20: 326–330.

[67] Vannote, Minshall, Cummins, Sedell, and Cushing, (1980), "River continuum concept."

[68] Hatfield, J. L., S. K. Mickelson, J. L. Baker, K. Arora, D. P. Tierney, and C. J. Peter. (1995). Buffer strips: Landscape modification to reduce off-site herbicide movement. *Clean Water, Clean Environment, 21st Century : Team Agriculture, Working to Protect Water Resources*. St. Joseph, MI, American Society of Agricultural Engineers; Soranno, P. A., S. L. Hubler, S. R. Carpenter, and R. C. Lathrop. (1996). "Phosphorus loads to surface waters: A simple model to account for spatial pattern of land use." *Ecological Applications* 6: 865–878.

[69] Dunne, T., and L. B. Leopold. (1978). *Water in Environmental Planning*. New York, W. H. Freeman.

[70] Ruhe, R. V. (1975). *Geomorphology: Geomorphic Processes and Surficial Geology*. Boston, Houghton Mifflin.

[71] Cooper, Gilliam, Daniels, and Robarge. (1987). "Riparian areas as filters for agricultural sediment."

[72] Karr and Schlosser, (1977), "Impact of nearstream vegetation."

[73] Gosz, J. R., F. H. Bormann, and G. E. Likens. (1972). "Nutrient content of litter fall on Hubbard Brook experimental forest, New Hampshire." *Ecology* 53: 769.

[74] Gorham, E., P. M. Vitousek, and W. A. Reiners. (1979). "Regulation of chemical budgets over the course of terrestrial ecosystem succession." *Annual Review of Ecological Systematicss* 10: 53–84; Bormann, F. H., and G. E. Likens. (1979). *Pattern and Process in a Forested Ecosystem*. New York, Springer-Verlag. p. 56–62.

[75] Omernik, J. M., A. R. Abernathy, and L. M. Male. (1981). "Stream nutrient levels and proximity of agricultural and forest land to streams—some relationships." *Journal of Soil and Water Conservation* 36: 227–231.

[76] Lowrance, R., R. Leonard, and J. Sheridan. (1985). "Managing riparian ecosystems."

[77] Yates and Sheridan, (1983), "Estimating the effectiveness of vegetated floodplains wetlands."

[78] Toth, R. E. (1990). "Hydrologic and riparian systems: The foundation network for landscape planning." in *International Conference on Landscape Planning*, University of Hannover, Federal Republic of Germany, June 6–8, 1990.

[79] Smith, R. A., R. B. Alexander, and M. G. Wolman. (1987). "Water-quality trends in the nation's rivers." *Science* 235: 1607–1615.

[80] Makarewicz, J. C., and P. Bertram. (1991). "Evidence for the restoration of the Lake Erie ecosystem—water-quality, oxygen levels, and pelagic function appear to be improving." *Bioscience* 41: 216–223.

[81] Lehman, J. T. (1986). "Control of eutrophication in Lake Washington." pp. 301–316, in *Ecological Knowledge and Environmental Problem Solving: Concepts and Case Studies*. National Research Council. Washington, DC, National Academy Press.

[82] Smith, Alexander, and Wolman, (1987), "Water-quality trends in the nation's rivers."

[83] Cooper, Gilliam, Daniels, and Robarge, (1987), "Riparian areas as filters for agricultural sediment."

[84] U.S. General Accounting Office. (1988). "Public Rangelands: Some Riparian Areas Restored But Widespread Improvement Will Be Slow." Report to Congressional Requesters. GAO/RCED-99-105.

[85] Platts, W. S., and J. N. Rinne. (1985). "Riparian and stream enhancement management and research in the Rocky Mountains." *North American Journal of Fisheries Management* 5: 115–125.

[86] Goudie, A. (1990). *The Human Impact on the Natural Environment*. Cambridge, MA, MIT Press; Karr and Schlosser, (1978), "Water-resources and land-water interface."

[87] Karr, J. R. (1988). "Kissimmee River: Restoration of degraded resources." in *Kissimmee River Restoration Symposium*, West Palm Beach, FL, October, 1988.

[88] Yarbro, L. A., E. J. Kuenzler, P. J. Mulholland, and R. P. Sniffen. (1984). "Effects of stream channelization on exports of nitrogen and phosphorus from North Carolina coastal-plain watersheds." *Environmental Management* 8: 151–160.

[89] Erman, D. C., and V. M. Hawthorne. (1976). "Quantitative importance of an intermittent stream in spawning of rainbow-trout." *Transactions of American Fisheries Society* 105: 675–681.

[90] Groeneveld, D. P., and T. E. Griepentrog. (1985). "Interdependence of groundwater, riparian vegetation, and streambank stability: A case study." pp. 44–48, in *Riparian Ecosystems and Their Management: Reconciling Conflicting Uses*, R. R. Johnson, C. D. Ziebell, D. R. Paton, P. F. Ffolliott and R. H. Hamre, ed. USDA Forest Service.

[91] Lowrance, Todd, Fail, Hendrickson, Leonard, and Asmussen, (1984), "Riparian forests as nutrient filters in agricultural watersheds."

[92] Manning, R. E. (1979). "Impacts of recreation on riparian soils and vegetation." *Water Resources Bulletin* 15: 30–43.

[93] Fergusson, B. K., and T. N. Debo. (1987). *On-Site Stormwater Management: Applications for Landscape and Engineering.* Mesa, AZ, PDA Publishers.

[94] Lowrance, Todd, Fail, Hendrickson, Leonard, and Asmussen, (1984), "Riparian forests as nutrient filters in agricultural watersheds."

[95] Karr, J., K. Fausch, P. L. Angermeier, P. R. Yant, and I. J. Schlosser. (1986). *Assessing Biological Integrity in Running Waters: A Method and Its Rationale.* Champaign, IL. Illinois Natural History Survey, Special Publication #5.

[6] Karr, J. (1991). "Biological integrity: A long-neglected aspect of water resource management." *Ecological Applications* 1: 66–84.

[97] Ibid.

[98] Steedman, R. J. (1988). "Modification and assessment of an index of biotic integrity to quantify stream quality in southern Ontario." *Canadian Journal of Fisheries and Aquatic Sciences* 45: 492–501.

[99] Barton, Taylor, and Biette, (1985), "Dimensions of riparian buffer strips."

[100] Cooper, Gilliam, Daniels, and Robarge, (1987), "Riparian areas as filters for agricultural sediment."

[101] Nieswand, G. H., R. M. Hordon, T. B. Shelton, B. B. Chavooshian, and S. Blarr. (1990). "Buffer strips to protect water-supply reservoirs—a model and recommendations." *Water Resources Bulletin* 26: 959–966.

[102] Mander, U., V. Kuusemets, K. Lohmus, and T. Mauring. (1997). "Efficiency and dimensioning of riparian buffer zones in agricultural catchments." *Ecological Engineering* 8: 299–324. See also Wenger, (1999), "A review of the scientific literature on riparian buffer width, extent, and vegetation."

[103] Bren, L. J. (1995). "Aspects of the geometry of riparian buffer strips and its significance to forestry operations." *Forest Ecology and Management* 75: 1–10; Bren, L. J. (1998). "The geometry of a constant buffer-loading design method for humid watersheds." *Forest Ecology and Management* 110: 113–125; Bren, L. J. (2000). "A case study in the use of threshold measures of hydrologic loading in the design of stream buffer strips." *Forest Ecology and Management* 132: 243–257; Xiang, W. N. (1993). "Application of a GIS-based stream buffer generation model to environmental-policy evaluation." *Environmental Management* 17: 817–827; Xiang, W. N. (1996). "GIS-based riparian buffer analysis: Injecting geographic information into landscape planning." *Landscape and Urban Planning* 34: 1–10.

[104] Lowrance, R., L. S. Altier, R. G. Williams, S. P. Inamdar, J. M. Sheridan, D. D. Bosch, R. K. Hubbard, and D. L. Thomas. (2000). "REMM: The riparian ecosystem management model." *Journal of Soil and Water Conservation* 55: 27–34.

[105] Lee, P., C. Smyth, and S. Boutin. (2004). "Quantitative review of riparian buffer width guidelines from Canada and the United States." *Journal of Environmental Management* 70: 165–180.

[106] Ibid.

[107] Budd, Cohen, Saunders, and Steiner, (1987), "Stream corridor management in the Pacific-Northwest."

[108] Cooper, Gilliam, Daniels, and Robarge, (1987), "Riparian areas as filters for agricultural sediment."

[109] Budd, Cohen, Saunders, and Steiner, (1987), "Stream corridor management in the Pacific-Northwest."

[110] Cooper, Gilliam, Daniels, and Robarge, (1987), "Riparian areas as filters for agricultural sediment; Toth, (1990), "Hydrologic and riparian systems."

[111] Hartigan, Douglas, Biggers, Wessel, and Stroh, (1979), "Areawide and local frameworks for urban nonpoint pollution management in northern Virginia"; Hartigan, J. P., and T. F. Quasebarth. (1985). "Urban nonpoint pollution management for water supply protection: Regional versus onsite BMP plans." in *International Symposium on Urban Hydrology, Hydraulic Infrastructures and Water Quality Control*, University of Kentucky, Lexington, July 23–25, 1985.

[112] Cooper, Gilliam, Daniels, and Robarge, (1987), "Riparian areas as filters for agricultural sediment."

[113] Kite, D. J. (1980). "Water courses—open drains or sylvan streams?" in *Trees at Risk*. London, Tree Council Annual Conference.

[114] Bormann, B. T., and J. C. Gordon. (1984). "Stand density effects in young red alder plantations productivity, photosynthate partitioning, and nitrogen-fixation." *Ecology* 65: 394–402.

[115] Karr and Schlosser, (1977), "Impact of nearstream vegetation."

[116] Ibid.

117 Lowrance, Leonard, and Sheridan, (1985), "Managing riparian ecosystems."

118 Baird, K. (1989). "High quality restoration of riparian ecosystems." *Restoration and Management Notes* 7: 60–64.

119 Brown, K. (2000). *Urban Stream Restoration Practices: An Initial Assessment.* Ellicott City, MD, Center for Watershed Protection; Gray, D. H., and A. T. Leiser. (1982). *Biotechnical Slope Protection and Erosion Control.* New York, Van Nostrand Reinhold Co.; Gray, D. H., and R. B. Sotir. (1996). *Biotechnical and Soil Bioengineering Slope Stabilization: A Practical Guide for Erosion Control.* New York, John Wiley and Sons.

120 Decamps, H., M. Fortune, F. Gazelle, and G. Pautou. (1988). "Historical influence of man on the riparian dynamics of a fluvial landscape." *Landscape Ecology* 1: 163–173.

121 Karr, (1988), "Kissimmee River: Restoration of degraded resources."

122 Parkyn, S. M., R. J. Davies-Colley, N. Jane Halliday, K. J. Costley, G. F. Croker. (2003). "Planted riparian buffer zones in New Zealand: Do they live up to expectations?" *Restoration Ecology* 11(4): 436–447.

123 Decamps, Fortune, Gazelle, and Pautou, (1988), "Historical influence of man."

124 Platts and Rinne, (1985), "Riparian and stream enhancement management and research"; Wineger, H. H. (1977). "Camp creek fencing—plant, wildlife, soil and water responses." *Rangemans Journal* 4: 10–12; Behnke, R. J., and R. F. Raleigh. (1978). "Grazing and the riparian zone: Impact and management perspectives." pp. 263–267, in *Strategies for Protection and Management of Floodplain Wetlands and Other Riparian Ecosystems: Proceedings of the Symposium.* Washington, DC, U.S. Government Printing Office; Apple, L. L. (1985). "Riparian habitat restoration and beavers." pp. 489–490, in *Riparian Ecosystems and Their Management: Reconciling Conflicting Uses.* R. R. Johnson, C. D. Ziebell, D. R. Paton, P. F. Ffolliott, and R. H. Hamre, ed. USDA Forest Service.

125 Davis, G. A. (1977). "Management alternatives for the riparian habitat in the southwest." pp. 59–66, in *Importance, Preservation, and Management of Riparian Habitat: A Symposium,* R. R. Johnson and D. A. Jones, ed. USDA Forest Service; U.S. General Accounting Office, (1988), "Public Rangelands: Some Riparian Areas Restored But Widespread Improvement Will Be Slow."

126 Ames, C. R. (1977). "Wildlife conflicts in riparian management: Grazing." pp. 49–57, in *Importance, Preservation, and Management of Riparian Habitat: A Symposium,* R. R. Johnson and D. A. Jones, ed. USDA Forest Service.

127 Platts and Rinne, (1985), "Riparian and stream enhancement management and research."

128 Apple, (1985), "Riparian habitat restoration and beavers."

129 Nassauer, J. I. (1990). "The Appearance of Ecological Systems as a Matter of Policy." in *Landscape Ecology Symposium,* Fifth Annual, Miami University, Oxford, Ohio, March 21–24, 1990.

130 Baird, (1989), "High quality restoration of riparian ecosystems."

CHAPTER 5

THE SOCIAL ECOLOGY OF LANDSCAPE DESIGN: APPLICATIONS FOR GREENWAYS

When we intervene in ecological systems, the effects of our actions reverberate across time and space, often in ways that are not at all obvious. This is true not just for the biophysical systems that surround us, but also for the connections between those systems and human society. In relation to that human realm, it is true not just in terms of topics commonly associated with greenways such as recreation and aesthetics, but in relation to broader more complex social themes such as economics, social justice, and civic interaction. A fully ecological approach to landscape design—that is, an approach that considers the full range of effects of our actions—calls for close attention to these and other social issues.

Although the role of humans in altering natural systems is increasingly highlighted in ecological studies, the implications of these changes for people and society are often narrowly conceived. Even as we have questioned outdated or simplistic ideas of "nature" as separate and apart from human influence, some new but still idealized state of nature often becomes the assumed endpoint, the goal being to protect or restore, if not "pristine" nature, then some new conception of "healthy" nature or "ecological integrity." That social benefits will follow is taken for granted.

This is not necessarily the case. Assuming that more protected land will be inevitably, of itself, good for people is akin to assuming that more species, regardless of whether they are native or invasive, will be "good" for ecosystems. Greenways affect a variety of social functions, and how they are designed can affect these functions profoundly, for good or ill. Moreover, because land protection involves the redistribution of finite resources—both financial and natural—it is inherently political and will benefit some groups over others. As with the concept of biodiversity, discussed in chapter 3, we need to look more deeply. To move from a goal of "ecological integrity" in a biophysical sense to a more inclusive goal of "landscape integrity" (as discussed in chapter 1), we need to look specifically at *how* protected greenspace will benefit society and at *who* specifically is most or least likely to benefit.

The next step is to bring a wider range of social questions into the ecological field of view. Although talk of the benefits of nature for physical health and psychological well-being is commonplace, other concerns that are more explicitly *social*—for instance, concerns related to communities, civil society, politics, equality, and justice—deserve consideration as well and are the primary focus of this chapter. Especially if nature is to be woven into the fabric of modified landscapes—which also means it will be woven through cities, neighborhoods, and, in a very real sense, through institutions and through perceptions and experience—we need to explore and understand a host of new connections and relationships.

How do greenways affect social interaction within and between neighborhoods? What are their economic impacts? What does the distribution of greenspaces mean for questions of environmental justice? Does the experience of nearby nature change the way we think about our homes or about more distant, "wild" nature? Questions like these can help in achieving designs that are effective for both people *and* nature—that are, in the broadest sense of the term, effective *ecologically*.

This chapter explores these and other practical questions related to the social-ecological design of greenways and discusses specific strategies, techniques, and examples. First, it is important to establish a common basis of understanding by sketching out how social-ecological systems work. The next section will take up this question by explaining how social factors can be incorporated into the framework of landscape structure, function, and change outlined in chapter 2, as well as examining how ideas and institutions guide social and ecological change.

Society and Nature: Understanding the Human Landscape

Structure and Function

We can view the physical structure of the *human landscape* (a perspective that emphasizes both people and the built environment) through the same landscape-ecological framework of patch-corridor-matrix discussed in chapter 2.[1] Fully incorporating people in our analysis, however, requires consideration of another, overlapping aspect of structure called *social structure*, which is related to the nature and distribution of social groups.

Much like plant and animal communities, human social groups are distributed in nonrandom patterns across the landscape. But with social structure, distribution is determined not just by biophysical relationships (e.g., people, like other animals, congregate around areas with ample resources), but also by processes of *social differentiation* related to factors such as occupation, wealth, race, and ethnicity, as well as a variety of cultural factors and lifestyle preferences. Also important is the related concept of *class*, which refers to the position of individuals and groups in the social hierarchy, typically marked by some combination of income, education, and occupational status. Although social structure does not always involve spatial separation—members of different groups being mobile and interacting with each other—it nonetheless is usually expressed spatially to some degree, as when members of different classes live in different neighborhoods, work in different parts of a city, and pursue different leisure activities in different places.

Both landscape structure and social structure are closely related to human-landscape *function*. If structure refers to how a landscape is put together, function refers to the dynamic processes that make things happen within the context of a given structure. Key functions include the flow, distribution, and accumulation of basic resources such as energy, raw materials, labor, and information, as well as their processing into more complex resources and benefits such as housing, transportation, psychological and physical health, manufacturing facilities, and educated citizens. As with the biophysical landscape, structure and function are closely related. Class structure, for instance, influences the accumulation of wealth and specialized knowledge (which concentrate in upper class neighborhoods) and the concentration of wage-labor and sometimes of pollutants (in lower class neighborhoods). Also as in the biophysical landscape, corridors, because they can connect otherwise disparate landscape elements together, can play a key role in human-landscape function. For example, the configuration of landscape elements, but especially of corridors such as greenways and roads, influences the time and energy required for transportation between those elements, while the existence and location of sidewalks or trails affect exercise and human health.

The social functions of greenways can be grouped into three categories, around which much of the discussion of greenway applications below will be organized. As both attractors of recreational use and conduits for the movement of people, greenways enhance *social connectivity*. Especially where they link together diverse populations, greenways can thus influence patterns of *social interaction* within and between neighborhoods. Aside from their physical attributes, greenways can also increase social connectivity and positive social interaction because they are so often supported by vigorous local, grassroots organizing and volunteer efforts. These effects, in turn, have the potential to help build *social capital*—the networks of social ties and interactions that provide a crucial basis for trust, cooperation, and successful social, economic, and political activity.

Because they provide for routine, direct experience of nature close to home, greenways also enhance *connectivity between people and nature*—typically more so than other forms of greenspace—because of their linearity, high ratio of edge to interior area, and thus greater accessibility. This, of course, creates opportunities for recreation and the experience of aesthetic beauty, but also can have a more profound significance because bringing nature into people's daily lives influences how they think about and experience their home environment.

Finally, greenways, like other forms of greenspace, can affect local and regional *economics*. This is true both in the usual sense of generating monetary wealth (through increased business activity or property values) and also through the production, ideally in an environmentally sustainable fashion, of material resources through community gardens and forests or, in a sense, the production of energy from nonmotorized transportation.

With regard to all of greenways' positive functions and especially their economic impacts, these benefits are often distributed unequally in space. For instance, some localities may be far better endowed than others with either existing public lands or the resources for acquiring them. *Environmental justice* thus becomes an important theme that, as with many of the ecological issues discussed in previous chapters, reminds us of the importance of thinking about greenways in their broader spatial contexts.

A key area where structure and function come together is in the related concepts of *neighborhood* and *community*. Although the size and boundaries of a given neighborhood will vary "depending on who is defining it and can range from the length of a street (block or blocks) to a district several square miles in extent," neighborhoods are fundamentally physical and place-based and have functional relevance for all the people living in a given area.[2] Although "community" is sometimes used in a similar way, it carries strong social and cultural connotations and suggests the existence of shared experience, interests, and understanding among community members. Unlike neighborhoods, communities are not necessarily defined spatially. A community may develop around the shared experience of place (a neighborhood, a town, a landscape), but it may also be based on interests or activities that are independent of place. We might thus speak of a professional community, a community of greenway enthusiasts and conservationists, or an online community. Neighborhood and community are closely related, of course, not least in the sense that "neighborhoods have long been thought to offer a sense of coherence and identity for those living in large cities" and so can be crucial in forming bonds of community.[3]

Defining what is meant by "community" is especially important because of the common but problematic invocation of community in planning and conservation initiatives in both a structural sense (i.e., a geographic area of focus) and a functional sense (as providing important values for its members and an appropriate arena for setting goals and making decisions). The rise of "community-based conservation" stems explicitly from a welcome attempt to reform top-down models for conservation that saw local residents more as a problem to be minimized than as active participants in ecosystems and potential allies in conservation. Conservation that actively incorporates the needs and contributions of local people—or better yet that *emerges from* local residents— is both an ethical imperative and a pragmatic improvement that can increase the likelihood of success compared to top-down approaches.[4]

However, the popularity of community-based conservation also rests partly on problematic assumptions of just what a community is. The notion of community, in its broadest sense, refers to relationship and connection among people beyond immediate blood relations. Historically, of course, community tended to be much more local than in today's world, in which many of us are tied through both work and personal connections, to people across the country and the world, and where many people will relocate multiple times through the lifespan. These trends account for a certain nostalgia for idealized local communities of the past, and nostalgia has the potential to obscure our understanding of how communities work.

Some community-based initiatives fall short of expectations—especially for marginalized groups—because popular conceptions of community suggest homogeneity, commonality, and agreement among residents and tend to downplay equally important characteristics of diversity, disagreement, and conflict, as well as crucial linkages at larger scales (i.e., between multiple communities of the sort envisioned by such initiatives).[5] To the degree that commonality and agreement do exist, they often cut across particular places and scales, linking together people who may live far apart but have similar orientations and interests. Likewise, stressing the supposed autonomy of local communities may draw attention away from the control exerted over resources by groups and institutions at larger scales. Some authors have suggested a move beyond simplistic assumptions about communities to a more flexible focus on *institutions*—the rules, relationships, and organizations that *cut across* multiple scales and actually govern human behavior toward ecosystems.[6] This approach, discussed further below, is useful because it pushes us to look beyond idealized conceptions of community and investigate more specifically how social systems function.

However, the idea of community—or more precisely, local community—remains important and will be used frequently in this chapter because of the special stake and potential influence of local residents who both understand and care about their landscape, and because, nostalgia aside, local connections among people and between people and nature constitute an important and powerful realm of human experience. The answer is not to abandon community as an object of focus, but rather to look more carefully at community structure and function and to consider relationships at multiple scales.

Change

As with natural landscape elements, components of the human landscape change over time. This can happen gradually as the result of ongoing functional relationships—as, for instance, when consistent inflow or outflow of population and resources results in economic development or decline—or because of more abrupt changes, such as mass migration, economic restructuring or rapid technological or political change.

A familiar type of human landscape change involves the spread of suburban residential matrix into rural areas. In addition to the loss and fragmentation of habitat, sprawl causes a variety of secondary environmental and social effects when compared with more dense, town-centered development. These effects may be either positive or negative—or, more likely, both simultaneously—ranging from relatively low land costs and a culturally valued lifestyle to increased traffic, energy consumption, and pollution, more sedentary and less healthy patterns of activity, and decreased civic interaction.[7] With parcelization and development of previously large land ownerships also come increased restrictions on travel across private lands and greater challenges for land protection, especially of greenways, which may cut across dozens or hundreds of individual ownerships.

As with alterations in biophysical landscape structures, human landscape change occurs unevenly across space. Patch dynamics may be prominent where change occurs within already developed areas (figure 5.1a). Any type of community may go into decline if the economic base is reduced. New industries or government-sponsored redevelopment schemes may help restore the economic base and turn things around. In many U.S. cities, deindustrialization in the late twentieth century opened the way for restoration of riverfront lands for use as greenways or high-end residential and commercial development (figure 5.1b). Where community groups can get involved early on in planning for these river corridors, the chances of steering use toward less expensive and more broadly beneficial uses are likely to increase. (For a good example, see the case of the Bronx River Greenway below.) Similarly, government subsidized brownfield development converts patches with toxic contamination to new productive uses.

Related but more problematic is the process of *gentrification*, which involves upward pressure on real estate prices in desirable areas, movement of middle- and upper class residents into less expensive, low income neighborhoods or towns, and renovation of housing stock, which causes

FIGURE 5.1

Two examples of urban landscape change. (a) An industrial waterfront (top) undergoes deindus- trialization, which opens the way for (bottom) ecological restoration along a greenway, which in turn triggers gentrifi- cation of a neighbor- hood on the left bank and introduces an uncertain future for a low-income neighbor- hood on the right bank. (b) Patch dynamics in an urban residential landscape. A working class neighborhood (left) undergoes economic decline, with the long-term result of abandoned hous- ing and vacant lots (right). In this case, some remaining residents have organized to create a community garden (lower left) to make use of vacant space, produce healthy foods, and enhance community. (Drawing by Joe McGrane.)

prices to rise in those areas. Although gentrification can infuse new energy and economic activity into an area, it can also force low-income residents, who tend disproportionately to rent their homes, to move elsewhere, while simultaneously limiting neighborhood social diversity.[8]

An example of how greenways can contribute to gentrification can be seen in Boston, where a fifteen-year project to bury the city's central artery highway is resulting in the mile-long Rose Kennedy Greenway. Although construction was ongoing and a fully realized greenway still a few years away in 2004, property values along the corridor had already increased seventy-nine percent since the project's inception in 1988, in comparison with a forty-one percent increase citywide. Especially for residential uses, property values have increased with unexpected speed, prompting some developers to switch from planned commercial development to high-end con-dominiums. As one economist put it, "People looking for residential condos are willing to pay an arm and a leg more to have a park as a neighbor."[9] The reaction in existing neighborhoods reflects the variable effects of gentrification, with some people enthusiastic about the change and others, especially in Chinatown, fearing that existing uses "will be displaced by a swank new urban scene" and pushing not just for open space but for "affordable housing to maintain a livable place for the many older people who live there."[10] Although the city favors affordable housing in principle, a lack of firm commitment may be related to the higher taxes that will come from high-end development and will help defray the city's share of the $15 billion price tag of the central artery project.[11]

Gentrification and spatial inequality more generally can also have complex ecological effects. Human-landscape analysis in Baltimore has shown that neighborhoods with higher incomes and levels of education have more and healthier vegetation than low-income areas with similar build-ing densities.[12] This might, at first glance, seem a purely positive outcome—both biophysically and socially—for the neighborhood as a whole. However, in addition to the social problem of spatial inequality, we might expect such situations to also involve increased fertilization and irrigation of landscaped properties. This, in turn, could lead to increased nonpoint source pollution, the effects of which will be borne by downstream residents and aquatic ecosystems.

In this case, change is tied to economic inequality and has mixed outcomes—positive for some people and ecological indicators, but negative for others. Adding social structure, function, and change to a landscape-ecological approach alerts us to important new processes of change and to the question of just who benefits and who does not. In the case of gentrification, provisions for main-taining a certain proportion of affordable housing or regulating real estate markets can make for fair-er and more equitable outcomes. From a biological standpoint, the relationship between social struc-ture and vegetation would suggest the need for management officials to encourage homeowners to use organic practices and perhaps to first target wealthier neighborhoods where problems are likely to be more prominent. In some cases, special zoning ordinances restricting fertilizer use might be called for.

Regional Scale Change

It is also important to consider structure, function, and change at the scale of metropolitan regions that constitute the larger context for greenway design. This is the scale at which the economic driv-ers of sprawl most often occur, and also at which distributive questions of environmental justice should be considered.

Change at this scale may involve the growth or decline of metropolitan regions or the reconfig-uration of their components. Technology, of course, is often crucial, as can be seen with the influ-ence of transportation—first railroads, then automobiles—in allowing people to commute long distances and thereby expanding the functional scale of metropolitan regions. Also important have been government policies, heavily influenced by special interest lobbies, that subsidize a sprawling network of roads and highways.[13] Suburban sprawl and the loss of natural areas cannot, thus, be written off as simply the result of technological change or the shortsightedness of individual decisions—the causes are complex and closely tied to interests, power, and politics.

A major cause of urban and regional expansion (as well as the growth of smaller towns and cities) is the ongoing competition to attract new business and industry by lowering costs, thereby creating economic growth and jobs. John Logan and Harvey Molotch have highlighted the question of who benefits from land development and economic growth at the metropolitan level by describing the role of coalitions of special interests that drive an "urban growth machine."[14] Driven by property owners and land speculators who profit disproportionately from population and economic growth, as well as by the business community in general and by government in search of tax revenue, this coalition works to produce a social consensus on the value of growth and keeps the political establishment oriented toward this as an overarching goal, despite the fact that growth machines perpetuate and even increase inequality and economic segregation. In actuality, Logan and Molotch point out, for many groups the benefits of growth routinely fail to measure up to expectations, as those places with the highest growth rates draw in-migration from other, less competitive regions and competition for jobs grows. Although many people clearly benefit from growth, for others the result may be a rising cost of living, especially housing costs, with little or no improvement in job prospects. Even for homeowners whose property values rise, that long-term gain in equity may be countered by rising property taxes (due to greater demand for services), as well as the now familiar litany of environmental and social problems that go unquantified.

Research on this question has produced variable results, with progrowth coalitions exercising more or less control and with growth producing a range of economic and employment effects.[15] In recent years, other groups pressing for land protection and quality of life issues have increasingly challenged the growth machine with measures such as urban growth boundaries and other growth control measures. There is growing recognition that increased development can do more to increase the need for services than to generate tax revenues, leading to skepticism about growth even from a purely fiscal standpoint. Yet the underlying principle—that both the causes of and the benefits from growth and sprawl are disproportionately tied to economic elites, property owners, and real estate speculators—holds true in most cases, and these interests continue to promote a progrowth ideology, usually with a high degree of success.

The concept of growth machines is of more than passing interest for greenway design. Although it would seem, at first glance, that land conservation is inherently antigrowth, to the extent that greenways and greenspace more generally increase business activity and real estate values— functions that are often touted as net positives by greenway supporters—they actually have the potential to worsen the effects of gentrification and economic segregation and even to further promote growth and development outside of designated protected areas. This counterintuitive problem and what can be done to prevent it will be discussed in more detail later in this chapter.

Demographic trends can also be an important driver of regional change. For instance, in the years following World War II many northern cities saw not only overall expansion but large migrations of African Americans from the south and their concentration in inner-city neighborhoods because of a booming urban manufacturing sector and housing made available by a middle-class migration to the suburbs. By the 1970s there was a shift toward Latino immigrants, while a decline in U.S. manufacturing contributed to high rates of unemployment and urban blight in many inner-city areas. This, in turn, caused accelerated "white flight" or movement of middle- and upper class residents to outlying suburbs.

Myron Orfield describes the feedbacks that today continue to increase this polarization between wealthy outer-ring suburbs and low- to middle-income inner cities and inner suburbs

> Once polarization occurs, the concentration of poverty, disinvestment, middle-class flight, and urban sprawl grow more and more severe. The increase of real property wealth in certain outer suburbs, aided by truly massive regional infrastructure expenditures, and its decline in the central city and inner suburbs represent an interregional transfer of tax base from some of the most poor and troubled communities in American society to some of the most thriving and affluent. The problems associated with these patterns are more complex and detrimental than any other set of challenges facing American society. There is essentially no federal urban policy left to deal with this polarization or its costs.[16]

In some cities, a booming economy in the 1980s and '90s brought further suburban expansion, but also a rediscovery and renaissance of urban life and gentrification of low-income areas. Gentrification further pushes low-income residents and recent immigrants to move to older, inner-ring suburbs or smaller, outlying cities where housing costs are lower but where a lack of public transit sometimes makes commuting to distant jobs, now increasingly located in outer suburban and commercial areas, difficult and expensive.[17] For example, the city of Fall River, Massachusetts, having lost much of its industrial base, became a relatively affordable place to live in the 1990s when real estate prices soared in the Boston metropolitan area. Fall River attracted low-income residents from Boston to the point where the city felt overburdened with the influx and tore down existing public housing rather than accept federal funds for renovation.[18]

Finally, low-density sprawl is hardly a cure-all even for those who are able to live in high-end communities. Although the suburban ideal is clearly desirable for many people, much-discussed problems such as social isolation, sedentary dependence on automobiles, and traffic congestion often lead to frustration with suburban living. For some, the next step is to escape even farther afield to weekend retreats and resort areas—which bring new pockets of sprawl to the country-side—or to exurbs at the far metropolitan fringe. In these ultra-low density suburbs, destinations are spaced still farther apart and long-distance driving becomes part and parcel of everyday life. Thus, the persistent drive to escape, rather than to solve, the detrimental effects of the automobile society results in the continual reinforcement of its underlying causes.

In sum, today's patterns of landscape and regional change, in addition to degrading natural ecosystems, have significant negative effects on low-income populations and are of arguable value even for those who are better off. Although greenways can hardly solve all of the problems created by today's patterns of landscape change, they have an important contribution to make. By making urban and dense suburban living more attractive and meaningful, greenways can help relieve development pressures on surrounding rural areas and reduce transportation and energy needs. However, in an era of increasing economic segregation and civic fragmentation, there is a pressing need to ask how to distribute the benefits of conservation equitably among different parts of a region and all sectors of society and how public spaces can encourage positive social interaction among diverse social groups.

Specific ways of achieving these goals will be discussed later in this chapter. First, we also need to look beyond this level of immediate, tangible issues to deeper root causes of the current situation. The next section will explore the history, concepts, and institutions that must be understood and responded to if we are to guide change in positive and lasting ways.

The Social Basis of Landscape Change: Ideas, Institutions, and Participation

Unlike other organisms, people can learn about and intentionally guide landscape change, as well as reflect on and alter their own behavior. Although our awareness is always incomplete and we inevitably bring about some combination of desired results and unexpected or negative change, considering the social processes that influence change increases the odds of success with any effort to plan for the future. We can more fully understand the human role in the landscape by stepping back from the tangible processes described above and examining cultural and institutional dynamics that shape how we perceive, think about, and modify our environment.

All human knowledge and behavior are, to a great extent, *socially constructed*. This means that in addition to reflecting basic biological traits of the human species, the shared concepts and the closely related institutions (rules, norms, and routine patterns of behavior) that characterize a group or society have been cobbled together over time and played out repeatedly to the point where they become widely accepted, habitual, and even taken for granted as inevitable or natural. Particular orientations toward nature, society, and environment are thus neither correct in any absolute sense nor purely a matter of personal conviction, but are closely related to particular cultural groups at specific points in their histories.

Although we all have an intuitive understanding of the concepts and institutions that must be negotiated in our daily lives, intervening successfully in complex human-ecological systems in ways that will pass the test of time requires that we look more deeply and more critically at the social and conceptual architecture that shapes those systems. The more fundamental and far-reaching our plans, the more important these deep patterns become.

This section will explore the significance of concepts and institutions for open space planning. First, it will consider contemporary western society's emphasis on distant wilderness as the home of the most important or "real" nature—an idea that is problematic because it draws attention from the places where most people actually live. By bringing nature into people's everyday lives, greenways and other forms of nearby nature can help us to rethink old ideas and forge new relationships that are healthier for both people and nature. Next, this section will consider institutions— ranging from informal practices to formal regulations and organizations—that guide specific behaviors and so tangibly affect social-ecological function and change.

This sequence is somewhat artificial, because ideas and institutions are always bound together, but it is intended to address two prominent misconceptions. The first is that deeply held ideas and values are stable and virtually unchanging. The second is, somewhat paradoxically, that on a more immediate and pragmatic level, changing specific ideas and understanding through education is the most important key to changing behavior. Regarding the first, there is a need to question and reflect on some of our most cherished ideas about nature if we are to meet today's environmental challenges. Regarding the second, it is important to understand that institutions (along with power that comes into play in changing them) are at least as important to pragmatic change as ideas and education.

Evolving Conceptions of Nature and Culture

It just may be that the most radical act we can commit is to stay home.
—TERRY TEMPEST WILLIAMS[19]

At a time when our relationship to nature is in flux, we would do well to reconsider our bedrock ideas about that relationship. Especially at this basic level, the process of social construction does not occur randomly, but is closely related to a society's means of material production. Before the industrial revolution, "nature" tended to be seen not as distant or separate from culture and society, but rather was recognized as the daily, immediate basis for agricultural production that most people depended on for their livelihood. Many of the images of pristine or scenic nature that today are held dear had little relevance. As late as the early nineteenth century, rugged mountains and distant, lonely places were generally seen as useless, forbidding, or even downright ugly by Europeans and their New World descendants.[20] Even today, less industrialized societies, as well as many rural residents in developed countries, do not share the popular yearning for wilderness and pristine nature.[21]

With the coming of capitalism and the industrial revolution, these places gradually took on new meanings. More and more people moved to cities built of concrete and steel. Urban air and water became dirty and unhealthy. Industrial workers performed monotonous, menial tasks day-in and day-out. A growing cadre of white-collar workers encountered their own brand of tedium and physical enervation in administrative offices. The upper classes fretted about growing masses of the poor and the foreign-born, despite their usefulness in maintaining reservoirs of cheap labor. Whatever the advantages of the new order, this was not only a harsh world for industrial laborers but also a time of change that inspired feelings of anxiety for those who were better off.

One response—first for the wealthy and eventually for the middle class—was to turn outward to the countryside. Although Henry Ford had the automobile in mind when he said, "We shall solve the city problem by leaving the city,"[22] this idea was clearly at work by the middle of the nineteenth century with the advent of passenger railroads and scenic tourism. There was a new fascination with what appeared to be the antithesis of the industrial city, a desire to witness a new aesthetic of the sublime exemplified in remote, rugged, and wild landscapes. Here could be found both an entertaining distraction from the industrial city and, on a spiritual plane, the transcendent qualities of God's creation in its purest form—qualities that helped to give a sense of meaning and stability in a changing world.

Paradoxically, the new notion of wild, nonhuman nature depended on the trappings of modernity, including not just changes in urban environments but also new forms of industrial transportation—steamboats, railroads, and eventually the automobile—that opened up easy access to remote places. With industrial capitalism and its twin inventions of urbanization and rapid mobility, fundamentally new conceptions of nature became prominent. Despite much variability, they have remained so to this day, as can be seen in the continued popularity of wilderness tourism and in the common suggestion that the most real or desirable nature is apart from human influence and away from our homes.

Unlike earlier societies that engaged mostly in *productive* uses of nature, stressing the need to grow food and make other material goods, modern industrial society has relegated material production to specialized economic sectors while stressing a more pervasive *consumptive* orientation to nature. This is true both in the sense that we emphasize the passive viewing or *aesthetic consumption* of scenic nature and in the sense that nature tourism has become a form of *material consumption* by stimulating demand for a variety of commodities, including energy, transportation, manufactured goods, and services.

This emphasis on distant nature has given rise to rich cultural and artistic traditions, provided respite from the stresses of urban life, and fostered the protection of ecosystems and biological diversity. Perhaps more important than any tallying of such benefits, however, this perspective is deeply embedded in our thought and traditions; it is an integral part of our relation to the world and so not to be lightly dismissed.

But it has also led to serious problems. There has been, for instance, a tendency to base international conservation on the wilderness ideal that is a vestige of colonialist thinking that places western ideologies over the needs of third-world residents.[23] This tendency has led to obvious ethical problems, as well as local resistance and poor conservation results with many top-down, authoritarian projects.[24] Similar relationships are often at work within developed countries, as urban-based environmentalists, well meaning but often naïve about their influence on rural society, seek to exert control over rural landscapes by appealing to metropolitan yearnings for the experience of wild nature.[25]

Fixating on wild and beautiful places far from home makes it that much easier to avoid more difficult problems of the urban environment and the implications of consumptive behavior—both in relation to nature tourism itself and in the less exotic places where we live and work—that lie, along with the current economic imperative of continuous growth, at the root of environmental damage. At the same time, it allows us to maintain the sense that we are doing the right thing if we contribute to popular environmental causes, despite the fact that such contributions are a tiny fraction of our total economic and resource expenditures—most of which contribute to environmental degradation in some way. Finally, the pervasive idea that the good life is to be found away from the city—be it in accessible enclaves of quasi wilderness or low-density suburbs that attempt to recreate a middle, pastoral landscape—encourages further development and sprawl in the very places we cherish for their beauty and wildness. In a complex and finite world, it is difficult to escape the likelihood that these notions about pristine and distant nature may do more harm than good overall.

An alternative approach stresses our connection to nature in the places where we live and work. For those of us who cherish wild nature, this shift may seem less rewarding in the short run, but it can lead to a deeper and more meaningful sense of place and relationship with community, as well as a more environmentally sound lifestyle. By creating more functional, beautiful, and meaningful spaces close to home, we can make clear that nature is not just "out there" in distant places, but that it takes diverse forms and surrounds us in our daily lives. By making nearby nature more of a focus for writing, art, and education we can stress the idea that experiencing and caring for nature is not just something for the wilderness but a practice to be integrated into daily life. By helping to make life at home more fun and interesting, we can decrease the demand for consumptive tourism and ever more distant suburban commuting. By designing greenspace that incorporates materially productive uses such as community gardens and forests, we can see nature not just as something out there to look at, but as the very basis of our survival and learn to participate actively in its cycles of life.

This is not to suggest that wilderness is unimportant. The question should not be one of either wilderness or nature close to home—a framing that simply turns the old dichotomy on its head. The importance of large wilderness reserves for biodiversity is demonstrated in chapter 3 of this volume, and the ability to experience such places has great cultural, psychological, and spiritual benefits. Instead of choosing one or the other, we should begin the large task of rethinking our relationship to nature as the world around us changes and as we ourselves change. An important first step is to pay more attention to how we experience and shape our home landscapes.

Institutions and the Regulation of Social-Ecological Systems

Institutions involve the norms, rules, and routine behaviors that guide human activity. Although today's popular culture surrounds us with the suggestion that we are all unique individuals in charge of our own actions, beyond a relatively narrow range of intentional choice, our behavior (as individuals and as groups) is shaped and constrained by institutions. Changing human behavior, then, is not just a matter of education or values, as is often suggested, but of changing the institutions that guide us. Understanding how institutions work, how they change, and how they *resist* change is crucial to learning about and guiding landscape change.

Institutions can be formal (laws, bureaucracies, religious ceremonies) or informal (customs, conventions, habits). For our purposes, relevant examples of formal institutions include land-use laws and regulations; property rights and boundaries; political jurisdictions; public agencies and private organizations; and official processes for public participation and decision making. Surrounding and infusing all of these are complex networks of informal institutions, such as those related to organizational culture, professional norms, traditional land uses, leisure and recreational behavior, and civic interaction.

Institutions are socially constructed in much the same way as—and closely related to—the concepts and ideas discussed in the previous section. As behaviors are played out over and over again, or *institutionalized*, they come to be taken for granted as simply the way things are done. Just as the idea of wilderness as an uplifting or virtuous place may seem entirely self-evident (and so becomes difficult to question), conventional activities such as hiking or nature photography or tourism tend to be taken as obvious pursuits in such a place—when in fact they would have seemed rather strange only a few centuries ago and may again in the future.

But institutions, like ideas, are not just subject to long-term, historical change. Formal institutions, of course, may be consciously reviewed and changed from time to time, or entirely new ones may be created. Change also occurs unintentionally, as individuals and groups adjust to new circumstances or perhaps simply learn how to do things better, and those new techniques become routine. Attempts to change complex, formal institutions such as political systems, bureaucracies, and, of course, laws and regulations, often encounter resistance because change affects the interests and habits of many different actors. *Power*, or the ability of individuals and groups to influence the behavior of others, thus becomes a fundamentally important aspect of institutional change.

The collection of institutions in a given setting can be thought of as a sort of ecosystem—an *institutional ecosystem*.[26] Like their biophysical counterparts, institutional ecosystems are highly complex. They have many overlapping, interdependent elements and cut across multiple scales, as well as organizational and political boundaries. Consider, for example, a streamside greenway. Here, the biophysical ecosystem is affected by the flow of water, nutrients, sediment, and species from upstream and adjacent land areas; air pollution from local and regional sources; invasive species originally from other parts of the world; and, in the long run, greenhouse gases and global warming. As described in chapter 2, an ecological approach to biophysical systems stresses the need to consider this diversity of processes and scales. Institutional ecosystems should be approached in the same way.

Those same biophysical processes are intertwined with a range of institutions, such as local traditions of recreational use; patterns of ownership and land use adjacent to and upstream from the corridor; customary resource uses such as hunting and fishing; local watershed associations and land trusts; town, state, and federal programs and regulations; and, in the broadest sense, regional and global patterns of material and energy consumption that influence pollution. Although it is not possible to address all of these elements comprehensively (just as it is impossible to do so with the full range of biophysical linkages), researchers and planners need to be aware of the full range and complexity of institutions so that, in a given case, the most important connections within and between biophysical and social systems can be identified, investigated, and addressed.

Especially worthy of discussion here are questions of institutional *alignment* (do institutions match up spatially with the key biophysical and social processes?) and institutional *adaptability* (are institutions sufficiently flexible and adaptable to stand the test of time as social and ecological conditions change?). Closely related to both of these issues is the need for broad public participation to guide and support institutions, a diverse topic to be addressed here and also in the following section.

Institutional Alignment

Most political boundaries were drawn long before ecology and environment were pressing concerns as they are today. This has resulted in boundaries, legal frameworks, and public agencies that match up poorly with ecological and related social processes (figure 5.2). Hoover and Shannon point out that:

> typically, in the USA, each jurisdiction through which a greenway might pass retains a set of institutional practices (e.g., land use plans, farming strategies, and tax structures), which have evolved locally over time, independent from surrounding jurisdictions. In terms of greenway conservation, the consequence of isolated, local institutions is a cacophony of competing, conflicting land use policies, none of which takes into consideration the greenway in its entirety.[27]

FIGURE 5.2

A typical case of institutional misalignment. Ecologically arbitrary property and political boundaries, which limit collaboration among property owners and agencies, are at odds with ecological flows in the landscape, such as excess nutrients running downhill from a farm (bottom right); effluent from a sewage treatment plant and a tributary into which it flows (center left); the greenway corridor itself, including the movement of people, water, and wildlife; and industrial pollutants emanating from a power plant.
(Drawing by Joe McGrane.)

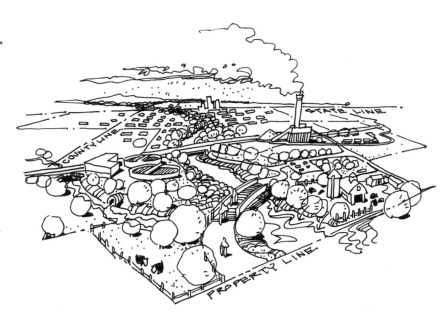

The same is true with property boundaries, which are crossed continuously by flows of air, water, and species. Compounding this spatial misalignment has been the tendency of many management plans to avoid this difficult problem altogether.[28]

Establishing functional alignment may involve collaboration between existing local institutions (e.g., town or county agencies or local land trusts); an existing overarching institution that can integrate management at the landscape scale (e.g., a watershed council, or state or federal government), or the creation of an entirely new, more precisely aligned institution such as a nonprofit organization dedicated to a specific greenway, greenway network, or watershed. To the extent that existing institutions can be adapted to new tasks or collaborate with neighboring institutions, this will often be more reliable and efficient than establishing entirely new ones.[29] Where existing broader scale institutions have a specific role to play (e.g., because of financial resources, technical expertise, or legal authority), this should be carefully balanced with the greater responsiveness of local organizations by planning for regular communication and collaboration across scales. If there are clear gaps in the institutional ecosystem (i.e., if existing institutions lack the resources or expertise needed or if effective collaboration proves infeasible), new organizations or agencies that are to be charged with collaborative cross-boundary design and management should be created with input from as broad an array of interested parties as possible. Management that transcends traditional boundaries "can be effective only by creating an interactive network of participants, information, and practices. This network should represent the diverse legitimate interests and capabilities of a pluralistic society."[30]

Designing and managing across boundaries also requires attention to informal institutions. As with biophysical ecosystems, some elements of institutional ecosystems are far more likely to be perceived than others through casual observation. Biophysical ecosystems contain large or obvious elements that strike us immediately as important to system function (for instance, trees, streams, and

BOX 5.1

Great River Greening: An Innovative Case of Institutional Alignment and Collaboration

Minnesota's Great River Greening is a young organization, founded in 1995, that has achieved impressive results in transboundary ecosystem restoration and management. Great River Greening has developed technical expertise and collaborative relationships with more than 400 organizations and businesses to restore native riparian communities along the Mississippi, Minnesota, and St. Croix rivers in the Minneapolis-St. Paul metropolitan area (figure 5.3). Here, the rivers cut across five counties, dozens of municipalities, and thousands of private land holdings.

The effort started with a project to restore 4,000 acres (1,619 ha) of derelict industrial land by planting 25,000 native trees—requiring the cooperation of ninety-three mostly corporate (and initially reluctant) landowners, recruitment of 7,000 volunteers, and collaboration with the University of Minnesota's Center for Landscape Studies to develop a plan for native restoration and techniques for bringing soils back to fertility. Since then, Great River Greening has expanded its area of focus within the metro area; become a partner in Metro Conservation Corridors, which coordinates the involvement of thirteen public agencies and private organizations; involved more than 15,000 volunteers; planted 41,000 native trees and shrubs and 73,000 native wildflowers and grasses; and controlled invasive nonnative species on 550 acres (223 ha).

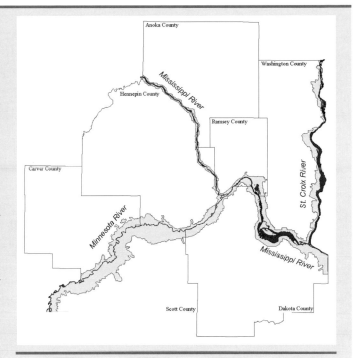

FIGURE 5.3

Great River Greening promotes functional alignment between institutions and the riparian ecosystems of the Mississippi, St. Croix, and Minnesota rivers by defining a large, ecologically functional area of focus and coordinating ecological restoration efforts among a range of organizations and agencies in a seven-county area surrounding Minneapolis-St. Paul, Minnesota.

Great River Greening's mission involves engaging "volunteers in the planting of native vegetation, removal of exotic weeds, native seed collection and stewardship work that results in an informed and involved citizenry." Working with so many diverse organizations and people is always a challenge but it is key to building long-term trust and commitment. Results in this case rest not just on technical expertise, but on the organization's ability to effectively cut across existing jurisdictions and ownership patterns by working collaboratively "as a catalyst, creating effective partnerships among agencies, municipalities . . . private landowners . . . and scientists."[1]

[1]Great River Greening. Retrieved August 9, 2005, (http://www.greatrivergreening.org).

large animals), but they also contain many far more subtle pieces that are, at least upon initial observation, harder to see and understand but that are still extremely important functionally (things like soil organisms that recycle nutrients and insects that pollinate flowering plants). Similarly, institutional ecosystems are likely to include both prominent, formal institutions and a range of closely related routine behaviors and relationships among politicians, managers, volunteers, landowners, and recreational users. Successful interventions typically require attention to both of these levels.

Consider a relatively simple scenario of a newly designated riverside greenway that must be consistently managed along its length to maintain water quality, runs through several towns, and is bordered by hundreds of private properties. The enthusiasm of activists and planners may give way to frustration as unexpected and even seemingly irrational obstacles emerge. Perhaps coordinating the towns requires a new cooperative management entity or coordination by county or state government. Either of these strategies might meet with resistance because it challenges the authority of town officials; redistributes funds that sustain departments, payrolls, and even political patronage systems; and requires the reformulation of work habits and relationships for employees. Meanwhile, landowners may be asked or required to change the customary use of their properties—say, limiting the size of suburban lawns, restricting the cutting of trees, or restricting the use of fertilizer. Such changes may be resented and resisted by some, while even the most sympathetic landowners may be tempted to rationalize noncompliance with the idea that just one exception won't make any real difference—a perfectly reasonable assumption in isolation, but disastrous when widespread.

In such a scenario, successfully intervening in the biophysical landscape requires three kinds of institutional change. The first and most obvious step, of course, is to change the locus of authority and decision making by acquiring property rights to the greenway corridor itself (either in total or partially with easements). This must be followed with changes to formal management institutions so that there is coordination and consistency across political boundaries and—perhaps most difficult—by changing the informal habits of the individuals and groups (e.g., landowners, recreational users, and land managers) who interact with those formal institutions. Depending on the situation, this last level of change might be accomplished through education, incentives, or—as a last resort—disincentives, in the form of fines or other penalties.

Even the most informal social interactions can be important to the long-term cultivation of common understanding and trust, which in turn facilitate formal institutional collaboration. In greenway-related research in the Tug Hill region of northern New York, Hoover and Shannon found routine contact and deliberation among stakeholders to be key to establishing trust and cooperation across boundaries and multiple scales.[31] In examining state and regional planning and regulatory programs that limited private-property rights and local autonomy in favor of landscape-scale ecological goals, they found that acceptance of state-level authority increased both where there was a history of the state working collaboratively with local communities and where there was a better developed network of informal communication and deliberation. They stress that there are important, long-term linkages between routine, informal institutions and acceptance of formal interventions: "policymaking in a participatory democracy context is a learning process where complex deliberative opportunities are built upon simpler ones."[32] Even seemingly insignificant communication and collaboration helps to build traditions of trust and understanding that can be crucial to reaching larger goals.

Adaptability of Institutions

The inherently dynamic nature of social and biophysical systems, as well as the rapid pace of change occurring in developing landscapes—and in the world at large—calls for designing institutional networks that are not just functional today but that will be adaptable in the future. The adaptability of institutions—their ability to perceive and respond to change—is closely related to the process of *social learning*. Social learning depends not just on individuals but is built into the operation of groups and organizations. It tends to increase when there are (1) diverse sources of information (e.g., public input and discussion on questions of values and goals, informal observation and monitoring among local resource users, formal scientific research, and formal political processes); (2) an experimental orientation toward policy and planning, whereby interventions are monitored, evaluated, and adjusted; and (3) regular communication and collaboration across scales and within and between communities, organizations, and agencies.[33] Although such practices will require greater effort and resources up front, to the extent that they are embedded in formal structures and procedures and embraced informally, institutions are more likely to learn and adapt as conditions change.

The importance of adaptability is driven home by Holling's comparison of twenty-eight cases of resource management from around the world.[34] He found a remarkably consistent pattern in which short-term success in managing a single resource, often with attention to just a single scale, resulted in increasingly centralized, inflexible management systems that became unable to anticipate or adapt to new or more systemic problems. In most cases the long-term result was pervasive degradation of ecosystems. Holling's research focused largely on regional-scale systems and on resource extraction (of timber, fisheries, grazing, etc.) rather than lands set aside for conservation. Although at first glance the relevance of these findings for greenway design may seem limited, it is important to consider the possibility that greenways could become just the sort of focused, highly successful initiative that might lead to inflexible institutional systems and a lack of ability to respond to changing ecological threats at larger scales. Such threats might potentially include, for instance, development pressures borne of regional demographic and economic trends or very large-scale processes such as acid precipitation or global warming. There is a real risk that successful greenways and other local initiatives can create a false sense of security and, counter-intuitively, diminish the response to larger, overarching problems.

It would be a mistake to assume that local conservation and activism can exist in isolation from or have nothing to contribute to these broader and more complex issues. To the contrary, there is growing evidence that successful long-term management of resource systems is closely linked to the ability to address issues at multiple scales and that information and institutional capacity at relatively small and local scales is key to developing this capacity.[35] For instance, widespread but decentralized, locally based ecological monitoring, often conducted by volunteers, increasingly helps to make up for the fact that most formal scientific studies cover short time frames and small spatial scales. Local monitoring has become an integral component of large-scale ecological assessment and management—examples include the Global Coral Reef Monitoring Network and Canada's nationwide Ecological Monitoring and Assessment Network.[36] Similarly, local grassroots groups can make important contributions to advocacy efforts focused on state, national, and global-scale issues, especially if they band together with other local groups. Planning and management institutions would do well to build a certain degree of broad, strategic analysis into their routines, including tracking larger ecological and social trends, assessing emerging problems, and exploring how they might contribute to larger goals of sustainability.

Adaptability is also important at smaller scales and with more focused agendas. For a given greenway, new issues may emerge, such as increased use of the greenway itself; intensifying uses of adjacent lands; heightened levels of air or water pollution, or changing political and fiscal contexts that affect both local threats and the capacity of management responses.

In some cases, new threats also have the potential to trigger new opportunities for strengthening institutional arrangements. For instance, an effective watershed management regime in Sweden had its origins in alarm at the new problem of acid rain in the 1980s.[37] A combination of concern among local fishermen and new government grants for liming lakes led to formation of a watershed association (a new institution that both filled a functional gap and transcended local political boundaries) and local-national collaboration on restoring water quality. The new institutional framework built on local traditions of crayfish harvesting, which was a major point of community-level social interaction, and set the stage for further innovation, especially a strong emphasis on social learning that integrates and applies informal information from local users, systematic ecological monitoring, and formal scientific sources. Social learning, in turn, is likely to maintain both a high level of collaboration and adaptability to new changes in the future.

Guiding Landscape Change through Participation

There are differing views about what, fundamentally, brings about behavioral and institutional change—and thereby guides planning interventions of all sorts. Some tend to see the key to change as educational—a matter of knowledge, ideas, values and attitudes. If individuals start to think differently, it is assumed that they will change their behavior, and if groups or society as a whole start to think differently that can be the basis for institutional change, which in turn will affect behavior. Others emphasize power and politics—the ability to control resources, decision making, and, once again, the institutions that guide and constrain behavior. In reality, both ideas and power are crucially important.

Faced with choices about how to act, people's ideas and values, along with their factual knowledge, play an important role in their decisions. At the same time, choices are very much shaped and constrained, as we have seen, by institutions, which in turn are the objects of political action, in which individuals and groups struggle to influence change in accordance with their own interests. Moreover, the two realms of ideas and power are very much connected, as ideas influence the nature of activism and political struggles and as power comes into play in determining the flow of information and ideas through, for instance, the funding of research, media presentations, or the design of school curricula. Thus, moving the human landscape toward a state that is both more ecologically sound and more socially beneficial requires attention to ideas and information and to the brass tacks of politics alike.

We focus here on public participation as an overarching realm that not only incorporates informational and decision-making functions, but, ideally, integrates the two into a deliberative process that fosters individual and social learning and inclusive, fair, and democratic decision making. It is important to keep in mind that landscape design is an inherently political process, even when goals may seem to be clearly in the public interest. If design is to be fair and socially responsive, this political act should be done with maximal participation throughout the process. Not only is there an ethical obligation to do this but, because the long-term prospects of initiatives will often hinge on broad public support, which in turn may depend on responsiveness to diverse public needs, it is also likely to be pragmatic.

Formal participation sometimes is seen as a matter of soliciting the preferences of individuals, which can then be incorporated into hierarchical, top-down decision processes. Often through public hearings, "ordinary citizens' opinions are heard, and sometimes integrated by experts into policy, but rarely are citizens asked to participate directly in the policy design process."[38] In other words, the flow of information is simple and one-way, power ultimately lies with official "decision makers," and there are typically relatively low levels of citizen commitment, civic interaction, and social learning. More robust, deliberative participation, however, involves a shift to horizontal power relations, complex and multidirectional communication, and collective learning. Participation becomes:

> a collective process for engaging in . . . reflective criticism. People work back and forth
> among the norms and theories to which they claim to subscribe, and the decisions they
> have made or are tempted to make. They seek to understand where their ideas conflict
> and where they are inconsistent with their actual practice. They explore those options they
> find most compelling as their grasp of the situation improves. Deliberation fosters 'civic
> discovery' . . . through such deliberations, opinions can be revised, premises altered, and
> common interests rediscovered.[39]

Like the closely related idea of adaptive institutions described above, such a process may require a significant commitment of time and resources but is likely to pay important dividends in the long run in the form of better decisions and greater public support. Deliberative participation may involve, instead of (or in addition to) single, large public hearings, more intimate forums, such as planning workshops, neighborhood meetings, citizens' advisory committees, and more sustained sequences of events that stretch across the duration of a project or series of projects. Such a level of commitment may not always be possible, but where it is the results are likely to include greater inclusiveness, clarification of underlying conflict and commonality among groups, the establishment of stronger long-term consensus and goals, and greater learning and commitment among participants.

Kristen Day provides an example from Costa Mesa, California that, although not specific to greenways, points to the importance of broad participation in all phases of a project.[40] This case is related to New Urbanism, a planning strategy that emphasizes neighborhood distinctiveness, an interspersion of residential and commercial areas, parks and greenspaces, and nonmotorized transportation—and so is often tied to greenway design. Costa Mesa's Westside neighborhood had become predominantly low-income Latino in the 1990s, and many Anglo property owners were disturbed by the area's appearance, including "deteriorating streets, littered sidewalks and overflowing dumpsters, few trees," and a generally "unkempt look."[41] The city developed a New Urbanist plan for Westside that emphasized physical and aesthetic improvements, including creating a greener and pedestrian-friendly, "traditional 'Main Street'" character and a shift from industry to "clean" high-tech businesses.

The plan was not implemented, however, because of concern among Latino residents that it would jeopardize existing industry and low-cost multifamily housing. Notably, during the project's public involvement phase, Latino residents' suggestions had focused not on planning and design, but on nonphysical issues such as communication between the city and residents, public safety, and "recreational and educational opportunities for youth."[42] But because "the decision to emphasize physical planning . . . was foregone and not open to serious debate" such concerns were never taken seriously—and this avoidance of diversity and conflict within the community ultimately led to the plan's demise. This incident of *a priori* problem definition is directly related to assumptions about the nature of community. Day concludes:

> An immediate focus on physical planning and design may mask underlying group differences that would be better acknowledged. . . . As a strategy to improve urban neighborhoods, New Urbanism prioritizes design and planning. Neighborhoods with diverse populations may first need, however, to build trust and to identify similarities and differences so that groups can eventually discuss priorities for planning and design. Focusing first on design may ensure disagreement, as groups define community in ways that exclude those unlike themselves.[43]

Involving the public at an early stage may not always be seen as a good thing for greenway enthusiasts because it takes greenways out of the realm of being an absolute good and raises the possibility that the larger community may have other priorities. Given the widespread appreciation and demand for greenspace in communities of all sorts, however, a more common outcome will be participatory guidance of greenway projects toward serving the needs of all stakeholders, not just those who are the most enthusiastic and organized. The end result will be initiatives that, whether focused on greenways or other priorities, respond more effectively to the range of public needs and that garner more effective and sustained public support.

Applications: Greenways as Part of a Reinvigorated Commons

Turning to specific applications for greenway design, it is important to be explicit about this chapter's vision of what is important and worth doing in the world. At the core of that vision is the idea that greenways are fundamentally a form of *common* space with important *social* functions. They are not only open for public use in a strict legal sense, but represent a relatively new and vigorous form of an old idea—that commonly held and commonly managed resources have a vital and far-reaching role to play in society.

Greenways are ideally both egalitarian and democratic. They are egalitarian in that they, at least in theory, offer important benefits to all citizens, regardless of wealth, power, or social standing. They are democratic in that they both depend on and further strengthen traditions of civic participation and collective decision making.

The commons, traditionally in the form of common agricultural and forest lands, have played a crucial role in many societies by producing shared resources and benefits, providing a safety net for the poor (and for all in times of scarcity), and serving as civic and cultural space. The commons, however, have been under assault in a capitalist economic system that relies on private ownership and competition. This long trend continues to the present day, marked by examples as diverse as the push for privatization and "structural adjustment" in

---

BOX 5.2

Rules of Thumb for Public Participation

In a discussion of community-based ecosystem management that considers both explicitly political questions and the role of civic interaction in building effective institutions, Moote et al. suggested several "key dimensions" or principles for public participation.[1]

- *Inclusiveness* and *diversity* are important to both democratic process and the efficient flow of information. "It is crucial that community members from diverse backgrounds actively participate from the beginning in planning, design, decision making, implementation, and monitoring." Special attention should be paid to overcoming power imbalances and ensuring effective participation of marginalized or disempowered groups.
- *Accessibility* is key to ensuring robust participation. Specific techniques should be tailored "to match the diverse needs and communication styles of affected groups." To ensure accessibility, practitioners should draw creatively on a range of techniques such as workshops, neighborhood gatherings, private meetings, written communication, multiple meeting locations and times, informal networking, and personal recruitment.
- *Transparency* of decision making is crucial to building trust, openness, and cooperation. It should be "clear who the participants are, what the schedule for decision making is, who has ultimate authority for making those decisions, and how input to the process will be used."
- *Mutual learning* means that participation should be active, participatory, and nonhierarchical. "Participation in activities such as field trips, field work (e.g., monitoring, training, rehabilitation, planting seedlings), and workshop tasks such as planning, problem solving, and analytical and information-sharing discussions fosters learning and understanding better than passive speeches, hearings, and videos. This type of active learning requires those people traditionally considered 'experts' to shift from primary presenters or speakers to join with other participants as resource people, facilitators of learning processes, and coordinators of interaction."
- Finding a *collective vision* should be a key goal based on the exploration of common values and interests. "Exploring interests and values not only defines vision and provides a basis for trust, it also provides a foundation for commitment. If a community is able to find broadly defined common values . . . it will have a stronger sense of itself and a basis for collective action.

[1] Moote, M. A., B. Brown, et al. (2000). "Process: Redefining relationships." pp. 97–116, in *Understanding Community-Based Forest Ecosystem Management*. G. J. Gray, M. J. Enzer and J. Kusel, ed. New York, Food Products Press.

---

international development and, in the United States, the property rights movement and renewed emphasis on commodity production on federal lands. For those who fear that the pendulum has swung too far toward private ownership, the vitality of the greenway movement comes as a welcome trend and a rallying point for further action. The popularity of greenways, and greenspace more generally, marks a broad recognition that there is much to be gained by bringing new attention to the commons for both social and ecological reasons. There are essential needs and functions that—as economists dating back to Adam Smith have recognized—simply are not provided by a pure market economy and that require the shared responsibility and commitment of public initiatives.

Greenways can play an especially important role in a revived commons because they are strategic repositories of concentrations of public values; because they literally tie communities and regions and other sorts of common space together; and because they are a new form open to experimentation and innovation. This reinvigoration of the commons also comes with the recognition that this is not just something for government, but can be a shared project between government and civil society, including incorporated nonprofit groups, organized community associations, and more dispersed citizen participation. With this diverse collaboration has come a new energy and expanded repertoire of options and strategies: land trusts, easements, watershed and community conservation groups, social movements and activism, public participation, and public-private partnerships. Although government initiatives at various levels are extremely important, this broad and innovative participation is the essence of an engaged citizenry and brings benefits for the health and integrity of landscapes and democracy alike.

The discussion that follows focuses largely on how greenways can best function as a modern-day form of common space. We examine how greenways can act as a platform for environmental education and environmental art, both of which are important to the long-term project of reexamining the relationship between society and nature, as well as providing more immediate understanding and inspiration. We proceed to a discussion of how greenways enhance social connectivity and facilitate positive social interaction and community well-being. Finally, we address the economic implications of greenways. This last topic, however, is not approached from a conventional perspective of neoclassical economics—a perspective that tends to ask how greenways can increase the private accumulation of capital, and which has been treated extensively elsewhere.[44] Instead, we consider greenways from the perspective of ecological economics, which asks more explicitly value-laden questions about the purpose and effects of economic activity (is it to accumulate dollars, or to produce useful goods in a sustainable fashion?) and about how wealth is distributed (does economic activity lead to a just distribution of benefits?). As we do with conventional economics, we also give minimal coverage of less specifically *social* questions related to physical and psychological health benefits, beauty and aesthetics, or the design of recreational facilities. These important topics have also been covered elsewhere.[45]

Environmental Education and Art: Rethinking People and Nature

Earlier, we argued that the American emphasis on distant, wild, and scenic nature is problematic and that greenways, because they encourage routine involvement with nature in the places where people live, have an important role to play in rethinking these relationships and habits. But this is not just a matter of abstract thought, and neither will simply establishing new greenways or even providing recreational facilities be enough. Environmental education and environmental art are tools that can help encourage and move this process forward by integrating experience and concepts in powerful new ways.

Greenways are especially important to ideas and experience of nature because their typically metropolitan location, as well as their linearity and high edge-to-interior ratio, makes them a widely accessible example of nature close to home and so well suited to exploring human relationships to nature. Linearity and the mobility that it facilitates also make greenways compelling places for using narrative—for telling stories. This section explores how greenways can be used for innovative forms of environmental education, as well as for environmental art. Artists, often in collaboration with communities and citizens, can further explore our changing relationship to nature and use those explorations to stimulate public awareness and involvement in local environments.

Environmental Education (by Lianne Fisman)

The goal of environmental education is to produce citizens who are knowledgeable about the bio-physical environment and its problems, aware of strategies that can be used to deal with these issues, and engaged in working toward their solution.[46] Traditionally, environmental education has focused on fostering knowledge (cognitive learning) about problems or issues, often in pristine or wilderness landscapes that tend to be inaccessible to many urban and suburban residents. This approach is troubling for a number of reasons. First, it neglects the importance of emotion in shaping people's environmental attitudes and behaviors. Second, it implies that remote landscapes are inherently more valuable and worthy of protection than one's home environment. Third, it fails to recognize the importance of sustained contact with a given place in building a sense of caring and commitment. Finally, focusing environmental education on "wild" nature reinforces the fallacy that human communities function independently of the ecosystems in which they are embedded. If designed and programmed appropriately, greenways offer opportunities for residents of all ages to experience nearby nature and learn about the biophysical and social environments of which they are a part.

Although factual knowledge is important in cultivating environmental awareness and responsibility, research indicates that emotional, or affective, learning is at least as important.[47] In the words of Charles Jordan, the recreation and parks director in Portland, Oregon: "What we do not value we will not care for. What we do not care for we will not own. What we do not own we will lose."[48] Opportunities to spend substantial amounts of time in a given location allow for the discovery of meaningful components of the landscape and the development of an emotional attachment to that place. For many people, landscapes that are readily accessible are those that are near to their home; these places seldom fit the image of wild nature associated with traditional environmental education.

Using nearby nature for educational purposes sends the message that the local environment has genuine ecological value. It also gives people sustained contact with natural areas—an essential component of the development of environmental knowledge and concern.[49] The importance of fostering a connection to the local environment is illustrated, for example, by the results of a study suggesting that environmental education built around wilderness experiences may actually diminish environmentally responsible behaviors amongst youth. These programs tend to reinforce the separation of pristine nature (that is worth protecting) from youths' home environments.[50] This does not mean that carefully designed wilderness experiences cannot be an effective part of a broader environmental education curriculum. It does, however, highlight the need to create programs that focus on the value of local environments.

Although all conservation areas are potential sites for experiential learning, many greenways are unique in their accessibility to a wide range of society, regardless of their resources. Some of these corridors run through urban neighborhoods, giving access to those who have not been included in the traditional environmental movement (with its focus on protecting wild nature). Greenways provide urban residents with opportunities to experience nature in their own locale. They can also serve as the starting point for formal education programs that are built around issues that resonate with neighborhood residents, such as preserving local flora or fauna, learning about the impacts of adjacent land uses (such as bus depots or dry cleaners) on the quality of the greenway environment, or the creation of amenities such as pocket parks and community gardens. Because greenways tend to enhance the aesthetics of the neighborhood, they may also foster a sense of pride and ownership that leads to further stewardship activities. Some of the cases described below illustrate the potentially powerful link between environmental and civic education.

A combination of affective and cognitive learning can be achieved through both formal and informal educational experiences. Greenways readily provide opportunities for informal, unstructured education. Moving along the greenway, people observe and develop knowledge about changes in the biophysical and social landscape. This learning may be tacit or made more explicit through the use of markers, such as signs, monuments, and public art that clarify the narrative of the greenway and promote cognitive learning. It is, however, important to remember that flagging a particular feature imbues it with meaning and implies that it is a significant part of the landscape. Consultation and cooperation with residents can help ensure appropriate signage that incorporates local knowledge and values and increases pride and ownership over local resources.

Valley Quest, a Vermont-based program, has a novel approach to narrating the landscape and fostering informal environmental education experiences. Community groups, classrooms, and individuals throughout the Connecticut River valley of Vermont and New Hampshire have created a series of treasure hunts (known as Quests) in their local environs that are published together in a book format. The Quests use natural and built components of the landscape (such as old mills, waterfalls, cemeteries, and one-room schoolhouses) as resources to promote environmental discovery and learning. Locals and visitors select a Quest in a particular area, and by following its clues, they learn about the ecology and social history of that place. The independent character of this activity means that questers have ample opportunity to explore, wonder, and discover landscape elements that are not explicitly identified in the hunt. Each Quest ends with a treasure box that holds a rubber stamp (to put in the back of the book) and a sign-in field journal. One of the most noteworthy aspects of this system is that it allows a broad range of local stakeholders to identify and share significant aspects of their environment. This model can easily be adapted to any greenway environment. (For more information see http://www.vitalcommunities.org/ValleyQuest/ValleyQuest.htm).

Formal learning typically takes place in schools or through classes and tends to focus on cognitive learning, particularly science and natural history.[51] Almost any area along a greenway can be used as an outdoor classroom and laboratory. Exploring the natural processes occurring in community gardens, parks, playgrounds, and disturbed areas helps people see their local environment as part of an important ecological system. An example of the diversity of spaces that can be successfully used in formal environmental education programs is found in the Open Spaces as Learning Places program. This program, which is run by The Urban Resources Initiative in New Haven, Connecticut, uses six very different open spaces to teach elementary school students ecology and environmental science. In-depth explorations of the children's schoolyard, a vacant lot, a local park, a river, a pond, and a cemetery provide learning opportunities for children about topics ranging from plant and animal adaptations to the local geology of New Haven.

Because a key goal of environmental education is to engage citizenry in action, it is important to consider some of the activities that seem to lead to civic engagement around ecological issues. Citizen science or participatory research explicitly engages people in ecological research and monitoring. In addition to generating scientific information, this approach helps foster a sense of ownership and commitment to the local environment.[52] Participatory research provides opportunities for people to learn about their communities and generate information that can be used to improve or better manage their environment. For example, monitoring air quality along a greenway allows residents to see the effects of various factors, such as traffic and vegetation, on air quality. Understanding these connections can lead to further questions about the links between ecological processes and human health and well-being. This information, combined with an increased sense of competence, can spur community activism and action.

Engaging schools or citizen groups in stream sampling along a greenway provides an illustration of how these open spaces can be used to teach about ecosystem connectivity and promote environmental action; participants learn about the scientific method and discover the impacts of upstream activities on the downstream environment. For example, The Urban Ecology Institute, a Boston-based nonprofit organization, works with elementary and high school classes to conduct a wide range of ecological monitoring projects, including water quality monitoring.[53] Some of the project sites are located adjacent to the participating schools, which provides opportunities for frequent visits by the youth. The same sites are used each year to provide long-term, comparative data, allowing the students to investigate and understand long-term trends and changes in their local environment.

Involvement in the planning and maintenance of greenways and linear parks provides residents with the opportunity to learn about the complex relationships among politics, culture, and their living environment. Boston's Southwest Corridor project is a case in point. In the 1960s, the swath of land that now comprises this greenspace was cleared to make way for a highway. The halting of the highway construction, and the subsequent design and construction of the greenway, was largely driven by the cooperation and activism of residents from the three neighborhoods abutting the project site. Residents became "experts" in land-use planning and learned about the connections between their local social and biophysical environments; inner-city youth received formal training through internships with consultants and engineers; and Harvard University and Massachusetts Institute of Technology faculty used this project as a field site to teach participatory environmental planning to their students.[54] The result of this massive educational and planning effort is a tremendous community resource that includes greenspace, basketball courts, community gardens, and a multiuse pathway. It also provides a poignant example of the overlap between civic and environmental education. Creating learning opportunities that foster an understanding of both the social and biophysical realms is critical if environmental education is to reach its goal of an environmentally aware and engaged citizenry.

The West Philadelphia Landscape Project is another example of the potential benefits of combining environmental and civic education. This project used the Mill Creek neighborhood in West Philadelphia as a classroom where students from Sulzberger Middle School and the University of Pennsylvania, "learned to read the neighborhood's landscape, to trace its past, understand its present, and envision its future."[55] Using old maps and photographs, students discovered that Mill

Creek is not just the name of their neighborhood, but an actual creek that was buried beneath their neighborhood more than sixty years earlier. Unpacking the environmental and social history of their community, students realized that the presence of the buried stream (whose pipes occasionally burst, causing basements to flood), combined with systematic economic disinvestments in their neighborhood, explained the subsidence and general disrepair of many dwellings along their streets. This program attracted the attention of the Philadelphia Water Department, which worked with the students and community members to create a plan for a storm water detention facility on a vacant lot next to the school. This site was designed to also be a wetland, water garden, and outdoor classroom for the school.

Not only did the Landscape Project give students a better understanding of local ecology, it taught the invaluable lesson that decisions made beyond neighborhood boundaries can have serious implications at the local level. This project is also noteworthy because it engaged and empowered youth who, as the future stewards of the environment, are an important demographic to consider in planning and education initiatives.

Chawla found that most environmentalists attribute their commitment to a combination of two sources: (1) extended periods of time spent outdoors in natural areas during childhood or adolescence, and (2) an adult who taught them respect for nature.[56] This finding highlights the importance of considering the types of learning opportunities that greenways provide for children and youth. Because effective learning in these early years lays the foundation for the development of adults who are knowledgeable and engaged community stewards, a priority for environmental planners and educators should be the provision of accessible natural areas and meaningful environmental education experiences for children and youth. Unfortunately, this is not usually the case—opportunities to explore and connect with the natural world are declining due to urbanization as well as increasing parental restrictions on children's movements. This is particularly true for disadvantaged children residing in urban areas.[57]

Well-designed greenways in urban areas provide "safe" spaces for urban youth to explore and connect with the natural environment, as well as important opportunities for intergenerational contact and knowledge exchange. They allow children to move independently and explore different environments, thereby increasing their ecological experiences and understanding. One of the most effective ways to create these spaces is to include children and youth in the planning and design process. Engaging these stakeholders ensures that the greenway includes spaces that they deem valuable and affords opportunities for the types of activities in which they wish to partake.[58]

Mixed-use corridors, where traditionally adult-oriented spaces (such as community gardens) are near playgrounds and basketball courts, create important opportunities for intergenerational contact and knowledge exchange. Although it is often assumed that knowledge flow is unidirectional (from adults to young people), it is important to realize that adults have a great deal to learn from youth, both about what makes a place appealing to young people and about the ecology of an area. A powerful example of youth serving as educators is found in the work of The Food Project, a sustainable agriculture organization. The Food Project engages inner-city and suburban youth in sustainable farming practices on lots in Boston's inner-city neighborhood of Roxbury (as well as on a thirty-one–acre (12.5-ha) farm outside of the city). The organization creates opportunities for youth to act as adult educators about sustainable agriculture. They are encouraged to talk with local residents and farm volunteers about sustainable growing practices and lead remediation, for example, and given support to present at regional and national agriculture conferences.[59]

The social and physical context of a greenway guides the type of environmental education that occurs in that space. Greenways that are located along river corridors may be used to teach about the relationship of wetlands to uplands or the function of riparian buffers. In contrast, a corridor running through a highly urbanized area may provide opportunities for educating the public about urban wildlife and urban forestry. Regardless of the specific lessons learned at each site, it is essential to keep in mind that greenways provide important opportunities for: (1) sustained contact with nature; (2) cognitive and affective learning about the biophysical environment and natural processes; and (3) building awareness about the role of humans in shaping their local environment. It is up to educators, planners, environmental professionals, and policy makers to work with residents to maximize these educational opportunities through the creation of innovative curricula and intelligent design.

Environmental Art

Since the 1960s, the field of environmental art has offered trenchant critiques of industrial society and helped push forward and disseminate new thinking about nature and the environment. Through collaborations of artists, planners, and communities, greenways can become places for creative expressions that tell stories of people, place, and history; challenge us to think about the world in new ways; foster social interaction and dialogue; and inspire social and ecological action.

Artist Ruth Wallen describes the range of possibilities:

> Today's environmental artists focus on the interrelationships between physical and biological pathways and the cultural, political or historical aspects of ecosystems and work to extend environmental principles and practices directly into the community. Ecological art can challenge perceptions, elucidate the complex structure of an ecosystem, examine a particular issue, i.e., a type of ecological relationship, or work directly to physically restore the biophysical environment.[60]

Especially when students or communities participate in collaborative art projects, "eco-art offers a vehicle to cultivate systems thinking, interdisciplinary problem solving, collaboration, and social and environmental responsibility."[61] By questioning underlying assumptions and perceived wisdom, art can help us rethink the modern duality of nature and culture. Even from the purely pragmatic standpoint of funding and public support, art can be "a positive contribution that makes a long-term restoration project immediately attractive to a wider audience."[62] By exploring both the biophysical function and cultural meanings of ecological processes and issues, environmental art also questions the common assumption that science and expert management can be objective and value-free.

Because art is by nature creative, exploratory, and experimental, specific "how-to" advice would hardly be appropriate here. Instead, this section offers several examples of innovative and successful projects that are either specific to or could be adapted for linear resources.

FIGURE 5.4

Ruth Wallen's Children's Forest Nature Walk in San Bernadino, California. (Photo by Ruth Wallen. Reproduced with permission.)

- Ruth Wallen worked with children in San Bernadino, California, to create "Children's Forest Nature Walk" (figure 5.4). Workshops with local children produced drawings and stories reflecting observations, experiences, and imagination at the site. Drawings were digitally scanned and grouped together with related text to produce permanent displays, which were then placed along a woodland interpretive path designed by the children. This project involves children in the creation of a special place that brings together nature and human experience, takes advantage of trails' linearity for educational and creative purposes, and increases community involvement and commitment to public space.
- Mark Brest van Kempen's "15 Cubic Meters of San Francisquito Creek" (figure 5.5) demonstrates the intricacy and processes of a reconstructed slice of a stream and riparian ecosystem. Visitors can view from all sides the structural and functional interactions of

FIGURE 5.5

Mark Brest van Kempen's 15 Cubic Meters of San Francisquito Creek. (Photos by Mark Brest van Kempen. Reproduced with permission.)

FIGURE 5.6

Steven Siegel's sculptures use postconsumer materials to create a "charged but subtle aesthetic" that juxtaposes the results of consumption with scenes of natural beauty. a) Oak, Korea, 2004. *b)* Freight and Barrel, Three Rivers Arts Festival, *Pittsburgh, 2004.*

Photos courtesy of Steven Siegel. (Reproduced with permission of Steven Siegel.)

ecosystem components that were painstakingly reassembled from photographs and measurements of the original system. At the same time, by highlighting rather than hiding a water pump and filter that sustains the enclosed system, van Kempen stresses connectivity and the need for linkages at larger scales to sustain life, as well as the fact that those connections can be either natural or human-made.

- Steven Siegel has produced visually striking sculptures made of postconsumer waste both to illustrate the transformation of nature into consumer products and to highlight issues of waste and recycling (figure 5.6). "Large boulders of compressed cans and plastic bottles and multilayered newspaper ridges" remind us "of the new human geology of landfills" and ask: "What is our aggregate impact on the earth? . . . It's as if Siegel uses our waste as punctuation amid pretty art parks and landscapes."[63] Environmental art need not focus on nature per se but can draw our attention to how it is transformed by human actions. Although not specific to greenways, works like Siegel's Trash Sculptures could effectively be arranged in sequence to give trail users a sense of discovery and surprise along their journey.

- Ichi Ikeda's "80-Liter Water Box" (figure 5.7) presents eighty liters (21 gallons) as the volume of water per day per person considered necessary for meeting basic quality of life. A translucent eighty-liter box with pictures of cupped hands is

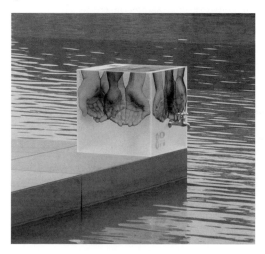

FIGURE 5.7

Ichi Ikeda's 80-Litre Water Box reminds viewers of the preciousness of water, especially in less advantaged parts of the world.

(Reproduced with permission of Ichi Ikeda Art Project.)

positioned at the edge of a stream or pond and combined with basic information on global water needs and distribution. Statistics on profligate water use in developed countries are contrasted with the fact that three-fourths of the world's people get by on less than fifty liters per day. In locations where the local importance of water is clear, this example expands people's thinking to similar, often more pressing issues in other places and at other scales. Ikeda's Water Box reminds us that what appears natural, sustainable, or just at the local scale may contrast dramatically with what is happening in other places and at larger scales.

These examples offer a sense of what can be done with environmental art and the different ways it can challenge our thinking. Such projects may take the form of commissioned art by professional artists, but this is not necessary. Especially projects like Wallen's could be carried out by volunteer groups or schools, perhaps with assistance from local artists, crafts people, or builders. Although professional art will be appropriate in some cases, the examples presented here can serve as inspiration for wide participation in creative designs that can have equally inspiring and educational results, while simultaneously stimulating broader community involvement.

Connectivity, Social Interaction, and Community

By enhancing social connectivity, greenways and the institutions that sustain them can influence social interaction within and between neighborhoods, as well as shared identity and sense of place that give meaning to people's home environment. The idea that landscape and the built environment can influence society has been debated for many years, starting with the work of architects and planners such as Ebenezer Howard, LeCorbusier, and Frank Lloyd Wright.[64] Although it has become clear that grand, utopian schemes tend to fall short of their goals and can even be counterproductive because of their ideological emphasis and detachment from real human needs,[65] more focused and modest attempts, especially those that consider and respond to the intricacies of social and economic life and to a range of public voices, can have considerable utility.

Greenways and Social Interaction

There has been growing concern in the United States in recent decades regarding social isolation and segregation. Although the country's population as a whole is more ethnically diverse than at any time in the past, segregation at the neighborhood level has been increasing in many cities for at least the past decade.[66] Although crime has decreased markedly in most states since the 1980s, the continued popularity of gated communities points to persistent fear and alienation and to a desire to be among people of similar appearance, backgrounds, and experiences. Segregation points not just to problems of inequality, but to the likelihood of reduced common experience and mutual understanding among different groups. Robert Putnam argues more broadly that social capital has declined over the course of several decades because of reduced participation in voluntary associations.[67]

It would be a mistake to think that such problems can be easily solved, but a growing body of evidence suggests that the existence and design of public space can have real influence on social interaction within and between neighborhoods. Based on a case study in Boston, Solecki and Welch argued that *boundary parks* that coincide with class and racial boundaries can serve as social barriers and reinforce spatial segregation.[68] Although Gobster found a similar situation in several Chicago parks, he also found an opposite situation, where a boundary park actually facilitated social mixing and interaction between neighborhoods.[69] Although he points out that the differences between these examples probably stem partly from factors unrelated to greenspace design— for example, the underlying segregation may be more or less pronounced—Gobster found design and management techniques that contributed to increased social diversity and interaction. In keeping with Jane Jacob's classic work on urban neighborhoods and parks,[70] these included locating popular facilities and uses on the park edge where they tie the park together with surrounding neighborhoods; spreading a variety of uses throughout the park; providing classes and programs for different age and cultural groups; and good physical maintenance and security. In short, this comes down to a design strategy of integration, diversity, accessibility, and safety. These findings suggest that boundary parks, instead of inevitably functioning as barriers between different groups, can become, at least in some cases, "*active* agents in counteracting boundary effects."[71]

Other researchers have demonstrated the importance of public space and greenspace in fostering social capital aside from the question of diversity. Kuo et al. examined inner-city public housing and found that the amount of vegetation in common areas was tied to both the overall use of those spaces and the development of social connections.[72] Similarly, Kweon et al. interviewed older adults (aged 64 to 91) in inner-city neighborhoods and found that "the use of green outdoor common spaces predicted both the strength of neighborhood social ties and sense of community."[73] Although these studies are not specific to greenways, the greater accessibility of linear greenspaces is likely to enhance such effects, especially if, in keeping with Gobster's findings, they are designed to support diverse uses. At the same time, greenways should ideally be combined with neighborhood-scale "mini-greenways" and "pocket parks." By infusing greenspace at multiple scales a variety of opportunities for use and for active participation in management will be created.

It is important, however, to resist simplistic interpretations of these studies. The fact of a correlation between greenspaces and social interaction, of course, does not tell us which variable comes first. It may be that neighborhoods with strong social ties are more likely to create greenspaces, rather than vice versa. The most likely case is that causality can run in either direction and that the two factors will often be mutually reinforcing. Some situations, such as new housing developments, may call for a focus on the design and planting of new public spaces. Others, such as older neighborhoods with little greenspace and little tradition of citizen involvement, may call for a combination of neighborhood organizing, assistance with design and maintenance, and provision of materials to jump-start local initiatives.

Linearity, Scale, and Network Structure

Although the high edge-to-interior ratio that comes with linearity presents problems for native wildlife and for water protection (as described in chapters 3 and 4), it provides increased accessibility for people—and, when greenways run through a variety of neighborhoods, for a greater diversity of people. For instance, Gobster and Westphal conducted research on the 150-mile-long (241 km) Chicago River corridor, which, like many river-based metropolitan greenways, "transects a spectrum of physical environments and human experiences."[74] These diverse social contexts, in turn, have the potential to open up opportunities for the sort of social interaction discussed above, both within and between neighborhoods.

Many discussions of greenways stress long-distance routes extending for tens and even hundreds of miles, rather than local networks that may be more functional from a social perspective.[75] Long-distance greenways seem to grab the attention of recreationists and greenway promoters because they appeal so strongly to the imagination. Their symbolism is not unlike what McQuillan described as the "mythology" of wilderness trails. "The essential claim of this mythology is continuity. . . . One is led to believe that . . . there is no fracturing of the landscape into city and country, public and private, wasteland and Eden: . . . one can still walk 2,015 miles in the woods [on the Appalachian Trail]."[76] Few greenways, of course, would qualify as wilderness, but the romantic draw of images of serene pathways stretching endlessly through protected natural corridors and tying together attractive features such as historic sites and scenic villages is similar. This emphasis is not altogether different from the problematic infatuation with wilderness described earlier and has the potential to perpetuate the symbolic divide between people and nature, albeit at a more local scale, rather than encouraging a synthesis of the two.

To be sure, there are positive aspects to long-distance greenways. They can be very effective from a promotional standpoint, fit well with biological conservation strategies, and provide for exploration and adventure relatively close to home. This emphasis, however, does tend to ignore the rarity of extended travel on such trails and can draw attention away from alternative network configurations. Even where length is not a priority, simple linear routes, especially where they follow protected riverside lands or railroad rights-of-way, are far easier to secure than more complex networks. For these reasons, many planners and greenway advocates follow a certain inertia in proposing single corridors, perhaps connecting a few major destinations, and the longer the better.

Gobster emphasizes the need to balance long-distance trails with more functional local networks.[77] He surveyed nearly 3,000 users of thirteen greenway trails in metropolitan Chicago and found that people using "local trails" (those where a majority of users lived within five miles [8 km]) used them more frequently to make shorter trips—and more often for commuting—than people using "regional" or "state" trails located farther from users' homes and typically accessed by car for recreation. These findings:

> suggest that local trails should provide the framework for a metropolitan trails system because they can more consistently meet people's everyday needs for recreation, commuting, and access to nature. Local trails might be linked to help meet functional needs, but simply linking trails to create an uninterrupted network of long-distance trails would be missing the point of what local trails provide. In some cases, small loop trails through existing parks and neighborhoods might be more useful on an everyday basis, and would be more cost effective in crowded areas where linear greenways would be difficult to develop. In other cases, boulevards or dedicated cycle lanes on streets that run alongside actively used rail and powerline corridors might form the basis for narrow 'mini-greenways' . . . while also providing a catalyst for reclaiming ribbons of nature throughout metropolitan areas.[78]

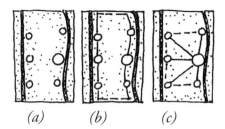

(a)   (b)   (c)

FIGURE 5.8

Alternative trail network structures in a metropolitan landscape described by Gobster (1995). (a) Original destination points (circles) along two linear resource features (bold lines). (b) "Regional development strategy" in which first-priority trails (continuous lines) and second-priority trails (broken lines) maximize a long-distance greenway trail network. (c) "Local development strategy" in which trails maximize functional ties between origin and destination points. (Redrawn from Gobster, P. H. [1995]. "Perception and use of a metropolitan greenway system for recreation." *Landscape and Urban Planning* 33: 401–413.)

To encourage local use, Gobster recommends a more diverse, local network of trails (figure 5.8) distributed so they are no more than five miles (8 km), and perhaps as little as one mile (1.6 km), from residences—the appropriate distance depending on the sort of population to be served. However, if we estimate conservatively that bicycling five miles (8 km) takes about a half hour and walking takes more than twice that, an upper limit of one mile (1.6 km) from the farthest residence—or of two miles (3.2 km) between trails—would be a more appropriate goal.

Aiming for such a density of trails would make Gobster's suggestion of linking greenways with "mini-greenways" and "ribbons of nature" especially compelling. Rather than building a relatively sparse and inaccessible network of long-distance recreational greenways, this strategy would integrate nature, common spaces, and travel corridors more fully into neighborhoods, decrease automobile and energy use, and increase healthy exercise for avid recreationists and casual or utilitarian users alike. Aside from connectivity, finer scale greenspaces are also valuable for neighborhood quality of life and environmental justice. "Micro-urban forest scales are the most relevant to issues of individual and household social justice, because individual trees and isolated tree stands bring about the kind of benefits that most substantially affect individuals and households."[79]

Still, the potential tradeoffs between such a model and the needs for longer and wider greenways to protect wildlife and water must be carefully considered. Ideally the two types of greenways can be meshed into a multiscale network, but where this is not feasible because of resource limitations, priorities and goals will have to be set—a task to be taken up in more detail in chapter 6.

Designing Meaningful and Adaptive Common Spaces

In addition to facilitating social interaction, common spaces can serve as a medium through which social identity, including sense of place, community, and citizenship, is influenced and reinforced.[80] To the extent that greenways are designed according to standardized, unimaginative conventions and without care for local diversity, one may look very much like another and this function of distinctiveness and community identity may fall short of its full potential. For instance, a straight-line paved pathway flanked by mowed grass, although surely an improvement on a narrow sidewalk or no pedestrian space at all, provides no diversity or rhythm for greenway travelers and may fail to take advantage of topography or local ecological and cultural features (figure 5.9).

FIGURE 5.9

Two alternative trail alignments along a riparian greenway. One (left) maintains a straight and rather monotonous path along the riverbank, while the other (right) periodically leaves the river to take people to a historic site (bottom left), over a hilltop with scenic views, and into a forested area (top).

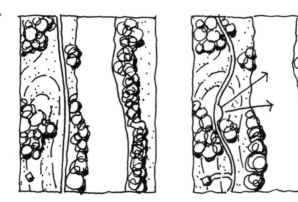

Emphasizing variety and local distinctiveness, on the other hand, makes a greenway something special and unique. Trails that meander across the landscape, multiple trails with different characters or configurations, and spurs that lead to locally significant places can offer variety, even if they have to make use of existing roads and rights-of-way in places. Where space is tight, adding occasional curves or creative landscaping can add distinctiveness and variety, while educational displays, environmental art, or spaces for public gatherings and events can promote learning, creative thinking, and dialogue among users and the community at large.

Such techniques can help build a common sense of place and belonging that may encourage increased communication and collaboration. Greenways can weave together communities not just physically, but in the sense of creating the distinctive common spaces and experiences that help to hold communities together. Ideally, locally distinctive design should not be a purely, or even primarily, professional endeavor, but should draw on community knowledge and participation.

Quayle and van der Lieck sketched out a hypothetical greenway model that offers important insights on how to facilitate such an approach, as well as how to combine and balance communal and private functions in the common space of greenways.[81] They point to the significance of everyday experience of routine neighborhood landscapes, which they say communicate two fundamental messages.

> The first one tells that indeed there is community, a measure of sharing or togetherness between the residents of a neighborhood. The second one is more personal, stating that within the community there are distinct individuals. Both messages . . . are increasingly difficult to communicate in the urban landscape.[82]

To counter this trend, they propose "hybrid landscapes" that combine formal communal space emphasizing commonality and citizenship with areas set aside for a range of evolving, more personalized uses. This emphasis on personal engagement reflects the notion that

> The act of making things and shaping places may be more important than the finished product. Yards and houses are places for creative tinkering, often serving as the objects being tinkered with. Gardening and its attendant psychological benefits of peacefulness and quiet take place in and create 'micro-restorative environments.'[83]

Quayle and van der Lieck (figure 5.10) envision a greenway as one possible example of a hybrid landscape. Their model stresses diversity, functionality, openness, and meshing with adjacent uses, and adaptation to evolving needs and contexts.

FIGURE 5.10

A depiction of Quayle and van der Lieck's (1997) vision of a greenway as a form of "hybrid landscape" that provides a diversity of spaces for public and private activities.

(Quayle, M., and T. C. D. van der Lieck. [1997]. "Growing community: A case for hybrid landscapes." *Landscape and Urban Planning* 39: 99–107.)

The backbone . . . is a pedestrian broadway through a neighborhood, linking the locales of everyday needs: homes, places of work and play, shops, and transit stops. Ideally, this greenway takes a position central in location and in the life of the community like the village or town square used to do. . . .

Along the greenway are pockets of activity, most importantly informal places of various sizes to gather and sit around. One space has to be large enough to hold a small market, a community meeting, and pumpkin sales at Halloween. Other spaces are small enough for intimate conversations, for family picnics or for solitary contemplation. . . .

Around the core are messy areas to temper the orderliness of the typical public landscape. A modicum of messiness is necessary to remove the deadening stiffness so typical of most urban green spaces. It also lures people into more natural areas, like children, bird-watchers, or seekers of solitude. . . .

The fringes of the hybrid landscape respond to adjacent land use. A school might have an environmental demonstration yard, a day care center might build a children's exploration garden or adventure playground, an apartment building might sponsor a tenant community garden or a senior citizen home might provide an outdoor gathering place under shade trees. . . .

Away from the main pedestrian traffic, but not out of sight, are tool sheds and covered work areas for craft projects too large or too dirty for apartments: stripping paint off old furniture, building soap box cars or fixing up cars. There could be potting sheds next to a seedling nursery for balcony produce, a large granite table for sessions of the neighborhood council, pavement chess sets, roller hockey rinks, bocce courts, maybe a rose garden or just thickets of blackberries.[84]

This scenario fits with the discussion of social interaction above and is in keeping with Walzer's differentiation between "single-minded space" used for limited purposes and "open-minded space . . . designed for a variety of uses . . . and used by citizens who do different things and are prepared to tolerate, even take an interest in, things they don't do."[85] It also highlights the complex, multifaceted nature of neighborhoods and opens the possibility of moving beyond dichotomized conceptions of homogeneous community and atomized, liberal individualism to an ideal of city life in which "social relations affirm—not deny—group differences. Multiple groups coexist side by side, maintaining their own identities, lifestyles, values, and so on."[86]

Making hybrid landscapes a reality, of course, will be no mean feat. Quayle and van der Lieck offered three basic rules: (1) responsibility and authority should be gradually transferred to the neighborhood level; (2) openness and an experimental, process orientation must be embraced; and (3) change should be incremental "so that frequent re-evaluations can be made, and the course of procedure redirected, if necessary."[87] Like ecosystems, neighborhoods and communities are heterogeneous and evolving. Embracing these characteristics will require the same sort of flexible, adaptive, experimental approach as managing biophysical ecosystems.

Economics and Justice: The Production and Distribution of Value

The economic implications of greenways are often raised by residents and landowners concerned about property values, by economic development agencies and activists, by government bodies that seek to bolster justification for public expenditures, and by conservationists seeking to build alliances and political support. Recent work has addressed these questions and pointed out that well-managed open space usually results in a net economic benefit for adjacent owners and neighborhoods.[88] Although there may be some risk of noise, litter, or vandalism, all of which can reduce property values, it is far more likely that the regular presence of managers and responsible users reduces such problems. Meanwhile, the amenity value of open space tends to make neighborhoods more desirable and to increase real estate values, while stimulating nearby businesses, especially those related to recreation and tourism.[89] Protected greenspace can also be a net benefit at the municipal or county level to the extent that developing the same lands would cause greater need for new services than it would generate income in new taxes.[90]

Although these benefits can be substantial and promoting them can help win support for a given project, the common emphasis on monetary valuation and on private gain from public initiatives will not always support—and may work against—broader social or environmental goals. If the larger social good is to be kept at the forefront, it is important to consider the context in which such issues are grounded. Most important are the distribution of monetary impacts (Do some groups or communities benefit more than others? Might some be harmed by gentrification and increased spatial inequality?) and the overall (i.e., not just local) ecological effects of new economic activity (Does it rely on nonrenewable resources or generate pollution? Does it produce benefits and goods that contribute not just to local quality of life, but to the larger goal of sustainability?).

Insights from *ecological economics* can be helpful in sorting through these questions. Instead of focusing solely on existing monetary indicators, ecological economics considers systems of production and consumption in their biophysical and social context.

> It treats human beings [and economics] not as outside nature, but rather as integral
> components of, and active participants in, the ecosystems that support them, . . . favors

biophysical assessments [over] monetary assessments, and emphasizes the equitable distribution of benefits over efficiency.[91]

Ecological economics emphasizes the finiteness of the global ecosystem and thus the impossi-
bility of infinite growth of the physical economy. This leads to an important distinction between
growth (the expansion of material and energy consumption) and *development* (qualitative
improvement of human well-being)—the latter being at least potentially independent of the former. Simple monetary measures (whether of a firm's profit or a country's gross national product)
fail to make this distinction, as well as ignoring *economic externalities*—negative or positive effects
(such as pollution or volunteer work) that are not part of the market and so have no dollar value.
This is not to suggest that dollars and cents should be disregarded—especially where greenways
run through low-income communities, monetary benefits may be crucial—but that monetary
values are an incomplete way of measuring costs and benefits and therefore need to be supplemented by an understanding of underlying ecological relations, nonmonetary values, and how
benefits are distributed to different groups.

The Nature and Goals of Productivity: Consumption Versus Production

In line with ecological economics is the movement toward *community economic development*
(CED), an approach that stresses local self-reliance, equitable distribution, and environmental sustainability. CED seeks to move toward a balance between production and consumption in a particular place and emphasizes "individual and community self-reliance through collaborative action,
capacity building, and returning control of business enterprises, capital, labor, and other resources
from the global marketplace to communities."[92] Reliance on local productive resources (whether
human or natural) reduces the need for long-distance transportation, encourages more efficient use
of resources, maximizes value added through labor and services, and helps make visible the underlying physical and ecological relations of production and consumption. By identifying ways to substitute local products for imports "people become more aware of the social and environmental
impacts of economic activities, and the benefits of supporting their local economy through wise
investment in local goods and services."[93] The idea of this strategy is not to isolate local economies.
Even if it were possible, this would be a dubious goal, because there are real advantages to trade
when one place can produce a certain good more efficiently than other places. Rather, the goal of
CED is to shift economic goals away from growth and accumulation at all costs and toward development and sufficiency with an awareness of social and ecological impacts.

This contrasts with a consumption-oriented approach adopted in many discussions of greenways
and economics. Closely related to the assumption that rising property values are economic good
news is the common emphasis on the role of greenways and other recreational open spaces in helping to bolster local economies by increasing consumer spending. This effect is highly variable but
has been documented in numerous cases.[94] As with property values, this effect can help make the
case for public investment in greenways, as well as being an important source of jobs and income.
But it is also important to consider the difference between *consumption* and *production*. Production

BOX 5.3
Greenspace, Community Farming, and Community Forests in Weston, Massachusetts

In the 1960s and 1970s, Weston, Massachusetts, took advantage of federal matching funds from the Land and Water Conservation Program and protected 2,250 acres—more than twenty percent of the town's total area—from development (figure 5.11).

In his book, *Reclaiming the Commons*, Brian Donahue documented the development of Weston's greenspace into a remarkable example of how nature protection can be combined with productive land use that provides healthy food, sustainable forest products, youth employment, and down-and-dirty, hands-on environmental education.[1] Although not technically a greenway network, Weston's greenspace has a high level of functional connectivity for both wildlife and people and suggests the sort of innovative programs that are possible.

Community farming in Weston started in the 1970s to provide activities for the town's young people and to provide low cost, healthy produce for Boston's Orchard Park housing project. At first vegetables were taken into the city, but eventually Orchard Park residents became involved and would drive out to Weston to help with the harvest, creating an exchange not just of calories but of mutual assistance and good will.

In 1980 a nonprofit called Land's Sake was formed and took over operations from Weston's Youth Commission while continuing to work town lands on a contract basis. This proved to be a crucial move in the program's development because it allowed for greater flexibility, including the ability to generate income through fundraising and contract work on private land, as well as rendering moot concerns among some in the town that the program was an unnecessary expense to taxpayers. Land's Sake works closely with the town and its residents to set goals for land management,

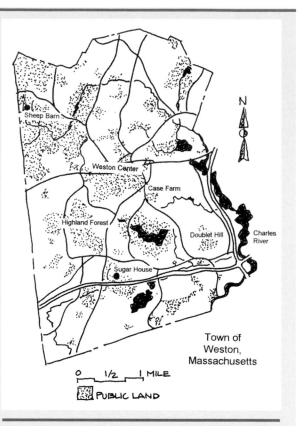

FIGURE 5.11

The greenspace network in Weston, Massachusetts, includes community-managed forests and agriculture. A network of locally managed trails links together many of these productive lands. (Redrawn from Donahue 1999.)

and consumption, of course, are the most fundamental economic activities, but often discussions of greenway economics focus entirely on consumption and the dollar income it generates.

Increasing consumption can benefit particular businesses and, to a lesser extent through the circulation of dollars, the community at large. This causes an absolute increase in local economic activity, but it may simultaneously draw spending away from other areas—which may, in turn, respond with their own growth-promotion efforts—the end result of which may be an overall increase in consumption, a dilution of local growth promotion efforts, or some combination of the two. In any case, benefits will typically go disproportionately to property and business owners. Especially when greenspace and recreation are used to promote tourism, the result will include increased energy use, pollution, and local traffic congestion. Thus, the combined assumptions that which involves farming, forestry, and the maintenance of a sixty-five–mile trail system that ties together natural areas, the town center, schools, and residences. All projects are guided by a multiple-use agenda and seek to balance four guiding principles of ecology, education, economics, and aesthetics.

Farming—mostly of vegetables, berries, and flowers—has been the most consistently successful and profitable activity, providing employment and educational experience for teenagers, supplying vegetables for a local farm stand and "pick-your-own" operations, and running in the black most years. Food is taken to homeless shelters on a regular basis, and annual strawberry and pumpkin festivals have become regular events for residents of Weston and neighboring towns.

Weston's forests are the other main site of activity. Fifty to one hundred cords of firewood are cut and sold each year, providing another area of work and education for youth, as well as funds for long-term timber stand improvement. Although the production of both firewood and lumber have been limited so far, it is expected that the town's 1,000 acres of high-quality timber lands are capable of sustainably producing 500 cords of firewood and 200,000 board feet of timber per year. Land's Sake calculates that that would be enough to build about twelve houses and substitute for 75,000 gallons of heating oil each year, even with ten percent of those lands set aside as ecological preserve and with a strong emphasis on ecologically sound forestry. Maple sugaring rounds out Weston's forest products, taking place each spring. The sugar house, where sap is collected and boiled down to syrup and sugar, is located adjacent to the town's middle school and has become a regular after-school hangout for youth.

In addition to being tied into high school biology units each year, Weston's forests have also become an important site of civic practice. Brian Donohue describes how

> Over the years we have moved our operation to different parts of the town forest, which means starting the saws and dropping trees behind a new neighborhood of forest lovers each time. Before we start cutting, we invite everyone interested to come for a Sunday afternoon walk, followed by coffee. . . . We spread the Forest and Trail Association map on the living room floor and discuss the philosophy of the overall town forest management program and the objectives of the particular cut. Our neighbors air their concerns, and we learn things that we should know and so modify our plans. . . . Not everyone will learn to love the sound of chainsaws, but you will have the weight of the neighborhood behind you.[2]

Weston's community farming and forestry could hardly compete economically with fully commercial operations—let alone with land speculation and housing development in one of the country's most expensive real estate markets. But as a use of public land, the combined benefits—production of food and fiber, education, civic involvement, service to low-income communities, and provision of recreation and scenic beauty—this example can serve as a model of how productive uses can be incorporated into local conservation.

[1]Donahue, B. (1999). *Reclaiming the Commons: Community Farms and Forests in a New England Town*. New Haven, CT, Yale University Press.
[2] Ibid., p. 264–265.

growth is good and that enticing people to spend tourism dollars in new places is inherently a net positive gloss over important problems.

Alternatively, it is worth emphasizing how greenways and greenspace networks can be places not for increased consumption but for local activities that *produce* energy and material goods in a sustainable fashion. For instance, the sort of local greenway networks described above that have many short links leading to practical destinations can increase nonmotorized transportation, which of course substitutes muscle power for fossil fuels and improves human health in the bargain. Fortunately, this is already a focus of many greenways. In Portland, Oregon, building trails for foot and bicycle travel has become part of the city's efforts to reduce energy use and the emission of greenhouse gases. Partly as the result of a 10 percent increase in commuting on foot and bicycle, Portland has reduced its carbon emissions per capita by 12.5 percent since 1990.[95]

Much less common are projects involving community gardens, farms, and forests that use organic and sustainable techniques and can replace distant sources that rely on heavy inputs of chemical fertilizer, pesticides, and energy. These uses, as well as ecological restoration projects, can be tied into experiential education programs and help build civic cooperation and capacity for community-based management. Community gardens on converted vacant lots or carved out of existing public lands can become nodes of activity, learning, and productive sustenance. Garden space allocated to individuals or families helps reinforce personal attachment to land and place and can be of considerable economic importance to low income people. Produce from community-based agriculture can also be sold at roadside stands or local farmers markets, with the proceeds used to fund land restoration or educational projects. Community forests can be tied into greenway networks and used to illustrate sustainable forestry practices, with wood going to local service projects or high school vocational programs, or sold to raise revenue. Incorporating these uses into greenways and recreational trail networks makes them more visible and accessible to the entire community. Overall, activities such as these can help show that nature is not a realm apart and separate from humanity, that we depend on its productivity for our daily lives and, in turn, that we can manage resources carefully in ways that simultaneously maintain ecological health and provide material benefits.

Greenways and Environmental Justice: The Distribution of Private and Public Benefits

Environmental justice has emerged as a major component of the environmental movement in the past two decades. Activists and scholars alike have criticized mainstream environmental groups for emphasizing wilderness, recreation, and generally middle- and upper-middle class constituencies; described numerous cases in which environmental risks from pollution and toxic waste have fallen disproportionately on low-income and minority communities; and galvanized a powerful, grassroots movement to address these issues.[96] More recently, some authors have started drawing attention to the unequal distribution of environmental *benefits*, especially with regard to access to natural resources in rural areas and access to greenspace and recreational resources in cities.[97] If greenways are to function effectively as a new sort of common space, they should be distributed equitably and work toward larger goals of social justice.

In some cases, river restoration and greenway planning have contributed directly to environmental injustice. This was the case in Denver in the 1990s, when, according to Lisa Headington, homeless people "who lived temporarily, seasonally, or relatively permanently along the river" were forcibly removed to make way for a greenway aimed at both providing for recreation and stimulating economic development.[98]

> The city argued that removal of the homeless was necessary to attract recreationists and investment to the river. Homeless persons were removed from the riverside spaces by means of 'sweeps,' new curfew and 'no camping' laws, and changes to the landscape to discourage sleeping or living along the river. Some homeless persons and advocates decry these measures as part of a larger trend to increasing criminalization of homelessness—particularly

since no new shelter or housing options were made available despite the [recent] loss of thousands of low cost housing units to gentrification . . . redevelopment unfairly cast the homeless as non-members of the commons, in opposition to a healthy and safe environment, and as impediments to the reclaiming of the river by the city and its people.[99]

A similar case occurred in Kathmandu in the 1990s, where a United Nations–sponsored river restoration and greenway movement vilified squatters along the Bagmati and Bishnumati rivers as causing river degradation and called for their removal. In fact, some squatters were actively engaged in river stewardship and their ecological impacts paled in comparison to contaminants flowing into the river from other parts of the city, largely because of their low rates of consumption.[100] In Kathmandu, squatters had more success than in Denver in fending off calls for their removal (more recently, political turmoil in Nepal has drawn attention away from these issues). But both of these cases reflect the international movement to reclaim previously industrial or "abandoned" river corridors as new common spaces—a positive impulse in principle, but one frequently coupled with the tendency to *exclude* marginalized groups from the newly defined commons. In Denver "persons living along the river have been considered a part of the spectacle of [a] 'forgotten landscape'" in need of purification "and not as members of the commons. In contrast to the phoenix-like promise of nature cherished along the river, the signs of humanity observed among the shelters of homeless people—plastic flowers, books, a jar of mustard—are gazed upon with voyeuristic horror akin to rubber-necking at an accident scene."[101]

Headington points out that although this conflict may at first seem insurmountable, the question of how, from a design perspective, to bring the homeless into the new commons has hardly been asked. Based on her research on the South Platte and other similar cases, she suggested some possible ways to help bridge this gap, such as designing trails to minimize the impacts of foot travel in high-use areas, offering camping permits in exchange for maintenance and stewardship work, and designating a part of the corridor as a camp that might evolve "into a permanent 'green' community."[102] Indeed, given the low levels of resource use of homeless people, these communities are already far greener than most. But most important, she stressed, is to make this issue visible in the public arena, develop a more respectful attitude toward the homeless, and direct the creative energy of designers, planners, and others toward finding creative solutions. As discussed earlier in this chapter, marginalized and low-income groups should be brought into policy and planning processes at the earliest stages.

A very different scenario has played out along the Bronx River Greenway in New York City, where in the 1990s activists from low-income neighborhoods set about restoring a highly industrialized and degraded river corridor and designing a continuous greenway along its length. The greenway's grassroots origins account for the explicit embrace of environmental justice principles by the new Bronx River Alliance, a public-private partnership that includes a wide range of community groups and agencies. Rather than focusing on attracting private development that, in the context of the city's skyrocketing housing costs, would accelerate gentrification,

the community groups are pressing for the inclusion of development projects they have conceived as ways to ensure that local people share in the economic benefits that the pathway and park will bring. Projects include: an educational and environmental center with a boat storage building; 400 units of affordable housing on a large brownfield site; and a combination travelers' hostel and residence for young people.

Housing is already an urgent need, and local activists are keenly aware of the two-edged nature of the changes they are working to bring about. As neighborhoods that are now among New York City's most environmentally degraded are transformed by the reclamation of the Bronx River, the low-income people now living there are threatened with displacement, as property values and housing costs rise. A number of strategies are being developed to address this pressing issue, notably the formation of community land trusts, and the implementation of inclusionary zoning.[103]

Beyond these river-specific cases, environmental justice issues occur more broadly in relation to the drive for economic growth in towns, cities, and regions. Amidst the emphasis in the media and among politicians on aggregate measures of economic growth, the question of how wealth is distributed in society is often given short shrift. Instead, there is a need to disaggregate such measures, to see exactly how the economy affects specific people and groups in their daily lives. For greenways and greenspace more generally, this means looking beyond popular arguments that they will stimulate economic growth and considering the effects of that growth in the context of urban growth machines described earlier in this chapter.

Although we tend to think of land protection as being inherently in opposition to growth, when it causes business activity and property values to increase, this assumption becomes less certain. To the extent that greenways stimulate economic activity and attract new residents, businesses, and even corporations—a role that has come to be often stressed by green space proponents—they may play a dual role, mitigating the negative effects of sprawl on a local level but paradoxically bolstering the growth machine and further accelerating the cycle of growth in the areas that surround protected greenspace and at larger, metropolitan scales. The overall effect of economic growth turns out to be more complex and variable than a simple accounting of dollars would suggest.

Although the link between land protection, growth machines, and the complex social dynamics of gentrification has not been considered by researchers, the link between protected greenspace and property values is much clearer. Property values often increase between five and thirty percent in metropolitan areas due to close proximity to greenspace.[104] Such figures are routinely cited by greenway advocates as a positive benefit, and of course this is true for property owners and for tax-collecting municipalities. It is the broader implications for environmental justice that are a concern. Although the larger social impact of such increases will be gradual, over time, economic segregation may increase, with wealthier groups able to take full advantage of public open space by living nearby and low-income groups living elsewhere.

The risk of such scenarios should not be taken as an argument against protecting greenspace, but rather points to the need to think more comprehensively about how it should be designed, distributed, and coordinated with related initiatives. Greenways, of course, have much to offer in relation to equity and justice because they are more likely to pass through a diversity of neighborhoods and provide more widespread access than traditional parks. Beyond that, a number of strategies can help ensure equitable access and minimize the problem of economic segregation. Towns, counties, and regions can explicitly focus on achieving an equitable distribution of open space across all scales by stressing the inclusion of low-income neighborhoods in particular projects, opting for smaller,

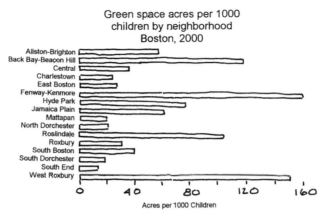

FIGURE 5.12

The Boston Foundation provides a yearly measure by neighborhood of acres of green space per 1,000 children.

more numerous, and dispersed acquisitions over large, showcase projects, and including distributional principles in town and county plans, state land acquisition programs, and the agendas of private organizations. Two nonprofit organizations already working toward more equitable distribution are the Boston Foundation, which includes a measure by neighborhood of open space acres per 1,000 children (figure 5.12) in its annual *Boston Indicators Report*, and the Trust for Public Land, which works with public and private groups throughout the country to secure endangered open spaces and has a strong focus on low-income neighborhoods.[105]

To minimize future problems stemming from amenity-based growth, towns and regions can encourage density of new development, rather than expansion, and consider limiting new development altogether with such tools as urban growth boundaries and municipal or regional zoning.[106] Because restrictions in one place have the potential to cause increased sprawl elsewhere, it is especially important that these efforts be coordinated where possible among neighboring jurisdictions or, ideally, at state or regional levels. Finally, because limiting development across large areas is likely to cause increased housing costs and push low-income residents to other areas that may lack greenspace, there is a need to maintain an adequate supply of affordable housing. As noted with the Bronx River Greenway above, with some conservation projects it may be possible to set aside acreage that is less environmentally sensitive for use in subsidized housing projects. Other mechanisms for addressing this problem include rent control and stabilization programs, public housing, requirements for including a certain portion of affordable units in new housing developments, and initiatives by community land trusts that focus less on conservation and more on housing issues.[107]

Of course, these sorts of efforts involve a host of political and economic issues that extend well beyond the purview of green space projects. The need is not for greenway planners to tackle all related issues, but rather to recognize those issues and establish communication and collaborative efforts with other professionals and agencies, as well as to inform politicians and other decision makers who are in a position to provide leadership on such issues. Such collaboration has been especially successful where there are formal institutions for planning and governance at the regional scale.[108] Although it may be tempting for environmental and social advocates to push their own agendas individually, a more collaborative approach will often be more fruitful.

Conclusion

Implicit in this chapter is an argument that social science and social issues need to become more routine components of the interdisciplinary mix that planners and designers draw on to inform their work. This means going beyond the common focus on recreational and aesthetic benefits or on idealized conceptions of community and "sense of place." It means putting social systems on a par with natural, biophysical systems (at least analytically, if not always in terms of a project's goals) with a view to the full range of processes and relationships that bind the two realms together into real-world landscapes. It means considering how natural and social connectivity of greenways influences social interaction, civic practice, ideas about nature, and environmental justice. It means looking beneath the surface of what may appear to be win-win situations to understand the heterogeneity and conflict inherent in human social systems, embracing those differences and the creative tensions they bring, and using democratic participation to empower citizens, resolve conflict, and identify common aspirations. Doing so can lead to more effective and more sustainable solutions for people and nature alike.

Notes

[1] This description of the human landscape is informed by Machlis, G. E., J. E. Force, and W. R. Burch. (1997). "The human ecosystem part I: The human ecosystem as an organizing concept in ecosystem management." *Society and Natural Resources* 10: 347–367; and Field, D. R., P. R. Voss, T. K. Kuczenski, R. B. Hammer, and V. C. Radeloff. (2003). "Reaffirming social landscape analysis in landscape ecology: A conceptual framework." *Society and Natural Resources* 16(4): 349–361.

[2] Gobster, P. H. (2001). "Neighbourhood-open space relationships in metropolitan planning: A look across four scales of concern." *Local Environment* 6(2): 199–212. p. 199.

[3] Ibid.

[4] Berkes, F. (2004). "Rethinking community-based conservation." *Conservation Biology* 18(3): 621–630.

[5] Agrawal, A., and C. Gibson. (1999). "Enchantment and disenchantment: The role of community in natural resource conservation." *World Development* 27(4): 629–649.

[6] Gunderson, L. H., C. S. Holling, and S. S. Light, ed. (1995). *Barriers and Bridges to the Renewal of Ecosystems and Institutions*. New York, Columbia University Press; Agrawal and Gibson, (1999), "Enchantment and disenchantment"; Berkes, (2004), "Rethinking community-based conservation."

[7] Orfield, M. (1997). *Metropolitics: A Regional Agenda for Community and Stability*. Washington, DC, The Brookings Institution; Calthorpe, P., and W. Fulton. (2000). *The Regional City: Planning for the End of Sprawl*. Washington, DC, Island Press; Hayden, D. (2003). *Building Suburbia: Green Fields and Urban Growth, 1820–2000*. New York, Vintage Books.

[8] Kennedy, M., and P. Leonard (2001). *Dealing with Neighborhood Change: A Primer on Gentrification and Policy Choice*. Washington, DC, Brookings Institution Center on Urban and Metropolitan Policy.

[9] Palmer, T. C. J. (2004). "For property owners, parks mean profits." *Boston Globe*. June 14. p. A1.

[10] Slack, D., and C. Reidy. "One neighborhood wary, another welcoming." *Boston Globe*. June 15. p. A1.

[11] Ibid.

[12] Grove, J. M., and W. R. Burch. (1997). "A social ecology approach and applications of urban ecosystem and landscape analyses: A case study of Baltimore, Maryland." *Urban Ecosystems* 1(4): 259–275. For related work linking human demography to vegetation characteristics, see Field, Voss, Kuczenski, Hammer, and Radeloff, (2003), "Reaffirming social landscape analysis."

[13] Hayden, (2003), *Building Suburbia*.

[14] Logan, J. R., and H. L. Molotch. (1987). *Urban Fortunes: The Political Economy of Place*. Berkeley, University of California Press.

[15] Logan, J. R., R. B. Whaley, K. Crowder. (1997). "The character and consequences of growth regimes: An assessment of twenty years of research." *Urban Affairs Review* 32: 603–631; Jonas, A. E. G., and D. Wilson, ed. (1999). *The Urban Growth Machine: Critical Perspectives, Two Decades Later*. Albany, State University of New York Press.

[16] Orfield, (1997), *Metropolitics*. p. 1.

[17] Calthorpe and Fulton, (2000), *The Regional City*.

[18] Goldberg, C. (2001). "Massachusetts city plans to destroy public housing." *New York Times*. April 12. p. 1.

[19] Williams, T. T. (1994). *An Unspoken Hunger*. New York, Pantheon. p. 134.

[20] Nicolson, M. H. (1959, reprinted 1997). *Mountain Gloom and Mountain Glory: The Development of the Aesthetics of the Infinite*. Seattle, University of Washington Press; Cronon, W. (1995). "The trouble with wilderness; or, getting back to the wrong nature." in *Uncommon Ground*. W. Cronon, ed. New York, W.W. Norton. pp. 69–90.

[21] For example, Gomez-Pompa, A., and A. Kaus. (1992). "Taming the wilderness myth." *BioScience* 42(4): 271–278; Guha, R. (1998). "Radical environmentalism and wilderness preservation: A third-world critique," in *The Great New Wilderness Debate*. J. B. Callicott and M. P. Nelson, ed. Athens, University of Georgia Press; Little, P. E. (1999). "Environments and environmentalisms in anthropological research: Facing a new millennium." *Annual Review of Anthropology* 28: 253–284; Dove, M. R., D. S. Smith, M. T. Campos, A. S. Mathews, A. Rademacher, S. B. Rhee, and L. M. Yoder. (In press). "A paradox of globalization: Revisiting the concept of Western versus non-Western environmental knowledge." In *Local Science Versus Global Science*. P. Sillitoe, ed. Oxford, UK, Berghahn Books.

[22] Quoted in Lazare, D. (2001). *America's Undeclared War: What's Killing Our Cities and How We Can Stop It*. New York, Harcourt. p. 131.

[23] Guha, (1998), "Radical environmentalism and wilderness preservation."

[24] Berkes, F., J. Colding, and C. Folke, ed. (2003). *Navigating Social-Ecological Systems: Building Resilience for Complexity and Change*. Cambridge, UK, Cambridge University Press.

[25] For example, McCarthy, J. (1998). "The good, the bad, and the ugly? Environmentalism, 'Wise Use,' and the nature of accumulation in the rural West." In *Remaking Reality: Nature at the Millennium*. B. Braun and N. Castree, ed. London, Routledge; Braun, B. (2002). *The Intemperate Rainforest*. Minneapolis, University of Minnesota Press.

[26] Imperial, M. (1999). "Institutional analysis and ecosystem-based management: The institutional analysis and development framework." *Environmental Management* 24(4): 449–465.

[27] Hoover, A. P., and M. A. Shannon. (1995). "Building greenway policies within a participatory democracy framework." *Landscape and Urban Planning* 33: 433–459.

[28] Berkes, (2004), "Rethinking community-based conservation."

[29] Hoover and Shannon, (1995), "Building greenway policies within a participatory democracy framework."

[30] Knight, R. L., and T. W. Clark. (1999). "Boundaries between public and private land: Defining obstacles, finding solutions." In *Stewardship across Boundaries*. R. L. Knight and P. B. Landres, ed. Washington, DC, Island Press. p. 181.

[31] Hoover and Shannon, (1995), "Building greenway policies within a participatory democracy framework."

[32] Ibid., p. 457.

[33] Berkes, Colding, and Folke, ed., (2003), *Navigating Social-Ecological Systems*.

[34] Holling, C. S. (1995). "What barriers? What bridges?" in *Barriers and Bridges to the Renewal of Ecosystems and Institutions*. L. H. Gunderson, C. S. Holling, and S. S. Light, ed. New York, Columbia University Press. p. 3–34.

[35] Gunderson, L. H. (2003). "Adaptive dancing: Interactions between social resilience and ecological crises." In *Navigating Social-Ecological Systems: Building Resilience for Complexity and Change*. F. Berkes, J. Colding, and C. Folke, ed. Cambridge, UK, Cambridge University Press.

[36] Environment Canada, Ecological Monitoring and Assessment Network. Retrieved August 12, 2005, (http://www.eman-rese.ca/eman/). United Nations Atlas of the Oceans, Global Coral Reef Monitoring Network. Retrieved August 12, 2005, (http://www.oceansatlas.org/servlet/CDSServlet?status=ND0xMjcyOC40NDk1NyY2PWVuJjMzPXdlYi1zaXRlcyYzNz1pbmZv).

[37] Imperial, (1999), "Institutional analysis and ecosystem-based management."

[38] Hoover and Shannon, (1995), "Building greenway policies within a participatory democracy framework." p. 436.

[39] Landy, M. (1991). "Citizens first: Public policy and self government." *Responsive Community* 1(2): 56–64, quoted in Hoover and Shannon, (1995), "Building greenway policies within a participatory democracy framework." p. 436.

[40] Day, K. (2003). "New urbanism and the challenges of designing for diversity." *Journal of Planning Education and Research* 23: 83–95.

[41] Ibid., p.86.

[42] Ibid., p.88.

[43] Ibid.

[44] National Park Service. (1992). *The Economic Impacts of Protecting Rivers, Trails, and Greenway Corridors*. San Francisco, National Park Service, Western Regional Office; Lerner, S., and W. Poole (1999). *The Economic Benefits of Parks and Open Space: How Land Conservation Helps Communities Grow Smart*. San Francisco, The Trust for Public Land; Quayle, M., and S. Hamilton (1999). *Corridors of Green and Gold: Impact of Riparian Suburban Greenways on Property Values*. Vancouver, University of British Columbia, Faculties of Agricultural Sciences and of Commerce and Business Administration; Irwin, E. G. (2002). "The effects of open space on residential property values." *Land Economics* 78(4): 465–480.

[45] Little, C. (1990). *Greenways for America*. Baltimore, Johns Hopkins University Press; Flink, C., and R. M. Searns (1993). *Greenways: A Guide to Planning, Design, and Development*. Washington, DC, Island Press; Fabos, J. G., and J. Ahern, ed. (1996). *Greenways: The Beginning of an International Movement*. New York, Elsevier.

[46] Strapp, W. B., D. Bennet, W. Fulton, J. MacGregor, P. Nowak, J. Swan, R. Wall, and S. Havlick. (1969). "The concept of environmental education." *Journal of Environmental Education* 1(1): 30–31.

[47] Kellert, S. (1999). *The Value of Life: Biological Diversity and Human Society*. Washington, DC, Island Press.

[48] Cited in Burch, W. R., and J. M. Carrera. (2000). "Out the door and down the street: Enhancing play, community and work environments as if adulthood mattered." in *Understanding Urban Ecosystems: A New Frontier for Science and Education*. A. R. Berkowitz, C. H. Nilon, and K. S. Hollweg, ed. New York, Springer.

[49] Sobel, D. (1996). *Ecophobia*. Great Barrington, MA, Orion Society; Hart, R. (1999). *Children's Participation: The Theory and Practice of Involving Young Citizens in Community Development and Environmental Care*. London, Earthscan; Vaske, J. J., and K. C. Kobrin. (2001). "Place attachment and environmentally responsible behavior." *Journal of Environmental Education* 32(4): 16–21.

[50] Haluza-Delay, R. (2001). "Nothing here to care about: Participant constructions of nature following a 12-day wilderness program." *Journal of Environmental Education* 32(4): 43–48.

[51] Kellert, (1999), *The Value of Life*.

[52] Bryant, B., and J. Callewaert (2003). "Why is understanding urban ecosystems important to people concerned about environmental justice?" in *Understanding Urban Ecosystems: A New Frontier for Science and Education*. A. R. Berkowitz, C. H. Nilon, and K. S. Hollweg, ed. New York, Springer.

[53] Urban Ecology Institute. (2005). Retrieved July 4, 2005, (http://www.bc.edu/bc_org/research/urbaneco/default.html).

[54] Peirce, N., and R. Guskind. (1993). "Boston's southwest corridor: People power makes history." *Breakthroughs: Re-creating the American City*. New Brunswick, NJ, Center for Urban Policy Research.

[55] Spirn, A. (2005). West Philadelphia landscape project. Retrieved December 8, 2005, (http://web.mit.edu/4.243j/www/wplp).

[56] Chawla, L. (1988). "Children's concern for the natural environment." *Children's Environments Quarterly* 5(3): 13–20.

[57] Chawla, L., and I. Salvadori. (2001). *Children for Cities and Cities for Children: Learning to Know and Care about Urban Ecosystems*. New York, Springer-Verlag.

[58] For a discussion of how to plan and implement a process that effectively engages children and youth, see Hart, *Children's Participation*; Driskell, D. (2002). *Creating Better Cities with Children and Youth*. London, Earthscan.

[59] For more information, see The Food Project, (http://www.thefoodproject.org).

[60] Rosenthal, A. T. (2003). "Teaching systems thinking and practice through environmental art." *Ethics and the Environment* 8(1): 153–168.

[61] Ibid., p.154.

[62] Spaid, S. (2002). *Ecovention: Current Art to Transform Ecologies*. Cincinnati, Contemporary Art Center, p. 3.

[63] Ibid.

[64] Fishman, R. (2000). "Urban utopias: Ebenezer Howard, Frank Lloyd Wright, and Le Corbusier." in *Readings in Planning Theory*, 2nd eds. S. Campbell and S. Fainstein, ed. Malden, MA, Blackwell. p. 21–60.

[65] Scott, J. C. (1998). *Seeing Like a State: How Certain Schemes to Improve the Human Condition Have Failed*. New Haven, CT, Yale University Press.

[66] Day, (2003), "New urbanism and the challenges of designing for diversity." p. 85.

[67] Putnam, R. D. (2000). *Bowling Alone: The Collapse and Revival of American Community*. New York, Simon and Schuster.

[68] Solecki, W. D., and J. M. Welch (1995). "Urban parks: Green spaces or green walls?" *Landscape and Urban Planning* 32: 93–106.

[69] Gobster, P. H. (1998). "Urban parks as green walls or green magnets? Interracial relations in neighborhood boundary parks." *Landscape and Urban Planning*. 41: 43–55.

[70] Jacobs, J. (1961). *The Death and Life of Great American Cities*. New York, Vintage.

[71] Gobster, (1998), "Urban parks as green walls or green magnets?" p. 54.

[72] Kuo, F. E., W. C. Sullivan, R. L. Coley, and L. Brunson. (1998). "Fertile ground for community: Inner-city neighborhood common spaces." *American Journal of Community Psychology* 26(6): 823–851.

[73] Kweon, B. S., W. C. Sullivan, and A. R. Wiley. (1998). "Green common spaces and the social integration of inner-city older adults." *Environment and Behavior* 30(6): 832–858.

[74] Gobster, P. H., and L. M. Westphal (2004). "The human dimensions of urban greenways: Planning for recreation and related experiences." *Landscape and Urban Planning* 68: 147–165.

[75] Gobster, P. H. (1995). "Perception and use of a metropolitan greenway system for recreation." *Landscape and Urban Planning*. 33: 401–413.

[76] McQuillan, G. (2000). "The forest track: Working with William Cronon's *The Trouble with Wilderness*." *College Literature* 27(2): 157–172.

[77] Gobster, P. H. (1995). "Perception and use of a metropolitan greenway system for recreation."

[78] Ibid., p. 409–410.

[79] Heynan, N. C. (2003). "The scalar production of injustice within the urban forest." *Antipode* 35(5): 980–998.

[80] Lindsey, G., M. Maraj, and S. Kuan. (2001). "Access, equity, and urban greenways: An exploratory investigation." *The Professional Geographer* 53(3): 332–346.

[81] Quayle, M., and T. C. D. van der Lieck. (1997). "Growing community: A case for hybrid landscapes." *Landscape and Urban Planning* 39: 99–107.

[82] Ibid., p.99.

[83] Ibid., p.102; "Micro-restorative environments" is from Kaplan, R., and S. Kaplan. (1990). "Restorative experience: The healing power of nearby nature." in *The Meaning of Gardens*. M. Francis and R. Hester, ed. Cambridge, MA, MIT Press.

[84] Quayle and van der Lieck, (1997), "Growing community: A case for hybrid landscapes." p. 104.

[85] Walzer, M. (1995). "Pleasures and costs of urbanity." in *Metropolis: Center and symbol of our times*. P. Kaasinitz, ed. New York, New York University Press. p. 321, quoted in Lindsey, Maraj, and Kuan, "Access, equity, and urban greenways: An exploratory investigation." *The Professional Geographer* 53(3): 332–346.

[86] Day, (2003), "New urbanism and the challenges of designing for diversity." p. 87.

[87] Quayle and van der Lieck, (1997), "Growing community: A case for hybrid landscapes." p. 105.

[88] National Park Service, (1992), The economic impacts of protecting rivers, trails and greenway corridors; Lerner and Poole, (1999), *The Economic Benefits of Parks and Open Space*.

[89] National Park Service, (1992), *Economic Impacts*; Lerner and Poole, (1999), *The Economic Benefits of Parks and Open Space*, Quayle and Hamilton, (1999), *Corridors of Green and Gold*; Irwin, (2002), "The effects of open space on residential property values."

[90] National Park Service, (1992), *Economic Impacts*; Lerner and Poole, (1999), *The Economic Benefits of Parks and Open Space*.

[91] Rees, W. (2003). "Ecological economics and an understanding of urban ecosystems." In *Understanding Urban Ecosystems*. A. R. Berkowitz, C. H. Nilon, and K. S. Hollweg, ed. New York, Springer.

[92] Roseland, M. (1998). *Toward Sustainable Communities: Resources for Citizens and Their Governments*. Stony Creek, CT, New Society. p. 160.

[93] Ibid., p.161.

[94] National Park Service, (1992), *Economic Impacts*; Lerner and Poole, (1999), *The Economic Benefits of Parks and Open Space*. Both of these publications provide literature reviews and practical advice related to the economic benefits of green space.

[95] de Steffey, M. R., E. Sten, D. Boyer, and S. Anderson. (2005). *Global Warming Progress Report: A Progress Report on the City of Portland and Multnomah County Local Action Plan on Global Warming*. Portland, OR: City of Portland and Multnomah County.

[96] For example, Bullard, R. (1994). *Dumping in Dixie: Race, Class, and Environmental Quality*. Boulder, CO, Westview: Dowie, M. (1995). *Losing Ground: American Environmentalism at the Close of the Twentieth Century*. Cambridge, MA, MIT Press.

[97] Mutz, K. M., G. C. Bryner, and D. S. Kenney, ed. (2002). *Justice and Natural Resources*. Washington, DC, Island Press; Headington, L. (2003). "The *other* tragedy of the commons: Redevelopment of Denver's South Platte River and the homeless." Department of Geography. Boulder, University of Colorado.

[98] Headington, (2003), "The *other* tragedy of the commons." p. iii.

[99] Ibid.

[100] Dove, M. R. et al. (In press), "A paradox of globalization."

[101] Headington, (2003), "The *other* tragedy of the commons." p. 366.

[102] Ibid., p.376.

[103] Byron, J. (2004). *Transforming the Southern Bronx River Watershed*. New York, Pratt Institute Center for Community and Environmental Development. p. 21.

[104] See Lerner and Poole, (1999), *The Economic Benefits of Parks and Open Space*; Quayle and Hamilton, (1999) *Corridors of Green and Gold*.

[105] The Boston Indicators Project (http://www.tbf.org/indicatorsProject/); Trust for Public Land (http://www.tpl.org/).

[106] Calthorpe and Fulton, (2000), *The Regional City*.

[107] Ibid.

[108] Orfield, (1997), *Metropolitics*; Calthorpe and Fulton, (2000), *The Regional City*.

CHAPTER 6

ECOLOGICAL

GREENWAY DESIGN

The previous chapters have focused on specific aspects and issues of greenways and their design. This chapter integrates these topics into an applied method of greenway design that is structured by answering a series of strategic questions.[1]

Greenways are much more complex and richer than the simplistic ways greenspace is often conceived of, as mere open—that is, undeveloped—space. Because of their capacity for flood control, water quality protection, and other environmental functions, greenways can be important mechanisms for helping fit development to the environment. In many situations urban greenways make the biggest contribution in just these ways, by reducing the impacts of development. In other cases, but less likely in urban settings, they may also protect and preserve rare biological resources. Beyond these functions, greenways play important roles in urban design, contributing to a metropolitan area's beauty, visual coherence, sense of place, and other social functions, as well as helping residents orient themselves as they move about (i.e., help them with way-finding).

The challenge for the greenway designer is in understanding and then designing with these rich but disparate issues in mind, and in doing so in ways that create a good and sustainable fit between the greenway and its setting so that important functions and features aren't overlooked. Due to the complexity of these issues and local landscape variation, there is no simple and universal cookbook approach to greenway design. There is, however, a great deal of useful information available to the greenway designer.

Urgency propels greenway design on several fronts. Reed Noss (chapter 3, this volume) observes: "If we are to halt a massive biological impoverishment of the earth, we need to reform our land-use planning dramatically and ensure that native species can maintain viable populations in landscapes dominated by humans, as well as in wilderness." Others feel a similar urgency for the benefit of human communities. They are concerned that if steps aren't taken quickly, development could forever preclude opportunities for nature to exist near where people live, greatly diminishing the quality of life for urban dwellers.

Many important greenway design issues have surfaced in a project in the Chatfield Basin, on the southwestern urbanizing fringe of Denver, Colorado. We present an overview of that effort because it may be typical of other projects in North American cities and because it is known firsthand to the author. Additional insights from this and similar projects are presented in text boxes throughout the chapter.

Chatfield Basin Conservation Network: An Example

In 1996 biologist Raymond Sperger (figure 6.1) was noticing changes at South Platte Park (figure 6.2) in Littleton, Colorado—changes other people were missing. He realized he hadn't seen black bear in the park since 1986 and the regular visits by herds of mule deer had stopped in 1990. He

FIGURE 6.1

Biologist Raymond Sperger, shown here, realized visits by black bear and mule deer to the natural area he managed had stopped. He wondered if this was a sign of things to come for all the protected areas in the Chatfield Basin.

also knew that more and more houses were appearing along the boundaries of this 700-acre (283 ha) natural area that straddles the South Platte River upstream from Denver. He also knew that nearby Douglas County consistently ranked as one of the fastest growing in the United States.

Because Sperger had experience in both ecology and environmental education, he looked for creative ways to tell others about what he thought was

FIGURE 6.2

Sperger works at South Platte Park, a 700-acre natural area along the river of the same name, in metropolitan Denver, Colorado.

happening—habitat fragmentation—and its likely results—species loss. He told people that South Platte Park and other nearby protected areas were becoming isolated islands of habitat in a sea of development. Because of habitat fragmentation, an investment worth millions of dollars, intended to support and sustain wildlife, was at least partially at risk.

To illustrate some of the impacts of fragmentation in terms he felt local decision makers could understand, he made a simple diagram showing what a house would look like if hallways didn't actually connect all rooms (figure 6.3). He made another illustration by cutting up a city street map and randomly reconfiguring the pieces so that not all houses could be reached by streets. Wildlife need connections across the landscape, just like we need in our homes and communities, he said simply, pointing to his illustrations.

He did more than tell people about the problems. He suggested something

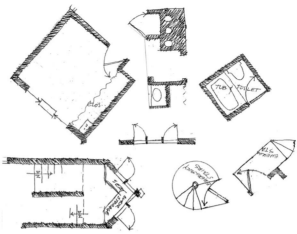

FIGURE 6.3

To help people understand the potential implications of habitat fragmentation, Sperger made a simple illustration: a house with rooms that were not all connected by hallways.

FIGURE 6.4

Sperger made a diagram on an aerial photograph highlighting the parks and other protected greenspace (with dark outlines) and connected them with swaths (striped areas), suggesting areas that should be studied to identify conservation connections.

could be done if people were willing to work together. A resource he found particularly helpful in sketching out potential solutions was *Saving Nature's Legacy*, by Reed Noss and Allen Cooperrider.[2] Using Noss and Cooperrider's book for guidance, Sperger drew a plan—a diagram really—on an aerial photograph of the 140-square-mile (363-km²) Chatfield Basin highlighting the various parks and other protected greenspace in dark green (figure 6.4). Then he did something bold. He drew broad swaths of light green connecting the dark green areas. He labeled his drawing: Chatfield Basin Reserve Network. The people he spoke with, who represented a wide range of perspectives from environmentalists to developers, got the point. There was work to do in these broad interconnecting areas. Working together they wrote a proposal to fund a conservation study of the area. Together they attracted funding and project participants. They used the money to hire a team of professional planners and ecologists to work with them.

In looking at the map Sperger had made, there was no mistaking what and where the dark green, already protected areas were. The job at hand was to determine a basis for further refining the light green swaths—the connections that stakeholders hoped would help sustain wildlife, provide routes for hikers and mountain bikers, help manage flooding, and reduce the amounts of phosphorus and other nutrients reaching the reservoir just downstream. They sought a system of greenways or a greenway network.[3]

Those tentatively drawn light green bands on the map prompted questions the group sought to answer. How and where should lands be protected to encourage wildlife movement (as discussed in chapter 3), trails and other human uses (chapter 5), and flood protection and water quality protection (chapter 4)? How could such an ambitious network be envisioned, implemented, and sustained in a metropolitan setting, in the face of rapid urbanization, with the disparate demands of society (chapter 5)?

These are the same fundamental questions that originally inspired this book, and these same questions frame the process of designing greenways presented here.

Design Makes a Difference

Through a simulation study, ecologists Richard Forman and Sharon Collinge concluded that it made a significant difference in the effectiveness of nature conservation whether land was developed through a random (i.e., unplanned) process or with spatial planning. In their exercise they found that over five times more area of high ecological value, including large patches, medium patches, and major streams, was retained with planning compared to a completely random sequence of development without planning.[4] This is the same conclusion—that thoughtful design makes a difference—reached by most designers and planners, and the impetus for this chapter.

Given the substantial development underway in many North American metropolitan areas, the prospects of a design strategy sometimes called "creative fragmentation"[5] has considerable appeal. It suggests that by designing greenspace in advance of development, it may be possible to guide development away from areas attractive for conservation and toward other more appropriate locales. This is a strategy beautifully articulated many decades ago by writer and urban observer William Whyte, who urged, "communities to plan linked open space systems ahead of development, then encourage developers to align their open spaces within the community framework. The landscape would determine the location of open space linkages by the very existence of riparian corridors. The community would accept nature's framework, then fill in elements such as parks, schools, and community centers."[6] With this approach, as in Forman and Collinge's simulation, a skeleton or framework of desirable areas would be identified and preserved in advance of development. This is a central tenet of the green infrastructure movement in North America. Critics of this approach sometimes wonder if this doesn't invite development, in either overt or subtle ways.

Dealing with the Complexity of Greenway Design and Confusion among Designers

Although some greenway projects may not have a professional designer participating, someone with broad integrative skills is still needed. An understanding of the complex social and natural contributions of greenways and a realistic appreciation of how nature functions in and around them is required for effective greenway design.

Anyone proposing to guide development and fragmentation across landscapes and regions

confronts the tremendous complexity of attempting work at that scale. Effectively implementing a greenway, and especially a greenway network in a metropolis, requires an incremental, multiscale, long-term perspective and approach,[7] and is not a casual undertaking. In addition to citizen participants, greenway design will require the contributions of many types of professionals, some of whom may have as strikingly different perspectives on nature as the general public.

Some designers, for example, claim that all landscape design should "show the hand of the designer." They say copying nature or otherwise intentionally obscuring that a place was manipulated by people is dishonest. Others take just the opposite tact, believing that landscape design that is mistaken for nature's work is the ultimate compliment to the designer. Still others seek to create obvious indicators— "cues to care," as Joan Nassauer has suggested—that humans are being effective stewards of the landscape, even of natural areas that may appear messy, but which are given orderly frames (figure 6.5).[8]

These different perspectives on the part of greenway designers can have very different outcomes on how a greenway is envisioned and implemented. Some designers may treat an undeveloped area as sacrosanct, even when it has been heavily disturbed by people, and others may treat it casually, even when significant ecological processes are present. What is needed is a realistic assessment of nature.

Greenways Can Be a Component of Sustainable Design

The greenway design approach presented in this chapter is ecological in a very broad sense, not just because it makes use of the sciences, especially landscape ecology, but also because it strives to be holistic, integrative, and process oriented. It aims for ecological fit or landscape integrity with a longer term goal of sustainability. English landscape architect Ian Thompson divided this goal into three aspects: ecology, community, and delight.[9] In his take on ecological design, University of Wageningen landscape architect Jusuck Koh also saw three fundamental principles: inclusive unity (integrating people and place), creative balance (change with balance), and complementarity (integrating people and nature). Although these principles imply a significant role for greenways and also offer specific guidance to the designer, they must be supplemented with concerns regarding social difference, inequality, and politics.

FIGURE 6.5

"Cues to care" are reminders that even if an area looks otherwise unkempt, people may still be actively serving as stewards. In these simulations an area is shown (a) managed as a natural grassland and (b) with regeneration and obvious signs of care: a birdbox and a sign.

(Reprinted from Hands and Brown. [2002]. "Enhancing visual preference of ecological rehabilitation sites," *Landscape and Urban Planning*, vol. 58. pp. 57–60, with permission from Elsevier.)

TABLE 6.1 Jusuck Koh's general principles of ecological design are here translated into greenway design objectives useful at two levels: 1) understanding the significance of greenways in urban and landscape design, and 2) developing design strategies for areas within and adjacent to greenways.

GENERAL DESIGN STRATEGIES[1]	POSSIBLE DESIGN OBJECTIVES APPLICABLE TO GREENWAY DESIGN
Connection to and expression of temporality and time: diurnal, seasonal rhythm; tidal cycle; processes of change, aging, development; expression of ephemerality, transience, lightness, impermanence.	Provide *visual and physical access* to greenway elements that express *seasonality* (e.g., leaf color, frozen water, fruit).
Use of recycled form, material, image; new use of the old and coexistence with the old; tradition; "closing the circle" (use of output/waste as input/source; conserving energy, knowledge, species).	Cleanse *stormwater* and other waste outputs from adjacent land uses before or as they enter the greenway.
Grounding, undergrounding, backgrounding: revealing the ground, and framing the background, responding to topography.	*Feature* significant *topography* in the greenway.
Sense of connectedness to nature, landscape: fitness (to function and program as well as to environment and context).	Use the greenway to provide visual and physical *access* ("connectedness") *to nature*.
Circular arrangement: equity, community.	Provide *equal access* to the greenway to all segments of the community. Target *underserved social groups* for greenway projects and address gentrification in adjacent neighborhoods.
Aesthetic and design participation: engagement, and user participation; void, room with openness, open-endedness, openable window, changeable and movable seats and walls.	Engage future greenway users in the greenway design process. Include in the greenway areas elements such as community gardens and adventure playgrounds that can be *manipulated by users*.
Aesthetic of frugality, voluntary simplicity, and modesty.	Use *local solutions* whenever possible in implementing aspects of the greenway.
View framing: vista, seeing without being seen, "Prospect/Refuge"; belvedere.	Create *vantage points* within and adjacent to the greenway where users can view wildlife, other greenway users, or interesting elements.
Immediacy (elimination of barrier, wall and proscenium arch, overcoming disinterested "aesthetic distance" for contemplation by the rich and noble), vividness.	Provide opportunities and aids within the greenway for users to have immediate and vivid *experiences with natural processes*.
Indoor-outdoor continuity and "deep integration": breathing wall, window or pavement; porous and permeable wall/boundary as membrane.	Whenever possible or appropriate, *extend greenway functions outward* from the greenway to integrate the greenway and its context.
Territorial articulation, identity and autonomy: dike, wall, fence, threshold, entry, stoop, passage, gateway, territorial marker, boundary, edge.	*Mark* the greenway, and especially all entrances, so it becomes known as a purposeful and distinct place.
Horizontal transition (from public to private): balcony, veranda, threshold, bridging; vertical transition (from topographical to architectonic, from commercial to residential, from profane to sacred).	Create *transition areas* (vestibules) for users coming into the greenway to help them realize and remember that they are entering a special place where appropriate behavior may differ from where they are coming.
Receiving, accepting the given (without erasing and obscuring).	Seek out *postindustrial* or other "denatured" areas in selecting greenway alignments if they are compatible with greenway objectives, and don't attempt to totally obscure their previous uses, pretending they were pristine areas.
Attention to detail: self-similarity and nested hierarchy (revealing how things are made); joint and joining between different material, construction, territory, etc.	Create elements along the greenway that *remind users* they are in the greenway and that give more information about the greenway's functions.
Revealing the process of construction and maintenance: scaffolding, layering.	Make obvious the human interventions in the greenway, instead of trying to obscure these, giving *cues to care*.
Differentiated edging: interfacing, bounding, territory.	Delineate the *edges of or entrances* to greenways so visitors know the rules are different within.
Human scale and form: embodied shape, pulse, breath, sensuality.	Include obvious places (e.g., trails and viewing blinds) for *people* in the greenway, as appropriate.

Multifunctioning and niche (time-sharing).	Provide *opportunities* for recreation and other uses, perhaps community gardens or forests, public gathering spaces, or farmers' markets.
Materiality: local material, natural material, tactile and haptic experience.	Use *local materials* in any construction (paths, bridges, etc.) within the greenway to emphasize what is unique to an area and gives an area its specific sense of place.
Directing/orienting/connecting to sun, moon, and landscape view: genius loci, identity of place and sense of place; allusion to known/sacred landscape images and memory (symbolic unity).	Align the greenway so that users have *views and experiences* that give them a sense of the landscapes they are passing through, even including signs or other marks that remind users of previous uses of the land.
Diversity, multiplicity, biodiversity, patch size, network (and other ecological and landscape ecological concepts).	In designing the greenway, work with and communicate the relationships of *pattern and process.*
Design expressions of regenerative, sustainable, healing design.	Seek out *degraded areas* to restore as part of the greenway project.
Ephemerality with endurance: change and continuity (unity with environmental and human change); tradition and innovation.	Design greenways to sustain their functions despite changes in *adjacent land uses.*
Flow/transience: revealing/daylighting stream flow.	Daylight streams that may have been piped and generally *make natural processes visible.*
Fluvial forms: stains, sedimentation, erosion of flow, erosion, decay, sedimentation; "sensitive chaos," "fractal," "self-similarity."	Make the greenway extensive enough to accommodate natural processes such as erosion, and thereby communicate the *complexity of the landscape.*

[1] Koh, J. (2004). Ecological Reasoning and Architectural Imagination. Inaugural address of Dr. Jusuck Koh, Wageningen, The Netherlands.

Language, Principles, and Models for Greenway Design

Given the conflicting and confusing language used to describe greenways and other greenspace (see table 1.1), it's not surprising that the ways of thinking about greenway function and design (i.e., principles and models) often have been simplistic and not always that helpful.

The author saw this two decades ago as a student of landscape architecture and planning. He was instructed in those pre-landscape ecology days that a generalizable landscape planning objective should be to maximize the amount of edge between habitat types as a means of encouraging wildlife. There was no discussion of what species of wildlife would be encouraged (edge species) or discouraged (interior species). There was no mention of landscape pattern or possible negative edge effects. It was a simple maxim (grown out of game management): make edges when you can and there will be more wildlife. As discussed in chapter 5, design and planning models of society, community, and the human dimensions of greenspace often have been equally inadequate to the task.

Ecological research has come a long way in the last twenty years. In this section I present concepts and principles from the previous chapters and a range of other sources, from the natural and social sciences, and from design and planning theory. It is my hope that these will aid the reader in formulating models of how greenways could succeed in his or her specific locale.

Sometimes the words "model" and "theory" can seem a bit formal, technical, and off-putting. Of course, they simply refer to ways of conceptualizing the workings of things around us. Frequently they attempt to simplify complex systems. In reminding us that "all models are wrong, some are useful,"[10] planner Chris Duerksen and his colleagues are saying that simplifications are needed but will inevitably have limitations. Scientists and nonscientists develop—and debate and refine, accept or reject—theories or representations of the landscape. Designers formulate models of how landscapes or other designed areas should work. All of these are wrong, to some degree, perhaps because of oversimplification or other faulty assumptions. But many of these models are still helpful. Models, in fact, are very much part of the way we humans deal with the world's complexity and are vitally useful in greenway design.

From Principles to Practice

We adapted the following greenway design objectives from the work of Jusuck Koh, who was a student of the eminent ecological planner Ian McHarg.[11] Through decades of practice and teaching, Koh has championed a richer, more complex sense of ecological design and an ecological aesthetic that embraces the complexities of natural and social systems. Because of the ecological orientation of what he called his "interrelated aesthetic languages and design strategies,"[12] it is easy to extrapolate from them to meaningful greenway design objectives.

Koh confronted the modernist sense of landscape design that finds its roots in architecture and art and that often seems at odds with ecology. He posited an ecological design that seeks a closer fit between people and nature. Environmental design and aesthetic theory, he noted, need not be at odds with each other.[13] He proposed a dynamic theory of creativity to replace a static, culture-bound concept of beauty.[14] His design perspective is very compatible with the ecological greenway design approach presented in this book (table 6.1).

Another landscape design theorist (and also a student of Ian McHarg's) offering useful insights relevant to greenway design, is Massachusetts Institute of Technology landscape architect Anne Whiston Spirn. She pointed out that landscapes have a *deep structure*, which in contrast to the "forms we see on the surface of the landscape" are a more "enduring structure, with distinctive rhythms, to which all organisms within that landscape respond."[15] She added that design—and we can specify greenway design—that reveals and responds to this deep structure is more likely to be functional, economical, and sustainable.[16]

Effective Greenway Design Is Collaborative

Designers have a special role to play in creating greenways because they are integrators in an age of intellectual fragmentation. They are generalists in a society that values specialists. This is not to say scientific knowledge and scientists aren't essential to greenway design, implementation, and management, because they clearly are. It has been pointed out that there are advantages of including both a deductive approach, such as a scientist might take, and a more inductive approach, as might be the tendency of a designer, planner, or other nonscientist.[17]

Denver planner Chris Duerksen and his planning and biologist colleagues offered a number of "operational principles of habitat protection" that are relevant to the discussion here. As a reminder to both scientists and designers, they suggested that we "be willing to use rules of thumb based on scientific findings that may someday prove to be false," and operate with an understanding that "complex environmental problems do not have a single, scientific solution founded on 'truth.'"[18]

BOX 6.1

Network Theory

Network theory may provide greenway network designers with suggestions of how greenway systems could come together and function. Although the following network types are simplified abstractions that bear little resemblance to real landscapes, they may suggest connections that might otherwise be overlooked. In applying such network configurations to a case study, a team of researchers found that the theory-based configurations were best used as guides, rather than as a specific desired outcomes.[1]

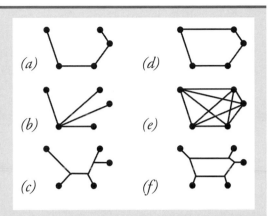

Possible network types include:[2]

a. *"Paul Revere,"* which would be a traditional, single greenway, connecting two or more points.

b. *Hierarchical,* in which one or a few nodes are important enough that it is desirable that all other nodes connect to them. This might be a greenway network that provides people with access to a school or other community resource.

c. *Least cost to builder* minimizes the length of all the connections for efficiency, but may be very vulnerable to disruption of wildlife movement with even a single break.

d. *"Traveling salesman"* is a single route, but gets you back to where you started. This can be an advantage for recreational users who have the option of not having to turn around to return to their starting point.

e. *Least cost to user* may be a good conceptual starting point in configuring a greenway network because it proposes connecting every node to every other node.

f. *Beckman topology* combines two types: least cost to builder and traveling salesman. Greenway users of this kind of network could move between any two nodes without passing through any others.

[1] Linehan, J., M. Gross, et al. (1995). "Greenway planning: Developing a landscape ecological network approach." *Landscape and Urban Planning* 33: 179-193.

[2] Hellmund, P. (1989). Quabbin to Wachusett Wildlife Corridor Study. Cambridge, MA, Harvard Graduate School of Design.

A Design Method: Getting the Greenway Vision

A landscape can seem overwhelmingly complex and the process of successfully identifying and protecting a greenway bewildering. Yet, by systematically answering the targeted questions offered in the design approach presented below, it should be easier to sort through this complexity. The method has been drawn from many other sources in addition to the previous chapters, including findings in the sciences (especially landscape ecology), interviews with people from across North America who have designed or managed greenways, the literature of ecological planning and design, and the authors' professional and academic design experience. The process is summarized in figure 6.7 and characterized in the following discussion. The balance of this chapter provides details of the five design stages and suggests where to find sources of input for the method.

The design method is not an attempt to present *the* definitive, universal procedure for greenway design according to some rigidly defined recipe of guidelines. Rather, it seeks to raise important issues of greenway design through a careful sequence of questions and then suggests ways of answering those questions. It is the job of the project designer to tailor the design process to local conditions and requirements, posing and answering questions about issues specific to the project.

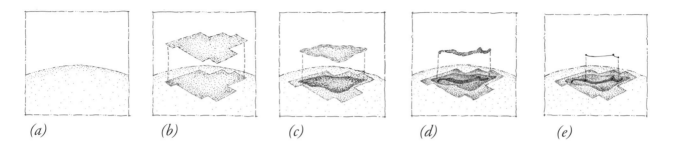

(a)   (b)   (c)   (d)   (e)

FIGURE 6.7

*Summary of the five-
stage ecological greenway
design method. The
questions posed at each
stage help narrow the
possible greenway
solutions in the region.
(a) Stage 1: Identifying
potential issues,
stakeholders, and
preliminary goals.
(b) Stage 2: Defining
a broad region to study.
(c) Stage 3: Selecting
nodes and swaths.
(d) Stage 4: Selecting
alternative alignments
and setting widths.
(e) Stage 5: Implementing
and managing.*

At each stage the designer is presented with one or more broad questions and, most often, several specific, subsidiary questions. (See table 6.2 for the characteristics of each stage.) By systematically answering these questions, project-specific goals, objectives, and actions can be identified. Associated with each stage are design guidelines that can be used for guidance in answering the questions. Further assistance is offered through the more specific steps or actions suggested with each subsidiary question. In this manner, at each stage greenway options are evaluated and alternatives narrowed.

The design method is flexible and can be used for many kinds of greenway projects. It is intended to bridge the gap between scientific and other knowledge, such as presented elsewhere in this book, and the practical design of greenways. It helps clarify the social and ecological context of greenway design and shows how to consider landscape fit, including landscape integrity and community health, at each design stage.

The approach is strategic in that it substitutes the complexity of attempting to plan the entire landscape with the more manageable task of identifying and protecting a linear network as a kind of sustainable framework for a landscape.[19] The method incorporates what Richard Forman and Sharon Collinge called "the spatial solution," or "the pattern of ecosystems or land uses that will conserve the bulk of, and the most important attributes of, biodiversity and natural processes in any region, landscape, or major portion thereof."[20]

This approach fits well with what has been proposed as a kind of intentional, "creative fragmentation," in which the eventual configuration of remnant habitat is anticipated in advance of fragmentation, rather than just being left with whatever is not put to other uses.[21] The approach is similar to what former U.S. Secretary of the Interior Bruce Babbitt called the "confluence of smart growth and conservation biology," a "collaborative weaving of the habitat needs of plant and animal species with the spatial requisites of the human species."[22]

A Strategic Process that Seeks a Framework on Which to Build

Geographically, the greenway design process starts by looking broadly, but then narrows as more detailed information is needed. This strategic approach saves time and resources that would be necessary if a more comprehensive approach were taken. At each stage (table 6.2) the method uses the best knowledge available to remove from consideration those areas of the landscape that do not meet project goals. But it does not use detailed information when more general information will suffice. Several times early in the process questions are posed about sustainability and whether a greenway appears to be the right priority.

TABLE 6.2 Characteristics of the five stages of the greenway design method.

STAGE	STAKEHOLDER INVOLVEMENT	DATA	DURATION
1. Identifying potential issues, stakeholders, and preliminary goals.	As many people as express interest. Look beyond traditional allies. The group may be small in the beginning.	Whatever is readily available. Paper maps may be enough. Onsite and aerial photographs.	Weeks to months.
2. Defining a broad region to study.	More stakeholders.	Can be paper maps or geographic information system (GIS).	Months to a year.
3. Selecting nodes and swaths.	More stakeholders.	GIS, but can be hand-drawn maps.	Months to years.
4. Selecting alternative alignments and setting widths.	More stakeholders.	GIS, but can be hand-drawn maps.	Months to years.
5. Implementing and managing.	Separate groups may focus on distinct portions of the greenway. Overall there will be many cooperating groups.	GIS, but can be hand-drawn maps.	Years to decades and ongoing.

Because the design process is divided into distinct stages, issues are addressed at the most relevant scales. Many greenway concerns are scale dependent and problems can result—or opportunities can be missed—if a concern is investigated at an inappropriate scale.

What you see about the landscape depends on the scale of the maps, aerial photographs, and other tools you use to make your observations. If you are standing in the middle of a patch of ancient bristlecone pine in California it may appear that the species is quite common. If you can lift off the earth in a hot air balloon or look at a vegetation map of the immediate area, you may see that there are other types of patches and species in the area. Ascending up even higher you may discover that bristlecone pine are quite rare across that larger area. Scale makes a difference in how you perceive such aspects of the landscape. We can reach different conclusions when we work at different scales. In the example of the bristlecone pine, we might say we started out with so narrow a focus that we could only estimate the abundance of that species on a very local scale.

Scale is characterized not only by extent—how broadly or how narrowly we look—but also by grain or resolution. Although broadening extent often introduces new landscape elements (e.g., more patches of bristlecone pine, as above), increasing grain (or resolution) offers more detail about the same area and landscape elements. For example, with greater resolution comes increased information about what is present in and around a habitat patch, its edge configuration, and other spatial patterns that will have implications for ecological processes there. With data of coarse grain, you may not be able to detect a corridor of vegetation running through an area. It may be invisible. Only with finer grain may the corridor become obvious.

A Collaborative Conservation Approach

Metropolitan and other regions may have complex patterns of ownership, jurisdiction, and management responsibility. Often there are multiple agencies and organizations working to conserve or manage various aspects of the landscape, from floodplains to wildlife habitat to recreational trails.

Sharing a Perspective: A Bus with a View

One activity Chatfield Basin Conservation Network members still talk about positively, years after it happened, is a bus trip they took together early in the collaborative planning process. The route was a loop through the 140-square-mile basin, with various stakeholders serving as tour guides at different places along the way. One particularly memorable stop was an overlook that afforded a panoramic view of much of the basin with its foothills and the Rocky Mountains behind. From that stop, with all the major landmarks laid out below, it was easy to see and discuss the importance of landscape connections. The trip provided an opportunity for participants to share time together in the field seeing resources they might otherwise talk about only in the abstract. It also strengthened working relationships and was a great touchstone for many years of working together.

Biking Together

While developing a plan for the South Platte River through Denver, project planners and stakeholders took a several-hour bicycle ride along the river to view conditions firsthand. Not only did seeing the corridor for themselves enhance later collaboration among stakeholders, but time together outdoors, away from the regular meeting room, also enhanced working relationships.

Zooming Together

Even if there is no prominent lookout point in a region, it may still be possible to gain an integrated perspective of the landscapes being considered for a greenway with the help of a volunteer-based environmental aviation organization or someone else with an airplane. The largest and oldest such organization in North America is Lighthawk (http://www.lighthawk.org), which for more than twenty-five years has been showing decision makers environmental problems and conservation opportunities from an aerial perspective. A low-budget but nonetheless effective means of achieving a similar aerial perspective is to use a free or inexpensive Web-based application that streams to your computer aerial photographs and other geographic information. These applications, such as Google Earth (http://earth.google.com) and NASA World Wind (http://worldwind.arc.nasa.gov), which allow you to simulate flying over the landscape, are surprisingly effective.

Although few of these organizations may have broad, integrated, greenwaylike goals, they each could likely contribute to a regional greenway effort. Typically, greenway creation in a landscape of complex ownership and management takes many players. No one group can likely do it alone, making collaboration essential. Even if you think your goal is to create a simple greenway connection in one limited part of a region, you quickly realize that your project would be vulnerable to— or may benefit by—factors outside that limited area. It will be very important for those guiding the greenway project to have or find effective facilitation and consensus-building skills to reconcile or accommodate differences.

The participation of private citizens will also be important during the process, and they may be the ones driving the greenway process. For some public projects there may be a legal requirement for public involvement. But more importantly, involving people can be the key to sustaining a greenway over the long term. When the people, especially owners of property adjacent to the greenway, understand and support the greenway and its goals, they may help monitor the greenway and notify managers when there are problems. Greenways' abundant edges can make intrusion and disruption easy (by people, pets, livestock, exotic plants, etc.), which can be difficult to manage. In some cases, greenways may not be publicly owned lands but legally or even informally designated thoroughfares across private lands.

Stakeholders—people or organizations that would have a direct stake in any greenway project—and members of the public can play important roles throughout the design, implementation, and management of a greenway. They can help identify project goals and provide volunteer services ranging from resource inventorying to modest site construction and maintenance. If stakeholders play a part in developing a greenway plan, they are more apt to understand the needs of the greenway and support it. The design process can help educate the public about what it takes to sustain a greenway and how they will benefit from the greenway. An advisory committee made up of members of the public, government officials, scientists, other technical experts, and representatives of interested organizations may be a helpful addition to the design process.

As discussed in chapter 5, anytime one or a handful of social groups are identified as those directly affected or interested in a greenway, it is useful to ask what communities aren't being considered. Such is the nature of community. By definition it is about inclusion, but implicitly then it is about excluding some people or social groups. An alternative to "community" as a basis of planning is accommodating social differences without excluding. With this approach, "Rather than a single, shared vision, neighborhood planning would support variety, including multiple and varied activities, lifestyles, and identities."[23] This is the challenge for greenway designers.

Project Vision and Goals

Developing a vision and supporting goals can bring focus to a project and greatly aid its progress, especially when many people are involved over many years. Sometimes developing a vision for a project and developing its goals can seem like mere formalities. Yet, without articulating these statements—agreements, really—it may be difficult for diverse groups to work together effectively over the time frames necessary to implement and maintain a greenway.

It is important to keep a project true to its goals and to know why a specific design or research activity is being carried out. In this method, goals lead to broad questions, broad questions are answered by researching subsidiary questions, and subsidiary questions are answered with the help of suggested steps and guidelines. This lineage means that every action should be traceable back to one or more project goals. If this tracing cannot be done, an action may not be directly supporting the project. This accountability keeps the design true to original intent and helps explain the rationale and development of the project to the public or to officials. Still, it will be important to demonstrate flexibility with project goals because information learned along the way may dictate that goals be reconsidered.

Protecting landscape integrity is a fundamental concern of the design method. (See chapter 1 for discussion of landscape integrity.) Recreation and other social goals are also included because the long-term sustainability of protected areas will depend on public support. Certainly many greenways have been and will continue to be created principally for recreation, but this does not relieve designers of the responsibility for protecting broader landscape integrity. Nor should greenway projects devoted primarily to protecting plants, animals, and water automatically dismiss recreation or other social goals if compatible forms of use can be accommodated.

Table 6.3 presents how practical techniques have been integrated into the greenway design method in support of each goal of the method.

Integrating an ecological perspective into the design of greenways—as challenging as it may seem—is crucial to the success of the greenway. Greenway ecology may differ significantly from the ecology of other, typically nonlinear, conservation areas. This difference is primarily because a typical

BOX 6.3
Early in the planning process for the Chatfield Basin Conservation Network, stakeholders agreed to pursue complementary goals related to wildlife, recreation, and water. In many cases the same areas were important for each of these goals. Having this diversity of stakeholders around the table meant it was easier to reach consensus. Also, because the area of interest was large (the entire basin), it was easier to shift some activities away from others, rather than fight over the same locations.

TABLE 6.3 Goals of the greenway design method.

DESIRED QUALITIES OF THE DESIGN METHOD	TECHNIQUES TO ACHIEVE THE GOALS
Scale sensitive so ecological and other issues are understood and addressed at an appropriate scale or scales, both temporal and spatial.	Distinguish the *scale* at which evaluations and decisions are made and historical landscape patterns are examined to understand the dynamics of change in the region.
Strategic, rather than comprehensive, to more efficiently use limited planning resources.	Examine broad questions at a broad *scale*, and later, more specific questions at successively narrower geographic scopes.
Politically sensitive, so that decisions are made at the appropriate level by the most relevant parties.	Make decisions at the narrowest or *most local scale* possible.
Stakeholder-driven, so that it works with all the important players who can help implement the greenway, especially those who might otherwise work against it or who might be politically marginalized.	Engage and involve *stakeholders* from the very start of the process, so they will feel a sense of ownership and be more inclined to actively support it over many years.
Adaptable so that the process can be *adjusted* for the uniqueness of local social and ecological conditions as they vary over time and space.	Raise questions about *local ecological and social conditions* and their spatial and temporal patterns. Once these are answered, use that new information to make subsequent decisions.
Driven by *specific* rather than generic or vague values.	Use *key uses* as lenses to view the landscape and make design decisions.
Systemic, in order to look at the landscape as an interrelated whole, rather than as isolated pieces.	Ground the process in concepts from ecology, human ecology, and other sciences, as well as ecological landscape design, that recognize the *dynamic, interrelated nature of landscapes*.
Frugal and *flexible in its use of data*, so that the method makes good use of the data available, even if it is limited, and can be updated as better information is obtained.	Investigate the *design questions* with whatever resolution data are available at the time, remembering to revisit those steps once better data are available.

greenway abuts many elements along its path. Also, because of their long, narrow shape, greenways have a high edge-to-area ratio and usually many more neighbors than a typical squarish park of the same size (figure 6.8). This narrowness can make desirable greenway functions, such as wildlife movement, water purification, or recreation, more vulnerable to influence by adjacent land uses than these functions would be in other parks of similar area. Along with more neighbors, proportionally more areas within the greenway are penetrated by edge effects, including potential intruders (pets, pollutants, people, etc.). (See discussions in earlier chapters, especially chapters 2, 3, and 4.)

The Role of Key Uses

The key-use concept is very broad and is fundamental to the design method detailed below. A *key use* is a use for which a greenway is designed and managed (figure 6.9). Using key uses is an antidote to watered down, generic design processes that try to be all things, but can easily become unfounded in the real world. The concept can be applied to such diverse issues as movement and habitat requirements of individual species or groups of plants or animals, the criteria associated with types of recreation (such as hiking or bird watching), urban design, and criteria for protecting water quality or providing flood control. Ranking the key uses will help during the design process if there are conflicts between the needs of different uses.

Any prospective greenway use for which criteria can be developed may serve as a key use. For example, for a project along the South Platte River, near Denver, use by humans (primarily bird-watchers) and six species of birds was considered key in the design process developed by the project planner. Although most of the bird species were rare or locally in decline, two of the species were selected because they were popular with birdwatchers. Use by humans was included as key because of the area's potential for birdwatching and other forms of recreation. Criteria for what it would take to accommodate these uses on the site were used to guide design decisions.[24]

Selecting key uses for a project deserves careful consideration. Sometimes there will be obvious candidates, other times not. Selecting key uses should grow out of the project goals. For a recreation goal, ask what kind of recreation is intended. For biodiversity protection, determine which species or guilds of plants and animals are intended to benefit from the greenway. For water protection, ask if the issue is controlling floods, maintaining water quality, or a combination of these issues. Because greenways have the potential to counteract some of the effects of habitat fragmentation, it may be useful to include a fragmentation-sensitive species as a key use. Because of the tremendous influence key uses have in the design process, their selection warrants careful consideration and advice from appropriate experts.

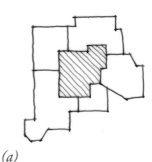

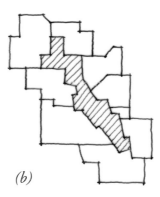

FIGURE 6.8

A typically squarish park (a) may have many fewer neighbors and less interaction with its neighbors than a similar size greenway (b).

(a)

(b)

Key uses should be selected on the basis of adequate information for identifying the needs of each. There may be a temptation to select many key uses, and certainly too few would not give a complete picture of greenway needs. But too many key uses can make the method unwieldy. The South Platte River project, which had as its two main goals protecting wildlife habitat and providing recreation, used people (birdwatchers) and six birds to represent the key uses.[25] The wildlife corridor component of another study used two: river otter for riparian corridors and fisher for upland areas.[26]

The criteria identified for key uses can be recorded as project-specific guidelines and used with other guidelines. For example, a scientific journal article may report that a certain species (one selected as a key use of the greenway) strictly avoids open areas. This information can be made into a guideline for use in designing the greenway. The more specific the guideline the better. For instance, is the species of interest never found any closer than a certain distance from the edge of a forest? If so, that fact would be very helpful in the rule of thumb. When measurements, especially of distance, are reliably known, they should be incorporated into guidelines because they will be useful in mapping habitat and movement requirements.

FIGURE 6.9

Greenways are designed and managed for key uses; these serve to ground greenway design in real-world requirements.

The Role of Questions

Questions play an important role in the design method. They prompt the designer to investigate issues that may prove significant at each stage of design. Answers to the questions also help keep track of sources of decisions and make the design process more transparent. The questions in this chapter are largely based on earlier chapters in this book. They are meant to raise issues and prompt other questions related to the specifics of a greenway locale.

The Method's Emphasis on Goals Setting

To locate boundaries and make other greenway decisions effectively, some means of evaluating the many alternatives must be considered. To do this evaluation requires *goals* that define the hopes for the greenway and what purposes it will serve. The better articulated these goals are, the better they can aid in making decisions.

Because of a widespread decline in opportunities for protecting biodiversity, preserving water quality, and providing nature near where people live, single-goal greenways are difficult to defend and should only rarely be proposed. Therefore, the design method presupposes that every greenway project will begin at least with goals related to biodiversity, water, recreation, and social equity. These goals are a reasonable starting point because most wildlife corridors also help preserve water quality, and many can accommodate recreation or some other social or economic goal without adverse impacts to wildlife and water quality.

Goals are not just for getting projects started; they influence the entire design and management process. The project goals and their supporting objectives can be referred to when choices must be made between alternative swaths, alignments, widths, network schemes, site designs, management plans, or other aspects of a greenway.

Greenway Design Method

Stage 1: Identifying Potential Issues, Stakeholders, and Preliminary Goals

The first stage of the method helps designers step back from a greenway project that they may already be too close to and look beyond obvious solutions to get an overall sense of how feasible a

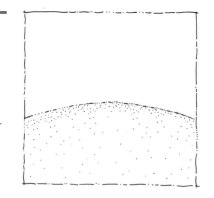

FIGURE 6.10

The first stage of the greenway design method helps designers look beyond obvious solutions, to get an overall sense of how feasible a project may be.

project may be (figure 6.10). Starting a project with a greenway alignment or firm project goals may cause designers to overlook a better alignment, neglect a more urgent need, or fail to recognize an important stakeholder, and ultimately limit success. Be skeptical of "solutions in search of a problem." Greenways are not automatically good for every situation, something that may not be obvious without considering a possible project from broader temporal and spatial scales and reviewing what they indicate about the likely sustainability of a greenway.

The start of a project "is a time for letting impressions sink in, for listening to people, not telling them, for questions, not answers, for dabbling and generally messing about within shadows that only slowly take form," wrote landscape architect John Lyle.[27] He warned designers against reaching premature conclusions that may seem all too obvious at the start of a project.

Greenways are effective in part when they maintain or enhance connections among nodes, that is, areas of interest or significance. However, refuges, parks, flood detention basins, and other greenspace already designated for some conservation or recreation purpose should not automatically be assumed to be effective greenway network nodes simply because they have some official designation. They may be totally or partially degraded or otherwise incompatible with specific greenway functions. The locations and sizes of these already designated lands should influence the alignment of a greenway only if they have qualities and uses that are consistent with the goals of the greenway or that, through restoration, could become consistent with the goals.

For instance, if a heavily used recreational area is planned as a significant intermediate node along a greenway that is intended for wildlife movement, that area may act as a barrier or otherwise affect the flow of wildlife. If because of such incompatibilities an alignment is found not to meet the project goals, then either another alignment needs to be found or the original goal needs to be reconsidered.

BOX 6.4
The principal organizer of a greenway project that focused on an urban river felt it was important to meet face-to-face with as many of the stakeholders as possible before the process got underway. Separate meetings were conducted with representatives of each organization, and the project was outlined to them. At each meeting the project organizer requested that the highest ranking representative of that organization be assigned to the project. Not only were businesses and government agencies well represented, but environmental and social action groups were also. This careful, somewhat time-consuming process of engaging stakeholders probably had much to do with the project receiving a $6 million grant within just a few years, followed by more funding shortly thereafter, and considerable success in implementation.

Resources and People at This Stage

This stage is intended to assess whether a greenway or greenway network is appropriate for the region and what its potential scope might be. Depending on the complexity of the region's resources and politics and on how much the project instigators already know about the region, this first stage can potentially be accomplished with a small group of people and without detailed analysis. Although it may be tempting simply to avoid people who don't seem favorably disposed toward a greenway project, it will be important to engage them and understand their perspectives if they are stakeholders.

An important aspect of this stage is getting an integrated view of what most people may see only as pieces—the aggregated protected or semiprotected lands. This can be accomplished through putting onto a map (paper or digital) the responses to each of the questions below and noting overlaps or potential conflicts.

Determining the Overall Extent of the Region

Starting from a possible project or area of interest, the first step is to expand the scope geographically to define the general region that is the project's context. A region has been defined as "an area, usually containing a number of landscapes, that is determined by a complex of climatic, physiographic, biological, economic, social, and cultural characteristics."[28] Determining the specific boundaries of the region may not be that important. Typically, it is easier to identify centers of regions than their boundaries, and all that is needed at this stage is a general sense of where and what the region is. Sometimes regions have names and their approximate bounds are known to residents. Other times, as with the Chatfield Reservoir in the Chatfield Basin project area, there is a feature that readily lends its name to a region that may not have previously been named.

Expanding attention out to the broader region should help overcome the common tendency to jump to conclusions regarding what is needed in a greenway, where it is needed, and who should be involved, without understanding possible important contextual relationships.

Questions to Gain a Better Sense of the Region, Its Resources, and Its People

Answering the following questions, which touch on very diverse topics, should help formulate a sense of the region.

- Where are the riparian corridors in the area and what are the limits of their watersheds and their general characteristics?

Stream corridors are such obvious potential links in a greenway system that they should be considered first in identifying a region. Often they already enjoy some level of regulatory protection because of the flood damage potentially associated with them or because of wetlands found there. It will be important to consider the watersheds these streams drain and their general health and other characteristics. In most cases the extent of a watershed can be readily determined based on topography and drainages. This watershed approach is especially appropriate for areas where flood management and water quality improvement are priorities.

- Do people in the area already perceive that they live in a region?

Sometimes because of geography or history, people already recognize that they live in a region, such as the Valley of the Sun, Southern Canmore region, or the Tri-City region. Practically every large city gives its name to its surrounding region, such as the Toronto region, the Shreveport region, and the Seattle region. People easily recognize watershed names drawn from the rivers that drain them, such as the Hudson, Blackstone, and Red River valleys. Sometimes the perceived region may be too large to be useful in framing questions at this stage, and some other basis should be used.

- What composite region is defined by overlapping the regions required for wildlife movement of species of interest?

Wildlife may define a region by their movements, such as elk that migrate seasonally between winter and summer habitat, uniting those habitats into a region. Without looking at the entire range used by wide-ranging wildlife of interest, it will be difficult to plan effectively for connectivity that is to serve such wildlife.

BOX 6.5
Initially the Chatfield Basin Conservation Network used very straight lines for some boundaries to acknowledge that where these boundaries were drawn was arbitrary and not based on extensive study. In later years, network members decided to extend the area of interest to more of the broader watershed.

- Generally, how fragmented is the region's habitat and other natural resources?

To consider levels of habitat fragmentation and how they might affect nature conservation, examine a map of the region's vegetation. Determine if there are significant areas that appear generally less fragmented than the rest of the region. Less fragmented areas, even if no more detailed information than that is known about them, may be good candidates for conservation because of the possible natural conditions that exist there.

In landscapes that are or have been mostly forested, fragmentation may be obvious because of the stark visual contrast between forested and open areas. Fragmentation in grasslands, on the other hand, may be much less obvious because the visual contrast between native grasses and exotic weedy species may not be as easily detected from aerial photographs or by an untrained eye. Even fragmented and degraded areas, however, through restoration may present opportunities to help meet the nature conservation goals of greenways.

A useful source of digital vegetation mapping for most of the United States is the Gap Analysis Program of the Department of the Interior, which has developed land cover mapping for much of the lower forty-eight states and Hawaii.[29]

- Where are opportunities for hiking, bicycling, and other ways of experiencing nature, and how well are these experiences linked into an overall system that is widely accessible?
- What are opportunities for greenway-related environmental education or art programs? What are important issues to explore through such programs and where are there natural or social elements to draw upon (e.g., habitats, species, historic sites, management examples, etc.)?
- Are there indications of flooding or water quality problems in the region? What kinds of controls have already been instituted to address these problems?
- What are the region's disturbance regimes and patterns that might affect the success of a greenway? Where are disturbances likely to occur and what corridor widths might be wide enough to accommodate fire, floods, or other likely disturbances?

Greenways may be subjected to natural disturbances, such as fire, flooding, and windstorms, and in most cases such disturbances are integral parts of the ecological health of the natural systems within and around a greenway. For example, cottonwoods may require exposed substrate and a high water table—the conditions associated with flooding—for their seeds to germinate. In areas where flooding is controlled, cottonwoods may not be able to regenerate.

If greenways are too narrow, some disturbances—even naturally occurring—may disrupt their functions and effectiveness. For instance, a naturally occurring fire, which supports germination of some plant species, may create a complete break in cover along a greenway, perhaps making it ineffective for targeted wildlife species. In a landscape with little or no development, there might be alternative wildlife corridors. With development, a greenway may be the only option for wildlife movement. Accommodating the typical dimensions of tree gaps in a forested landscape could also help set the width of a greenway so that it is more resilient to these disturbances. Redundant greenway links may make a system less vulnerable to some of these disturbances.

• What are the general conservation trends in the region?

How much greenspace is already protected in the region and how much is being pursued by others may have an effect on any greenway project. A proposal for a tax to purchase greenspace in Larimer County, Colorado, was met with skepticism by some in the county who felt fifty percent public ownership of the county was enough, even though most of the (federal) government lands were located in a mountainous area of the county at some distance from where a majority of residents live. If residents and others perceive that there is "enough" conservation in the region, it may be difficult to gain support for a greenway project.

Another potential challenge is if other conservation or recreation projects already underway. These may be attempting to attract some of the same funding that the greenway would take. Look for ways to collaborate or otherwise avoid competition.

• What are the development trends in the region?

You can gain helpful guidance for implementing a greenway by considering existing patterns of development such as housing, commerce, industry, and roads. By looking at development trends—how much new development, what types, and where it is going—you may be able to identify aspects that are either supportive of greenways or that may make it difficult to develop and sustain a greenway.

Sadly, greenspace is most often just what remains after development, typically because it lacks some quality attractive for development. If green infrastructure enhances the quality of life in an area, it is reasonable to demand that development and conservation be planned together and that greenways and other greenspace not be mere leftovers. Rather than seeing them as competitive, it is helpful to attempt to locate the best places for each.

Talking to realtors and planning officials can help you identify development trends that may be threats to conservation and other greenway objectives. Especially note linear forms of development—infrastructure such as roads and canals, and power, telephone, and gas lines—because they are likely to cause breaks in any greenway. In some cases, they may also create opportunities along their lengths for recreation or wildlife habitat.

Having some sense of which areas may get developed in the future can also alert greenway planners to areas that might be served by future trails or otherwise provide residents with close-to-home access to nature.

• What social groups are found in the area, where are they located, what differences and similarities do they have?
• What evidence is there of inequality or segregation and is it likely that increasing "amenity values" could exacerbate these problems by contributing to gentrification?
• What attitudes do different social groups in the area hold toward greenways and more generally to greenspace?
• How are people likely to respond to the changes proposed with a greenway project? Are there ways to include children even at this early stage in the process?

BOX 6.6

When Denver parks planners proposed naturalistic drainages with native plants as improvements to greenways in a low-income neighborhood—an attempt to find more ecologically sensitive design solutions—some residents asked instead for the same highly maintained, bluegrass linear parks they saw in most of the city's more affluent neighborhoods. They wondered if the naturalistic proposal was some kind of discrimination. This was a reminder to planners that typically education must accompany such projects if they are to be understood and appreciated.

TABLE 6.4 Examples of agencies and organizations conserving lands in Colorado's Chatfield Basin.

AGENCY/ORGANIZATION	OBJECTIVES IN CONSERVING LANDS IN THE CHATFIELD BASIN
State parks	Conserve nature, provide recreation, protect scenery
County open space department	Conserve nature, provide recreation, protect scenery
County department	Keep most development away from floodplains
Federal government	Protect wetlands, manage forests and grasslands and other ecosystems
Local and national land trusts	Manage growth, conserve nature, and other objectives
State archeological society	Protect archeological resources

Rather than consider the public as a monolithic group, it is important to separate it into constituent social groups, perhaps identified by ethnicity, race, economic status, or other characteristics. Not only may separate groups have differing views toward nature and recreation, but they will likely differ in the amount of influence they wield. What are the economics, transportation issues, recreation needs, civil society and patterns of participation among different groups and how might these relate to greenway planning? It is important to understand who is included or excluded in these various groups, whether there are conflicts between groups, and whether one group or another is more likely to benefit from a greenway project. In a market system, improving quality of life, or some aspect of it, can have complex and often variable effects across social groups. Not every group may benefit and it is the obligation of the greenway designer to understand these dynamics and seek social equity.

- Generally which areas within the region are already protected, by what organizations or agencies, and for what purposes?
- Are there areas adjacent to or near protected areas that are also deserving of protection?

Looking within the region, determine which areas already are protected or have been designated for some compatible objective—social or natural. Such objectives might include nature conservation, floodplain protection, outdoor recreation, scenery protection, farmland preservation, or urban buffering. Determine which agencies and organizations protect these areas and their stated purposes for doing so (table 6.4).

It should be relatively straightforward to locate maps of lands already protected by public and private land management agencies, such as the U.S. Forest Service, Parks Canada, a provincial or state greenspace department, or The Nature Conservancy. Less obvious may be other lands that are protected by laws, such as floodplain legislation, other zoning, or wetlands regulations, or that are privately owned, but have conservation easements.

Taken together these lands represent the starting point for considering greenway planning. Often, when these diverse pieces are considered together, project proponents are surprised at how extensive a region's protected greenspace already is.

• Which unprotected areas have already been targeted as nodes for conservation or
other greenway objectives?

By reviewing plans and reports and talking with the authoring agencies and organizations, you
may be able to determine areas beyond those already protected that have been identified for future
protection. This shows you where these organizations could be active in the near future and therefore where partnerships might be likely. Review such documents as county or city comprehensive
plans, park and open space department acquisition plans, habitat conservation plans, and Nature
Conservancy ecoregional plans.

Sometimes stakeholders and others will consider the specific location of targeted properties as
too sensitive to reveal, or least to map. They may be negotiating on a property or not want to tip
their hands in ways that might make it more difficult to reach a deal. Still, some such stakeholders may be willing to give you orally at least a general sense of priorities.

• Are there significant unprotected and untargeted areas that might be part of a
greenway network?

Even after answering the previous questions, important unprotected and untargeted areas may
be overlooked, having been missed by others. Just because nature conservation may have been more
thoroughly examined in the area of interest, don't forget to consider opportunities and constraints
for water resources, outdoor recreation, urban separators, and any other factors that might not have
been given as much attention.

In particular, look for lines of all kinds in the landscape, as they may represent important greenway opportunities (see box 6.7). Such lines may range from the more obvious, such as rivers and road
rights-of-way, to more subtle lines, such as ridgelines, irrigation ditches, and jurisdictional boundaries.

Playing connect the dots is another way of uncovering greenway possibilities. Identify attractive nodes, destinations, or other "dots" for a greenway network and then see what lies between
them, across broad bands.

Determining the significance of various features and processes is not necessarily easy.
Judging local significance may be relatively straightforward because the locale may be well
known by a number of people. Judging significance related to successively broader areas is progressively harder because fewer and fewer people know the larger areas from personal experience. The Natural Heritage Program of most states and provinces and other countries in Latin
America, for example, can help determine the relative significance of plant and animal species
and communities in an area.[30] If national, state, or local government agencies or private conservation organizations have been working in an area, there may be an extensive understanding
of its ecology and conservation needs.

Before it is possible to identify which of a region's natural features might be protected by a
greenway, it is necessary to understand what a greenway can effectively protect and what it is
not good at protecting. Other chapters in this book, other books and websites on greenways,
and articles in conservation and recreation journals can help describe the characteristics of
successful greenways. Two organizations, one an agency of the U.S. government and the other

BOX 6.7

Landscape Lines

Lines of many kinds and origins may represent significant opportunities for greenways. The Niagara escarpment, the edge of a thick series of naturally occurring dolomitic layers, arcs across hundreds of miles of North America. It contains along its length the most ancient and least disturbed forest ecosystem east of the Rocky Mountains, with thousand-year-old cedar trees and a wide diversity of plants and animals, including threatened or endangered species such as lady's slipper orchid, Massasauga rattlesnake, and Hart's tongue fern.[1]

The Cold War relict 4000-mile Iron Curtain corridor, stretching from the Barent Sea to the Black Sea, has a tremendous array of natural and cultural resources (figure 6.11). With the end of the Cold War, visionaries quickly saw its potential as a greenway.[2] Similar possibilities for greenways exist along equally unusual lines such as the Korean Demilitarized Zone[3] and the former Panama Canal Zone.[4]

While most communities may not have such dramatic examples, there may be smaller line-conserving opportunities that are regionally important.

FIGURE 6.11

The Iron Curtain corridor is an example of a line (albeit, an especially long one) that exists for reasons totally unrelated to conservation and recreation, but which has tremendous greenway potential. (Photo by Klaus Leidorf/BUND–Project Office Green Belt)

[1] Escarpment Biosphere Conservancy. (2004). Escarpment Biosphere Conservancy. Toronto, Ontario, Canada. Retrieved October 31, 2004, (http://www.escarpment.ca/).

[2] Leupold, D. (2004). Biologist with Umweltamt Salzwedel (Nature Conservation Agency). Salzwedel, Germany.

[3] Bradley, M. (2000). Korea's DMZ a rare chance for conservation. ABC Science Online, Australian Broadcasting Corporation. Retrieved July 2, 2004, (http://www.abc.net.au/science/news/stories/s142141.htm).

[4] Funk, M. (2004). "The Route to Prosperity." *Audubon.* Retrieved December 22, 2005, (http://magazine.audubon.org/features0408/panama.html).

a private, nonprofit organization, may be of particular assistance: the U.S. National Park Service's Rivers, Trails, and Conservation Assistance program and The Conservation Fund's American Greenways program.[31]

- Where are already protected corridors? What organizations or agencies are protecting them? For what purposes?
- Where are targeted or untargeted but still unprotected corridors?
- Where are postindustrial waterfronts, brownfields, vacant lands in inner cities, or other degraded sites that could be reclaimed as part of a greenway?

Although it might seem logical to avoid areas lacking qualities attractive for a greenway, just the opposite can also be true. With degraded areas, such as brownfields and other postindustrial sites, it may be possible that the resources devoted to creating a greenway can be applied to reclaiming the degraded area for community use (figure 6.2). Sometimes a degraded area may be the missing link in an otherwise interconnected system. For example, in Denver, an important link of a regional greenway network was discovered buried under three feet (0.9 m) of concrete at the city's abandoned international airport.[32] Westerly Creek has since been daylighted,

BOX 6.8

In some cases, areas that are perceived to be degraded or highly industrial may in fact be rich in wildlife, such as the once highly contaminated Rocky Mountain Arsenal near Denver, which is now part of the U.S. National Wildlife Refuge System and home to hundreds of deer, eagles, and other wildlife.[1] Visual blight should not be confused with ecological functioning. Just because an area may be perceived by people as ugly or trashy doesn't mean wildlife will not find it useful. Before the buildings were dismantled and land filled, Denver photographers Wendy Shatil and Robert Rozinski recorded some of the ways production and storage facilities at the arsenal were used by deer and other wildlife.[2]

A key factor in making such places attractive to wildlife seems to be the absence of people. For obvious reasons, arsenals and military bombing ranges are places where the public is excluded. But wildlife displaced by development may thrive in these places. For instance, many of the approximately 30 military bases in Virginia, totaling 200,000 acres have become safe havens for wildlife, including threatened and endangered species.[3]

[1]Hoffecker, J. F. (2001). *Twenty-Seven Square Miles: Landscape and History at Rocky Mountain Arsenal National Wildlife Refuge.* Denver, U.S. Fish and Wildlife Service.

[2]Shattil, W., and R. Rozinski (1990). *When Nature Heals: The Greening of Rocky Mountain Arsenal.* Boulder, Colorado, R. Rinehart, in cooperation with the National Fish and Wildlife Foundation.

[3]McCloskey, J. T. (1999). "Aiding Wildlife on Military Lands." *Endangered Species Bulletin* 24(1):16-17.

reconfigured, and replanted with a range of native and adapted plants. It plays important roles in managing stormwater and improving water quality.

Because the cleanup requirements for greenspace uses may be lower than for residential or other uses—and therefore the costs associated with cleanup may be lower—greenspace may be a very attractive alternative for a postindustrial site.

Postindustrial sites may offer important opportunities for conserving nature conservation, and they also have important history lessons to present. Artist Tim Collins, who has worked on the Nine Mile Run Greenway in Pittsburgh, suggested that postindustrial public space should, among other things, "reveal the legacy of industrialism, not eradicate it or cloak it in nostalgia; create images and stories, which reveal both the effect and the cause of the legacy and reveal ecological processes at work in the city, not eradicate them; build infrastructure which embraces ecosystem processes and a philosophy of sustainability."[33]

- What could be the key uses of greenways in the region?

Based on what you have learned about the region's resources and community greenspace

BOX 6.9

The potential reuse of postindustrial sites is only just beginning to be discovered, and some such sites may hold considerable promise as future multipurpose greenways. The 245-acre August Thyssen AG steelworks site in Duisburg-Nord, Germany, was transformed into a very popular, decidedly postmodern park: Emscher Landschaftspark (figure 6.12). Through it flows the Emscher River. It is best known for the fantastic steelworks ruins, which are used for various forms of recreation, such as rock climbing, scuba diving, and strolling. But large portions of the site are wooded areas primarily for conservation.

FIGURE 6.12

Emscher Landschaftspark in Duisburg-Nord, Germany, illustrates the considerable potential for postindustrial properties to be transformed into innovative urban greenspaces.

desires, what are the logical uses greenways might support in this region? It may be helpful to think of these uses in at least two categories, those for which there are strong resources and support and those with at least some resources and support. For each of the uses describe the potential ecological, social, or other characteristics of greenways most supportive of that use. Determine where such conditions might exist in the region.

It is much easier to imagine extending uses to new areas in a region if they already take place there. With a bit of brainstorming it may be possible to develop a list of appropriate uses, some of which may be new to the region. For example, with plans to renovate a very urban stretch of Cherry Creek through Denver came the possibility of introducing punt boats on which visitors could be ferried through the heart of downtown.

- Who are the potential stakeholders of a greenway project at this stage?

Many stakeholders will be identified through answering the previous questions. Some may not know they have a stake and something to gain in the greenway design process, while others may even be antagonistic or hold competing goals.

- What are the factors that might limit the changes needed to implement a greenway and what would be needed to overcome them?
- Are there problems, such as rising land costs, that make conservation more difficult?

There may be institutional, economic, or other factors that could inhibit change in the region, the change needed to create a greenway. What will be needed to overcome these factors? Could it be education, activism, technical change to formal institutions, or some other effort?

BOX 6.10

Badgers as Key Users

Badgers and their corridors are getting special attention in the city of Inverness, Scotland, reported the newspaper *The Scotsman*. The Scottish Natural Heritage (SNH) program and other organizations recommended that wildlife corridors be integrated into proposed developments to enable badgers to move around safely.[1] An SNH spokesperson told a reporter that "the expansion of the city could place extra pressures on the local badger population, so it is important to provide a badger strategy as an integral part of the local planning process." While badgers are not considered especially rare in Scotland, they have some legal protection, and in this case, considerable regard.

[1]Ross, J. (2004). "Badgers set to influence city's growth." *The Scotsman*. Edinburgh, Scotland.

BOX 6.11

The Chatfield Basin Conservation Network quickly grew from a few dozen stakeholder organizations to as many as 75 member organizations. The groups included:

- State fish and game agency
- U.S. Forest Service
- Open space departments of two counties
- State parks regional office
- Two state parks in the basin
- Two local land trusts
- A national land trust
- State department of transportation
- County planning department
- Developer of a major new town development
- County weed management supervisor
- A major manufacturing corporation cleaning up a contaminated site

The people who originally organized the Chatfield Basin Conservation Network decided that the network should be inclusive, even if it meant members collectively could only take positions that were middle-of-the-road, rather than weigh in on some controversial projects. At one point, several of the members were battling each other in court over a separate issue, but still participated fully in the joint work of the network. Although for various reasons some stakeholders may not participate, it is important to keep them informed of progress on the greenway project.

BOX 6.12

Several greenways in Longmont, Colorado are known for sculptures that relate to or encourage exploration of their settings. "101 Faces" by artist Jerry Boyle, for example, located along Lefthand Greenway, is a series of concrete faces hidden in various locations along a path, inviting discovery. (Photos by Lauren Greenfield).

• Where are there opportunities for greenway-related education and art?

Some areas may be especially appropriate for environmental education because of resources there and their juxtaposition are conducive to teaching. Other areas may lend themselves to environmental art.

• What areas within the region figure prominently in conveying a regional identity or sense of place and for whom?
• Are there diverse definitions of and aspirations for sense of place that will need to be accommodated?
• What might be the preliminary mission and goals of the greenway?
• What ecological, water, recreational, community, or other issues of the region, discovered through the previous questions, should be addressed by the greenway mission?
• Setting a preliminary mission and supporting goals can help focus efforts and also attract stakeholders with similar interests.

Should the Greenway Project Go Forward?

After reviewing the relative significance of the region's features and functions, the degree to which they are protected, the threats to the region's landscape integrity, the potential level of stakeholder support, and other needs within the region, it is important to ask whether creating a greenway should be a priority for the region. These early investigations may lead to some other conclusion: perhaps the greatest need is not for a linear conservation area but instead for protecting an extensive area of wildlife habitat or a key point of a watershed or taking on some very different community goal. To take a project forward, by the end of Stage 1 there should be strong indicators that the resources and stakeholders exist within the region to warrant a greenway project.

Stage 2: Defining a Broad Region to Study

Through most of the first stage, the project may have had no definite project goals or study boundaries. To go much further, however, a project needs more specific direction as a basis for decision making. Thus, the purposes of the second stage of the method are to select goals to guide the development of the project and to identify a preliminary geographic area of study—a region (figure 6.14).

This stage has four main parts: 1) continuing to enlarge the group of active project participants, 2) revisiting the Stage 1 questions with that larger group, 3) conducting a rapid assessment to better understand a possible framework for a greenway in the region, and 4) answering additional questions to set goals and identify a study area.

Mapping at this second stage, as at the first, will probably be very broad-brush. But because general locations are now important, maps will probably be overlaid or combined in some fashion. They may be hand-drawn maps, such as might be drawn as overlays to or directly on topographic maps from sources such as the Canadian National Topographic System or the U.S. Geologic Survey. With the abundance and inexpensiveness of digital spatial data—for use in geographic information systems—it may be convenient to conduct the analysis by computer, completely or in part.

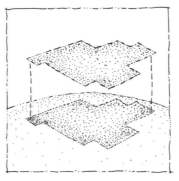

FIGURE 6.14

In Stage 2 greenway designers select goals to guide the project and to help identify the broad region to be studied as the greenway's context.

Continue to Expand Stakeholder Involvement

Convene a meeting of all stakeholders identified in the first stage and ask representatives of each organization or other individuals to bring copies of all relevant plans and related documents. Invite other experts who may not view themselves directly as stakeholders, but who may have expertise in such topics as community issues, ecology, recreation, planning, or conservation. Ask participants to identify anyone else who may have been left out, but who can contribute in a meaningful way.

Stakeholders may be from planning departments, state fish and game agencies, parks and recreation organizations, conservation organizations, land trusts, and social action groups, but also developers, transportation departments, construction companies, homeowners associations, affordable housing proponents, homeless advocates, educators, and property owners. Look broadly across the region to identify who might be interested in or affected by a greenway project.

Consider carefully who will issue the invitation to this meeting. In some situations it may be best for an organization or person who is not directly part of a government agency to take a leadership position in bringing together stakeholders. Undoubtedly government agencies will play a major role in most greenway projects, but if they take the lead that may discourage stakeholders suspicious of government actions and intentions.

Revisit the Stage 1 Questions with the Expanded Group of Stakeholders

Present the preliminary findings from the first stage to the stakeholder group and ask them to comment and develop more detail, especially in response to the following concerns and questions.

What Would Be the Key Uses for Greenways in this Region and Where Are Destinations or Other Already Protected Nodes for These Key Uses?
Carefully selected key uses may have specific, documented requirements that can guide goal setting and decision making. For this reason the design method identifies a greenway's key uses and their supporting criteria rather than pursuing generic goals such as encouraging wildlife movement or making the community more sustainable, which alone may not be especially meaningful.

BOX 6.13

Of great interest to the Chatfield Basin Conservation Network were properties owned by a large corporation that was closing down its manufacturing operations. These properties included ecologically significant stretches of one of the last streams in the Denver metro area that was not dammed or channelized. Representatives of the corporation were invited to participate without any preconception of the outcome. Later the corporation donated extensive streamside lands to the county for greenspace.

- Which areas are specifically already managed for biological diversity, water resource protection, flood control, recreation, or other targeted greenspace purposes?
- Which other areas within the region have the qualities needed to serve as nodes for a greenway?
- Are there any significant nodes, such as what Forman and Collinge called "last stands,"[34] or areas of greatest biodiversity value?
- What are the habitat and movement requirements of the key uses?
- What are the destination and movement requirements of the key users?
- Who owns degraded areas potentially of greenway interest and what is the general condition of these lands?
- Who are the likely developers of new growth in the region and what is planned?
- What are the region's disturbances and where are they likely to be found?
- Are there areas of wildlife habitat that once were connected where connectivity could be restored?
- Are there nodes or destinations that would be useful to connect for people?

Reviewing old maps and other historical documents may reveal the locations of areas in the region that are degraded today but were formerly corridors or part of the landscape matrix that had high levels of connectivity for wildlife. If such lost links are restored ecologically, it is possible they could serve as wildlife corridors again. Ecologist Reed Noss warns *against* creating artificial or very narrow connections that may compromise conservation goals by encouraging weedy species (see chapter 3). With the possible negative impacts on genetic variability and population viability associated with creating connections in the landscape, restoring former connectivity or maintaining existing connectivity is the prudent course.

Conduct a Rapid Assessment of the Region

Richard Forman and Sharon Collinge suggested that "Society does not have to wait for detailed ecological surveys before taking effective action,"[35] and then they went on to suggest ways of conducting rapid landscape assessments. Elsewhere they enumerated some of the landscape elements to look for in a "general survey of landscape-wide patterns and processes, . . . [including] the distribution of aquifers, major streams, large rare habitats, apparent high-biodiversity areas, large home-range or wide-ranging species, major centers of movement or flow, and major areas of different human land-uses."[36] Also valuable, they wrote, is more detailed knowledge of "localized land uses and bits of nature, such as small rare habitats, characteristics of water bodies, or localized rare species and soils."

This is the level and scope of the effort needed at this stage—a quick assessment of the area, with the understanding that more detailed investigations will follow. These efforts aim to start developing what Forman and Collinge called the "spatial solution" (figure 6.15), which is the "pattern of ecosystems or land uses that will conserve the bulk of, and the most important attributes

FIGURE 6.15

Major components of the "spatial solution" according to Forman and Collinge (Forman, R. T., and S. K. Collinge. (1997). "Nature conserved in changing landscapes with and without spatial planning." Landscape and Urban Planning 37: 129-135.) The important patterns are:

- *indispensable patterns, including a few large interconnected patches of natural vegetation (i1, here remnant forest patches), vegetated major streams corridors (i2); and "small patches of nature scattered through the ecologically less-suitable matrix" (i3, here small remnant forest patches surrounded by houses).*

- *aggregate-with-outliers pattern, which is comprised of large patches (aggregates) of natural vegetation (N), cultivation (C), and pastureland (P), with carefully interspersed smaller patches (outliers) of the same land uses.*

- *strategic points (s), such as site characteristics that are rare and positions key for protection, control, or access, relative to the size and shape of the landscape. Here these include stream confluences and where roads enter wilderness.* (Drawing by Joe McGrane.)

of, biodiversity and natural processes in any region, landscape, or major portion thereof."[37] Greenways can protect important linear elements of a spatial solution, especially when their functions are understood in reference to that larger spatial solution.

Although Forman and Collinge focused on nature conservation, their overall approach can also be broadened to look at all the functions relevant to greenway design, as is done here. This stage is also a means of identifying topics needing more in-depth research.

The "Indispensable Patterns" of the Region

There are four landscape patterns indispensable to ecological functioning: 1) a few large patches of natural vegetation, 2) connectivity between the patches, 3) vegetated corridors along major streams, and 4) "bits of nature" scattered through the ecologically less-suitable matrix.[38] Large patches of native vegetation are likely to provide habitat for wildlife needing interior conditions not present in smaller patches. Connections between these patches can help overcome some of the conditions associated with habitat fragmentation. Providing this connectivity, which may function through stepping-stones instead of continuous habitat, may be the major contribution of a greenway. Vegetated corridors along streams can contribute considerably to flood management, water quality protection, and nature conservation. Small patches of nature in less hospitable surroundings can play a role as stepping-stones and provide habitat for species that are not adversely affected by the small patch size.

"Strategic Points" in the Landscape

Strategic points are locations in the landscape with exceptional and long-term ecological characteristics. They are key positions for protection, control, or access relative to the size and shape of the landscape.[39] For example, headwater streams are important to protect because of their disproportionate influence over stream water quality. Stream confluences may be strategic points to protect for wildlife movement. Urban development patterns may limit trail access in a neighborhood to a few strategic points.

First Removals

If there are broad areas lacking qualities that would support the identified greenway goals, then it may be useful to exclude them from consideration and the need for data gathering. If the greenway is primarily intended to protect sensitive wildlife, it will less likely pass through a nearby urban center, such as a downtown or suburban commercial district. A study to protect a riparian corridor may not need to investigate areas that are outside the stream's drainage basin. The kinds of areas that can be reasonably ignored will depend on the scope of the intended greenway network and its goals. It may be easy to eliminate areas as unimportant if the project is attempting, say, to create a short greenway segment. But if the intent is to design an intricate regional network of greenways with very diverse goals, then it may be necessary to investigate the entire region. First removals should not include areas that, with restoration, could serve greenway objectives.

Aggregate with Outliers

Reviewing Richard Forman's proposal for ideal land-use relationships, the "aggregate with outliers" principle, may highlight areas of interest for a greenway that might not otherwise have been obvious.[40] Briefly stated, the model proposes aggregating similar uses, such as development, agriculture, and conservation. It recognizes a role for small patches (outliers) of other uses in these larger aggregations and corridors connecting the large patches of similar type. Accordingly, larger areas of agriculture work better than separated, smaller areas. The same is true with habitat areas: in general, the larger the better, because large patches may contain conditions for wildlife not found in smaller patches. The same approach is also suggested with development: aggregated development is more efficiently served by infrastructure and many other services. This model explicitly endorses the greenway concept in proposing corridors between separated areas of similar land use.

> **BOX 6.14**
> The Chatfield Basin Conservation Network did a rapid assessment by creating subgroups of stakeholders and experts around three main themes: wildlife, recreation, and water. Members of each subgroup met several times, drawing on maps to combine their knowledge. Later the results of each subgroup process were combined into one overall concept plan.

Opportunities or Constraints for Wildlife and General Nature Conservation

- What is the full range of movement requirements for the species of interest?
- What is the range of habitat requirements of nonmigratory species?
- What are the dispersal requirements of the species of interest?
- Are there important plant species in the area dispersed by animals that might benefit from corridors?
- Are there species of interest in the study area for which dispersal corridors are not needed?
- What conditions are needed within the landscape matrix to support functional connectivity— a measure of the continuity along the corridor's length that is needed for some use, such as the movement of an animal species or the pollution-buffering ability of streamside vegetation.
- Are there weedy or other species within the study area for which a strategy of discouraging dispersal would be desirable?
- Are there roads and road edges in the study area that are supporting biological invasions of nonnative plants or pests?
- Where are there locations of frequent road kill that might indicate the need for an under- or overpass?
- Are there patches in the study area that at one time were connected that could be usefully reconnected through restoration?
- Are there bird species in the area that could benefit from corridor preservation?
- Is there a logical overall alignment of corridors within the study area that should be protected if global warming is taking place and its rate is not too rapid to preclude timely wildlife relocation?
- What is the relative significance of the wildlife species in the area from a local, regional, national, and global perspective? Which species have the greatest significance?
- Are there roadless or near-roadless areas that could be included in the greenway to benefit wildlife?

- Where are distinct travel routes used by wildlife?
- Also see chapter 3 for more discussion of these topics.

Opportunities or Constraints Related to the Region's Riparian Corridors

- What order streams are in the region and what are the characteristics associated with these orders?
- Are there lower order streams in the area that if protected would yield the greatest benefits for the stream network as a whole?
- What are the likely characteristics of streams in the area based on the river continuum concept?
- Where are wetlands and what are their types and functions?
- Are there stream confluences within the area or other nodes that deserve special attention?
- Also see chapter 4 for more discussion of these topics.

Alignment of Political, Watershed, or Other Relevant Boundaries

- If political, watershed, or other relevant boundaries don't coincide, what additional jurisdictions need to be included?
- Will there be cross-boundary coordination problems?
- Are there resource experts who understand both sides of such boundaries?
- Also see chapter 5 for more discussion of these topics.

Urban Design Opportunities

- Are there places where a greenway could make urban or suburban development more attractive, compatible, and integrated into the region?
- What are the social structure and distribution of human populations in the area and how might these relate to a greenway project?
- Are there community activities, pedestrian flows, types of social interaction, or other aspects of the populations relevant to a greenway?
- What potential greenway uses would match the needs of surrounding populations?
- Are there land uses or areas that should be separated by a greenway because they might disturb each other?
- Is the region already so developed that any trail routing will have to adapt its routing and construction standards to connect to where people live?
- Is there an opportunity to plan interconnected networks in advance of new development?
- Are there opportunities to complement the greenway's linear recreation with nodes that promote local interaction, such as public gathering spaces, picnic tables, performance centers, community gardens and forests, open-air markets and businesses, camping, fishing, and hunting, outdoor classrooms, long-term routes, and network linkages to provide for adventure and exploration?
- Can the greenway be conceived of as a component of a larger smart growth or other planning effort?
- Also see chapter 5 for more discussion of these topics.

Likely Institutional Setting of the Greenway

- What are the full range and complexity of institutions in the region, both formal and informal, that will determine the success of the greenway?
- What are the most important connections within and between biophysical and social systems that will determine the success of the greenway?
- How supportive will existing social and institutional structures be of the greenway project, especially if project goals are far-reaching (spatially, temporally, or thematically) and the change they represent is fundamental?
- What are the factors likely to inhibit the change necessary to accomplish the greenway and what is needed to overcome these factors? Education? Activism? Technical change to formal institutions? Buy-in of disparate stakeholders?
- Will you be able to work from the bottom up, coordinating with higher levels or broader scales, as appropriate, but primarily engaging participants at the local level?
- How are people likely to respond to the changes proposed with a greenway project?
- Does the project have the right mix of public information (regarding the value and functions of greenways), political participation and activism, and analysis and potential for institutional change to succeed?
- Have you compensated for any lack of empowerment of some groups by making extra efforts to involve them and making sure their concerns are taken seriously? Have you resisted pressure from powerful constituencies? Are you missing important opportunities by taking a middle-of-the-road approach that ignores fringe ideas? Are you missing opportunities by avoiding conflict rather than dealing with it head-on and resolving it?
- What are effective ways of aligning both biophysical and institutional ecosystems spatially and functionally in this region? Have you found ways of promoting institutional learning and change to facilitate planning interventions and ensure adaptability in the face of future social and ecological change? Have you considered broader scale issues to which greenways and their institutions are or should be connected?
- Are there important existing informal institutions or individualized behaviors that will support or resist project goals or specific changes? What forms of participation, dialogue, education, or incentives could help address these issues?
- Are there diverse sources of information informing the greenway design process? Are there ways of taking an experimental approach toward policy and planning, whereby steps toward the greenway are monitored, evaluated, and adjusted? Is there regular communication and collaboration across scales both within and among communities, organizations, and agencies?
- Are the project goals more specific for immediate issues with a high degree of certainty and broader and more flexible when there is uncertainty?
- Also see chapter 5 for more discussion of these topics.

Likely Economic or Other Social Impacts of the Greenway

- What are the purposes and likely effects of economic activity (including distribution of wealth) related to the greenway? Is the purpose of the greenway to accumulate dollars? Or to distribute income or other benefits widely or to the groups that most need them? Or to produce useful goods in a sustainable fashion?
- Would economic activity related to the greenway likely lead to a more or less just distribution of wealth?
- Would a greenway contribute to an equitable distribution of greenspace when looking across a broader perspective, not just locally? If not, can adjustments be made in alignment to make it more equitable?
- Are there opportunities to tie a greenway project into affordable housing by emphasizing shared goals between conservation and social advocacy groups or by setting aside some acquired land for housing?
- Are project economics such that projects will consume or produce energy and materials? Are there ways of shifting more toward the latter, except in cases where income is badly needed and will clearly be distributed widely in the community?
- Have you developed effective mechanisms so that public participation is regular and two-way? Are you using multiple techniques (e.g., private meetings, outreach through community leaders, and written correspondence) that recognize the diversity of cultures and the fact that some groups may not be comfortable with, or may be skeptical of, formal involvement?
- Are there special links between any biophysical resources that might be included in a greenway and any specific social groups that value these resources?
- Where are distinct recreational routes already used by residents?
- Also see chapter 5 for more discussion of these topics.

Educational and Art Opportunities of a Greenway

- Are there opportunities for real education in support of the greenway (which ideally will encourage critical thinking about greenway-related issues and larger issues of sustainability) and not just public information and project advocacy?
- What opportunities are there for both formal and informal education?
- What are the specific sites, resources, or topics of greatest relevance, interest, or value? What relationships can be explained or elucidated, such as natural processes and society-nature relationships?
- What issues lend themselves to critical reflection relative to the greenway?
- What unseen connections can be made visible through art and education? Who are the audiences?
- Are there themes that can be related to people's real lives?
- How do local and global issues come together in the greenway and where do local residents fit into this?

- Are there special educational opportunities for children and youth and how can young people be included in the design process?
- What opportunities are there for storytelling along the greenway?
- Also see chapter 5 for more discussion of these topics.

Study Area Boundaries and Project Goals

At this stage, greenway boundary locations are still not as important as they will be later. They should be drawn very wide and inclusive rather than narrow and exclusive. Revise the mission statement from Stage 1 and develop greenway goals with stakeholders that embody the needs of the key uses.

Stage 3: Selecting Nodes and Swaths

In this stage the focus shifts from that of the entire region down to an area more manageable for study, called here a swath (figure 6.16). In this way some areas are elevated for consideration and further study and other areas are eliminated from consideration.

In a general sense, a *swath* is a long broad strip or belt.[41] The way the concept is used here is close to the U.S. Geologic Survey's definition of "all data received from a spacecraft on a single pass. . . ."[42] The concept is simple: a swath is a wide sweep of land that includes elements of interest about which information is gathered (figure 6.17). It is broad-brush and general.

More than one viable swath may be identified at this stage. If so, the one that appears to hold the greatest potential for supporting the key uses could be selected for study first, or several could be carried forward to create a greenway network.

The following considerations will guide this scale transition from the broad region to one or more swaths.

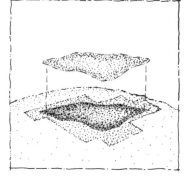

FIGURE 6.16

In Stage 3 some areas are elevated for consideration and further study and other areas are eliminated from consideration as the focus shifts from that of the entire region down to an area more manageable for study, called here a swath.

The Project Team

The most efficient way to accomplish this stage of the process is through extensive stakeholder involvement because stakeholders will have useful knowledge and because they have a stake in the future of the area.

Convene a meeting of all the stakeholders identified in the first two stages and ask representatives of each organization to bring copies of all relevant plans and other documents. At the meeting(s) present the preliminary findings from the first two stages and ask for comment.

Because the stakeholder group may be large, it may be necessary to have a core working team that is made up of key stakeholders and other advisers. It

FIGURE 6.17

A swath is a wide sweep of land that includes elements of interest about which information is gathered. The greenway will be identified within the swath.

BOX 6.15

In the Chatfield Basin in Colorado, green infrastructure planners readily defined the riparian corridors based on flood control and water quality protection, for which there were designated floodplains, mapped alluvial deposits, and other studies. It was much more difficult to develop habitat and movement criteria for wildlife in open grasslands, because much less is known about the size of patches or the width of movement corridors required for individual species.

may be convenient to have subcommittees of the stakeholder group examining specific aspects of the project. Work may be greatly facilitated if there are funds to hire professional consultants to aid in the project. Some projects have greatly benefited from having professionals lent to the project from participating governmental agencies.

General Node and Movement Requirements of Key Uses

For each key use identified in the previous stages, identify criteria for nodes—which may be lakes, parks, extensive habitat patches, or other areas or destinations—and movement. For some uses this may be relatively straightforward, while for others it will be vexingly difficult. Use the best knowledge available and record and communicate to all interested parties how and why these criteria were set. Be prepared to adjust these criteria as new information is obtained.

Nodes

Using the key-use criteria and the knowledge and expertise of the stakeholders, map the locations of possible nodes.

- Which nodes serve which key uses?
- Are some nodes more important than others?

Swaths Connecting Nodes

The swath should be a broad zone that connects nodes and then extends out to a natural, visual, or other logical boundary such as the limits of a watershed or viewshed. This is a way of defining a study area for the next stage that is large enough to include features attractive for a greenway, as well as the areas around them that will play a part in the analysis. At this stage don't try to identify detailed alignments to meet the criteria, but instead look for broad swaths that seem likely to include the qualities needed.

Should the Project Go Forward?

Even at this stage it is important to review whether the project should continue.

- Did the outcomes of this stage provide evidence that a greenway project is worth carrying forward?

Stage 4: Selecting Alternative Alignments and Setting Widths

In this stage the key uses serve as frames of reference to obtain more detail about areas within the swath(s) that may become parts of the greenway. Those uses then guide the identification of alignments and determination of how wide (figure 6.18) the greenway segments need to be. Because of the potential complexity of determining the precise boundaries of a greenway, it is helpful first to select from within the swath a general alignment for the greenway without setting definite widths. Alignments are selected for *each* key use, one at a time. This procedure helps keep the criteria separate and ensures that alignments meant to serve a key use will serve it. If uses are grouped, it can be more difficult to verify that the separate sets of criteria are being met for each use. Later, all of the alignments are examined at the same time.

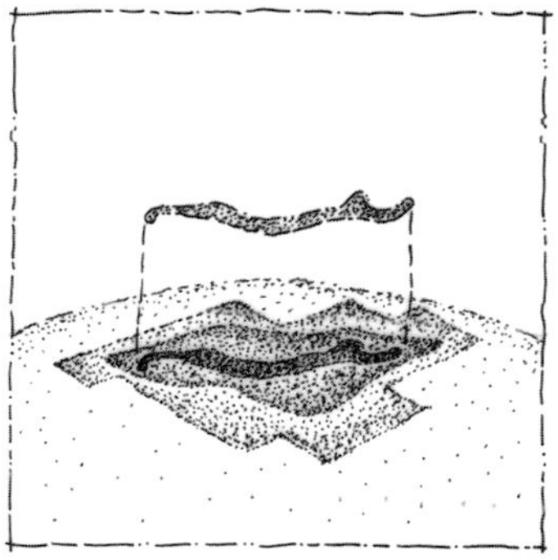

FIGURE 6.18

In Stage 4 the greenway designer considers the key uses to identify greenway alignments and to set segment widths.

Additional Stakeholders, Especially Those Whose Focus Is Very Local

This stage is best accomplished by involving adjacent property owners, local stakeholders, and key regional stakeholders—especially people who are very familiar with local conditions in the priority areas. Additional stakeholders with very local concerns will likely be interested in joining the greenway efforts once specific projects are identified. There are stakeholders, including property owners, who may be major contributors at the local level, but for a variety of reasons, are not interested in participating earlier in the process. There may be many more stakeholders participating at this stage than previously, depending on the number of local greenway projects that are initiated simultaneously. Some local stakeholders may not immediately see the benefit of participating in the project and others may be antagonistic to the project.

Best General Alignment for Each Key Use

The best alignment for a key use is one that makes effective connections (i.e., has good functional connectivity) for that use. The alignment may be a corridor that presently exists, one that reinstates historical connections, or one of stepping-stones that function without being physically connected. Artificially increasing connectivity by making connections where there have been none should be undertaken only after very careful consideration and review by experts (see chapter 3).

It probably comes as no great surprise that some of the greatest and most frequent disrupters of greenway networks are the networks of infrastructure that humans build, especially roads. Achieving a high degree of connectivity tends to be a fundamental goal of both green and gray infrastructure. Hence they frequently are in conflict. Rarely have wildlife and water quality been better off because of such conflict, as evidenced by the staggering estimates of wildlife road kill in North America and the substantial amounts of contaminants reaching streams from roads. Where intersections of the two types of networks cannot be avoided, structural separators, such as underpasses or overpasses, should be considered.

BOX 6.16

In the Chatfield Basin, some partners saw considerable benefit in participating when it provided them the opportunity to join others in applying for grants related to land management. For example, a county open space department worked in cooperation with the U.S. Department of Agriculture Natural Resources Conservation Service to secure grants available to local land owners for land management. An even broader group of stakeholders worked together successfully to win major funding for a range of conservation and recreation projects.

Disturbance Characteristics of the Swath that Might Affect Greenway Alignment or Width

Particular note should be made of those landscape disturbances—both human-caused and natural—that occur in the region. Education, policing, and other management approaches should be implemented to limit human disturbances that might disrupt the greenway.

Determining the range in size of natural disturbance patches will help in setting greenway widths. If, for example, large, wind-caused gaps are common in a forested landscape, then greenway width should be set so that functions within the greenway will not be disrupted if the width is narrowed by such a gap. A similar analysis could be undertaken in landscapes where fires are common. Ecologists and other scientists familiar with the region will be aware of the kinds of disturbances that could potentially disrupt greenway function. Long-term studies of ecosystem dynamics from areas similar to the swath should help determine the range of sizes for disturbance patches. In some situations, aerial photographs may help in estimating the dimensions of such patches.

Given that many kinds of landscape disturbance, including wind or fire, occur naturally, some readers may wonder why the design of a greenway should be adjusted for such natural phenomena. In many landscapes dominated by development, natural corridors are few in number. The loss of one corridor in such a landscape, even if due to natural disturbance, could have a serious impact on a greenway's ability to function in intended ways.

Combining the Best Alignments into a Single Unified Greenway

With this step, if there are multiple nodes and swaths, the plan of the greenway concept can start to resemble a messy spaghetti-and-meatballs arrangement (figure 6.19). Later it will be refined to a more recognizable greenway system. Even at this stage, it is important to keep track of which alignments and nodes serve which specific key uses. Depending on how many key uses and nodes there are, this step of the process can become complex.

If an alignment or one of its links can serve more than one use, then that segment may be an especially important part of the greenway, as long as the uses do not conflict. Often alignments that nearly coincide can be accommodated in one corridor if widths are carefully set (a later step in the method) to avoid conflict. Even if an alignment serves only one key use, it must remain part of the greenway if that link is required for that use. When looking at what may seem a tangle of routes, the designer should try to identify a single alignment that serves all of the uses. This can be considered the core alignment, and it has the highest priority for further study. Additional links should be added if they provide qualities that support the key uses.

For instance, a portion of a greenway may follow a stream and have sufficient habitat to support wildlife movement,

FIGURE 6.19

Alignments for individual key uses are overlain, and similarities and differences are noted.

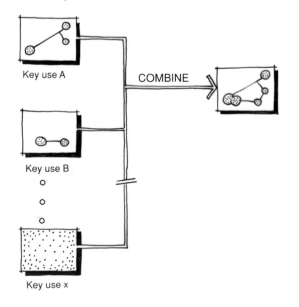

Key use A

COMBINE

Key use B

Key use x

but be too steep for a bicycle path, which might be accommodated by a separate greenway loop. Including redundant connections for wildlife is a good way to reduce the impact of future breaks to the system.

Setting Widths Locally in Response to the Needs of Key Uses

Typically, one of the strongest determinants of where greenway widths are drawn is the location of existing property boundaries. Existing patterns of ownership and the availability for purchase or donation of individual properties usually have a tremendous effect on the configuration of a greenway. (Exceptions can occur in new towns, such as The Woodlands, Texas, or in planned unit developments, where all the land uses, including greenspace, are planned simultaneously.) A frequent strategy for creating a greenway is to identify an approximate alignment for the greenway and then, working within the confines of existing property boundaries, try to secure the minimum amount of property to make a continuous greenway. Sometimes a set minimum

FIGURE 6.20

Constant width boundaries (dashed lines) may not correspond to landscape functions (stippled areas).

greenway width is used, based upon some vague sense of ecological conditions (figure 6.20). Yet given the heterogeneity of most landscapes, it is difficult to imagine that a constant width can be trusted, unless it has been very liberally set.

An alternative approach—the one proposed here and supported in earlier chapters—is to adjust greenway widths in response to locally varying ecological conditions. With this approach the greenway is less likely to be too narrow to accommodate its intended uses. A potential route will not have to be rejected because in one place it was restricted to a width that did not meet the arbitrary minimum even though it could support the greenway functions at that point.

Making widths responsive to local conditions may make acquisition more challenging and costly, but it is worthwhile to the degree that it ensures the integrity of the greenway. For example, consider a greenway project that has as a major goal of protecting a movement corridor wide enough for a species that avoids open areas and requires continuous interior-forest conditions. Using a constant width along the greenway does not recognize that the parts of the greenway near high impact land uses may have edge effects that extend considerably farther into the greenway than they do elsewhere. Depending on how generously the width was set, the greenway may be compromised for that species.

A similar situation may exist when a constant-width greenway is intended to protect water quality. If the greenway has the same width adjacent to a farm that uses heavy applications of fertilizers and pesticides as it does next to an area of undisturbed forest, the set width may not be sufficient to buffer the stream next to the farm. Greenway function is better protected when width responds to the specific characteristics of adjacent uses.

Local conditions change, not only over space, but also over time. The effective width and

FIGURE 6.21

The effective width and functional connectivity of a greenway may change from season to season, as, for example, when leaf fall in a deciduous forest reduces the amount of cover available for wildlife, when snow accumulation makes certain portions of a trail impassable for recreationists, or when frozen ground reduces the filtration effectiveness of slopes above a stream.

functional connectivity of a greenway may change from season to season (figure 6.21) (for example, before and after leaf fall along an upland corridor or with winter application of road salts along a stream) and even from day to day (with and without high levels of weekend visitors) or from hour to hour (during daylight and after). Also, as years pass, development surrounding a greenway may change dramatically and with it the kinds and intensities of inputs to the greenway. A greenway's dimensions have to accommodate all of these changes if it is to be consistently effective.

A common response to these many unknowns is to add extra width where possible along the greenway. This response may be the best way to deal with a complex situation, but it works best if it comes only after careful examination of the present and (likely) future factors affecting width.

The miles-wide approach to setting widths that is sometimes suggested for wildlife movement and habitat corridors may partially be in response to the potentially confounding complexity of variable width setting and the need for adding a contingency. But even with an approach that sets a very liberal width, there needs to be a constant reading of landscape changes along the greenway. These kinds of readings not only help set or evaluate dimensions, but also flag potential management problems that may need to be monitored. For instance, through setting widths it may be noticed that extensive erosion is taking place on adjacent property. Ongoing monitoring of the situation may be necessary to detect threats to the greenway.

Computer programs—specifically geographic information systems (GIS)—can facilitate setting widths that respond to local ecological conditions when sufficient digital data are available. Using techniques of combining maps called cartographic modeling (or geoprocessing),[43] appropriately detailed data, and carefully developed criteria, a GIS can set widths at intervals along the length of a greenway. The success of this process depends, among other things, on how well articulated the criteria are and how detailed the supporting data. Completely automating the process of width setting would most likely take very sophisticated cartographic modeling, but even partially computerizing the process can be very helpful.

One simple GIS technique that can be useful in setting greenway widths is establishing a buffer around those landscape elements that could potentially harm greenway function. These buffers might approximate the major influence zones of the harmful elements, such as noises from highways or the home range of aggressive pets coming from neighborhoods. The width of the buffer depends on the extensiveness of the impacts. These buffers and the elements they surround should be avoided when the greenway alignment is identified.

Greenway designers are frequently confronted with limitations—political, right-of-way, financial—that would compromise greenway width setting. In some cases, creative solutions might be possible. For instance, if adequate width cannot be acquired in an area such that greenway functions could be compromised, it may be possible to reach an agreement with adjacent landowners to manage for greenway functions on their land.

Concerns in Setting Greenway Widths

Answers to the following questions should help identify the issues that will guide setting greenway widths.

Width Issues Related to Wildlife
- What edge effects should be expected along the greenway? Are any of the corridors under study primarily used by edge species? Which species? What impact would these species likely have on the species the greenway aims to support?
- Are there larger animals in the study area that are sensitive to human influence and that might require wider corridors for adequate cover and seclusion? If so, what kinds of dimensions might be necessary?
- Are there species present in the region for which regional movement is important and for which miles-wide greenways may be needed? Are there locations within the area where such dimensioned greenways are feasible to protect?

Width Issues Related to Riparian Corridors
- Are there areas where stream habitat is fragmented and movement of fish and other aquatic organisms is reduced due to alteration of uplands and riparian vegetation or extreme changes in water quality caused by urban and agricultural development? Are there opportunities for restoration?
- If most areas along a stream are not vegetated, where are the areas with vegetation and what is their contribution to stream health? If most areas along the stream are vegetated, where are the areas without vegetation that may be good candidates for restoration?
- Are there stream banks infested with invasive exotic plants or with such potential? What are the prospects for management? What would grow there if the invasive species were removed?

- What is the quality of water within the area and what is the condition of the riparian functions of hydrologic regulation, filtration of sediment and dissolved nutrients, stabilization of stream structure, and regulation of water temperature, related to water quality?
- Are there areas near streams that are sources for excessive inputs of sedimentation, nutrients, or other contaminants? What are the present and likely future conditions of areas between these sources of contamination and nearby streams?
- Where are upland sources of nitrogen, other nutrients, or other contaminants and what can be done about them?
- What are ways of limiting upland sources of nitrogen, especially where there is no intervening vegetation to filter it out? What is the capacity of intervening vegetation or wetlands to filter out nitrogen?
- Are permeable soils present that overlay impermeable material (subsoil or bedrock) such that groundwater will remain in or near the zone where roots can absorb nutrients and these vegetative stream buffers can be particularly effective?
- For projects in the temperate zone, are the timing, composition, and concentration of inputs of excessive nutrients and sediment to waterways (based on seasonal growth patterns of riparian vegetation) creating specific problems?
- What is the likely filtration capacity of riparian forests in the area, based on the slope and width of the floodplain and the nature of the vegetation, including density, successional stage, and seasonal variation of growth and senescence (i.e., aging, decline, and death)?
- Are there likely to be pulses of runoff-borne pollutants at times of the year when lack of buffer zone plant growth makes riparian areas seasonally ineffective?
- Where is riparian vegetation effective at shading the water surface (especially of any small, headwater streams) in summer, preventing temperature extremes?
- Are there areas of major human activities, such as agriculture, urbanization, forestry, transportation, recreation, flood control, and withdrawals for water supply, that may be affecting water quality and the ecological integrity of riparian corridors? Or could such areas become a problem if there was a loss of riparian vegetation between the areas and nearby streams?
- Where is the natural meandering span of the stream, that is, the geomorphic floodplain, riparian forest, or area over the stream's shallow groundwater system (including groundwater recharge areas in uplands)?
- Where are the 100-year or other recurrence-interval and legal floodplains? Are there areas that could be included within a greenway that could buffer impacts from degraded up-slopes?
- What is the likely effectiveness of any stream buffers considering such factors as chemical characteristics of contaminants, soil properties, buffer width, and runoff rates found in the area?
- What and where are the point sources of contaminants into streams?
- What are the nonpoint sources of contaminants in the area?
- Where are major areas of agriculture and to what degree do they contribute to water quality degradation?

- Are there areas within the riparian corridor being used for livestock grazing where stream banks are being trampled, vegetation is being denuded, and waste is adding nutrients to the stream?
- Are there stretches of streams that have been channelized or buried and where stream conditions have been degraded? Are there opportunities for dechannelizing or daylighting any of these areas?
- Are there areas of stream diversion or groundwater extraction where stream conditions have been degraded? Are there opportunities for modifying or ending these practices?
- Have roads or utilities been built in stream corridors such that they have major impact on the stream?
- Is recreation having an impact on riparian corridors?
- Where are major urbanized areas and what impact are they having on riparian corridors? Where are major impervious surfaces that release surface flows directly into streams? Are there buffer areas between streams and major impervious surfaces?
- Are buffer strips of riparian vegetation currently or likely to be overwhelmed and degraded by upland activities?
- What is the ecological health of aquatic systems according to the index of biotic integrity (IBI) (see chapter 4) or another method?
- Is the stream corridor under study in the headwaters, middle, or lower reaches of the stream and what are the implications of this?
- Are there opportunities to connect a variety of habitats (e.g., upland and riparian) with a greenway?
- Through what sort of landscape does the stream flow? How does the corridor function in relation to the other components of the landscape? To what extent has the surrounding landscape been modified by people? For what kinds of uses?
- Is the riparian corridor important for wildlife?
- How does the corridor segment affect, and is it affected, by other segments upstream and downstream?
- Is the greenway project investing adequately in studies to define the riparian corridor, recognizing that such studies are a useful long-term investment in the development and management of the greenway?

Width Issues Related to Human Ecology
- Which elements of the greenway affecting social groups are short-term and which have the potential to bring about fundamental, long-term change? Are any short-term solutions incremental and likely to build toward a long-term solution or do they potentially reduce the severity of the immediate problem and thereby risk reinforcing dysfunction?
- Where are places that would be interesting to explore as part of a greenway and what are the resources (e.g., published literature, local schools and colleges, professionals and specialists, local adults with special knowledge) for taking advantage of these opportunities?
- What opportunities are there for both formal and informal education? What are the specific

sites, resources, or topics of greatest relevance, interest, or value? What relationships can be explained or elucidated? What issues lend themselves to critical reflection? How do local and global issues come together in the greenway and where do local residents fit into this?

- What unseen connections can be made visible through art and education? Who are the audiences?

- Where are opportunities for citizen science, which explicitly engages people in ecological research and monitoring of the greenway?

- Are there opportunities to create adjacent places within the greenway where adults and children can spend time near (and learn from) each other, such as community gardens and playgrounds?

- Where are places for collaboration among artists and community members for creative expression, including telling stories of people, place, and history and thinking about the world in new ways?

- Where along the greenway edge could popular facilities and uses be located so that the greenway and neighborhoods are tied together?

- Are there opportunities to maximize accessibility through short-distance trails that connect residential areas to the greenway and to public transit hubs, commercial districts, schools, and other such destinations? If the greenway has long-distance trails, can they be thoroughly integrated with shorter, more local trails?

- Are there specific places where a greenway could make dense development more attractive and desirable while providing close access to nature?

- What opportunities are there to work with developers and city and county planners so connections into development are effective and movement is discouraged where it should be?

- What opportunities are there to work with developers and public planners to coordinate appropriate trail connections into developments?

- Do homeless people rely on open lands that are slated to become a greenway? How can they be brought into the greenway design process as stakeholders and worked with collaboratively to deal with any conflicts?

- Should barriers to wildlife movement be created in any areas adjacent to the greenway where such movement could put wildlife in danger, such as open space that dead-ends in dense development?

Evaluation of the System after It Is Initially Pieced Together

Once widths have been set, it is important to determine how well the entire system might serve the key uses. This kind of reexamination, much of which might take place in the field, should be carried out as if the greenway design were being approached for the first time. Any shortcomings of the greenway in meeting the project goals and accommodating the key uses should be carefully noted. If significant problems are identified that cannot be corrected by adjusting widths or alignments, then there may have to be a looping back in the design process. How far back in the process the project will have to go, will depend on the kind of problems discovered and whether they are concerned with the goals, uses, and criteria identified for the project or with the quality of data used.

Although an intuitive approach to configuring a greenway might be most common, other approaches have been recommended. For instance, some researchers have proposed a technical approach using a gravity model.[44] The gravity model helps estimate the interaction between pairs of nodes, that is, how likely it is that connections between nodes are important to wildlife. Nodes have more interaction with increased node size, the closer the distance between them, and the lesser the degree of landscape "friction," or resistance to movement, between them. Such an approach can lead to better informed decisions about which links to conserve in a system; intuition alone may not yield the most efficient results.

Stage 5: Implementing and Managing

The final stage of the greenway design method is really just the beginning of the greenway. With implementation comes a different kind of work, typically a need for fund-raising, and incremental accomplishments on the ground (figure 6.22). With a shared overall vision and coordination, it will be possible for separate efforts to work simultaneously on different parts of the greenway.

It is difficult to predetermine the steps for this final stage of the work because of the site-specific nature and wide range of the activities. Identifying the type of facilities that will be needed and their locations has to be in response to specific site conditions and in support of specific project goals. Accordingly, this stage of the greenway design method depends on the designers' ability to read and understand the landscape in the field. Specialized texts and experts on specific topics, such as ecological restoration and environmental management, should be consulted. The following questions should help frame important issues related to implementing and managing the greenway.

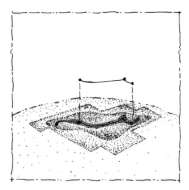

FIGURE 6.22

In the final stage, Stage 5, the first parts of the greenway plan are implemented, sometimes by separate groups united by a shared overall vision and plan.

- What is the priority for acquiring and implementing each segment of the greenway?

The significance of each segment of the greenway should be ranked according to its contribution to greenway functions, the degree and immediacy of threat from development, the number of landowners, and any other important project-specific criteria. This ranking helps determine which segments to acquire and complete first.

- What is the design program for the greenway?

With the familiarity of the greenway and its key uses gained in the previous stages of the design process, a preliminary list can be composed of the kinds of facilities that will likely be built in the greenway. These facilities, such as trails, wildlife underpasses, and check dams, are the items, large and small, that are needed to support the key uses of the greenway. Collectively they are known as the design program. Even as it is important to trace every step in the design process back to one or more goals, so every element constructed in a greenway should be tied to at least one goal.

The scope of the design program will depend on the intensity of the key uses and the sensitivity of the greenway's sites. For some greenways, such as those that have little or no recreational use and are primarily for wildlife and water quality protection, only modest construction may be needed to facilitate the greenway goals. Other greenways, especially those that are recreational, may have abundant facilities to serve recreationists, such as trails and toilets. Still other facilities, such as barriers and bridges, may be needed to protect the greenway's natural features and processes from overuse by recreationists.

- Where should facilities (such as trails, wildlife underpasses, and bridges) be sited and how should they be implemented?

To maintain landscape integrity the design of every facility should be as ecologically sensitive as the other phases of greenway planning. Sustainable design practices and best management practices should be consistently adopted. Particular care should be given to designing and siting facilities so that these elements do not interrupt connectivity for a key use. Also, the materials and means used in constructing the facilities should be carefully selected so that they do not introduce elements into the greenway that will compromise its integrity.

Greenway facilities need to be designed to respond to the dynamic natural processes of the greenway. If the greenway is susceptible to seasonal flooding, for instance, then this must be considered when designing trails and wildlife underpasses.

Facilities should be sited in such a way that they complement the key uses of the greenway. If use by wildlife is the highest priority, then trails should be sited so that they meet recreational goals without interfering with the wildlife functions of the greenway. Thus, facilities constructed in support of one key use cannot disrupt another key use if both uses are intended for the same segment of the greenway.

Dividing the greenway into distinct zones that reflect each area's intended uses can be an effective way to avoid treating the entire greenway as if it were a homogeneous unit. With such zoning, facilities and uses are allowed only in zones where they will not be ecologically or socially disruptive. The type and intensity of allowable recreation, for example, might be limited to those zones that can accommodate it. This same system of zoning can also function in greenway management.

Siting facilities requires fieldwork and, most often, careful, extensive mapping because specific directions of where and how to construct the facilities must be developed for the construction to take place. Some facilities, such as trails, may be laid out directly in the field.

- How should ecological restoration be accomplished where it is needed?

Some degraded areas will likely be included within the greenway. These should be restored ecologically if they are to support greenway functions. Plans should be formulated to carry out this restoration in consultation with restoration experts.

- How should the greenway be managed?

There may be a tendency to believe that because greenways are often natural corridors, once they have been created they can be left without management. Typically, there is too much interaction between greenways and their neighbors, however, for this to be true. Depending on the greenway's uses and ecology and on what surrounds it, the greenway may require more maintenance than similar acreage in a typical nonlinear protected area.

The time it takes to design and implement the greenway may seem lengthy, but that time is short in comparison with that spent maintaining the greenway. Ideally greenway management philosophy and practice grow directly out of the project goals set early in the design process and out of all of the lessons learned during that process. The same goals given for the design process also apply to management, because both greenway design and management are concerned with the same natural phenomena. It would not make sense, for instance, after giving biodiversity or water quality very close attention during the design process to allow maintenance vehicles to frighten wildlife or to pollute water.

No amount of planning will anticipate all the adjustments required in greenway management over the years. For this reason an adaptive management approach makes the most sense. With this approach, management activities are used as research opportunities. Careful monitoring and evaluation will be required of the effects of these activities, which can then lead to adjustments in how things are being managed. For example, if there is uncertainty about the best timing of an activity, such as an annual mowing of trailside grasses, alternative times could be tested and evaluated for impact on butterflies or other key uses. The maps developed for greenway design, especially any digital data in a geographic information system, can also be extremely useful in managing the greenway adaptively.

An institutional analysis will also be helpful to determine if the organizations and procedures supporting the greenway are effective. A more extensive evaluation can be carried out by reviewing each of the design process questions above to see how well the greenway is living up to its potential.

Written guidelines and management protocols will be needed to communicate the relative importance of each aspect of the greenway to managers and field personnel. In addition, they will need to be trained in ecological management techniques, which may be quite different from the more traditional greenspace techniques used in most places.

- How can the purposes of the greenway be communicated to a broad audience so that the greenway is not viewed merely as open space, available for utilities and any other uses that don't readily fit elsewhere?

The people on the front lines managing greenways and other greenspace frequently say that one of the biggest challenges to managing for landscape integrity is the numerous demands for rights-of-way for utilities, through roads, or new uses. It is as if greenspace—"open" space—is land without a permanent or significant use. It is easy to see why it might appear so to utility planners, who are trying to site a utility corridor and may feel there is little choice because all lands have been developed except for the greenway. One suburban natural areas manager observed that in recent years he barely finishes restoring habitat after one utility line is constructed before the request for the next such project comes along to disturb the same area.

Some of these requests may be inevitable, but building widespread understanding and support for the greenway may make it easier to say no to such proposals. In one midsized U.S. town a federal agency proposed to the city's greenspace department temporarily storing a sizeable amount of fill dirt on a designated protected natural area. The outcry from the public was immediate and the proposal was withdrawn.

Sources of Information for the Greenway Design Method

The design method relies on a gradual inventory of natural and social features. Inventorying is not one of the stages of the method; it is something that happens throughout. It may be tempting for greenway designers to rely on books such as popular field guides to answer ecological questions about an area. These books, however, need to be used very carefully and only to respond to very general questions because they are, for the most part, generalized discussions of regions, not detailed descriptions of specific areas.

Because few greenway designers are conversant in all the ecological and sociological topics needed to complete a project, professional help will usually be needed. Many kinds of professionals devote themselves to the study of the issues related to greenway creation and may be useful as consultants on a project. In addition, the journals these professionals read and write for may have articles that can help greenway designers (table 6.5). Some of these professionals, especially those at universities or local, state, or federal agencies, may offer their services at little or no charge.

As mentioned earlier, general assistance in creating greenways may also be obtained from the U.S. National Park Service's Rivers, Trails, and Conservation Assistance program or from the American Greenways program of The Conservation Fund in Arlington, Virginia, both of which have been involved with several statewide greenway efforts. Natural Heritage programs in the United States and Canada use a standard approach to evaluate the presence of threatened and endangered species or critical natural communities.[45] Although such programs may not reveal the exact location of a project's key species, generalized maps of the locations of federally and state-listed species and important communities can be supplied.

There are also many informal sources of information that may prove useful in designing greenways. Experienced naturalists, bird watchers, hunters, trappers, and other people who spend considerable time outdoors often have firsthand experience with a landscape over many years. Specific soil characteristics, other than what is given in county soil surveys, are sometimes difficult to discover without fieldwork, but farmers and others may be able to help because of their highly developed abilities to read a landscape's soil conditions. Possible future development patterns can sometimes be learned from realtors, developers, private land planners, government planners, or others who are abreast of an area's development trends. Road maintenance departments may have records of where the most frequent automobile accidents occur with wildlife. Such locations may indicate the presence of important wildlife movement paths.

Finding and Using Maps

With the design method, detailed information is gathered only when its specific use is known and then only with the detail that is necessary to a particular scale or stage of work. This

TABLE 6.5 Professionals involved in greenway design, their locations, and journals to which they contribute.

PROFESSIONALS	LOCATIONS	JOURNALS
Plants and Animals		
Wildlife biologists, ecologists, landscape ecologists, biologists, botanists, conservation biologists, fisheries biologists	Departments of biology at universities and colleges, departments of fisheries and wildlife in state and federal governments, private consultants, state Natural Heritage programs, private nonprofit conservation organizations	*Conservation Biology, Biological Conservation, Journal of Biogeography, Ecology, Journal of Applied Ecology, Environmental Management, Wildlife Monographs, Wildlife Management Bulletin, Wildlife Resources News, Wildlife Abstracts, Wildlife Review, Journal of Mammalogy, Ark, Condor, Wilson Bulletin, Landscape Ecology, Landscape Journal, Habitat Suitability Models of the U.S. Fish and Wildlife Service, Natural Areas Journal, Journal of Wildlife Management*
Water Resources		
Water resources specialists, hydrologists, limnologists, aquatic ecologists, landscape ecologists, environmental engineers, agricultural engineers, physical geographers, environmental scientists, agronomists	Departments of ecology, agricultural engineering, and geography at universities and colleges, departments of soil and water conservation in state and federal governments, private consultants, private nonprofit conservation organizations, U.S. Environmental Protection Agency, private land trusts	*Ecology, Environmental Management, Journal of Soil and Water Conservation, Environmental Science and Technology, Environmental Conservation, Ecological Applications, BioScience, Ecological Engineering, Journal of Environmental Quality*
Design		
Landscape architects, landscape designers and planners, recreation planners, regional planners, ecological planners, environmental planners, community planners	Departments of biology, landscape architecture, and planning at universities and colleges, National Park Service, local, regional, and state outdoor recreation commissions, U.S. Forest Service	*Landscape Architecture, Landscape Journal, Landscape and Urban Planning*
Outdoor Recreation		
Outdoor recreation planners, foresters, landscape architects	Departments of outdoor recreation at colleges and universities, National Park Service, local, regional, and state outdoor recreation commissions, U.S. Forest Service	*Biological Conservation, Journal of Applied Ecology, Journal of Environmental Management, Journal of Wildlife Management, Natural Areas Journal, Restoration and Management Notes, Journal of Forestry*
Social Ecology		
Sociologists, planners	Departments of urban sociology and urban and regional planning at colleges and universities	*Human Ecology, Harbinger—a Journal of Social Ecology*

approach recognizes that gathering and analyzing data can be very time-consuming and costly. Furthermore, different techniques for analyzing maps may be appropriate at different stages. Cruder, more general mapping approaches, such as in the first two stages, may be all that are necessary early on.

Beginning a project with a comprehensive resource inventory can therefore be a big mistake. How can appropriately scaled and classified maps be gathered before the questions have been articulated? An overview of maps, however, a kind of environmental scan, is helpful; it can, in fact, be crucial to understanding a project's setting. But it is generally best not to start mapping without a clear reason, not to skip what John Lyle called "a time for letting impressions sink in . . . for questions, not answers."[46]

There is no such thing as a standard list of maps needed for designing a greenway. But as you identify goals and objectives and carry out the steps of the design method, including identifying key uses, it will be clearer what kinds of maps will be needed. Some sources of national and international geographic information system data include:

- GIS Data Depot-U.S. (http://data.geocomm.com)
- Geobase-Canada (http://www.geobase.ca)
- Google Earth (http://earth.google.com)

There are also many sources of state/provincial and local data, such as:

- Massachusetts Geographic Information System (http://www.mass.gov/mgis)
- Manitoba Land Initiative (http://mli.gov.mb.ca)
- City of Fort Collins, Colorado (http://ci.fort-collins.co.us/gis)

Conclusion

As this chapter's presentation of the design method makes clear, much attention and care are required if the process of designing a greenway is to fulfill its potential for people and nature. The design method is an open, flexible, question-driven process. If through the method an effort is made to discover and understand the social and ecological workings of a landscape and this information is applied to greenway design, then greenways can do much to protect landscape integrity. The results of applying the design method to a greenway project will depend on the thoughtful care taken at the many steps along the way. The result will be less of a sudden outcome and more of an ongoing dialogue between what is being discovered about the nature and people of a greenway and how design and management can best respond to that knowledge.

Notes

[1] Design is used here in the sense of intentional change in the landscape, at a variety of spatial scales, as proposed in Lyle, J. H. (1985). *Design for Human Ecosystems*. New York, Van Nostrand Reinhold Company. It is "giving form and arranging natural and cultural phenomena spatially and temporally," as proposed in Ndubisi, F. (2002). *Ecological Planning: A Historical and Comparative Synthesis*. Baltimore, Johns Hopkins University Press. Thus it refers not only to the manipulation of landscape elements at the site scale, but also to interventions at much broader areas, which is often called planning (e.g., ecological landscape planning). However, design is not used here to refer to activities also called planning that focus on organization, administration, or development of policy.

[2] Noss, R. F., and A. Y. Cooperrider. (1994). *Saving Nature's Legacy: Protecting and Restoring Biodiversity*. Washington, DC, Island Press.

[3] See Chatfield Basin Conservation Network Working Group (1998). *Chatfield Basin Conservation Network Concept Plan*. Also see (http://www.ChatfieldBasin.org) for more information about the plan Sperger and colleagues developed.

[4] Forman, R. T., and S. K. Collinge. (1997). "Nature conserved in changing landscapes with and without spatial planning." *Landscape and Urban Planning* 37: 129–135. This same thought is echoed by Carroll, C., R. F. Noss, et al. (2004). "Extinction debt of protected areas in developing landscapes." *Conservation Biology* 18(4): 1110–1120.

[5] Laurance, W. F., and C. Gascon. (1997). "How to creatively fragment a landscape." *Conservation Biology* 11(2): 577–579.

[6] Quoted in Girling, C. L., and K. I. Helphand. (1996). *Yard, Street, Park: The Design of Suburban Open Space*. New York, John Wiley & Sons, p. 112.

[7] Cook, E. A. (2000). *Ecological Networks in Urban Landscapes*. Wageningen, Netherlands, University of Wageningen, p. 201.

[8] Nassauer, J. I. (1995). "Messy ecosystems, orderly frames." *Landscape Journal* 14(2): 161–170.

[9] Thompson, I. H. (2000). *Ecology, Community, and Delight: Sources or Values in Landscape Architecture*. London, E & FN Spon.

[10] Duerksen, C. J. (1997). *Habitat Protection Planning: Where the Wild Things Are*. Chicago, IL, American Planning Association.

[11] Koh, J. (2004). "Ecological reasoning and architectural imagination." Inaugural address of Prof. Dr. Jusuck Koh, Wageningen, Netherlands.

[12] Ibid, p. 15, 26.

[13] Ibid.

[14] Koh, J. (1987). "Bridging the gap between architecture and landscape architecture." Council of Educators in Landscape Architecture Annual Meeting. He adds, writing elsewhere, "What we are designing in this ecological view, I believe, are not 'form', 'space' or 'function' as Modernists had led us to believe, but 'system', 'process', and our 'embodied experiences' thereof." Koh, J. (2004). "Ecological reasoning and architectural imagination."

[15] Spirn, A. W. (1993). "Deep structure: On process, form and design in the urban landscape." p. 9–16, in *City and Nature: Changing Relations in Time and Space*. T. M. Kristensen, S, E. Laresen, P. G. Moller and S. E. Petersen, ed. Odense, Denmark, Odense University Press, p. 9.

[16] Ibid, p. 12.

[17] Cook, E. A., and H. N. van Lier, ed. (1994). *Landscape Planning and Ecological Networks*. Amsterdam, Elsevier.

[18] Duerksen, C. J. (1997). *Habitat Protection Planning*.

[19] Ahern, J. F. (2002). "Greenways as strategic landscape planning: Theory and application," Ph.D. Dissertation. Wageningen, Netherlands, Wageningen University.

[20] Forman and Collinge, (1997), "Nature conserved in changing landscapes with and without spatial planning."

[21] Laurance, W. F., and C. Gascon. (1997). "How to creatively fragment a landscape."

[22] Babbitt, B. (1999). "Noah's mandate and the birth of urban bioplanning." *Conservation Biology* 13(3): 677–678.

[23] Day, K. (2003). "New urbanism and designing for diversity new urbanism and the challenges of designing for diversity." *Journal of Planning Education and Research* 23: 83–95.

[24] "South Platte River, Brighton, Colorado," in Smith, D. S. (1993). "Greenway case studies." p. 161–206, in *Ecology of Greenways*. D. S. Smith and P. C. Hellmund, ed. Minneapolis, University of Minnesota Press.

[25] Ibid.

[26] "Quabbin to Wachusett Wildlife Corridor Study, Massachusetts," in Smith, D. S. (1993) in "Greenway Case Studies" p. 161–206, in *Ecology of Greenways*. D. S. Smith and P. C. Hellmund, ed. Minneapolis, MN, University of Minnesota Press.

[27] Lyle, J. H. (1985). *Design for Human Ecosystems*. New York, Van Nostrand Reinhold Company.

[28] Forman, R. T. T., and M. Godron. (1986). *Landscape Ecology*. New York, John Wiley & Sons.

[29] See U.S. Geological Survey, Gap Analysis Program. (http://www.gap.uidaho.edu/).

[30] See NatureServe. (http://www.natureserve.org).

[31] See also The Conservation Fund, What Is Green Infrastructure? (http://www.greeninfrastructure.net) and the Defenders of Wildlife's Conservation Network Design Web site. (http://www.biodiversitypartners.org/habconser/cnd/index.shtml).

[32] Kopperel, J. (2004). Landscape architect and project manager with EDAW, Inc. Personal communication.

[33] Collins, T. (2000). "Interventions in the Rust-Belt, The Art and Ecology of Post-Industrial Public Space." *British Urban Geography Journal, Ecumene* 7(4): 461–467.

[34] Forman and Collinge, (1997), "Nature conserved in changing landscapes with and without spatial planning."

[35] Ibid.

[36] Forman, R. T. T., and S. K. Collinge. (1996). "The 'spatial solution' to conserving biodiversity in landscapes and regions." p. 537–568, in *Conservation of Faunal Diversity in Forested Landscapes*. R. M. DeGraaf and R. I. Miller, ed. New York, Chapman & Hall.

[37] Forman and Collinge, (1997), "Nature conserved in changing landscapes with and without spatial planning."

38 Ibid.

39 Ibid.

40 Forman, R. T. T. (1995). *Land Mosaics: The Ecology of Landscapes and Regions*. New York, Cambridge University Press.

41 Merriam-Webster Online Dictionary. (2004). Definition of "swath." Retrieved July 5, 2004, (http://www.m-w.com/dictionary).

42 U.S. Geologic Survey. (2004). Definition of "swath." Retrieved July 5, 2004, (http://edcsgs9.cr.usgs.gov/glis/hyper/glossary/s_t).

43 Tomlin, C. D. (1990). *Geographic Information Systems and Cartographic Modelling*. Englewoods Cliff, NJ, Prentice-Hall.

44 Linehan, J., M. Gross, et al. (1995). "Greenway planning: Developing a landscape ecological network approach." *Landscape and Urban Planning* 33: 179–193.

45 Pearsall, S. H., D. Durham, et al. (1986). "Evaluation methods in the United States," p. 111–133, in *Wildlife Conservation Evaluation*. M. B. Usher, ed. London, Chapman and Hall.

46 Lyle, J. H. (1985). *Design for Human Ecosystems*. New York, Van Nostrand Reinhold Company, p. 136.

LANDSCAPE LINES
TO HOLD

In the midst of a controversy over coastal planning along the New South Wales coast, Australian Fran Kelly put it succinctly and well in speaking to a reporter from the Australian Broadcast Corporation: "You can't just clear everything, get rid of any wildlife corridors, just build and build and build, and then at the end of the day go 'oh dear, we've got nothing left.'"[1]

Increasingly residents and officials of metropolitan and other areas across North America are taking steps to ensure that there will be greenspace left at the "end of the day." In many urbanizing locales this amounts to a kind of "creative fragmentation," working to identify and save key components of greenspace in advance of development, accepting that development will come and natural areas will become fragmented and potentially isolated. The challenge is in knowing which pieces to save and how these eventual remnants will function once their matrix has dramatically changed. Most likely the least desirable situation is when these fragments are small and unconnected. But even if interconnected, where connections are identified as simplistic links drawn on paper and without much understanding of what is in the field, this system risks having "arbitrary boundaries that look so tidy on a map [but that] are extremely difficult to hold on the ground," as William Whyte wrote of greenbelt planning. He went on to observe that "the kind that work follow the idiosyncrasies of the land; the ridges and valleys, and especially the streams and rivers. Here is the line to hold."[2] To Whyte's physiographic recommendations, we feel impelled to add other lines that may be more difficult to visualize, but that are equally vital to sustaining greenspace. These are existing and future connections in service of people. They are defined by residents' needs, experiences, and aspirations. Sometimes they are already clearly expressed. Other times they are connections and destinations that will become significant only as a city grows on the ground or in social capital.

Some of these special greenway opportunities for nature and for people are illustrated here.

A. Keep aspects of functioning nature in greenways near where people live, no matter how urban the area.

B. Give people access to nature and recreation in greenways and thereby facilitate social interaction.

C. Reclaim postindustrial and other degraded areas as greenways and thereby serve residents and accommodate natural processes while restoring the land.

D. Link diverse neighborhoods with a greenway to encourage social interaction and promote environmental justice.

E. Manage for greenway objectives away from (e.g., upstream of) and as a complement to metropolitan greenways to enhance water quality protection or other greenway functioning within the metropolis. Similarly, avoid sending exacerbated floodwaters or other problems downstream of the greenway.

F. Promote greenway objectives away from a greenway in its landscape matrix, rather than considering such areas as totally incompatible and not worthy of attention.

G. Protect linear vegetated areas as greenways wherever they occur, and especially if they connect large patches of vegetation.

H. Include in greenways sustainably managed community gardens, farms, and forests that can replace distant sources of food and materials that rely on heavy inputs of chemical fertilizer, pesticides, and energy.

I. Set aside less environmentally sensitive areas within or adjacent to greenways to meet compatible community needs, such as subsidized housing.

J. Seek out situations where there is social conflict, but where a greenway project might be an appropriate vehicle for bringing together diverse perspectives, thereby empowering citizens, identifying common aspirations, and potentially resolving the conflict.

K. Create many short trails that link people to schools and other practical destinations, thus reducing reliance on motorized transportation.

Some additional greenway opportunities include:

• Create greenways along appropriate community-recognized landscape lines, such as irrigation canals, trails, or abandoned railroad corridors to build on the identity they may already hold for residents.

• Look for possible greenway alignments that already are of interest to diverse, but possibly uncoordinated (or perhaps conflicting groups) and bring these groups together to consider a greenway.

• Seek out parties who may not think of themselves as greenway proponents, but who may have things to gain from participating or are otherwise in positions to affect the success of a greenway.

[1] Australian Broadcasting Corporation. (2004). "Taree council rejects conservation criticism." ABC Online. Retrieved December 21, 2004, (http://www.abc.net.au).

[2] Whyte, W. (1968). *The Last Landscape*. Philadelphia, University of Pennsylvania Press, p. 162. Originally published in Garden City, NY, by Doubleday.

INDEX